65.00

TAX SHELTERED FINANCING THROUGH THE R & D LIMITED PARTNERSHIP

WILEY PROFESSIONAL BANKING AND FINANCE SERIES
EDWARD I. ALTMAN, Editor

THE STOCK MARKET, 4TH EDITION
Richard J. Teweles and Edward S. Bradley
TAX SHELTERED FINANCING THROUGH THE R & D LIMITED
PARTNERSHIP
James K. La Fleur
CORPORATE FINANCIAL DISTRESS: A COMPLETE GUIDE TO PRE-
DICTING, AVOIDING, AND DEALING WITH BANKRUPTCY
Edward I. Altman

TAX SHELTERED FINANCING THROUGH THE R & D LIMITED PARTNERSHIP

JAMES K. LA FLEUR

Chairman, President, and CEO
GTI Corporation
San Diego, California

A Wiley-Interscience Publication
JOHN WILEY & SONS
New   York   •   Chichester   •   Brisbane   •   Toronto   •   Singapore

Library of Congress Cataloging in Publication Data:

La Fleur, James K., 1930-
   Tax sheltered financing through the R & D limited partnership.

   (Wiley professional banking and finance series)
   ''A Wiley-Interscience publication.''
   Bibliography: p.
   Includes index.
   1. Limited partnership—Taxation—United States.   2. Tax shelters—
Law and legislation—United States.   3. Research, Industrial—United
States—Finance.   4. Limited partnership—United States.   I. Title.
II. Series.

KF6452.L33   1981   343.7305'2662   82-16012
ISBN   0-471-87066-8   347.30352662
Printed in the United States of America
10 9 8 7 6 5 4 3 2 1

Series Preface

The worlds of banking and finance have changed dramatically during the past few years, and no doubt this turbulence will continue through the 1980s. We have established the Wiley Professional Banking and Finance Series to aid in characterizing this dynamic environment and to further the understanding of the emerging structures, issues, and content for the professional financial community.

We envision three types of book in this series. First, we are commissioning distinguished experts in a broad range of fields to assemble a number of authorities to write specific primers on related topics. For example, some of the early handbook-type volumes in the series concentrate on the stock market, investment banking, and Financial Depository Institutions. A second type of book attempts to combine text material with appropriate empirical and case studies written by practitioners in relevant fields. An early example is a series volume on the management of cash and other short-term assets. Finally, we are encouraging definitive, authoritative works on specialized subjects for practitioners.

It is a distinct pleasure and honor for me to assist John Wiley & Sons, Inc. in this important endeavor. In addition to banking and financial practitioners, we think business students and faculty will benefit from this series. Most of all, though, we hope this series will become a primary source in the 1980s for the members of the professional financial community to refer to theories and data and to integrate important aspects of the central changes in our financial world.

EDWARD I. ALTMAN
Professor of Finance
New York University, Schools of Business

Preface

This book started as a research project in the fall of 1978 as part of Pepperdine University's P/KE (Presidential/Key Executive) MBA program. The assignment was to pick a topic of direct concern to the business that each participant was currently managing.

The funding of R & D programs had been a matter of concern to me for a number of years. Obtaining sufficient funds for new product development is difficult even for established corporations; for small companies or lone investors it is often impossible. I had heard of the 1974 *Snow* decision through my accounting firm and had had some vague understanding that the implications of that Supreme Court decision might affect future funding tactics for R & D programs.

My immediate business problem at that time was developing some financial strategy to obtain much needed R & D funds for GTI Corporation. As President of that company I was concerned with simultaneously reducing debt and initiating several new product development programs. Debt reduction was necessary in light of anticipated high interest rates while new products were needed to replace aging product lines. Current cash flow was not sufficient to do both. The R & D partnership, utilizing outside investors, appeared to be a possible solution, so the R & D partnership was chosen as my research project.

As the study was underway, it became apparent that here indeed was a powerful new financial tool available to the corporation in need of development funds. Further, the R & D partnership seemed to represent a real financial breakthrough for inventors and small businesses—a business format that allowed control of the new products to be retained while gaining access to an almost unlimited pool of investment funds.

The original study ended with Chapter 5. After the project was completed in April of 1980, I formed such a partnership. Based on my experience, Chapter 6 was added during the spring of 1982 along with Appendixes M through T. With these new additions, the title was changed from "R & D

Limited Partnerships: A New Investment Vehicle to Reinforce Corporate New Product Development Efforts," to "Tax Sheltered Financing Through the R & D Limited Partnership." I would hope that the information presented here can contribute in some small way to this country's efforts to regain the technological momentum it seems to have lost.

JAMES K. LA FLEUR

Los Angeles, California
October 1982

Abstract

On May 13, 1974, the United States Supreme Court decided *Snow* v. *Commissioner*, in which a partnership had been formed to develop a trash burner. The Internal Revenue Service argued that the partners were not carrying on an existing "trade or business" for the year in question and could not deduct the research and development expenditures. The Supreme Court decided that the expenses were incurred in connection with a "trade or business" even though not yet actively conducted, and therefore allowed the deductions. This result has not been changed by subsequent legislation, including the Tax Reform Act of 1976, the Revenue Act of 1978, or the Economic Recovery Tax Act of 1981. In effect, individuals or partnerships are now in the same position as corporations with regard to offsetting current income against R & D expenditures even if the two are unrelated in any direct fashion.

This study was undertaken to determine how such limited partnerships could be structured to provide attractive investment vehicles for high-income investors while simultaneously assisting inventors, small businesses, and corporations in their new product development programs. It was felt that the *Snow* decision had wide implications for the directing of investment funds into development programs essential to the national interest.

The hypothesis for this study is as follows: R & D limited partnerships will be formed involving American inventors, small businesses and corporations in need of financial assistance for new product development, and high tax bracket American investors.

The basic and exploratory nature of work in this field to date suggests that inferential analysis and testing are most appropriate for accepting or rejecting the hypothesis. The nature of the data does not warrant the application of rigorous statistical analysis. Certain "key" characteristics of existing limited partnerships were compared with those that exist in R & D limited partnerships. The data indicated that R & D limited partnerships possessed a preponderance of those characteristics. The study also indicated that both small businesses and large corporations in the United States are in need of the benefits of accelerated new product development. Because of the adverse effects of inflation, they are hard pressed to generate the funds required for such development. Hence, within the limitations of inferential analysis, the hypothesis should be accepted.

The study cautioned that organizers of such partnerships, rather than pressing minor legal points to gain additional advantages, should abide by the intent of Congress in forming such partnerships and thereby avoid adverse legislative action in the future. The underlying profitability of the project must be considered of equal importance to near-term tax benefits, to establish a sound reputation and to insure future public support of the R & D limited partnership.

The final chapter provides a step-by-step procedure for organizing, funding, and managing a partnership of this type, using as an example Electronic Equipment Development, Ltd., an R & D partnership organized by the author after completion of this study. The Appendixes contain numerous legal documents required to organize and operate the partnership.

Contents

TAX SHELTERED FINANCING THROUGH THE R & D LIMITED PARTNERSHIP

CHAPTER ONE

Introduction

On May 13, 1974, the United States Supreme Court decided *Snow* v. *Commissioner*,[1] in which a partnership had been formed to develop a trash burner. The Internal Revenue Service argued that the partnership did not have an existing "trade of business" for the year in question and could not deduct the research and development (R & D) expenditures. The Supreme Court decided that the expenses were incurred in connection with a "trade or business" even though not yet actively conducted, and therefore allowed the deductions. This result has not been changed by subsequent legislation, including the Tax Reform Act of 1976, the Revenue Act of 1978, or the Economic Recovery Tax Act of 1981. In effect, individuals or partnerships are now in the same position as corporations with regard to offsetting current income against R & D expenditures even if the two are unrelated in any direct fashion.

Since 1974 several limited partnerships have been formed solely to engage in some specified R & D project, thus affording the limited partners the opportunity of offsetting current income against expenditures which they hope will lead to the development of a marketable product, while the general partner, often the inventor of the product, gains access to a large pool of investment funds while still retaining total control of the invention. This type of investment vehicle therefore would seem to offer definite advantages to individuals in high tax brackets, provided the research projects are well chosen and the R & D activities are professionally managed. Individual inventors and small businesses will find the availability of funds and the opportunity to retain control irresistibly attractive.

On the other hand, many American corporations, both large and small, find themselves in positions in which they are unable to generate sufficient cash from their present operations to successfully update their current product lines through normal R & D activities. This situation has been brought about by a combination of adverse factors such as high and continuing inflation, which in effect erodes their asset base, foreign competition, and

1

aging product lines. Assuming this to be true, few options are available to the corporate management. Funds could be made available by increasing debt, or new equity funds could be obtained. In many instances, neither of these alternatives is attractive. For one thing, by the time a company finds itself in this position, its debt-to-equity ratio may already be dangerously high and speculative borrowing, even if the banks would cooperate, may not be considered prudent. With regard to new equity funds from the public market, the stock of many companies is selling either below book value or at very low multiples of earnings; hence new equity issues for a company in this position may not be attractive to the present stockholders even if such an issue could be marketed successfully. Furthermore, many privately held companies are excluded, either by choice or by lack of experience, from the public equity market altogether. Failure, however, to take any action to introduce new products will inevitably lead to the failure of the company.

A third alternative would be for the corporations either to form or cause to be formed a limited R & D partnership specifically to develop those products for which the corporation feels there is a market and which it has the capability to manufacture and market, but which require more cash for successful development than is presently available. The corporation could act as the general partner if desired or could make arrangements with another corporation or individual to act as the general partner. Further, it would contribute to the limited partnership ideas and any preliminary development work or available patents pertaining to those ideas, in return for interests in the partnership. These ideas then would be the focal point of the R & D partnership's activities. After formation of the partnership, the partnership could contract with the original corporation to perform the required research activities, if the corporation happened to have the required facilities and available personnel. If not, an independent commercial laboratory could be assigned the work. Arthur D. Little, The Battelle Institute, The Carnegie Mellon Institute, and many others are organized to perform such activities. The partnership would own the new products developed and would expect to recover the investment through the sale of the developed product to the corporation that originated the idea or to an outside third party if the project proved to be beyond the financial capability of the original corporation. Such buy-back arrangements could be prearranged so long as the partnership assumed the technical risks of meeting pre-set specifications. Such a sale, properly structured, would be treated as the sale of a capital item. Another possibility would be for the partnership to exchange its developed product for shares of stock in a new corporation formed exclusively to manufacture the entire product, or perhaps parts of it, for sale to the original corporation for final assembly and marketing. One of the virtues of the partnership form of business organization is its extreme flexibility; in this instance, flexibility may be one of the most needed characteristics of the organization, because successful execution of a new product development program demands ingenuity of a rather high order to satisfy not only the technical problems involved but the legal and tax problems as well.

If the organization is properly formed and well managed, the investor could defer taxes on current income while receiving capital gains income from the sale of the finished products whose market may very well have been assured by the original corporation at the outset. Certainly a wide range of risk-to-reward ratios seems to be possible within the framework proposed here.

The corporation originating the ideas, on the other hand, benefits in two ways: first, ideas for products being constantly generated could be developed and marketed instead of being "shelved" due to lack of funds. While it would be true that some of the profit must be returned to the partnership in one form or another, it may prove on the average that higher profit margins earned by new products will allow significant payments to be made to the partnership and yet provide more profits than are being produced by present, aging product lines. Another advantage to the corporation would be the opportunity to build up a large and diversified research group, if the corporation chose to undertake the actual development effort. This research staff could then be used on a continuing basis, assuming the early projects do, in fact, start to increase the total revenues to the corporation. A further advantage is that no dilution of the present stockholders' interest in the corporation will occur, in many instances a factor of some importance.

Finally, in those instances where effective individual tax rates are higher than the corporate rate, the limited partnership will risk less after-tax funds than the corporation would risk to achieve the same result. This "spread" of risk dollars expended provides the key basis for negotiation when the partnership is formed. Several sound reasons seem therefore to exist for corporations and high tax bracket investors to collaborate in R & D activities in the manner suggested here.

The hypothesis for this study is as follows: R & D limited partnerships will be formed involving American inventors, small businesses and corporations in need of financial assistance for new product development, and independent high tax bracket American investors. Partnerships formed as described in the hypothesis, if successful, could provide a significant flow of development funds into American industry. The results of this study support the hypothesis.

Fundamentally, the questions posed for this study are as follows: Does a market exist for such a business form (Is there a need?); does this form properly respond to that market (Can it fill the need?); and are there participants who want to play the game by the rules that presently exist (Can the risks be reduced to levels acceptable to all parties?)?

With the questions formulated in this manner, it becomes obvious that the need for R & D activities should be explored; that the basic principles underlying the limited partnership form of business organization should be investigated; that the legal framework in which such an organization must operate should be stated (What are the rules of the game?); and that the attitude of the potential investors toward assuming risks and their capabilities of assuming those risks should be ascertained. Obviously this line of reasoning leads immediately to questions as to what the risks are and whether they can be minimized to the point of acceptability to a sufficient number of investors to develop programs of significance that can be carried to a successful conclusion. The above statements and questions set the basic framework in which this study was carried out.

Chapter 2, divided into seven sections, reviews literature pertaining to the questions posed above. The first section provides a general background of limited partnerships, including historical significance, the legal structure that presently exists and how it developed, the impact of recent legislation and what the impact of future legislation is likely to be, how partnerships are formed, what businesses may be engaged in, and how much this form of business organization is utilized at the present. The second section of Chapter 2 looks into various aspects of R & D partnerships in particular. The *Snow* v. *Commissioner* case, the cornerstone of the structure, is examined in some detail. Various Internal Revenue Code provisions pertaining to limited R & D partnerships are explored particularly as pertains to the definitions of R & D activities and the tax treatment of deductions and subsequent income that could be expected from such an undertaking. The third section reviews two actual limited partnerships formed since the *Snow* v. *Commissioner* case was decided in 1974. The next section of the literature review looks briefly at published accounts of the need for R & D expenditures in the United States, as well as the relationship between United States R & D expenditures in recent years as compared to those of its major trading partners, Germany and Japan. A brief look is taken at information available, to determine whether a correlation between long-term profitability and R & D expenditures has been quantitatively established. Incidentally, the answer seems to be in the negative, although adequate data apparently are available to determine whether such a correlation exists. This possibly could be an appropriate subject for another project. The fifth section looks at literature pertaining to the need of United States companies for funds. Does a shortage of funds exist? Here the impact of inflation, the product life cycle, recent cash flow trends, and the behavioral aspects of management toward such a project [the N.I.H. (not invented here) factor—"If we didn't invent it, it can't be any good"] are examined. Also, at least a superficial look is taken at whether any correlation between bankruptcy and failure to expend R & D funds has been established (it apparently has not—again the data exist but have not been examined with the idea of establishing this fact). Next the investor is looked at. What motivates the investor? Can it be predicted in advance whether sufficient investors are available to support specific projects; and if so, what are the key factors that must be present to provide the incentive required to assure an adequate supply of risk capital? The final section of Chapter 2 examines the chances of success in the introduction of a new product and discusses ways to reduce the risk.

Chapter 3 is concerned with the methodology applied in this study. Simply stated, the methodology consisted of studying the characteristics of successful limited partnerships in other fields and assessing whether such conditions are present or can be developed for R & D projects.

Chapter 4 presents the results of the study. In summary, it appears that because the limited partnership is such a flexible business form in regard to both organizational structure and methods of compensation, and the projects available in the development field are so varied, a wide range of risk-to-reward ratios can be predicted. As a result it seems inevitable that, unless present laws pertaining to limited partnerships are drastically altered, large amounts of development funds are going to be directed into this form of business. Interestingly, while many business people seem to be complaining that the government is not doing enough to encourage new investment into American industry, this form of incentive has been available since 1974 and very few people seem to have noticed it. That it exists is not accidental. The committee hearings in Congress discussing various tax provisions relative to R & D expenditures specifically mentioned that the laws, as presently enacted, should encourage investment in development projects and that these laws (Section 174 in the Internal Revenue Code in particular) would be particularly beneficial to small and beginning businesses.[1] Congress apparently meant what was said as subsequent legislation, specifically the Tax Reform Act of 1976, the Revenue Act of 1978, and the Economic Recovery Act of 1981 did not alter any major aspect of tax law relative to R & D development activities.

Chapter 5 summarizes the study, draws some conclusions based on the results presented in Chapter 4, and suggests further studies in this field. Specifically it points out the significance of the tax incentives available in R & D limited partnerships to individuals and corporations to attack the nation's energy-related problems as well as other vital technological areas. With a step-change in energy costs occurring over such a short time period, tremendous opportunities exist on a level never seen before. Alternate forms of energy must be made available. This type of program can materially aid in the development of these energy sources. Further, while it is obvious that these alternate energy sources will be more expensive than the nation has been accustomed to in the past, it is not so obvious that the entire industrial base of the United States must be redesigned to efficiently utilize these new sources of energy. And this retooling of the entire country will require tremendous quantities of investment funds. This chapter explores some of these implications.

Chapter 6 discusses in some detail the key steps required to actually form and operate an R & D limited partnership, using as an example Electronic Equipment Development, Ltd., an R & D limited partnership that was organized and is presently being managed by the author.

The Appendix contains documents to verify the legal issues involved in the R & D limited partnership field as well as key documents and forms required to create and operate such a partnership. These documents were included so that this publication would be immediately useful to anyone wishing to form or cause to be formed a limited partnership in the R & D field. This is not meant to be a complete do-it-yourself handbook for the non-lawyer reader; competent legal assistance should always be obtained. Sufficient documentation in its original form is included to assure that the establishment of such an enterprise rests on firm legal ground and can be done at a minimum cost to the organizer.

Note for Chapter 1

[1] Appendix H, "*Edwin A. Snow et ux, Petitioners* v. *Commissioner.*"

CHAPTER TWO

Literature Review

An extensive literature search was conducted to locate information to either support or reject the hypothesis introduced in Chapter 1. Although considerable material was examined, only a very small percentage of the total is represented here. A comprehensive review of the tax aspects of limited partnerships alone would be unmanageable in a project of this nature. In addition, as related to limited partnerships, a complete analysis of legal problems, SEC problems, corporate profitability questions, value of R & D, behavioral aspects of investors, and problems involved with the successful introduction of new products to the marketplace would be beyond the scope of this book. However, a reasonable cross section of the available material is presented here, a rather comprehensive Bibliography is provided following Chapter 6, and some of the key documents are included in the Appendixes for ready reference.

GENERAL BACKGROUND INFORMATION FOR LIMITED PARTNER-SHIPS

Three basic forms of business organization are recognized by statute in the United States: sole proprietorships, partnerships, and corporations. In this context, partnerships include "partnerships, joint ventures, syndicates, groups, pools, and most other associations of two or more persons organized for profit that were not specifically classified by the Internal Revenue Code as Corporations."[2]

A Limited Partnership is further defined by statute as a partnership consisting of at least one general and one limited partner. It has traditionally offered two quite basic business advantages that have not simultaneously been available to any other form of business operation—limited liability and single level taxation.[3]

Because of the ability to pass through profits and losses to the limited partner, limited partnerships can, if properly structured, be one form of tax shelter. Before getting too far into the statutory basis for the limited partnership, and to dispel any notion that the limited partnership is a new gimmick whose sole purpose is to provide tax shelter for high tax bracket investors, a brief look at the history of this form of business organization would seem to be in order.

Unlike general partnerships, which derive their legal basis from Engligh common law, limited partnerships are totally a product of legal statutes. A State of New York statute in 1822, establishing authority for the limited partnership, was the first example in the United States of adoption from a legal system other than that of England and it was not until 1907 that England adopted similar legislation. Until that time limited partnerships had been recognized only in civil law countries such as France and Italy. Interestingly, those countries derived the limited partnership concept from its early usage by merchants during the Middle Ages. Stephen Frank Matthews notes the reference to the 1822 New York statute in this quotation from surrogate L. Alexander W. Bradford's opinion rendered in *Ames* v. *Downing* in 1850:

> *The system of Limited Partnerships, which was introduced by statute into this state, and subsequently very generally adopted in many other States of the Union, was borrowed from the French code . . . it had existed in France from the time of the Middle Ages; mention being made of it in the most ancient commercial records and in the early mercantile regulations of Marseilles and Montpelier . . . in the statutes of Pisa and Florence, it is recognized as far back as the year 1160; also in the ordinance of Louis-Le-Hutin of 1315; the statutes or ordinance of Marseilles, 1253; of Geneva of 1588. In the Middle Ages it was one of the most frequent combinations of trade and was the basis of the active and widely extended commerce of the opulent maritime cities of Italy. It contributed largely to the support of the great and prosperous trade carried along the shores of the Mediterranean; was known in Languedock, Provence, and the Lombardy, entered into most of the industrial occupations and pursuits of the age and even traveled under the protection of the arms of the Crusaders to the city of Jerusalem. . . .* [4]

By the time the Uniform Limited Partnership Act was proposed in 1916, all states except New Mexico had adopted some form of the Limited Partnership Act, most following the language of the New York statute. Matthews raises the question here as to why, if this form of business had been around since the Middle Ages, it had not been used more extensively in the period between 1822 and 1917, the date when the Uniform Limited Partnership Act was first adopted by a state (Pennsylvania). He feels the answer lies in the rather strict interpretation by the courts of the limited partnership statutes, which restricted the investors' ability to limit their exposure. Matthews offers the following quotation from a commentator of the times, which neatly sums up the judicial attitude prevalent in the United States during the nineteenth century:

> *First: That a limited (or as he is also called a special) partner is a partner in all respects like any other partner, except that to obtain the privilege of a limitation on his liability, he has conformed to the statutory requirements in respect to filing a certificate and refraining from participation in the conduct of the business. Second: The limited partner on any failure to follow the requirements in regard to the certificate or any participation in the conduct of his business, loses his privilege of limited liability and becomes, as far as those dealing with the business are concerned, in all respects a partner.*[5]

In other words the risks were very high that a slight infraction of the statute would render the limited partner fully liable for all activities of the partnership; and for those wishing to avoid this risk, it seemed safer to become a corporate shareholder or at the least a creditor who received a share of the profit in lieu of interest. This factor alone seemed to limit the popularity of the limited partnership for almost one hundred years after its introduction into the United States. With the introduction of the Uniform Partnership Act, the limited partner was once more able to contribute capital to a business, acquire a profit interest, and exercise some control over the business "provided creditors have no reason to believe at the times their credits were extended that such person was so bound."[6]

The Uniform Limited Partnership Act (hereafter ULPA) has now been adopted in all states except Louisiana. Louisiana law is based on the French Code and in general differs from the remaining states. For further discussion of Louisiana law, Matthews suggests reference to "Partnership in Commendam—Louisiana's Limited Partnership," 35 *Tulane Law Review* 815 (1961).

Legal Basis of Limited Partnerships—The Uniform Limited Partnership Act of 1916

The ULPA was proposed in 1916 not only as a remedy to overly strict judicial standards applied to the limited liability aspects of the various state statutes as mentioned above, but also to standardize to the greatest extent possible the multitude of states laws in existence at the time. The ULPA, consisting of thirty-one sections, is included as Appendix A.

Section 1 of the ULPA defines a limited partnership as "formed by two or more persons" and of course differentiates between the limited and general partner. The use of the word "person" immediately raises the question as to whether a corporation or other entity not a person can be either a general or a limited partner. The answer turns out to depend on a number of factors, the most important of which is the state laws pertaining to allowable activities of the various non-person entities mentioned. Most state laws do not prohibit such activity; in fact, in absence of any specific statutes to the contrary, corporations are permitted to be both limited and general partners.[7]

Section 2 of the ULPA requires the execution of a certificate and its filing with the designated office. California Corporation Code Section 15502 sets forth the requirement that the certificate must be filed with the office of the county recorder in the county where the partnership is doing business.[8] (The form of the certification is in Appendix A, and the locations of the designated offices for each of the 50 states are included in Appendix N.)

Section 3 of the ULPA is titled "Business Which May Be Carried On" and leaves a blank to be filled in by the state if it desires to exempt certain types of businesses. California exempts banks and insurance.[9] The language of the section preceding the blank simply says that a limited partnership can carry on any business that a general partnership can.

Section 4 requires the limited partners' contribution to be either cash or other property but not services.

Section 5 restricts the use of a limited partner's name in the partnership's name except under certain circumstances. The purpose here is to avoid misleading creditors into believing that the limited partner is liable for the partnership's obligations.

Section 6 concerns false statements made on the certificate. In essence it provides relief for anyone who suffers a loss by relying on the false statement.

Section 7 provides that a limited partner shall not become liable as a general partner unless he takes part in the control of the business. As stated by Don Augustine and Peter M. Fass,

> *Probably the most serious problem encountered in drafting and carrying out a Limited Partnership agreement is that of determining what constitutes taking part "in the control of the business" of a limited partner. The problem is serious because the penalty for taking part in the control of the business of the Limited Partnership is general partner liability.*[10]

A further complication is that certain state laws require that the limited partners have certain rights, particularly in the area of removal and replacement of the general partner. The implications of these so-called democracy laws will be discussed in more detail in the next section on tax aspects as well as in Appendix C on California blue sky laws.

Section 8 states that additional limited partners may be admitted by amendment if done in accordance with Section 25. The major item of Section 25 is one of being in compliance with Section 2(1A) which in turn enumerates what must be in the certificate. Section 25 also specifies that all members, including those to be admitted, must sign and swear to the amendment. This signed amendment must then be filed for record at the appropriate office (county recorder's office in California).

Section 9 defines the rights, powers, and liabilities of a general partner. The general partner has all the rights and powers allowed those in a general partnership except the seven listed in Section 9. Unless the written consent to a specific act by all the limited partners is given, a general partner (or partners) has no authority to:

a. *Do any act in contravention of the certificate.*
b. *Do any act which would make it impossible to carry on the ordinary business of the partnership.*
c. *Confess a judgment against the partnership.*
d. *Possess partnership property, or assign their rights in specific partnership property, for other than a partnership purpose.*
e. *Admit a person as a general partner.*
f. *Admit a person as a limited partner, unless the right so to do is given in the certificate.*
g. *Continue the business with partnership property on the death, retirement or insanity of a general partner, unless the right to do so is given in the certificate.*[11]

Section 10 specifies certain rights the limited partners have regardless of Section 7. While these rights can be contractually altered by the partnership agreement, in the absence of such alteration, the rights of the limited partners are as specified in this section. In general they are concerned with the rights of access to the books and other information relating to the business as well as a right to share in the profits of the partnership.

Section 11 provides an exit for an investor who erroneously believes himself to be a limited partner, and Section 12 allows a person to be both a general partner and a limited partner in the same partnership at the same time.

Section 13 allows a limited partner to make loans to the partnership, but conditions the receipt of any payment, conveyance, or release from liability upon there being sufficient assets of the partnership to discharge partnership liabilities to persons not claiming to be general or limited partners at the time of the receipt.

Section 14 allows an agreement to be made that one limited partner has preference over another in distribution of profits or losses; but in the absence of any agreement, all limited partners are considered to stand on an equal footing. Section 15 requires the partnership to remain solvent following a distribution of profits to the limited partners.

Section 16 defines the situations allowing the limited partner to withdraw his contribution, and Section 17 provides that a limited partner is liable for any promised but unpaid contributions as stated in the certificate.

Section 18 states that a limited partner's interest in the partnership is personal property, and Section 19 provides that a limited partner's interest is assignable much the same as a stock certificate. There are few markets for secondary sales of limited partnership interests. However, the new assignee does not become a new limited partner unless all the members consent thereto, or unless the assignor had that power by the certificate.

Section 20 states that the death, retirement, or insanity of a general partner dissolves the partnership, unless the remaining general partners continue the business under a right to do so stated in the certificate or with the consent of all members. Section 21 states that should a limited partner die, his executor or administrator shall have all the rights of a limited partner; furthermore, the estate of the deceased limited partner shall be liable for his liabilities as a limited partner.

Section 22 is concerned with the rights of creditors of limited partners. In general it states that a court of competent jurisdiction may charge the interest of the indebted limited partner to the extent of the unsatisfied amount of the judgment debt.

Section 23 provides for the distribution of assets. Creditors are satisfied first, then limited partners, and finally general partners. Section 24 describes the circumstances requiring the certificate to be cancelled or amended. Section 25 describes the mechanical procedure for amending or cancelling a certificate.

Section 26 states that the standing of a contributor, unless he is a general partner, is nonexistent in proceedings by or against a partnership, except where the object is to enforce a limited partner's right against or liability to the partnership. The meaning is simply that a limited partner cannot sue the partnership nor file a suit on behalf of the partnership except in the specific instance of enforcing particular rights relative to the partnership.

Section 27 identifies the Act as the Uniform Limited Partnership Act.

Section 28 declares the canon on construction that "statutes in derogation of the common law are to be strictly construed" shall be inapplicable to this Act. The section provides guidance to the courts that they should not strictly adhere to the language of the limited partnership statutes. This derived from the former practice; for example, if an address was wrong on the certificate or if a name was spelled wrong, the limited liability protection of the partnership could be lost. Strict adherence to the language caused the limited partnership to remain unused for many years. Section 28 was added to prevent those sometimes trivial court decisions from abrogating the intent of the ULPA.

Section 29 states that the rules of law and equity shall govern in cases not provided for in this Act. Section 30 provides for the continuing of existing limited partnerships after the adoption of the ULPA, provided that a proper certificate is filed and that there is sufficient partnership property to discharge liabilities to persons not claiming as general or limited partners as well as an amount greater than the sum of the contributions of its limited partners. A limited partnership may continue to exist under previous statutes, except that such partnership shall not be renewed unless so provided in the original agreement.

Section 31 would repeal, except as affecting existing limited partnerships, to the extent set forth in Section 30 any prior statutes for limited partnerships.

Certainly the ULPA is a simple and straightforward document. It allows for a "cookbook" type of approach to setting up and administering the partnership. It has, as was previously noted, been adopted by every state except Louisiana. From reading through the Act, one would believe that no problems exist at all in setting up a limited partnership. Unfortunately that is not strictly true. Problems arise from at least two directions. First, the fact that the limited partnership has become highly popular for use as a tax shelter because of the single level of taxation coupled with its limited liability feature (actually the very heart of the whole concept) has inevitably attracted the attention of the Internal Revenue Service. Generally, if the IRS could successfully claim that a partnership was a corporation for tax purposes, the level of taxation would be much higher.

The second problem arises from lack of control which the limited partners must have in order to preserve their limited liability status.[12] Somehow, the fact that those who invest the most money (the limited partners) have the least to say about the running of the business seems to bother various state authorities. It seems rather undemocratic to them. As a result, state laws have been enacted to "protect" the rights of the limited partner. Giving more control to the limited partner, however, goes directly counter to the concept of limited liability; so these so-called democracy laws try to draw a fine line between the two positions and end up further complicating the drafting of an agreement that will satisfy all of the sometimes conflicting ground rules that currently exist. As most of these conflicts eventually get down to tax questions, the next section of the literature review is primarily concerned with tax problems related to limited partnerships.

Taxation Aspects of Limited Partnerships

A huge volume of material is available on tax aspects of limited partnerships compared to an almost total lack of literature on how the various projects undertaken by these partnerships can be made to operate profitably. As will be seen later, the average investor is in fact preoccupied with the tax shelter aspects of investment and unfortunately does not always consider the soundness of the business venture in the more conventional sense. While it is not a particularly popular notion to view the government's attempts in the field of taxation as having any particular virtues at all, it would appear that much of the controversy surrounding taxation of limited partnerships, which are promoted and marketed primarily for their value as tax shelters, could be avoided if in fact the purpose behind the particular venture was to operate a normally profitable enterprise. The government seems to attempt in many ways to discourage this view as it would appear that an excessive amount of investment capital becomes diverted from useful projects into projects whose main virtue is the avoidance of taxes. Be that as it may, people do dislike taxes. Many make prodigious efforts to either avoid paying any at all or defer payment to some date in the future. It should not be implied from this observation that anything is wrong with minimizing the taxes that must be paid, for as Judge L. Hand commented in *Newman v. Commissioner*,

> *. . . if I understand the Commissioner, he wishes us to consider that these deeds may have been a preliminary step in a reprehensible scheme to lessen . . . income taxes. There is not the faintest ground for imputing any such purpose to the parties at bar; and, if there were, it ought not to count. Over and over again courts have said that there is nothing sinister in so arranging one's affairs as to keep taxes as low as possible. Everybody does so, rich or poor, and all do right, for nobody owes any public duty to pay more than the law demands; taxes are enforced exactions, not voluntary contributions. To demand more in the name of morals is mere cant.*

Limited partnerships provide a way of "so arranging one's affairs as to keep taxes as low as possible."[13] This section will review those key aspects which form the basis of "sheltering" a portion of a taxpayer's income from normal taxation.

The key to the partnership's ability to shelter income lies in the fact that the Internal Revenue Code treats the partnership differently for accounting purposes than for taxpaying purposes. Under the partnership provisions of the Internal Revenue Code (Sec. 701–771), a partnership is generally treated as an entity for accounting purposes and treated as a conduit for taxpaying purposes.[14] It is an entity for purposes of calculating taxable income and many particular items of income, deduction, and credit (Sec. 703). It is also an entity for purposes of reporting information to the Internal Revenue Service (Sec. 6031).

However, a partnership is a conduit for purposes of income tax liability and payment. Each partner takes into income his own "distributive share" of the partnership's taxable income and the separately allowable items of income, deduction, and credit (Sec. 702[a]). The liability for income tax payment is that of the partner, and not of the partnership (Sec. 701).

On the profit side, this means that income is taxed at only one level—the partner's level (as distinguished from the corporation, where income is taxed at the corporate level and dividends are taxed at the shareholder level). Also, this means that the partner is taxed on the partnership profits even though none of those profits may be distributed to the partner.

On the loss side, this means that partnership losses, deductions, and credits pass through to the partner and can be used to offset other income, thereby reducing the income tax liability of the partner. The amount of losses which a partner may deduct under these provisions for a particular year is not to exceed the amount of the adjusted basis of his partnership interest (Sec. 704 [D]), which at the inception of the partnership equals the sum of capital contribution to the partnership plus his share, if any, of partnership liabilities.

It should be noted that the Tax Reform Act of 1976 and the Revenue Act of 1978 modified the provision that the partner's basis can include liabilities in excess of "at risk" contribution to the partnership for all limited partnerships except those dealing in real estate.[15] This provision will be discussed in more detail in the next section of this chapter.

Also, it should be noted that all partnerships, not just limited partnerships, are treated for tax purposes as described above. Limited partnerships have the additional feature, as noted in the above sections of this chapter, of permitting at least some of the partners to limit their liability to the extent of their interest in the partnership. The limited partnership is therefore somewhat of a hybrid—exhibiting at times the characteristics of a corporation and sometimes those of a partnership. This dual nature tends to introduce extensive complications into the tax picture, as will be discussed at some length in the following paragraphs.

Generally, from the government's viewpoint, if the limited partnership could be classed as an association (the Internal Revenue Code treats an association as a corporation), revenues would be increased.[16] From the partnership's viewpoint such a classification would amount to double taxation and must be avoided at all cost. The regulations pertaining to the determination of whether an entity should be treated (for tax purposes) as a corporation or as a partnership are complex and are subject to constant attack by the Internal Revenue Service (IRS). These regulations were scrutinized recently by the Court of Claims in *Zuckman* v. *United States* and by the Tax Court in *Larson* v. *Commissioner*. In both cases, the IRS attacked the partnership classification of a limited partnership; in both cases, the IRS lost. Before going into the details of the regulations, a brief look at the history of the courts' attempts to determine whether a partnership should be taxed as a corporation or a partnership should help in putting into perspective the problems encountered today in assuring that a new limited partnership actually will be taxed as such.

The problem started when Congress decided to tax unincorporated "associations" as corporations, while continuing to treat partnerships as "conduits" for tax purposes. This has been a part of American law since 1909. Unfortunately, Congress chose not to define either "corporation" or "association" so the problem of determining which is which has necessarily fallen to the courts and to the Treasury Department.[17]

The Supreme Court first considered the distinction between corporations and partnerships in the 1911 case of *Flint* v. *Stone Tracy*. The Court at that time elaborated upon the advantage of doing business in the corporate form as follows:

These advantages are obvious, and have led to the formation of such companies in nearly all branches of trade. The continuity of the business, without inter-

ruption by death or dissolution, the transfer of property interests by the dis-position of stock, the advantages of business controlled and managed by cor-porate directors, the general absence of individual liability, these and other things inhere in the advantages of business thus conducted, which do not exist when the same business is conducted by private individuals or partnerships.

This case was important in that it upheld the distinction between partnerships and corporations based upon the business advantages of the corporate form.[18]

The Supreme Court's latest analysis of the classification problem came in the 1935 case of *Morrissey* v. *Commissioner. Morrissey* required the Court to distinguish an "association" taxable as a corporation from a pure "trust." While the Court declared there was no constitutional question involved as to whether Congress had the power to tax corporations, associations, trusts, and partnerships differently or identically as it chooses, the vagueness of the provisions allowed the Treasury considerable flexibility in its determinations.[19]

Chief Justice Charles Evans Hughes then set out the limits that could be used for administrative construction of the term "association." Simply stated, he ruled that what was important was whether the enterprise resembled a corporation. Labels and names were not of any importance.

The Court then listed five salient features of the corporation: the power to hold title to property as an entity, centralized management through representatives of the members, continuity of life of the enterprise despite the death of a member, the ability to transfer interests in the enterprise, and the limitations of personal liability. . . .[20]

Because these factors were present, the Court found the organization in-volved in *Morrissey* and its companion cases to be associations. Unfortu-nately the *Morrissey* decision did not resolve the classification problem. The Treasury Department's regulations issued shortly thereafter still failed to clearly state any tests that could be used to determine with any degree of certainty whether an entity was an association or a partnership.

Another complication, in the 1950's, was caused by the Internal Revenue Service's determination to prevent doctors and other professionals from gaining the advantages of a corporation (pension and profit-sharing plans) by incorporating their practices. The IRS unsuccessfully challenged the as-sociation status of these professional organizations in a series of cases high-lighted by *United States* v. *Kintner*.[21] Apparently somewhat miffed that they were unable to stop the professional corporations, the Treasury Department issued the present regulations in 1960 in what was viewed as an attempt to overrule *Kintner* by administrative rules. The rules established two threshold tests for an association: the organization must have associates and must have "an objective to carry on business and divide the gains therefrom." An entity possessing these attributes is classified as an association if it has more than half of the remaining four corporate traits: continuity of life, centralized management, limited liability, and free transferability of interests. The regulations, which require a preponderance of corporate characteristics, are definitely weighted toward finding partnership tax status and thereby making it more difficult for the professional organizations to take advantage of corporate taxation.[22]

But the regulations failed to stop the professional corporations; and despite Treasury's attempts to tax the professionals as partners regardless of their legal status as corporations, the Federal Courts of Appeals uniformly refused to support the government's position. In 1969 the Treasury Department surrendered, conceding that:

> *Organizations of doctors, lawyers and other professional people organized under state professional association acts will, generally, be treated as corporations for tax purposes.*

Not only did the *Kintner* regulations fail to prevent professional associations from enjoying corporate tax status, but, as they were weighted toward partnerships they " . . . also had the unintended effect of guaranteeing the desired tax status to the limited partnership tax shelters."[23]

In summary, as the regulations now stand, a partnership will be taxed as such if it can prove that it lacks any two of four corporate characteristics: continuity of life, centralized management, limited liability, or transferability of interest.

As noted in the *Harvard Law Review* recently,

> *Two recent cases,* Zuckman v. United States *decided by the Court of Claims, and* Larson v. Commissioner, *decided by the Tax Court, illustrate that a limited partnership may achieve virtually all the practical advantages of corporate status and yet be taxed as a partnership.*[24]

However, to achieve this status requires careful structuring of the original partnership agreements as well as actually operating the entity so that it continues to resemble a partnership more than a corporation.

A brief summary here of typical interpretations of whether the four listed corporate characteristics are present will illustrate the care needed to assure partnership tax status. At least two of these characteristics must be absent in order for the desired status to be attained.

Continuity of Life

The regulations stipulate that an enterprise has continuity only if no member has the power to dissolve it at will, and specified involuntary events such as death or bankruptcy of a member will not trigger dissolution. The ULPA permits a general partner to dissolve at will, although this right may be surrendered by contract. Thus any partnership formed under the ULPA would seem not to possess "continuity of life."

Centralized Management

While many if not most limited partnerships would appear to have centralized management,

> The regulations specify, however, that organizations conforming to the ULPA "generally do not have centralized management" unless the limited partners own "substantially all" the interest.[25]

Limited Liability

An organization possesses the corporate characteristics of limited liability according to the regulations only if no member is personally liable for the firm's obligations. Someone in a limited partnership is always liable. Even if the general partner were merely a dummy (a person or corporation with no assets, for instance), "Under ULPA, if the general partner is a dummy the limited partners become personally liable—again preventing a finding of limited liability." Obviously, then, it is impossible under the regulations to find that a limited partnership possesses limited liability.[26]

Free Transfer of Interests

Most limited partnerships have some restrictions on the transfer of interest; but as noted in the *Harvard Law Review*,

> Even under Larson's interpretation, free transferability will not exist any time a general partner has a substantial interest, because transfer of his interest would work a dissolution.[27]

The Practical Accountant, in an article entitled "How to Avoid the Major Limited Partnership Problems" by Stefan Tucker, provided a convenient checklist to use when setting up a limited partnership, which takes into account most of the problem areas outlined above. The principal danger to avoid, of course, is being taxed as an association. In addition, the article discusses other tests that the IRS might use, as described in various Revenue Procedures.[28]

In spite of the fact that it appears relatively simple for a partnership to avoid being taxed as an association, the IRS continues to attack the tax shelters, even though it has managed to tie itself up with its own *Kintner* regulations. One approach the IRS has taken is to refuse to issue advance opinions unless certain conditions are met. The effect of this ruling appears to be an attempt by the IRS to get around its own regulations, as failure of a partnership to get an advance ruling throws a certain degree of uncertainty into the project, making marketing of it more difficult. This uncertainty is not only undesirable but unnecessary. For, as Robert N. Davies points out,

> *As to future business enterprises, the basic rules should be sufficiently concise, and consistent private rulings should be available so the fundamental form of taxation of the enterprise is subject to reasonable certainty at the outset.*[29]

However, if past history is any guide, it would seem unlikely that the IRS will avoid trying to make its own rules as seems necessary; and it would seem equally unlikely that Congress suddenly will start issuing clear and unambiguous tax regulations.

In summary then, the principal tax issue in limited partnerships is to assure that the original partnership agreement is drafted so that, insofar as possible, the partnership is taxed as a partnership and not as a corporation. Regardless of the cynicism exhibited by some writers, a limited partnership that is straightforward and avoids gimmicky constructions can, with reasonable assurance, count on being taxed as a partnership.

Evolution of Tax Law

A brief commentary on the evolution of the tax laws as they pertain to limited partnerships would seem to be in order here. The problem started a long time ago. At the time of the formation of the United States and during the debates and conventions that led to the writing of the United States Constitution, comments were made to the effect that it was a mistake to attempt to write down the Constitution in place of relying on unwritten English common law, a system that had evolved over many centuries. The argument was that once committed to writing the most obvious set of circumstances can be distorted out of perspective by a skilled lawyer trained to logically argue the "meaning" of words. Common sense has a tendency to get lost in a sea of logical rhetoric, and what sometimes starts out to be fair and understandable becomes distorted and incomprehensible. The common sense, fairness, and simplicity of the United States Government as envisioned by the country's founders have been distorted beyond recognition by arguments relating to the "general welfare" clause in the Constitution. Originally limited only to enumerated powers, the government has expanded interpretation of law beyond recognition, based on belief that the general welfare clause not only allowed government to take any action whatsoever if the action promoted the "general welfare," but also required it to do so.

The tax laws as reviewed above follow the same pattern of development as was followed in interpreting the Constitution. Regardless of the legal arguments presented, everyone who has given any thought to it at all "knows" what a corporation is and what a partnership is.

A corporation, an entity created solely by government decree, consists of several persons who wish to pool their resources to accomplish some task that they are unable to accomplish separately and who wish not to be liable for the obligations of the resulting organization beyond the value of their investment in the enterprise at any particular time. If they "advertise" this limited liability aspect of their business and if those who do business with the firm have no cause to believe that the individuals involved will personally guarantee the obligations of the firm, the law will recognize the limited liability of the organization. A corporation is United States Steel. A corporation was Standard Oil of New Jersey, now Exxon. A corporation is *not* a group of doctors who keep a minute book, elect directors, and pass resolutions. Doctors and other professional people, whom the public in the past held in high regard, are individuals highly trained to discharge a personal service and ready to be accountable as individuals for their actions. They have no personal need for large amounts of capital (hospitals are a different matter). In order, however, to provide a diversity of services and some backup for their clients in the event of personal incapacity, and to share some common but minor expenses, partnerships were formed. A partnership is just what it implies, a group of persons sharing a common profession and desiring to work together and share the proceeds of their endeavors in some prearranged manner, but still remaining personally responsible for not only their actions but those of their associates.

As can be seen from the above summary of the historical usage of the limited partnership, a third form of business organization evolved which represented a hybrid form of the corporation and partnership. The limited partnership was a response to the situation when at least one person desired to accept the full responsibility for the obligations of his business but for various reasons more capital was required than he personally was able to contribute to the endeavor. On the other side, there were persons who had surplus funds to invest but for various reasons did not have the time or perhaps the requisite skills to involve themselves in the management of the business. While they were willing to invest their money and keep out of management, it seemed to be necessary to them, particularly since they would take no part in the management decisions, that they be responsible for the obligations of the enterprise only to the extent of their investment in the venture at any given time. Of course, in order not to misrepresent this "limited" liability of the "silent" partners, it was necessary that potential creditors be made aware of this fact. Thus it is seen that the three forms of businesses evolved from a very real need. When properly utilized, they have satisfied a wide variety of situations found in the world of commerce. But, as in the problems that evolved from having a written constitution, as persons attempted to distort these rather simple ideas for their own benefit to the detriment of the public, the public responded by writing ever more complex defenses. While a simple return to basic morality and the willingness to accept responsibility for one's actions would solve the various problems, this seems to be a highly unlikely turn of events. Thus, the battle will go on.

In this particular case, the opening skirmish seems to have been Congress' determination, shortly after the turn of the century, to tax corporations differently than partnerships without either specifying why this was done or properly defining the terms used. As noted in the *Flint* v. *Stone Tracy* case in 1911, the Supreme Court recognized the distinction between partnerships and corporations and enumerated the advantages of doing business in the corporate form.[30] Next, Chief Justice Hughes, in *Morrissey* in 1935, further described a corporation but still tried to rely on "what looked like a corporation is a corporation." That seemed to be the last time common sense was to prevail. When the doctors in Montana tried to gain the advantages of a corporate form of business (primarily, it would seem, to gain the fringe benefits that Congress had allowed corporations but not individuals, rather than to avoid personal liability), the government tried to argue that groups of professional people were not corporations. They did not look like corporations; they did not act like corporations; and therefore they were not corporations. This would seem to be the last time that anyone has tried to make a common-sense type of argument in this field. For they were right, of course. A doctor is not a corporation. A doctor is a doctor. But the courts did not see it that way, and found for the doctors. Doctors can now be corporations if they so choose—at least in the eyes of the law.

The IRS, properly miffed that common sense had failed, decided to swing the other way and rigidly define rules. Granted, the rules were slanted toward preventing non-corporations from becoming corporations, but the IRS seemed to be saying that if the courts are going to remove common sense from the scene, there might as well be a good set of rules to go by. Subsequently, of course, IRS representatives found themselves arguing against their own rules as other events occurred which made it advantageous to be considered a partnership. The IRS returned to its attempt to have common sense prevail even in the face of its own rules. The *Larson* and *Zuckman* cases mentioned above seemed to represent the epitome of the failure of the courts to use common sense when faced with a definitive set of rules, regardless of the ludicrous outcome. Both *Larson* and *Zuckman* had a sole corporate entity as a general partner. In neither case did that corporation have substantial assets. Zuckman, for instance, capitalized at only $500, was subject to the complete control of J. H. Kanter, a limited partner with 21 percent interest in the partnership.[31] In other words, the limited partner owned the corporation that was the general partner but no assets were available in the corporate entity to satisfy creditors. This is what was meant above by a "gimmicky" situation. Regardless of the court's opinion, *Zuckman* represents a gross distortion of the original intent of the limited partnership concept of business organization. Once started down the path of "logic," however, it seems unlikely that common sense will ever again prevail. Nevertheless, when contemplating organizing a limited partnership, it is well to consider the question of whether "if it's legal it's right." Keeping in mind the original concept and designing an organization in reasonable conformance to that concept will result in very few difficulties in receiving the blessings of the various governmental bodies involved.

Moving on to the next "battle scene," the effects of the Tax Reform Act of 1976 (TRA 1976) on limited partnerships will now be reviewed.

Impact of the Tax Reform Act of 1976 on Limited Partnerships

The Tax Reform Act of 1976 was signed into law by President Ford on October 4, 1976. This act

> . . . is, without doubt, the most sweeping tax measure to clear Congress since enactment of the Internal Revenue Code of 1954 . . . tax shelters are a top target for the Act.[32]

This "sweeping tax measure" was brought about in large measure by the greatly expanded use of the limited partnership as a tax shelter, particularly when this type of organization was formed primarily to take advantage of various peculiarities in the tax law that emerged from an increasing tendency on the part of the courts to literally interpret the law even at the expense of common sense, as in the cases of *Larson* and *Zuckman* cited in the previous section.

The staff of the Joint Committee on Internal Revenue Taxation prepared a position paper on tax shelters which was published on September 13, 1975, for use by the Committee on Ways and Means. For the most part this paper provided historical background on tax shelters and limited partnerships for the use of the committee members. Having filled in the background, the staff went on in Section 2 to outline the "problem" as they saw it:

> It is argued that because the limited partnership is the form of business most suited to tax shelters, the tax provisions should be modified so as to restrict its use in this regard. Others argue that it is the tax shelter deduction provisions, not the limited partnership provisions, which require modification. . . .
>
> Criticism has been directed at the provision of the income tax regulations (Sec. 1,752-1[E]), which allows a limited partner to increase the basis in his investment, and therefore the amount of losses that he may deduct by a portion of nonrecourse indebtedness. Under this regulation, the investors are able to use borrowed funds with respect to which they have no personal liability to generate deductions in amounts larger than what they have at risk in the Limited Partnership. On the other hand, it has been argued that this provision of the income tax regulations applying to limited partners is no more than an adaptation of the principle of [the] Supreme Court case [of Crane v. Commissioner, 331 U.S. 1 (1947)], where nonrecourse indebtedness, regardless of the form of business involved, is added to the owner's basis of the property.[33]

Other somewhat minor points in dispute were then discussed by the staff, but toward the end of the paper they raised an issue that could have developed into a devastating blow to most tax shelters if the final Act had attempted to "correct" this problem:

> . . . *some maintain that many of the large syndicated Limited Partnerships which closely resemble corporations should be treated as corporations for tax purposes. In response it is noted that an entity that qualifies for partnership tax treatment under the income tax regulations is lacking in at least two of the four characteristics peculiar to corporations. Such an entity, it is maintained, should not be subject to corporate tax treatment. However, as has been noted above, it is frequently possible to simulate the absence of the corporate characterisitc of transferability of interests merely by providing that the general partner has the power to reject a transferee of a Limited Partnership interest when, as a practical matter, it is understood that the general partner would not exercise that right.*[34]

Several alternative actions were suggested that the committee might adopt to alleviate the problems as they saw them. Finally, after much soul searching, the Act was presented to Congress and, as noted above, was signed into law by the President on October 4, 1976. Whether the resulting tax laws are any fairer remains to be seen. However, Edmund Burke noted some years ago that "to tax and to please, no more than to love and be wise, is not given to men."[35] Fair or not it is now the law of the land. As noted above, it has wide impact, particularly on tax shelters. Taken in the context of the comments made above about common sense as applied to legal interpretations, the changes for the most part eliminated practices that seemed irrational anyway. Certainly, though, the changes will cause and probably already have caused the redirecting of sizable investments from projects that primarily are concerned with tax avoidance to those primarily concerned with profitable undertakings. Despite the grinding and gnashing of teeth by many, if more emphasis were placed on operating businesses at a profit and a little less emphasis on what to do with the losses, it might all be for the best.

Major Changes Dictated by TRA 1976

The first class of changes has to do with personal income taxes and concerns this discussion only to the extent that potential limited partners will want to participate in only those ventures that can benefit them the most. This book is not concerned with delving into extensive details on personal income tax problems, but those changes that seem most to affect limited partnerships have to do with changes in the minimum tax rate and the addition of new items of tax preference. Arthur Andersen lists these items as follows:

One-half of net long-term capital gains,
Excess itemized deductions,
Accelerated depreciation on leased personal property,
Accelerated depreciation on real property,
The excess of fair market value of stock over the option price at date of exercise
  of a qualified or restricted stock option,
Intangible drilling costs, percentage depletion,
Amortization of certified pollution-control facilities,
Amortization of railroad rolling stock, and
Amortization of on-the-job training and child care facilities.[36]

Income that is counted as a tax preference item tends to raise an individual's tax rate because such income decreases the amount of income that is subject to the 50 percent maximum rate on earned income. Most persons would attempt to avoid earning tax preference income if possible; hence tax shelter investments will begin to be structured to avoid, insofar as possible, earning tax preference income.

The major impact of TRA 1976 fell on the key factor in tax shelters— leverage. The ability to deduct more losses from a project than had originally been invested rested on the fact that non-recourse debt could be included as part of the partners' basis. Simply stated, if a partnership bought a piece of equipment (intended for lease) for, say, $100,000, but put only $10,000 down and borrowed the rest on a note in which it was stated that the lender had no recourse in the event of default except recovery of the piece of equipment, the partners would have a basis of $100,000 and could deduct losses on the project up to that amount. Assuming legitimate front-end costs and first-year depreciation, which could be accelerated by various methods, totaled $50,000 at the end of the year, and assuming each partner was in the 50 percent tax bracket, tax savings of $25,000 could be realized as a result of a $10,000 investment. TRA 1976 now essentially prohibits that type of arrangement through two of its sections: Section 213 and Section 204.

Arthur Andersen explains Section 213 as follows:

Deductions in excess of investments—"Catchall at Risk"—losses flowing through a partnership to a partner are only deductible to the extent the partner has tax basis. Tax basis heretofore has included nonrecourse debt. Generally, the Act does not allow nonrecourse debt to be added to a partner's tax basis for the purposes of deductibility of losses. This is known as the "Catchall at Risk" provision and does not include activities to which the "activity at risk" pro-visions apply (see below) nor does it include real estate activities. Effective for liabilities incurred after December 31, 1976.[37]

It should be noted that the above applies only to partnerships, not to individuals or corporations. Section 204, an explanation of which follows, excludes certain specific activities from deducting losses in excess of investment. As this item is of major importance to the tax shelter concept, Arthur Andersen's explanation is quoted in its entirety:

Section 204 Deductions in Excess of Investment Activity "at Risk"—The "activity at risk" provisions generally follow a philosophy similar to the "catchall at risk" above. The "activity at risk" rules apply to all taxpayers (other than corporations that are neither electing small business corporations nor personal holding companies) that engage in the following activities:

Holding, producing, or distributing motion pictures films or videotapes;
Farming (except farming operations involving trees other than fruit or nut trees);
Equipment leasing; and
Exploring for, or exploiting, oil and gas resources.[38]

Interestingly, real estate, the basis of more partnerships in 1975 than the next eight categories combined, was excluded from all "at risk" provisions in TRA 1976.[39]

The remainder of the changes affecting partnerships as such are of a somewhat less important nature but interesting in light of the "strict" interpretation of the law discussed in the previous section. For example, the Act provides that income or losses will be allowable to a partner only for the portion of the year in which the person is a member of the partnership, a provision that sounds reasonable. It is a little hard to justify, but in the past, a new partner could enter the partnership on the last day of the year and receive a full year of "deductions" for one day of participation in the partnership. As Arthur Andersen comments,

Existing practice has been for many individual taxpayers to "shop around" for tax shelters during the latter part of the year, hoping that they will be able to obtain the same tax benefits as if they invested during the early part of the year. As a result, many promoters have concentrated their marketing of tax shelters late in the year. This change should eliminate that practice and encourage that partnership investments, to the extent still viable, to be made before any significant deductions are incurred.[40]

Another example is the requirement that special allocations must have "substantial economic effect." As the ULPA allows partners to allocate profits and losses in any manner they see fit without regard to any known economic effect, it had been the practice to make such allocations for the sole purpose of reducing taxes paid by the partners. While the IRS had required that economic effect be considered in the past before the allocations were allowed, that practice has now been raised to the level of a statutory requirement.

Another practice in the past was to take accelerated depreciation in the early years of owning residential property. When a sale was made, the profit, that is, the difference between the depreciated value and the sale price, was treated as capital gains. This is no longer possible, as Section 202 requires that all depreciation in excess of straight-line depreciation be recaptured to the extent of gains realized at the time of sale. (Commercial property is already treated in this manner.)

Equipment leasing is one of the activities for which the law limits the deductible loss attributable to leased property to an amount for which the taxpayer is "at risk." In general, the amount "at risk" is defined to include the amount of money advanced to acquire the equipment and recourse indebtedness (if any). However, as Arthur Andersen notes,

> *The law states that the amount at risk will be reduced by any losses deducted with respect to the activity. However, it is anticipated that the calculation of the amount at risk in future years will be similar to the calculation of a partner's basis in a partnership, i.e. the initial "at risk" amount will be increased by (1) additional cash contributions, (2) profit, and (3) increases in liabilities on which there is personal liability and will be decreased by (1) cash distributions, (2) losses deducted, and (3) decreases in personal liability.*[41]

Farming operations also are affected by TRA 1976. As Arthur Andersen notes,

> *Farming operations conducted by entities other than regular corporations will be subject to the new "activity at risk" rules which prohibit an investor from claiming tax losses in excess of amounts he personally stands to lose.*
>
> *Farmers involved with trees, other than fruit or nut trees, will not be subject to the "activity at risk" rules, but partners in any type of farming partnership will face additional hurdles in deducting losses in excess of personal liability due to changes in overall partnership tax rules.*[42]

Interestingly, the farmers themselves advocated these changes. The impact of limited-partnership, tax-sheltered farming enterprises was so great that a rollercoaster effect seemed to be injected into the normal supply-and-demand relationships. While this was seen as detrimental to the farmers, it is interesting to notice how powerful a device the limited partnership is in its ability to attract investment capital into one type of business or another. This point will be brought up again later in a consideration of the probable impact on research and development activities from recent court decisions allowing this type of activity to be conducted in the limited partnership form in a tax-advantaged manner.

In stating the position of the farmers on this issue, Arthur Andersen notes that,

> *If "farmers" can be kept in the business of farming and "nonfarmers" can be kept from going in and out of farming, then industry spokesmen believe*

that a constant supply of farm products can be supplied and a fair profit can be returned to the farmer.[43]

Many changes were also made in TRA 1976 affecting the motion picture business, possibly because extraordinary abuses of the tax laws (if common sense is to be a guideline) occurred in past years in this field. There is no need to enumerate the change here or to describe the past; but, as Arthur Andersen notes,

In all probability, the use of motion pictures as a tax shelter will be a thing of the past . . . the possibility of economic gain if the film is successful (rather than tax losses) will become the primary incentive for an investment in a motion picture.[44]

Considering the investment picture in the United States as a whole, changes that will tend to channel investment into useful and profitable ventures rather than "gimmicky" losers, regardless of tax results, would seem to be beneficial.

Again, along the same lines, while the real estate industry escaped relatively unscathed in TRA 1976, enough changes were made to shift the emphasis, perhaps ever so slightly, from the "gimmicky" to the quality project. As Arthur Andersen notes,

The ability to shelter taxable income by offsetting losses resulting from real estate investments will be much more limited than in the past. There will be a much greater emphasis on economically justifiable real estate rather than upon mere tax gimmicks. Futhermore, the ability to convert ordinary income into capital gains through the use of rapid depreciation write-offs will be much less attractive. . . . As mentioned above the investment posture for the real estate industry will shift to an emphasis on quality and yield.[45]

While many adverse comments were made following the enactment of TRA 1976, the tendencies noted above to drive investments into more realistic activities seem to justify the efforts made by Congress to get it passed. It steps on a lot of toes. But it seems to have corrected a number of excesses; and for that alone, it seems to be working.

It is important to note the tremendous influence of tax legislation on directing the flow of investments from one activity to another. If developing alternate engery sources is in fact a high priority in this country, and if greatly increased research and development activity can help to resolve the problem, as it most likely can, then Congress has an ideal tool readily at hand to encourage such effort. In fact the effort has already been started, not entirely accidentally, by a Supreme Court decision that was handed down over eight years ago. But before elaborating on that decision, this seems an appropriate place to review another major participant in the arena of tax shelters and limited partnerships, the Securities and Exchange Commission (SEC). The next section will look in some detail at the role played by the SEC in the field of limited partnership tax shelters.

The Securities and Exchange Commission and Limited Partnerships

The sale of interests in a limited partnership must be treated as the sale of "securities" and hence is regulated by the federal government under the authority granted to it under the Securities Act of 1933. While subsequent sales of limited partnership interests are not normally conducted, any such sales would also come under federal regulations as a consequence of the Securities Exchange Act of 1934. The Securities Act of 1933 is known as a "disclosure" statute as it does not authorize the government to pass judgment on the merits of any particular issue but simply to assure that adequate disclosure of pertinent information has been made to "enable investors to evaluate the securities of these companies on an informed and realistic basis."[46]

To comply with "proper disclosure" as defined by the Securities and Exchange Commission (hereafter, the SEC), the SEC generally requires that a registration statement be filed containing certain prescribed information. Before sale of securities begins, the statement must become "effective" and the investors must be furnished a "prospectus" containing the most significant information in the registration statement. Some securities and some transactions are exempted from the registration requirement, although it should be noted that while it is possible to be exempted from the registration requirements of the Securities Act, the anti-fraud provisions of the Act are always in force. As most limited partnership securities issued claim exemption from registration, the SEC rules pertaining to such exemptions will be discussed in some detail in the following sections.

Before discussing the details of the SEC exemption rules, it should be noted that the various states also have securities regulations generally classified as "blue sky" laws. The pertinent blue sky laws for California are included in Appendix C. It is important to note that blue sky laws differ from state to state and the need to know and comply with these laws in the state where the partnership is doing business is essential. In many cases, compliance with these laws can be more time-consuming and costly than SEC compliance. Because of the limited scope of their discussion however, no attempt will be made to detail any of the state laws beyond the comments made above. A reference list for securities regulations in all 50 states is included in Appendix S.

With regard to federal laws, however, it would seem worthwhile to go into some detail. First, if there is any doubt that interests in limited partnerships are in fact "securities" as defined by the Securities Act of 1933 (hereafter, the Act), here is the definition from the Act:

Section 2. When used in this title, unless the context otherwise requires—(1) the term "security" means any note, stock, treasury stock, bond, debenture, evidence of indebtedness, certificate of interest or participation in any profit-

sharing agreement, collateral-trust certificate, preorganization certificate or subscription, transferable share, investment contract, voting-trust certificate, certificate of deposit for a security, fractional undivided interest in oil, gas, or other mineral right, or, in general, any interest or instrument commonly known as a "security," or any certificate of interest or participation in, temporary or interim certificate for, receipt for, guarantee of, or warrant or right to subscribe to or purchase, any of the foregoing.[47]

If that statement alone is insufficient, the Supreme Court's flexible and liberal approach in construing offers to be securities, as found in *Secy. v. W. J. Howey Co.*, should be convincing.

In this case the court chose to provide a definition of "investment contracts":

[An investment contract] is where individuals were led to invest money in a common enterprise with the expectation that they will earn a profit solely through efforts of the promoter or of someone other than themselves. . . .

. . . In other words, an investment contract for the purpose of the Securities Act means a contract, transaction or scheme whereby a person invests his money in a common enterprise and is led to expect profits solely from the efforts of the promoter or a third party. . . .

. . . The statutory policy of affording broad protection to investors is not to be thwarted by unrealistic and irrelevant formulae.[48]

Sale of an interest in a limited partnership is a sale of a "security." It should be treated as such.

At the time the Securities Act of 1933 was enacted and for some period thereafter, anyone not wishing to register an issue simply claimed that it was not a public offering. As expected, the SEC challenged many of these issues in court and gradually a body of law evolved around what was or was not a public offering. Unfortunately, many of the court decisions were not particularly clear and great confusion resulted. To clarify the situation, the SEC issued over a period of time several "rules" describing certain conditions which, if complied with, would give reasonable assurance to an issuer that a particular issue was in fact exempt. Three "exemption" rules exist at present: Rule 146, Rule 147, Rule 240. These rules are reproduced in Appendixes E, F, and G. A new rule, Rule 506, has been issued effective April 15, 1982, to replace Rule 146. A comparison of Rule 146 and Rule 506 is given in Appendix T. The intent of Rule 146 remains unchanged, but investors eligibility requirements have been significantly relaxed. Thus fundraising activities should be considerably simplified.

Exemption Rules

Rule 146 is known as the "safe habor" rule and is the most widely used for unregistered issues, particularly in the limited partnership field. It does not limit the amount of funds that might be raised but does limit to 35 the number of people who may purchase the issue (with some exceptions). This rule will be discussed in more detail in the following paragraph. Rule 147 exempts issues that are conducted entirely within one state. This rule is avoided by most attorneys because of extreme difficulty of containing an issue within a single state (and proving it) under the definition within the rule. Rule 240 limits the amount of money raised to $100,000 but allows up to 100 persons to purchase securities. This rule is infrequently used because of the low limit of funds that could be raised in relation to the legal costs that are inevitably associated with any fund-raising efforts. It should be noted that claiming exemption under any of these rules is not an "election." Claim can always be made to the appropriate section of the Securities Act of 1933 in a general sense; to obtain exemption under any one rule, however, all of the conditions set forth must be met.

Rule 146 became effective April 23, 1974, and was amended on May 7, 1975. The conditions set forth in this rule were the result of a gradual evolution of legal thought that developed from the inception of the Act through 1974. Generally it was believed that whether a transaction involves a public offering depends on the circumstances surrounding the issue. The following factors were thought to be relevant: (1) the number of offerees, (2) the relationship of the offerees to each other and to the issuer, (3) the number of units offered, and (4) the manner of offering.

In *SEC* v. *Ralston Purina Co.* [346 U. S. 119 (1953)] the Supreme Court added: (1) whether the offerees need the protection of the Act or can fend for themselves, (2) whether the offerees have access to the same kind of information that registration under the Act would provide.

Historically there has been no rule of thumb that could determine how many offerees may participate in a private offering, but 25 was the number frequently used. Rule 146 sets the number at 35 but exempts from the court anyone who purchases $150,000 or more of the particular issue. This is, of course, a major exception, as it would be possible to raise any number of people providing each was to purchase $150,000 of the issue. Certain other factors began to seem relevant as time passed: whether the various members of the group knew each other and shared some common interest, whether the relationship was such that each had access to the same information regarding the issue, and whether each member was in fact purchasing the issue for investment purposes and not for resale. It became well established that the burden of proving that an offering is exempt rests with the issuer.

All of these considerations were included, in various forms, in Rule 146.[49] Following is a summary of that rule.

1. *Manner of offering (Rule 146[C]).* No form of general solicitation or advertising is permitted including meetings, seminars, or written communications unless only qualified offerees (or their representatives) are included.

2. *Nature of the offeree (Rule 146[D]).* No offer may be made unless the issuer has reasonable grounds to believe, and believes, that the offeree has sufficient knowledge and experience in financial and business matters to evaluate the merits and risks of the investment or, alternatively, is able to bear the economic risk of investment.

3. *Access to or furnishing of information (Rule 146[E]).* The offeree must either have access to the same kind of information that would be included in a registration statement or the issuer must provide the kind of information specified in Schedule A of the Act. The issuer must also give each offeree or offeree-representative the opportunity to ask questions of and receive answers from the issuer and to obtain any additional information necessary to verify the accuracy of the information given by the issuer.

4. *Number of purchasers (Rule 146 [G]).* The issuer shall have reasonable grounds to believe, and after making reasonable inquiry shall believe, that there are not more than 35 purchasers of the securities; certain relatives of a purchaser, certain controlled entities, and persons who purchase for cash, in a single payment or installments, securities which in the aggregate amount to $150,000 or more are excluded from the count.

5. *Limitations on disposition (Rule 146[H]).* The issuer must exercise reasonable care to assure that the purchasers of the securities are not underwriters within the meaning of Section 2(11) of the Act. To do so the issuer must at least:

    a. Make reasonable inquiry to determine that the purchaser is acquiring the securities for his own account,

    b. Place on the certificate or other document evidencing the security a legend that refers to the restrictions on transferability and sale,

    c. Issue stop-transfer instructions, and

    d. Obtain a written agreement from the purchaser that he will not sell without registration under the Act or an exemption.

6. *Locating offerees (Rule 146[C]).* All written communications with potential offerees are prohibited unless the issuer has reasonable grounds to believe the potential offeree is qualified. Note that while this may make it difficult to locate offerees, certain investment bankers aware of this problem gather necessary information and make it available to their clients.

7. *Qualifying the offeree.* Once a potentially qualified offeree is located, the next step is to determine whether he has sufficient knowledge and experience or is able to bear the economic risk. The principal considerations to determine qualifications are that he has the financial ability to hold the securities offered for an indefinite period of time and has the financial ability, at the time of purchase, to sustain a complete loss of the investment.

8. *Access to and furnishing of information.*

Access. Rule 146 provides that if an offeree has access to the kinds of information that would be provided by a registration statement it is not necessary to furnish the information. From a practical standpoint it is probably unwise to depend on the offeree's having access, so most issuers elect to furnish the required information in order to insure compliance.

Furnishing of information. Companies that are subject to the reporting requirements of Section 13 or 15(D) of the Securities Exchange Act of 1934 may satisfy the disclosure requirements by furnishing the offeree the information contained in the Form 10-K, Form S-1 Registration Statement, or Form 10 Registration Statement, whichever is the most recent.

Most limited partnerships will not fall into this category and thus are required to furnish the information that must be included in the registration statement; but they

> *. . . may omit details or employ condensation of information if, under the circumstances, the omitted information is not material, condensation of information does not render the statement made misleading.*[50]

Note, though, that the burden of proof is on the issuer to prove that the resulting information is not misleading. Also, the rule allows any issuer who does not have an audited financial statement and cannot obtain one without "unreasonable effort or expense" to submit one on an unaudited basis.

As noted above, the issuer also is required to provide the opportunity for the offeree to "ask questions and obtain additional information." This requirement usually is fulfilled by a "due diligence" meeting hosted by the issuer, to which the offerees are invited. Notes are taken or the meeting is taped, because the burden of proof of compliance rests, as noted above, with the issuer. If the issuer is a public company at the time of the "due diligence" meeting, some problems could arise because of the discussion of "insider" information. Recipients of such information become "tippees" under the Texas Gulf Sulphur Rulings and risk getting involved with possible violations of Rule 10B-5. However, since most limited partnerships are not public, this complication happily can be avoided.

The above summary of Rule 146 is provided only as an indication of the various complexities that can arise from attempts to comply with the requirements to issue unregistered securities. While in theory a lawyer is not required to comply with Rule 146, great difficulties could be encountered by taking a do-it-yourself approach. The cost of legal help to insure compliance is of course the major expense involved in launching a limited partnership. While any estimates of costs of compliance would be only estimates, a representative cost of approximately $10,000 for the legal costs of a Rule 146 offering for $750,000 worth of securities was obtained during the preparation of this book.[51] An interesting comparison of costs can be obtained from SEC publications indicating the costs of registered issues for the years 1971–1972.[52] In those years a total of 116 limited partnerships made public offerings. The size of the offerings ranged from $2 million to $100 million, with an average cost of 9.33 percent. This was actually a lower average than common stock offering costs but still, for the $750,000 unregistered offering mentioned above, it would seem that a registered offering would cost in the range of $75,000 as opposed to $10,000 for the unregistered issue. Thus, familiarity with Rule 146 is essential if key front-end legal costs are to be kept to a minimum. Besides minimizing legal expenses, knowledge of the details of Rule 146 can prevent an organizer from inadvertently violating the law during the fund-raising phase of the project.

In summary, an interest in a limited partnership is a "security" and issuance of it comes under the jurisdiction of both the federal and state authorities. Private offerings are possible at a relatively low cost, provided the appropriate rules are precisely followed. Complete, honest, and realistic disclosure of all pertinent information is the basis of the regulations and is the key to successful launching of a new venture. The regulations are available to everyone to study, but competent legal assistance is required to minimize the risk that legal difficulities will occur when they are least expected.

Survey of Leading Activites Pursued by Limited Partnerships

While the ULPA does not place any limitation on the type of activities that may be pursued by limited partnerships, statutory restrictions contained in some state laws as well as practical considerations have precluded limited partnerships from participating in some activites. The California Uniform Limited Partnership Act, paragraph 15503, states, in conformance with the format of the ULPA, that

> . . . *a limited partnership may carry on any business which a partnership without limited partners may carry on, except banking and insurance.*[53]

With regard to restrictions in other states, Matthews summarizes the situation as follows:

> *A major portion of the states make no exception as to the business which a limited partnership may carry on, including Colorado, Florida, Missouri, Montana, New Mexico, Utah and Wisconsin. Among those states restricting business activity in Section three (of the ULPA) most insert banks, insurance companies, railroads with combinations of the three. Vermont prohibits a limited partnership from engaging in a business in which a corporation formed under the general corporation law may not engage. Arkansas seemed to stretch its resources by prohibiting any business as hereafter prohibited by law.*[54]

In addition, some activities are not particularly suited to the limited partnership form. As Moore, Ayers, and Pope noted.

. . . a partnership is usually an unsatisfactory legal entity for conducting man-
ufacturing and marketing (activities) due to its lack of limited liability. . . . [55]

The limitations mentioned above do not seem to have dampened enthusiasm for the limited partnership concept. Limited partnerships have been
used for real estate, oil and gas exploration, cattle feeding and breeding,
vineyards, citrus growing, nuts (the kind that grow on trees), egg production,
figs, olive trees, mobile home parks, oil and gas drilling, gold exploration,
motel, cable television, auto racing, mining, general equipment leasing, nur-
series, theatrical productions, and commodities, just to name a few.

Research for this publication failed to turn up a single centralized source
for determining the status of all limited partnerships in the United States,
although several sources were located from which some implications of major
limited partnership activity could be drawn. All states require that a certificate be filed with an "appropriate office" within the state; this office is most
often the County Recorder's Office. It was felt that a county-by-county
gathering of data was beyond the scope of the study. At least three sources
were found from which significant implications could be drawn, however.
All partnerships, both general and limited, are required to file an income tax
return with the IRS even though the liability for paying income tax rests
with the individual partner. These income statistics are published each year
by the IRS and are available about two years after the closing of the calendar
year; the three catergories of business forms listed are sole proprietorships,
partnerships, and corporations. The weakness in these data for the purpose
of this study is that no distinction is made between limited and general
partnerships.

The second source of information was the National Association of Security Dealers (NASD), which maintains statistics on tax-sheltered filings.
Again though, not all tax shelters are limited partnerships (although most
are) and not all tax shelters are registered. The last source located was the
SEC data on registered limited partnerships and while this source will include
all registered limited partnerships, very few limited partnerships, as noted
above, raise funds through registered offerings.

Based on the business income tax returns for 1973, the following were
the ten leading partnerships (general and limited) activities of ranked numbers (in thousands) of partnerships:

1. Building rentals (244)
2. Holding and investment companies (86)
3. Livestock farms (58)
4. Field crop farms (38)
5. Non-building real estate rentals (128)
6. Legal services (28)
7. Eating places (22)
8. General building contractors (20)

9. Gasoline service stations (20)
10. Grocery stores (17)[56]

On the other hand, NASD listed for 1972 the following tax shelter filing ranked by number of filings:

1. Real estate (243)
2. Oil and gas (226)
3. Cattle and breeding (30)
4. Farming (21)
5. Miscellaneous (11)

The numbers in parentheses are total filings (not in thousands as were in the listings under the business tax returns). Note that real estate still ranks number 1 even though this is not an apples-to-apples comparison. Oil and gas partnerships numbered 12,000 in 1973 in the business income tax returns listing not among the top ten, yet number 2 in the tax shelter filings the year before.

For registered limited partnerships, the SEC indicates the following ranking (again by number of partnerships—1972):

1. Extractive, including oil and gas (56)
2. Finance and real estate (44)
3. Commercial and other (15)

While the above data are of only limited utility because of their lack of common base and their failure to apply exclusively to limited partnerships, the data would seem to support Matthews' statement in 1974:

Though the limited partnership is not the exclusive route to obtain tax shelter, it is widely and frequently used in the major tax shelter industries of real estate, oil and gas exploration and cattle feeding.[57]

It is interesting to note that while the Tax Reform Act of 1976 was thought to be motivated primarily by the desire to limit the use of tax shelters, by its exclusion of real estate from the restrictions against the use of non-recourse financing to increase the taxpayers' basis for deducting losses, apparently the largest activity utilizing this type of shelter (real estate) was left untouched. An interesting speculation is whether this was done to promote socially acceptable ends (divert investments from oil and gas exploration to real estate investment) or to satisfy political problems. (Was the real estate lobby stronger than the oil and gas lobby?) Superficially, it would seem, in view of the increasing dependence of the United States on foreign oil imports, that the government should have moved in exactly the opposite direction; that is, to encourage investment in oil and gas and slow down investment into energy-consuming real estate developments. But this imparts a belief in government rationality as opposed to political expendiency, probably a utopian thought at best. It would be hoped, of course, as the energy problems becomes more threatening and at last the public realizes that it might be better to let those engaged in domestic oil and gas exploration and development make a profit rather than either to go to war over the right of access to foreign energy reserves or to do without petroleum products altogether, that the very powerful tool of tax benefits, as represented by tax shelters, would be directed toward solving vital problems at the national level rather than satisfying the most vocal political faction. At any rate, the tools are available.

This section has outlined what limited partnerships can accomplish in the way of channeling investment funds into various industries. The next section of this chapter will investigate how a Supreme Court decision in 1974 opened up a whole new application for the limited partnership just when the need for it was becoming critical to this country.

BACKGROUND OF R & D LIMITED PARTNERSHIPS

The possibility of forming an R & D limited partnership, which would permit the partners to deduct partnership expenditures for R & D activities from their individual incomes and then allow income from the sale of the successfully developed invention to be treated as capital gains income, first became a reality on May 13, 1974, when the Supreme Court handed down its decision in the *Snow* case. This section will review the available literature pertaining to two key aspects of this case: the decision itself, including the legal precedents involved, and some details of the tax consequences.

A Review of the *Snow* Decision

The formal announcement of the decision appears as follows:

> *Edwin A. Snow et ux, Petitioners v. Commissioner of Internal Revenue, Respondent. U. S. Supreme Court, No. 73-641, May 13, 1974. Sixth Circuit, 32 AFTR 2 73-5400 Reversed. Year 1966. Decision for taxpayer.*[58]

This decision, in which a taxpayer, Snow, was allowed to deduct from the income he earned as an executive his pro-rata portion of the expenditures made by a partnership in which he had made an investment, solely for research and development work even though no sale of the product took place in the year the expenses were incurred, is the foundation upon which this book is based. To base a judgment on the future utilization of this type of limited partnership, it would seem useful not only to study the decision carefully but to look into its legal background. As it now stands only three events could occur that would materially change the law. First, Congress could explicitly disallow R & D deductions by individuals or partnerships by enacting a new tax statute; second, the Supreme Court could reverse itself at some future date; finally, the Commissioner could interpret the decision on a narrow basis and such an interpretation could be upheld, if it were litigated, by the courts.

As the case was summarized,

Petitioner Edwin A. Snow, who had advanced part of the capital in a partnership formed in 1966 to develop a special-purpose incinerator and had become a limited partner, was disallowed a deduction under Section 174(A)(1) of the Internal Revenue Code of 1954, on his individual income tax return for that year for his prorata share of the partnership's operating loss. Though there were no sales in 1966, expectations were high and the inventor-partner was giving about a third of his time to the project, an outside engineering firm doing all the shopwork. The Tax Court and the Court of Appeals both upheld expenditures which are paid or incurred with his trade or business as expenses which are not chargeable to capital account.

The Court held that it was an error to disallow the deduction,

. . . which was "in connection with" petitioner's trade or business, and the disallowance was contrary to the broad legislative objective of the Congress when it enacted Section 174 to provide an economic incentive, especially for small and growing businesses, to engage in the search for new products and new inventions. Pp. 2–4. 482 F.2 1029, Reversed.[59]

Several comments can be made on this summary. First, the statement that it was "in error" to disallow the deduction, which was "'in connection with' petitioner's trade or business," raises at least two further questions: What does "in connection with" mean and what was the "petitioner's trade or business"? This is not just a question of semantics but raises several key legal issues which will be discussed later in this section. Secondly, it should be noted that the court ruled that "the disallowance was contrary to the broad legislative objective of the Congress. . . . "[60] This implies that the "broad legislative objective of the Congress" can in fact be ascertained twelve years later. The implication will be pursued later in this section; suffice it to say here that such a determination is not easy—it presumes that Congress, when it enacts a law, does in fact have "a broad legislative objective." Does a group as large as Congress, composed of so many persons with widely divergent opinions on the role of government, really have a single objective when it passes a law; or does that law, when passed, mean different things to different representatives?

Under the Constitution it falls to the Supreme Court to make that determination, rightly or wrongly. In this instance, the Court's decision was remarkably brief, and as such perhaps it is less liable to misinterpretations or reinterpretation than a longer, more complicated opinion. A closer look at the decision itself may answer part of the question of congressional intent.

Justice Douglas delivered the opinion of the Court:

> *Section 174(1) of the Internal Revenue Code of 1954, 26 USC 174, allows a taxpayer to take as a deduction "experimental expenditures which are paid or incurred by him during the taxable year in connection with his trade or business as expenses which are not chargeable to capital account." Petitioner was disallowed as a deduction his distributive share of the net operating loss of a partnership, Burns Investment Company, for the year 1966. The U.S. Tax Court sustained the Commissioner, 58 TC 585. The Court of Appeals affirmed, 482 F.2 1029 (32 AFTR 2 73-5400) (CA6 1973). The case is here on a writ of certiorari because of an apparent conflict between the Court of Appeals for the Sixth Circuit with that of the Fourth Circuit in Cleveland v. Commissioner, 297 F. 169 (8 AFTR 2 5989) (CA4 1961). . . .* [61]

It should be noted here that the Sixth Circuit Court supported the Commissioner against the taxpayer primarily on the grounds that the taxpayer was not engaged in "any trade or business" nor were efforts sufficiently continuous or regular to represent his engaging in a trade or business. The Fourth Circuit Court in Cleveland supported the taxpayer against the Commissioner, in similar circumstances stating that the taxpayer had entered the inventing business and could claim the Section 174 deduction.[62] This conflict of opinion between the courts was at least one reason why the Supreme Court agreed to hear the case.

Continuing the opinion of the Court,

> *Petitioner was a limited partner in Burns, having contributed $10,000 for a four-percent interest in Burns. . . .*
>
> *Burns was formed to develop "a special purpose incinerator for the consumer and industrial markets." Trott was the inventor and had conceived this idea in 1964 and between then and 1966 had made a number of prototypes. His patent counsel had told him in 1965 that several features of the burner were in his view patentable but in 1966 advised him that the incinerator as a whole had not been sufficiently "reduced to practice" in order to develop it into a marketable product. At that point Trott formed Burns, petitioner putting up part of the capital. Thereafter various models of the burner were built and tested. . . .* [63]

Here it is clear that at the time the partnership was formed, the invention had not been "reduced to practice," a significant point as will become apparent when the pertinent IRC sections are reviewed later. Also, as noted in the summary above, no sales occurred in 1966 even though prototypes were built.

Trott did obtain a patent on the incinerator in 1970 and, at the time of the Court's decision (May 1974), it was being produced and marketed under the name "Trash-away" by the Burns Investment Corporation. Snow was the Chairman of the Board of Burns.

The opinion went on to say,

> *Section 174 [of the Internal Revenue Code] was enacted in 1954 to dilute some of the conception of "ordinary and necessary" business expenses under Section 162 . . . adumbrated by Justice Frankfurter in a concurring opinion in Deputy v. Dupont, 308 U.S. 488, 499 (23 AFTR 808) (1940), where he said the section in question . . . "involves holding one's self out to others as engaged in the selling of goods or services." The words "trade or business" appear, however, in about 60 different sections of the 1954 Act (Saunders, Trade or Business, its meaning under the Internal Revenue Code, So. Cal. 12th Inst. on Fed. Tax. 693 [1960]). Those other sections are not helpful here because Congress wrote into Section 174 "in connection with" and Section 162 is more narrowly written than is Section 174, allowing "a deduction" of "ordinary and necessary expenses paid or incurred . . . in carrying on any trade or business." That and other sections are not helpful here.*

The issue raised here, as noted above, is the meaning of "engaged in trade or business" as mentioned in Section 162 as compared to the same words in Section 174. The Court here seems to be saying that because Section 174 prefaces the phrase with the words "in connection with" rather than "in carrying on," as used in Section 162, a wider interpretation of "engaged in trade or business" was permitted and in fact required by Congress. The opinion continued to explain its reasoning,

> *The legislative history makes fairly clear the reasons. Established firms with ongoing business had continuous programs of research quite unlike "small or pioneering business enterprises" (Hearings on H.R. 8300, 83rd Cong., 2 Sess., P I, 105.)*[64]

Congressman Reid of New York, Chairman of the House Committee on Ways and Means, made the point even more explicit when he addressed the House on the Bill (100 Cong. Rec. 3425 [1954]):

> *Present law contains no statutory provisions dealing with the deduction of these expenses. The result has been confusion and uncertainty. Very often, under present law, small businesses which are developing new products and do not have established research departments are not allowed to deduct their expenses despite the fact that their large and well-established competitors can obtain the deduction. . . . This provision will greatly stimulate the search for new products and the new inventions upon which the future economic and military strength of the nation depends. It will be particularly valuable to small and growing businesses.*[65]

The Court established its rationale for believing that the "intent of Congress" was to permit businesses just getting started to deduct research and development expenses in the same manner as their "large and well-established competitors." It could perhaps be argued that a "small and growing" business is not the same as one that is not yet "engaged in any trade or business"; but other statements made by various members of Congress, which will be discussed later in the section, seem to reinforce the Court's opinion here although these statements were not cited in the opinion.

The opinion continued:

> *Congress may at times in its wisdom discriminate taxwise between various kinds of business, between old and oncoming business and the like. But we would defeat the congressional purpose somewhat to equalize the tax benefits of the ongoing companies and those that are upcoming and about to reach the market by perpetuating the discrimination created below and urged upon us here.*
>
> *We read Section 174 as did the Fourth Circuit Court of Appeals in Cleveland "to encourage expenditure for research and experimentation." 297 F.2, 173. That incentive is embedded in Section 174 because of "in connection with," making irrelevant whether petitioners were rich or poor.*[66]

Here the Court is again arguing that the intent of Congress was to encourage research and experimental efforts similar to those in which Snow was engaged, and to sustain the lower court's ruling would operate counter to the intentions of Congress.

With a brief answer to a possible challenge that the petitioner was engaged in a "hobby" as defined under Section 183, rather than in a business for profit, the Court concluded its opinion:

> *We are invited to explore the treatment of "hobby-losses" under Section 183. But that is far afield of the present inquiry for it is clear that in this case under Section 174 the profit motive was the sole drive of the venture. Reversed.*[67]

The Court's decision was based on two key points: First, by including the words "in connection with" in writing Section 174, Congress intended a wider interpretation of being engaged in "a trade or business" than was the generally accepted interpretation of Section 162, which is concerned with deductions of ordinary business expenses. Second, the Court concluded that it was the intent of Congress that Section 174 be written to "encourage expenditure for research and experimentation" and a ruling supporting the Sixth Circuit Court would act contrary to this objective. A brief study of the history of both the legislative and legal aspects of the tax treatment of research and development expenditures will tend to reinforce the Supreme Court decision.

Historical Perspective of the *Snow* Decision

In the Spring of 1974, John W. Lee published a paper in Tax Lawyer titled "Preoperating Expenses and Section 174: Will *Snow* Fall?" Written after the Supreme Court had agreed to hear the *Snow* case but before a decision had been reached, it was a thorough and painstaking analysis of the issues facing the court in this case. Lee started out by commenting that while expenditures to develop new products unrelated to existing product lines may qualify under Section 174,

> . . . *for over a decade the Tax Court and lower federal courts, at the time this paper was written, held that the "going trade or business" requirement is not met unless the taxpayer "holds himself out to others as providing goods or services."* [69]

Under this view, there would be no deduction for expenditures for R & D that is undertaken when the taxpayer is just beginning an operation and does not have any product to sell. Thus, a small enterprise undertaking R & D for its first invention, which in unrelated to any mainline trade or business, would not be entitled to a Section 174 deduction, but a venture already engaged in the business of experimentation and developments of new products, i.e., inventing or general business, would be able to deduct R & D expenditures for new products even though not related to current product lines or manufacturing processes.

This appears to be discriminatory against a new or small business; and while there seems to be no issue at stake involving the right of Congress to so discriminate, there is an issue of whether this was Congress' intent. Lee stated four issues upon which the Supreme Court's decision could rest:

> *(1)   Whether Section 174 requires a distinction between trade or business expenses and expenses preparatory to engaging in a trade or business;*
>
> *(2)   Whether the trade or business concept includes a requirement of holding one's self out to others as providing goods or services;*
>
> *(3)   Whether the trade or business of a partnership is imputed to a limited partner, and, if so, whether that treatment affects the character of the partner's activities in another separate partnership; and*
>
> *(4)   Whether a tax shelter motive should affect the timing or deductibility of expenses.* [70]

As Lee pointed out, prior to 1926 tax regulation permitted either expensing or capitalization of expenditures for experiments intended to improve facilities or products. In 1925, the Board of Tax Appeals ruled in *Gilliam Manufacturing Company* that amounts expended to acquire patents were capital expenses and that a taxpayer could not deduct those expenses as incurred. The Treasury deleted that option from the regulation in 1926.

In the Goodell-Pratt Co. case (3 B.T.A. 30 [19251]), for instance, the Board of Tax Appeals reasoned that R & D expenditures must be capitalized because "they were expended expressly for the purpose of increasing the earning capacity of the enterprise in acquiring something of permanent use in the business." This reasoning was relied on throughout the thirties and forties and in many instances this case was cited as authority. In 1951, however, Representative Camp, a member of the House Ways and Means Committee, inserted in the Congressional Record a summary explanation of a proposed Revenue Revision Act of 1951, submitted by the American Bar Association. That explanation, in describing a provision quite similar to Section 174, stated:

> *In order to clarify the existing confusion in respect to the tax treatment of such expenditures, and to prevent tax discrimination between large businesses having continuous programs of research and small or beginning business enterprises, Section 154 provides generally that expenditures made in industrial or commercial products, service or processes may, at the election of the taxpayer, be deducted as expenses or capitalized and charged off over a period selected and designated by the taxpayer.*[71]

Representative Camp included the words "small or beginning" in describing the businesses which his proposed tax amendment would benefit. Three years passed before this proposed change was incorporated into the 1954 Code and emerged as Section 174, but the intent of Congress at that time was clear. The House and Senate Committee Reports on the 1954 Code recognizes the uncertainty in the existing law and made clear that the purpose of Section 174 was jointly to eliminate the uncertainty and to encourage taxpayers to carry on research and experimentation by allowing them the election of either current deduction or a deferred deduction of R & D expenditures until the invention is first put to an income-producing use, followed thereafter by amortization of such deferred expenditures over a 60-month period.

The Chairmen of the Congressional Tax Committees repeated, in their explanation of Section 174 to their respective Houses of Congress, that it was intended to

> *. . . eliminate the competitive disadvantage under the current law to small businesses that attempt to develop new products without established research programs since they were frequently not permitted to deduct their expenses, unlike large and well-established competitors with expansive regular research budgets.*[72]

However, while Congressional intent may be clear from the reading the above comments from the Congressmen involved, the Tax Court, in 1961, seven years after the enactment of the 1954 Code, ruled in *Koons* that the term "trade or business" in Section 174 was used in the sense of a "going" trade or business.[73] The taxpayer in *Koons* had contracted with a research laboratory to develop an invention, then in a primitive state, to the stage of commercial acceptance. The court held that development activity of this type was preliminary to the existence of a trade or business of the taxpayer and that Section 174 applied only to R & D expenditures made in connection with an existing trade or business. The Tax Court in *Koons* looked to the decision under Section 162 on business investigation and concluded that expenditures made in investigating a potential business or preparatory to entering into a business were not made in connection with an existing trade or business, and hence were not deductible.

It is interesting that *Koons* was not carried to a higher court. Snow was turned down first by the Commissioner, then by the Tax Court, and then by the Circuit Court before he received a favorable decision in the Supreme Court. Would the results have been the same had Koons persevered? Apparently the "law" to a great extent depends on how far and to what extent a litigant is prepared to expend resources to prove a point. This is a somewhat dreary conclusion considering that the government has virtually unlimited resources at its disposal while the taxpayer generally has limited funds, particularly in cases of this sort where the issue primarily centers around an individual's rights.

The Sixth Circuit Court in *Snow* noted that the Tax Court's ruling against Snow had applied the term "trade or business" as that phrase had been construed at the time of the Congressional enactment of Section 174 and that the definition had been made by Justice Frankfurter and later cited in the *Richmond Television Corporation* case as "holding one's self out to others as engaged in selling."[74] Interestingly, the court concluded that the above-quoted comments by Representative Camp could not set aside such "settled interpretation" of trade and business as used in Section 174. What of congressional intent? Apparently it can be ignored when convenient, at least in the lower courts.

Lee, however, went on to ask, "What then was the Congressional intent in incorporating a trade or business requirement into Section 174?" He submitted that

> . . . Congress only contemplated imposition of profit motive and continuity requirements—that the R & D activities must be carried on with an expectation of economic return as an end product of the R & D, and that the taxpayer must devote substantial portions of his time to the activities or there must have been extensive or repeated activity over a substanitial period of time.[75]

Prior to the *Snow* decision but after the enactment of the Internal Revenue Code of 1954, deductions were permitted under Section 174 for R & D which in itself did not constitute a "going business" where a corporation was seeking to develop a new product unrelated to its past line of products. In *Best Universal Lock Co.*, for example,

> . . . a corporation whose regular line of business was the development of locks sought a section 174 deduction for expenditures made in research for the design of a new air compressor. The court allowed the deduction, saying that section 174 extended to expenses incurred in developing a new product unrelated to

the past line of goods. In this respect one might observe the absence of any substantive difference between the kind of expenditures made by a business in its initial stage and those made by an ongoing business which undertakes the development of a new item unrelated to its regular line of goods.[76]

Lee went on at some length to follow the historical development of the different tax treatments afforded three basis types of business expenses: investigatory, pre-operating, and operating expenses. As he pointed out, investigatory expenses are never deductible, pre-operating expenses are usually capitalized, and operating expenses are always expensed. The controversy in *Snow* is centered around the treatment of pre-operating expenses: the same expenses may be judged pre-operating for a start-up situation but pure operating expenses for a "going" business. Research and development expenses seem to fall into this category and Lee spent considerable time developing arguments as to how pre-operating expenses should be handled. The more one reads the arguments surrounding Section 174 the more one concurs with the conclusion reached by Hinderer in *The Missouri Law Review*:

The opposing results reached by the Tax Court and the court of appeals, holding for the Commissioner [in Snow] and the Supreme Court, for the taxpayer, reflect a basic ideological conflict on how to interpret section 174. The Code does not define the term "trade or business." A precise definition, adequate for all situations, may be impossible. The traditional elements considered in determining the existence of a trade or business have been a profit motive and an enterprise characterized by regularity of activities and the production of income. The presence or absence of income, in itself, is not decisive.[77]

In other words, the classification of R & D expenditures as pre-operating expenses to a small or beginning business and hence not currently deductible, as opposed to classifying them as operating expenditures to a going corporation depends on two lines of thought: what were Congress' intentions when Section 174 was enacted and does this line of thought overrule previously "established" definitions. The lower courts did not seem to make much effort to determine Congressional intent and, while recognizing in passing that the intent might be different from previous case law, the courts chose to ignore it. The Supreme Court, on the other hand, looked at Congressional intent, satisfied itself as to what the intent was, and ruled that the intent superseded prior case law.

The last two issues raised by Lee in his pre-Supreme Court decision paper on the *Snow* case, while not subsequently brought up the Supreme Court, are of interest in considering R & D limited partnerships. First is the issue of the trade or business status of the limited partner: Is it imputed that his status is the same as that of the partnership? Finally there is the issue of tax shelter motive.

While it is beyond the scope of this discussion to present these arguments in any complete form, and in fact no conclusive arguments are available, the nature of the problems should be noted. With regard to the trade or business status of the limited partner, two significant issues are raised: (1) Is a partnership's trade or business status imputed to the partners, or does partnership profit or loss merely maintain the same trade or business status for tax return purposes in the partner's hands as it had in the hands of the partnership; and (2) assuming that a partner has obtained trade or business status either through attribution from another partnership, or independently through individual activities, does this status affect the character of distributive share of partnership income or loss which, in the hands of the partnership or in the hands of another partner, would not be incurred or earned in a trade business? As Lee pointed out, "The answers to these two inquiries have consquences in contexts other than Section 174."[78] For example, a question currently has been raised whether the profit motive of Section 183 (the hobby issue) is determined at the partnership or partner level. If the former, would a partner's motive override that of the partnership? Commentators have also frequently discussed whether a taxpayer who is a dealer, for example, in real estate may obtain capital gains treatment for a sale by a non-dealer partnership in which the person is a partner. These issues in essence turn on the competing "entity" and "aggregate" theories of partnership taxation, which the Supreme Court recently declined to address in *Basye*. (*United States* v. *Basye*, 410 U.S. 442 [1973].) As Lee concluded,

> Only the Supreme Court or Congress can now resolve whether the "entity" or "aggregate" approach is to apply here. The legislative history, a slight majority of commentators, and the imputation cases militate towards the aggregate approach. The government has blown both hot and cold for the entity approach, albeit heretofore usually hot.[79]

The last point raised by Lee was whether the tax shelter motive should affect the timing of the deductibility of expenses:

> The Sixth Circuit in Snow noted that the taxpayer had income in 1966 in excess of $200,000, so that his investment in the partnership was made as a high bracket taxpayer. It then concluded that two laudable public purposes were therefore in direct conflict: (1) stimulation of R & D by inventors and small businessmen, and (2) the desirability of strict interpretation of the laws so as to prevent unintended tax shelters.

Lee further noted:

> . . . as shown in the preceding section not just strict but erroneous interpretation as well of Section 174 is necessary to support the result reached by the lower court in Snow."[80]

A final point raised is the principle of matching income with expenses. Is this the intent of Section 174? At least one example to prove the inappropriateness of this concept is the example of advertising expenses. Current deductibility of these expenses is allowed and yet benefits accrue sometime in the future. The same might be said of R & D expenditures. There is no doubt that allowing currently a deductible expense in an enterprise that has no other business except R & D permits a taxpayer to shelter unrelated current income and hence defer income taxes until some later date when the process or invention produces taxable income. Yet it appears, as Lee noted that

> . . . *Congress contemplated that a taxpayer could offset R & D expenditures against substantial income from other sources and that a temporary loss of revenue (the deferred taxes) would result.*

Representative Camp's comments on the ABA prototype to Section 174 pointed out that

> *Merely providing for deductibility of such expenditures probably would be satisfactory to most large businesses. However, a small business which has unusually large expenditures in connection with a research program, or a new or beginning business enterprise, must be allowed the right to capitalize such costs and recover them by amortization deductions over the estimated useful life, in order to insure equality of treatment with large businesses, which can and usually do deduct the full amount of such expenditures from current income. . . . It is provided that the taxpayer may designate the period over which the capitalized costs of a specific research project or undertaking shall be amortized. Any temporary loss of revenue resulting from a taxpayer's selection of an unreasonably short amortization period will ordinarily be recovered in later years when no amortization deductions will be allowable.*[81]

Lee concluded:

> *Unless the Supreme Court decides to fashion a requirement that start-up costs are to be deferred until their related income is produced and are then deductible against such income as earned, which is not the same as capitalizing them, it should reverse* Snow.[82]

As noted above, the Supreme Court did reverse the lower courts as correctly predicted by Lee.

In spite of all the above arguments, including of course the Supreme Court decisions relating to the *Snow* case, there have been dissenting views, as noted by Hinderer:

> *The [Supreme] Court stated that this section was enacted to allow small businesses the same tax advantage as that previously enjoyed only by larger businesses with established research departments.*

Persuasive arguments can be made that Congress did not intend such a result. The Treasury Regulations for section 162 use the phrases "connected with or pertaining to" and "in connection with" as the apparent equivalent of the statutory language, "in carrying on." In other sections of the Code where the term "trade or business" has appeared, legislators, courts and the Commissioner have relied on the interpretation of the term as developed under Section 162.[83] . . . It would seem that if Congress had intended section 174 to be broader than section 162, it would have used words such as "any profit-seeking activity" rather than "trade or business."[84]

However, this sounds a little bit like sour grapes. The discussions by both Houses prior to enactment of Section 174 specifically stated that a wider interpretation of section 162 was desired and the Supreme Court concurred.

However, Hinderer quoted the Court of Appeals as follows:

. . . a decision in favor of Snow *makes possible a tax shelter for persons in high income brackets. Such a taxpayer will be able to take current deductions for sums advanced to an inventor-partnership.*

Hinderer went on to say,

The tax benefits do not end there. Once a marketable product is developed, the partnership, rather than proceeding with its manufacture whereby the proceeds would be ordinary income, may sell the invention to an established manufacturer. . . . The amount received from the sale would then be taxed at the more favorable capital gains rate. In this way, a taxpayer who advances funds to a limited partnership which is developing only one product will be in a more advantageous tax position than either a large business with an established research department or a taxpayer who invests in a corporation that is totally devoted to research. One probable consequence of Snow *will be to enhance the use of limited partnership as a one-shot investment medium for new product development.[85]*

Hinderer concluded by noting that, in the future,

The application of Section 174 should depend upon the substance of the expenditures or the purpose of them, rather than upon the stage of advancement of the business when the expenditures are made. Therefore, if an expense is of the same type that a large business would attribute to its research department, then it will probably be eligible for a deduction under Section 174, even though the taxpayer might not be engaged in a "trade or business" as defined in cases arising solely under Section 162.[86]

This appears to be a wholly rational and desirable outcome of the *Snow* case. If R & D expenditures will be allowed as deductible expenses based upon the "substance" or their "purpose" instead of some ill-defined state of advancement of the business enterprise, the intent of Congress to promote increased R & D efforts will probably be fulfilled.

At the beginning of this section it was stated that only three events could occur which would eliminate the R & D limited partnership as a viable legal entity: (1) Congress could explicitly change the law in view of the *Snow* decision, (2) the Supreme Court could reverse itself, (3) the Commissioner could disallow some aspects of a limited R & D partnership based on a narrow interpretation of the *Snow* decision. Based on the information presented here it would appear that if Congress had felt its intentions were misinterpreted by the *Snow* decision, it had an opportunity to correct this misunderstanding in the Tax Reform Act of 1976, the Revenue Act of 1978, or the Economic Recovery Act of 1981. Congress was well aware of the *Snow* decision, yet no attack on this decision was made in any of these pieces of legislation. Whether the Supreme Court would reverse itself is of course impossible to predict. However, the decision was short and simple, and without a change in the tax laws by Congress reversal would seem unlikely. With regard to a narrow interpretation by the Commissioner, again the decision was short and simple. It will be difficult to attack.

Key Federal Tax Code Provisions Relating to R & D Limited Partnerships

Favorable tax treatment for taxpayers engaged in research and development activities was the incentive held out by Congress when Section 174 of the 1954 Internal Revenue Code was voted into law. That favorable tax treatment for individual taxpayers, as opposed to the corporate taxpayer, was indeed the intent of Congress was reaffirmed by the Supreme Court in the *Snow* decision in 1974. While it is to be sincerely hoped that most, if not all, business ventures would be founded on the hope of achieving profitable status, many individual taxpayers are, in fact, preoccupied with the tax-planning aspects of business ventures. As Matthews noted,

> *Of the various responses to the question of what the limited partners viewed as the advantages of their investment in the* [cattle feeding] *fund, the most frequent response was tax shelter, accounting for nearly 80% of the responses.*[87]

While the IRS views business ventures structured primarily for the tax consequences and possessing no other "economic utility" as somehow immoral and subsequently attacks them when the opportunity arises, it is interesting to note that the tax laws are written by Congress—in many instances, precisely with the intent to encourage one type of economic activity over another by offering tax incentives for the desired activity while often providing tax disincentives for the undesirable activites. As an example, in a previous section of this chapter the Tax Reform Act of 1976 was discussed. In that Act nonrecourse financing of motion pictures was disallowed,[88] discouraging the channeling of investment funds into unrealistic enterprises. Section 174 of the 1954 Code was written to "greatly stimulate search for new products and the new inventions upon which the future economic and military strength of the nation depends.[89] So, while "economic utility" should be present in any business venture, not only to satisfy the IRS but to gain ultimate benefit for the investor, the tax aspects of the venture are always of major consequence.

Review of IRC Sections 174 and 1235

The two key Code provisions that pertain to R & D limited partnerships are Section 174 and Section 1235. Before the events that transpired following the *Snow* decision in 1974 are reviewed, the pertinent portions of these sections will be discussed.

Section 174 was incorporated into the Code in 1954. The circumstances surrounding its adaptation were discussed in some detail in the previous section of this chapter and will not be repeated here. Section 174 was litigated by *Snow*, finally resulting in a Supreme Court decision in favor of the taxpayer in 1974. (Section 174, is reproduced as Appendix K, for reference purposes.)

Section 174(a)(1) states:

> *In general, a taxpayer may treat research or experimental expenditures which are paid or incurred by him during the taxable year in connection with his trade or business as expenses which are not chargeable to capital account. The expenditures so treated shall be allowed as a deduction.*

This, of course, is the crux of the issue and the basis of the *Snow* decision. Note the use of the words "in connection with" in referring to the taxpayer's "trade or business." As noted by the Supreme Court, this is looser construction than contained in Section 162 where the words "in carrying on" are used supporting, in the Court's view, Congress' intention that Section 174 be available for use by "small and beginning companies," and hence not confined to use by ongoing businesses.

Section 174(a)(2) allows the taxpayer to take the deduction without the consent of the Secretary, provided this method is adopted the first taxable year in which the expenses were incurred. With the consent of the Secretary, this method may be adopted at any time.

Section 174(b) allows the taxpayer to amortize research expenses over a period of not less than 60 months provided that the taxpayer makes the election to do so in the manner prescribed in Section 174(b)(2).

Section 174(c) specifies,

> *. . . This section shall not apply to any expenditure for the acquisition or improvement of property to be used in connection with the research or experimentation and of a character which is subject to the allowance under section 167 (relating to allowance for depreciation, etc.) or section 611 (relating*

to allowance for depletion); but for purposes of this section allowances under section 167 and allowances under section 611 shall be considered as expenditures.[90]

Section 174(d) states that this section does not apply to

. . . any expenditure paid or incurred for the purpose of ascertaining the existence, location, extent, or quality of any deposit of ore or other mineral (including oil and gas).[91]

Section 174(e) provides a cross reference:

"For adjustments to basis of property for amounts allowed as deductions as deferred expenses under subsection (b) see section 1016(a)(14)."[92]

While the above section is simple, short, and to the point, it would seem its implications are far reaching. Precise definitions of many of the terms used are not provided in the original statute but subsequent statutes, revenue rulings, and case law are gradually filling in the blanks. Appendix I provides the explanations and definitions required to more fully explain Section 174. Pertinent Revenue Rulings are included as well as the more obvious definitions of exactly what a "research and experimental expenditure" is.

Section 174 provides for the deductibility portion of the tax benefits that can accrue to an R & D limited partnership. After such a partnership has incurred the expenditures required by the product at hand, the next step is to arrange for the sale of the product, assuming the research and experimental expenditures were made in such a manner as to produce a saleable item. It would be most desirable to the limited partners if such a sale could result in capital gains income as this income would be taxed at the present time at a maximum rate of 20 percent as opposed to a maximum tax rate of 50 percent if the income were classified as ordinary income. Such treatment is possible if the invention or product is sold to a second party under the conditions specified in Section 1235 of the 1954 Code, titled "Sale or Exchange of Patents."

Section 1235(a) states that

. . . A transfer (other than a gift, inheritance, or devise) of property consisting of all substantial rights to a patent, or an undivided interest therein which includes a part of all such rights, by any holder shall be considered the sale or exchange of a capital asset held for more than . . . one year . . . regardless of whether or not payments in consideration of such transfer are—

(1) payable periodically over a period generally coterminous with the transferee's use of the patent, or

(2) contingent on the productivity, use, or disposition of the property transferred.[93]

In other words, so long as "all substantial rights" are sold, the proceeds can be counted as long-term capital gains regardless of whether payment is received in a lump sum, over a period of time, or contingent on other events such as the number of units sold. Note that this section refers only to the sale of a "patent"; yet when the definition of a patent is discussed, it turns out that an actual patent is not needed if the requirements of this section are otherwise met. Specifically,

> *1.1235-2(A) Patent. The term "patent" means a patent granted under the provisions of Title 35 of the United States Code, or any foreign patent granting rights generally similar to those under a United States patent.*
>
> *It is not necessary that the patent or patent application for the invention be in existence if the requirements of Section 1235 are otherwise met.*[94]

The Commerce Clearing House explanation further elaborates on this important point as follows:

> *. . . apparently, therefore, the term "patent" includes "invention." This is supported by the fact that the regulations provide that a person may qualify as a "holder" whether or not he is in the business of "making inventions" or in the business of buying and selling patents. The regulations could be interpreted, however, as requiring that a patent must eventually come into existence. The Tax Court has held . . . that percentage payments received for the transfer of ownership of an unpatented invention were capital gains, overruling the Commissioner's contention that ownership of the invention could not be transferred because it had not been patented. The Commissioner acquiesced in this holding.*
>
> *The Court of Appeals for the Fifth Circuit . . . holds that secret formulas and trade names are sufficiently akin to patents to warrant the application, by analogy, of the tax law that has been developed relating to the transfer of patent rights, in tax cases involving transfers of secret formulas and trade names.*[95]

This means, of course, that a "know-how" type of product can be sold and receive capital gains treatment under Section 1235 if all other requirements are met.

Section 1235(b) defines a "holder" as used in Section (a):

> *For purposes of this section, the term "holder" means—*
>
> *(1) any individual whose efforts created such property, or*
>
> *(2) any other individual who has acquired his interest in such property in exchange for consideration in money or money's worth paid to such creator prior to actual reduction to practice of the invention covered by the patent, if such individual is neither—*

(a)   the employer of such a creator, nor

(b)   related to such creator (within the meaning of subsection [d]).[96]

It is interesting that in defining a "holder" the Code recognizes two levels of invention, that of the original idea and that of reducing that idea to practice. Different persons can be involved at each level and if different persons are involved, each can be a "holder" and qualify for capital gains treatment upon the sale of "all substantial rights" to an unrelated party. This concept is key to an individual partner's receiving captial gains income from the sale of a developed product. Without this definition it would be impossible for any other than the originator of any idea to qualify. But Congress recognized the value of the contribution of the means to reduce such an idea to "practice" and afforded those who made this contribution the realization of capital gains if the product were successfully developed and sold. It should also be noted that, while a partnership cannot qualify for the capital gains treatment as an entity,

Reg 1.1235-2(D) provides that, " . . . each partner who is an individual can qualify for capital gains treatment as to his share of a patent owned by the partnership." Each individual partner's distributive share of income from the transfer of all substantial rights to a patent or an undivided interest therein would be capital gains.[97]

"Reduction to practice" is defined in Section 1.1235-2(3) as follows:

. . . for the purpose of determining whether an individual is a holder under paragraph (D) of this section, the term "actual reduction to practice" has the same meaning as it does under Section 102(G) of Title 35 of the United States Code. Generally, an invention is reduced to actual practice when it has been tested and operated successfully under operating conditions.

This may occur either before or after application for a patent but cannot occur later than the earliest time that commercial exploitation of the invention occurs.[98]

Section 1235(C) states:

Effective Date.—This section shall be applicable with regard to any amount received, or payments made, pursuant to a transfer described in subsection (a) in any taxable year to which this subtitle applies, regardless of the taxable year in which such transfer occurred.[99]

Section 1235(d) provided the definition of "related persons" as used in Section 1235(B)(2)(b) and states:

Subsection (a) shall not apply to any transfer, directly or indirectly, between persons specified within any one of the paragraphs of section 267(b); except that, in applying section 267(b) and (c) for purposes of this section—

(1)   the phrase "25 percent of more" shall be substituted for the phrase "more than 50 percent" each place it appears in section 267(b) and
(2)   paragraph (4) of section 267(c) shall be treated as providing that the family of an individual shall include only his spouse, ancestors, and lineal descendants.[100]

Section 1235(E) is simply a cross reference relating to nonresident aliens. This topic is covered in Section 871(A) of the Internal Revenue Code of 1954.

The IRS has held that a patent transfer failing to meet the technical requirements of Section 1235 may qualify for capital gains treatment under the general capital gains provisions of the Code, but a comprehensive review of those provisions is beyond the scope of this study.[101]

Tax Treatment of Purchaser

A final key point in the tax treatment of the various participants in an R & D limited partnership is the treatment of the purchaser of the partnership's invention. It would of course be beneficial to the partnership, as well as to the purchaser, if the purchaser were able to deduct payments to the partnership, that is, if these payments could either be deducted as "ordinary and necessary expenses" under Section 162 or could be capitalized and depreciated under Section 167. This is normally the case, unless the sale represents "know-how" for which it is not possible to determine a "reasonable life." In that event, if the sale of know-how is classified as a capital gains license, the licensee is not able to deduct the license payments, either currently or through amortization, because "know-how" generally does not have a reasonably determinable useful life."[102]

Robert W. Anestis and Alan H. Finegold of the law firm of Kirkpatrick, Lockhart, Johnson and Hutchinson presented a paper to the Pittsburgh Tax Club on December 11, 1979, entitled "The R & D Limited Partnership—A Flexible Response to the Invitation of Section 174." This paper which contains an extensive analysis of the Code as it pertains to R & D limited partnerships, is reproduced as Appendix J.

Mertens' Laws of Federal Income Taxation also provides a thorough analysis of federal income tax law as applied to patents and inventions.[103]

With the above outline of the key tax provisions in mind, the events that have transpired since the *Snow* decision can now be reviewed.

The *Snow* decision was handed down by the Supreme Court on May 13, 1974. The November 1974 issue of the *American Bar Association Journal* carried a brief, four-paragraph summary of the case with no comments as to its possible implications.[104] The *Missouri Law Review* reviewed the *Snow* decision in the Fall of 1975 and commented:

One probable consequence of Snow will be to enhance the use of the limited partnership as a one-shot investment medium for new product development.[105]

Apparently potential users of R & D limited partnerships are not prone to read the *Missouri Law Review*. At any rate, from that point until May 1977, very little seems to have been published although it is possible that promoters were privately preparing R & D limited partnerships that had not yet surfaced publicly. In the May 1977 issue of the *CPA Journal* a small article appeared commenting on how a taxpayer can elect to defer and amortize R & D expenses.[106] No comments were made concerning the possibility of setting up limited R & D partnerships as a means of increasing the "efficiency" of R & D expenditures or the possible tax shelter advantages.

On November 15, 1977, a private offering of an R & D limited partnership was made under the name "R & D Associates." While it cannot be determined with any degree of certainty whether this was the first, it certainly was one of the early ones.[107] This was a private offering, probably claiming exemption under SEC Rule 146. The success or failure of that venture is not known at this time. However, a short time later, on March 25, 1978, Oppenheimer and Co., Inc., offered a private placement valued at $20,000,000 of Delorean Research Limited Partnership; this placement was immediately successful, raising the entire $20,000,000. An analysis of this partnership will be made in the next section of this chapter.

Finally, in September 1978, Moore, Ayers, and Pope published an article in *The Journal of Taxation* entitled "How Limited Partnerships Tax-Shelter the R & D of New Products or Technology."[108] Over four years had elapsed between the *Snow* decision and public recognition of some of the major implications of that decision.

While much of their material covered ground already reviewed in this chapter, the comments of Moore, Ayers, and Pope tend to confirm some of the statements made above. In summing up the tax advantages of the R & D limited partnership, these authors said:

> Such "R & D tax shelters" allow an individual investor to immediately deduct the portion of his capital contribution which is expended for research and experimentation and, if properly structured, to obtain long-term capital gain treatment on his investment return when the results of the research are commercially exploited.[109]

The details of how this partnership might be structured and the tax pitfalls to avoid have been reviewed above. However, Moore, Ayers, and Pope saw this device as being useful mainly for an inventor who wishes to see his invention "reduced to practice" while still controlling the enterprise. This is undoubtedly one use of the concept but, as will be discussed later, this may not be the area where the greatest application will be made. Moore, Ayers, and Pope listed the following advantages to an investor and an inventor if they choose to use the limited partnership vehicle:

> First the partnership approach enables the inventor to retain more control over his creation. . . .

A second major advantage for the inventor of the partnership approach is a reduction in his economic dilution relative to the corporate approach. Upon purchase of a limited partnership unit, an investor immediately recovers a portion of his investment through income tax savings. Additionally, if the partnership is carefully structured, the income generated by the partnership can be taxed at favorable long-term capital gains rates probably without ordinary income recapture of prior deductions. These income tax benefits reduce both the cost and risk of the investment and these factors will be included in the investor's risk-reward analysis.[110]

As has been noted above, the Code does currently provide for such advantages; because of these advantages, an inventor should be able to retain more of an interest in his invention while still rewarding the investor more favorably then if the corporate form had been used. Note that if a corporate form is used, the investor receives no immediate tax benefits and can deduct the investment only at such time as the stock were to become worthless. Even if successful, the investor can only hope for fully taxed dividends or a capital gain from the sale of the stock, which is difficult to realize in a privately held corporation unless a total "buy-out" is arranged. Thus, as the writers noted, "under the partnership approach, both the inventor and the investors benefit without cost to the other"[111]

A third consideration offered by Moore, Ayers, and Pope was "the source and timing of investor returns." As they pointed out,

Partnership investors commonly share in the invention's economic performance based on gross sales rather than on bottom line profitability as would shareholders.[112]

A fourth consideration is that:

The partnership approach results in immediate use of research deductions to offset investor income taxable at rates as high as seventy percent. It will normally be several years before a start-up corporation can use these deductions through carryforwards and their eventual utilization will generally be at a lesser forty-eight percent corporate rate.

Finally, these authors pointed out that,

. . . in the event the product is a market success, most investors would prefer the benefits of equity ownership. This would seem to be an advantage of the corporate approach; however, a corporation subject to a royalty obligation to the partnership may attempt to buy out these royalty rights in exchange for corporate stock in order to relieve itself of the cash flow burden. Thus, without prearrangement, there is a possibility that partnership investors may part with equity ownership of the invention's rights only to subsequently regain an equity participation in the manufacture and sale of a successful product.[113]

Moore, Ayers, and Pope went on to analyze the tax laws and court rulings in much the same fashion as was done by the other authors reviewed above, but they offered an interesting comment on nonrecourse vs. recourse partnership financing:

> . . . nonrecourse leveraging traditionally available to tax shelter investments prior to the 1976 tax reform act are now unavailable to most of these investments, including R & D limited partnership. . . . [However], as research provides no collateral for indebtedness, leverage in an R & D situation would seem to require the right of recourse against the other asset of the partners or the purchaser. [Anyway] . . . in contrast to nonrecourse leveraging, recourse leveraging may be a valuable marketing attraction for R & D partnerships. Recourse leveraging allows the limited partner to put up minimal cash while using recourse borrowing to complete his capital contribution. This borrowing can be in the form of a personal guarantee of partnership loans, an irrevocable letter of credit, or other similar devices; if the project is successful, the debt is paid by the partners' share of partnership cash flow. However, if the project is unsuccessful, the investor must ultimately honor his guarantee. This ultimate personal liability distinguishes recourse from nonrecourse leverage. R & D partnerships are good vehicles for recourse leveraging due to their significant front-end deductions and the opportunity for a rapid return of capital if the research should be successful.[114]

Following the publication of this article several other journals picked up the idea. In the September 1979 issue of *NewTech*, a brief article titled "R & D Tax Shelters: High Payoffs for High Technology" appeared which highlighted the tax advantage that can accrue to an inventor by utilizing a limited R & D partnership.[115] The November 1979 issue of *INC*. Magazine carried a brief article under "Ideas You Can Use" entitled, "Use Partnerships to Finance R & D."[116] While not directly referencing Moore, Ayers, and Pope's article in the *Journal of Taxation*, the article did refer to "a new financing alternative for companies ready to begin research and development of second generation products." While it offered nothing new, it seems to be the first article suggesting the use of R & D limited partnerships by corporations.

Finally, on December 11, 1979, Anestis and Finegold presented the paper noted above (and reproduced as Appendix J). This was the first presentation among the literature researched that wrapped up the complete tax package from all sides of a deal. This presentation took into consideration not only the partnership's tax consideration but that of the purchaser of the developed product as well, a key consideration when a deal is being struck. Obviously the more tax advantages that can be received, the higher will be the value of the product to the purchaser.

Certainly the tax basis of the R & D partnership had been firmly established by the many publications reviewed here. As noted by Moore, Ayers, and Pope,

That Congressional approval of this R & D exemption still exists can be sup-
ported, through negative implication, by the passage of Sections 461(G), 464
and 189 in the Tax Reform Act of 1976 which eliminated current deductions
for prepaid interest, prepaid expenses for farming syndications, and construc-
tion period interest and taxes, without altering Section 174.[117]

In other words, as noted above, Congress is aware of the *Snow* case and
its implications and seems to agree that its intent is being implemented. If
for some reason it did not agree, it has had ample opportunity to make
changes in the law as it saw fit. Since it has not done so for the past eight
years, there is reasonable cause to believe that partnerships organized to
benefit from the provisions of Section 174 are in fact utilizing the law as it
was intended by Congress and supported by the Supreme Court.

The next section of this chapter will review two R & D limited partnerships
which were organized during the 1977–1978 period, to provide background
material for what an actual partnership looks like as opposed to the extensive
analysis just conducted as to what they are allowed to look like.

RECENTLY FORMED R & D LIMITED PARTNERSHIPS

"R & D Associates"

A private offering of "R & D Associates," an R & D limited partnership,
was made on November 15, 1977. The amount of money to be raised by this
offering was $6,400,000 and the offering was framed in such a manner that
exemption under Rule 146 was probably expected. Units were limited to
$160,000 and the minimum purchase was one unit. Units were offered only
to those investors who

. . . the general partners (and any broker-dealer assisting in the placement of
units) believe have knowledge and experience enabling them to evaluate the
terms and risks of the offering and are able to bear the economic risk of the
investment.

The language of Rule 146 is apparent here. In addition, units would be sold
only to

. . . investors who represent in writing that (I) their taxable income is such
that a portion thereof is subject to federal income taxation at a rate of fifty
percent (50%) and that they have a net worth of $100,000 (excluding home,
furniture and automobile) and (II) they are acquiring units for their own account
for investment purposes and not with a view to resale or distribution thereof.[118]

The partnership would be formed under the Maryland Uniform Limited
Partnership Act, assuming the offering was at least 50 percent subscribed

and would have one corporation and one individual as general partners. The promoters did not seek an advance ruling from the Internal Revenue Service with respect to classification as a limited partnership, nor with regard to whether the allocation of income and losses among the partners had "substantial economic effect" as required by the Tax Reform Act of 1976. Instead they chose to rely on the opinion of a United States Counsel.

The objectives of the partnership were to acquire from an Israeli nonprofit research laboratory four distinct concepts (three in energy-related fields and the fourth in the crime-detection field) and to enter into an agreement with the same firm to perform the required research and experimental work to reduce these concepts to practice. The research firm would then commercially develop the products, if that were feasible, utilizing only Israeli-based manufacturing and marketing firms. It was contemplated that two agreements between the partnership and the research firm would be entered into to accomplish the proposed objectives; the first was an acquisition agreement, and the second, a research and development agreement. The effect of these two agreements was, simply stated, that the partnership and the research firm would share equally in the benefits of commercial exploitation of the concepts after the partnership had recovered its investment and the research firm had recovered its expenditures for the commercial exploitation aspects of the venture.

The partners would in turn share as follows: Until such time as the original investment had been recovered, the limited partners would receive 99 percent of the revenues and the general partners would receive 1 percent. After recovery, the general partners would receive 25 percent and the limited partners 75 percent. In addition the general partners would receive management fees of $150,000, payable out of the proceeds from the offering.

Bank financing had been arranged so that about half of the money could be borrowed, contingent on the bank's approval of the individual's credit, on a recourse note. The other 50 percent could be borrowed utilizing the partner's interest in the partnership as collateral, but whether this would increase the partners' basis for tax deduction appears doubtful under the conditions imposed by the Tax Reform Act of 1976 (Sections 704[D] and 465); whatever the final arrangements, the financing was available.

The offering contained the usual precautions regarding the "high degree of investment risk" and numerous disclaimers as to the feasibility of the entire project. While these disclaimers are always included in offerings, whether public or private, and are even required by law, they should not be laughed off as a bureaucratic requirement. These agreements are written by the attorneys for the promoters and are definitely slanted to protect their interests to the greatest extent permitted by law. The risks associated with successfully bringing such an enterprise to a truly profitable conclusion are high. But, as has been repeatedly pointed out in this study, the first concerns of the investor seem to be the tax aspects of the investment, particularly the front-end tax aspects as opposed to the eventual total consquences that must finally be faced. As such, it would appear that if the deductions can be made and the project has sufficient "schmaltz" to appeal to the particular investor, the eventual profitability of the venture is at least relegated to a somewhat minor role.

An item of note in this venture is the almost total lack of control that the limited partners have in the expenditure of their funds. While the general partners do acknowledge their fiduciary responsiblity to the limited partners, it is noted that

> *In this regard, investors should note that while the general partners will monitor the research and development activities of the [research firm] on the projects, the actual conduct of those activities, and expenditures of funds will be performed by [the research firm] without significant control by the partnership. The obligations of the research firm are set out in and limited by the provisions of the acquisition agreement and the research and development agreement. [The research firm] is not accountable to the investors as a fiduciary.*[119]

If the limited partners are attracted to Israel, solar energy, crime detection, and tax deductions, this project should be a desirable investment, but profitability and accountability for their funds may be more difficult to achieve.

The objective here is clearly as foreseen by the *Missouri Law Review* in its comments on the consequences of the *Snow* decision:

> *One probable consequence of* Snow *will be to enhance the use of the limited partnership as a one-shot investment medium for new product development.*[120]

The next R & D limited partnership reviewed was definitely not set up as a one-shot development effort, at least as construed by the *Missouri Law Review*; it was part of a broad plan to finance a major new enterprise.

Delorean Motor Company

John Z. Delorean, former Chevrolet division manager and vice president of General Motors, formed the Delorean Motor Company in 1975; in December of that year he transferred to it all the initial development work previously performed by JZDC (a company owned 100 percent by Delorean) on the DMC-12, a two-passenger sports car. Delorean's objective seemed then, as now, to successfully introduce a new automobile into the American market, a feat that has not been accomplished by a new company in some time. As Delorean noted,

> *In more than the last 25 years no United States enterprise, other than established motor car companies, . . . has successfully completed development, manufacture and sale in commercial quantities of a new automobile.*[121]

The company subsequently transferred all of its rights to the DMC-12 to the Delorean sports car partnership and from December 1974 through October 1977 the company and the partnership continued the design and development of the DMC-12 in the course of which two full-size running models were produced. In October 1977 the company acquired all of the outstanding interests in the Delorean sports car partnership and caused it to be dissolved. Once again the company had acquired all of the rights to the DMC-12. In March 1978 a private offering was made with the intent of setting up a new R & D limited partnership to continue the development of the DMC-12. This offering was for $20,000,000 and was successfully placed in a rather short period of time. During this same period, additional shares in Delorean Motor Company were sold as part of a program to set up a national dealer network in the United States. The dealers were required to buy 5,000 shares of Delorean stock at $5.00 per share and had to agree to buy a specified number of cars over the two-year period following commencement of production. At the same time, Delorean was arranging for approximately $60,000,000 in financing to obtain a manufacturing facility, hire and train production personnel, and acquire tooling and initial inventory preparatory to going into production. This was a well-organized and well-orchestrated effort on the part of the Delorean management team.

The following quotation from the company's business plan indicates that all of this activity was part of an overall financing plan that utilized exactly the correct business entity at each stage of development:

The development of a new automobile involves four major areas of activity, some of which may be carried on concurrently. Those are: (I) initial design and marketing analysis, (II) experimental engineering design and market development, (III) production design and engineering and (IV) manufacturing.

JZDC substantially completed the initial design and market analysis of the DMC-12. Delorean sports car partnership completed the experimental engineering design, produced two full-size running models, engaged in market development activities and initiated preliminary production design engineering.

The major activites to be completed involve completion of production design engineering for the DMC-12, which is to be carried on by the [new] partnership, and completion of the marketing program and establishment of a manufacturing facility by the company. The required engineering, design and testing leading to production designs for DMC-12 are to be carried on by the [new] partnership. . . . [122]

The utilization of the R & D limited partnership at the two stages of development where the intent of IRC Section 174 was exactly appropriate indicates not only astute judgment on the part of Delorean but seems to produce the results desired by the House Committee on Ways and Means when Section 174 was discussed in 1954.

The partnership was formed under the Limited Partnership Act of the State of Michigan, the provisions of which correspond to the Uniform Limited Partnership Act. The partnership was organized to acquire from the general partner (Delorean Motor Company) the existing technology and know-how with respect to the DMC-12 and nonexclusive rights with respect to certain technology, patents, and patent applications concerning the elastic reservoir molding process for producing reinforced plastic (the "ERM process") and to conduct continuing research as required to prepare the car for production. This technology represented the general partner's contribution to the capital of the partnership. It is anticipated that when all of the funds have been expended on this effort the partnership and DMC will enter into a license agreement whereby the partnership will grant a license to DMC to utilize the technology in return for royalty payments.

Delorean Motor Company will be allowed to purchase the assets of the partnership at the earlier of January 1, 1983, or at such time as an amount is realized sufficient to distribute an aggregate of twice the amount of royalties as the limited partners originally paid in. Delorean Motor Company can purchase the assets either with common stock of DMC or cash, the method to be decided by a majority vote of the limited partners.

The general partner receives no compensation for its services to the partnership but receives 1 percent of the royalty payments until the limited partners have received $40,000,000 after which time the general partner will receive 20 percent and the limited partners 80 percent.

The remainder of the agreement contains the usual disclaimers, details of royalty payments, marketing studies, estimated budget, exhibits of various documents, and a detailed, thorough opinion of counsel as to the tax consequences of the partnership. Details of the risk and benefits consideration of this partnership will be treated in Chapter 4 as this partnership is one of those studied in support of the basic hypothesis of this book. To date, however, this is the best example of how the limited partnership, properly executed, can be utilized in the pursuit of legitimate research and development goals.

The next section of this chapter investigates the available literature to ascertain the extent of the demand in the United States for research and development activities. The magnitude of this demand will determine how extensively the R & D limited partnership can be expected to be utilized in future years.

THE NEED FOR R & D EXPENDITURES

It appears to be almost axiomatic that sustained progress in a technological society requires continuing expenditures of research and development funds, for if no seed money is returned to the laboratory, no improvements in present technologies can be expected. In the so-called post-industrial societies this fundamental truism tends to get buried under an avalanche of socially desirable programs which are inevitably proposed because the benefits of the most recent technological advances allow such programs to be realized. What is frequently forgotten is that without the underlying technologically based industries, none of these programs would be financially feasible, no matter how desirable. It is not possible, however, to stop at any one point, due in part to the increasing populations of the various societies around the world. Even if the populations were to be stabilized, vast numbers of persons in the world still exist at bare survival level and their only hope for betterment lies in developing new technologies.

Redistribution of wealth, as the British have found out (and as, it would be hoped, the Americans will discover before it is too late), is not nearly as effective, as a means of increasing the general welfare, as increasing the total wealth. An increase in total wealth can take place only in a free society that is willing to invest at least part of its current income back into the system that produced the wealth in the first place. Any farmer knows better than to eat his seed corn. It is time that the industrialized societies, as well as those that want to become industrialized, learn that fundamental lesson.

The "seed corn" of industry is research and development activities, for it is in the laboratories that new ideas and developments are born and nurtured into useful products and processes. The United States is blessed with an abundance of trained and dedicated research personnel. This country consistently has produced more Nobel prize winners than any other country and its schools, universities, and industrial laboratories compare favorably with the best in the world. But a continual stream of investment funds must be available if this critically needed national resource is to continue to provide the flow of ideas essential to the country's continued growth and prosperity.

What then is the present state of R & D activities in this country, what are the trends, and how do this country's activities compare with those of its major trading partners in the world? This section of the literature review will attempt to provide answers to those key questions.

The section is divided into four sections: a general overview of R & D spending on a worldwide basis, a review of United States activities in this field, a brief look at Japan's attitude toward research, and finally a very brief look at an attempt (the only one this author could find) to determine statistically whether a valid industry-wide hypothesis can be stated which will establish the appropriate correlates of R & D spending.

Overview of R & D Spending Worldwide

As stated above, it seems almost axiomatic that industrial progress requires investment in new ideas. As Michel Domsch puts it,

> The importance of R & D for the future of society and the economy is beyond
> question. It is accepted that R & D is a major causal factor in the progress
> of technology. On it depends the profitable growth of individual companies
> and thus, by extension, the whole national and international economy. In West

*Germany for example, expenditure on R & D has more than quintupled in
the period from 1962 to 1976. In 1976 it amounted to more than DM 24
BN. . . . [123]*

Domsch notes that due to disproportionate growth rates between GNP
and R & D, the amount spent on R & D in Germany, expressed as a percentage of GNP,

*. . . rose from 1.2 percent in 1962 to 2.4 percent up to 1971. After that the
annual growth rate flattened off to roughly that of the GNP which resulted in
a constant percentage of 2.2 percent.*

*Expenditure of a similar order can be observed internationally amongst other
highly industrialized countries. Here too, according to the latest figures of the
OECD-science resources unit R & D accounts for about two percent of the
GNP. . . .*

*According to the OECD the vast majority of R & D expenditure commercially
is concentrated on only five areas: electrical group, chemical group, aircraft,
transport group and machinery. . . . [124]*

Domsch indicates that within those groups about 50 percent of the expenditures is equally divided between the electrical group and the aircraft
group while the remaining three groups more or less share the remaining
half of the expenditures. Domsch further states that

*. . . empirical research has shown that with many companies in the chemical
group, R & D expenditures accounted for more than 4–5 percent of their
turnover, and with some electrical companies it even came to 6–10 percent.
These figures must also be seen from another point: the results of successful
R & D are multiplied in improved production techniques, marketing success,
higher quality of life, etc. . . . [125]*

Interestingly, while the amount spent on R & D appears to be about the
same as in the other highly industrialized countries when expressed as a
percent of GNP, it should be noted that the total spent in 1973 by France,
Japan, and the United Kingdom amounted to only about one half of that
spent in the United States. It would seem unquestionable that the United
States dominates worldwide R & D efforts and will continue to do so for
some time to come, but trends indicate that trading partners of the United
States are aware of the value of R & D and are closing the gap. As the
confrontation between these industrialized countries and the Third World
countries upon which they depend for critical raw materials intensifies during
the eighties, competition for more efficient utilization of those raw materials
will become keener and the ground on which this battle will be fought will
be the research laboratory.

Research and Development in the United States

Robert F. Dee, chairman of the board and chief executive officer of the Smith Kline Corporation, remarked in a speech to shareholders in 1977 that

> . . . *it's evident that research improves the quality of our lives. It gives us new treatment for disease, new energy sources, new ways of solving environmental pollution problems, better communications, improved transportation.*
>
> *It's not so evident, but nonetheless true, that research is the cornerstone of a sound economy. Through research we're able to find better techniques for doing and making things. These techniques in turn give us increased industrial output. Increased output gives us lower costs and lower prices for commodities and services.*
>
> *This process, going from new technology to lower prices, is the tried-and-true way by which our economic system keeps itself in natural balance. It's a process that can drive down inflation, make U.S. exports competitive in world markets, reduce our balance of payments deficit, boost the value of the dollar, and create more work and consequently more jobs . . . research spending in the United States hit a peak in 1968. Since then, as measured in inflation-adjusted dollars, it has flattened out at a level far below what we need for national economic growth. . . .* [126]

Dee felt the United States was not spending enough on R & D and that the trends indicated no improvement. What then has the United States been spending, what is it being spent on, and who is spending it?

In January 1974, *Industrial Research* carried an article entitled "$33 Billion for Research." It summarized the research situation in the United States by saying,

> *Industry will assume a much larger share of R & D funding in 1974 and this, coupled with increased federal spending, will produce a year of real growth in R & D activity.*

Of this total of $33 billion that was forecast to be spent in 1974, the article estimated that 68 percent would be spent by industry, 14 percent by the federal government, 12 percent by universities, and the remainder by federally funded research centers and other nonprofit institutions. Of the industrial portion, it was estimated that 68 percent would be spent on product development. While this prediction is favorable in supporting the hypothesis of this book, the fact that so much is being spent on development as opposed to basic research is viewed by some with misgivings:

> *Industry continues to shorten the time frame in which it is looking at its R & D efforts and to shift to the right toward applied research and development and away from more basic research.* [127]

William P. Sommers, senior vice president and director of Booz, Allen and Hamilton, a management consulting firm, saw this as a further indication that there is a

> *. . . continuing trend towards applications and development, that industry and the government is looking towards applications and development, that industry and the government is looking toward getting something worthwhile for the money and they are not measuring this by new technology, but by salable products.*
>
> *[Dr. Sommers noted] that marketing people are increasingly directing the spending of the R & D money—a market is identified and then the research and development is put into motion. He classifies this as the age of marketing for many industries. New product development is taking a larger and larger share of the total research and development budget. . . .*
>
> *. . . in the short run, this trend is not all that bad, but it does indicate that we may run into some problems in the long term if we don't somehow increase the effort expended in basic research. . . .* [128]

The major push, according to *Industrial Research*, will be in chemicals, instruments and related high-technology products, electrical machinery, food and kindred products, and transportation; increases will be substantial in areas related to the energy situation such as natural gas, oil, and electric utilities. The article further noted that, as usual, the physical sciences and engineering will receive the major portion, about 63 percent, of the total funds for R & D although this portion continued to decline, losing one percentage point in 1974 compared to 1973. The loss was picked up by the life sciences which then took about 30 percent of the total. [129]

However large the United States' R & D efforts seemed in absolute terms, the adverse trends that had begun to show up since 1968 were becoming of some concern. In November 1976, *Iron Age* carried an article entitled "Is R & D Investment Being Short Changed?" The article was concerned that decline in research and development investment in the United States could affect the nation's ability to provide the jobs needed. The article stated:

> *The best route to economic growth is through technical innovation. It means more productivity at home and the ability to compete in the world marketplace. And it creates jobs.* [130]

The theme is repeated in article after article: R & D creates jobs. Few writers, however, identify the cause of the apparent decline. The blame is placed, if it is placed at all, on the government. Thomas A. Vanderslice, vice president and group executive of General Electric Company's special systems and products group, was quoted by *Iron Age*:

> *Yet, I believe, there are trends that, unless corrected, could lead to a rapidly maturing crisis, such as the United Kingdom is now undergoing in translating*

her technology into economic growth. . . . If the decline in research and de-
velopment investment by the U.S. is not reversed, it could seriously affect the
nation's economic leadership and our ability to provide the eighteen million
new jobs we must generate in the next ten years. . . . In the U.S., the percent
of GNP devoted to R & D has dropped steadily for more than nine years.
Meanwhile other countries have registered substantial gains. Underlying the
gains of Japan and West Germany were continuous large increases in funding
from both industry and government. . . . [131]

Again, Germany and Japan are singled out as prime examples to illustrate
that R & D activities, properly funded, lead to increased productivity. The
relative decline in United States spending for R & D appears to be the result
of cutbacks by the federal government. As Vanderslice noted,

. . . the share of the federal budget represented by R & D and by R & D plant
programs has declined continuously from 1965, not even keeping pace with
inflation. . . . Corporate spending for R & D, on the other hand, has just about
managed to keep pace with inflation, remaining nearly constant for most of
the period at around one percent of GNP. . . . The record suggests that Amer-
ican industry more fully recognized the value of maintaining constant, contin-
uing levels of support for R & D than the federal government. [132]

Here the issue of what role the federal government should play in the R
& D picture is raised. Certainly the motives of industry and government are
not the same, at least on the surface. Industry is a profit-oriented group;
government is a politically oriented entity concerned not only with re-
election, as the cynics are prone to believe, but with longer-term social goals.
If anything, it would seem that basic research may very well be the proper
field of interest for the government while development activities are more
properly carried out by industry. Perhaps the subtler role of providing tax
incentives to industry for development work rather than directly funding
these activities is the more proper one for government. Direct government
funding of product development projects can have disastrous results, as
any who followed the Concorde project in England and France could have
observed. There is no market discipline in government projects that would
force the cancellation of uneconomic projects as there is in private industry.
The control is simply not there. But the long-term view of desirable social
goals can be maintained by the government, and such a view can properly
be reduced to the sponsorship of certain critical research activities. The
long-term funding of fusion research in this country as well as others is
probably as good an example as any of the proper applications of government
effort.

Vanderslice went on to comment:

The basic anachronism in these adverse trends is that the polls tell us that
most Americans still believe that the best way to achieve the complicated and

sometimes competing goals we now seek remains the same: through economic growth . . . and economists tell us that the best route to economic growth is through technical innovation. . . . We cannot trade our natural resources for increased wealth as, say, a small oil or mineral-rich nation can.[133]

Regarding a quantitative value for R & D, Vanderslice continued:

Low technology companies, in a period of generally rapid growth for the U.S. economy, have had a job formation rate of about two percent per year; high-technology companies have created jobs five times as fast. They have also had a growth in sales double that of low-technology companies.

He concluded:

In the long run . . . I can think of nothing that can give us more leverage on all of the problems that confront us now and in the future, than to protect the "seed corn" of scientific and technological competence that resides in our universities, industry, government in-house and privately-funded research organizations infrastructure.[134]

Regardless of the trends, however, an increase of 12.7 percent in total outlays for 1977 was estimated by the Battelle Memorial Institute in an article published by *Industry Week* on January 3, 1977. The article noted that although half of that increase would be offset by inflation, the federal budget for 1978 was estimated to call for a 3 percent boost in basic research, even after the effects of inflation had been discounted. But the magazine still noted:

. . . the bad news is that R & D spending as a percentage of gross national product has been declining, and even with the proposed increases for 1977 it won't match the share it held a decade ago.

Concern over energy is a rising influence of Federal R & D spending, and the Energy Research and Development Administration is one of four Federal Agencies that together account for 87 percent of Government R & D spending.

Four industry groups will boost R & D more than the 13 percent average, reports Battelle. Leading the way is wood products and furniture (30 percent) followed by chemicals (23 percent), glass (19 percent), and transportation equipment (18 percent).

Despite the higher spending in 1977, Dr. W. Halder Fisher, Battelle's research economist, worries that much of the spending will go into practical R & D, rather than the basic research that is so important to the long-term economic health of the U.S. . . . [135]

Concern is expressed over the lack of basic research, but it seems apparent that the profit-oriented portion of the economy continues to recognize the value of R & D, albeit if slanted more to near-term profits, and that segment continues to increase. Of course there is a fundamental problem with basic research: it does not produce near-term benefits and hence its effects are difficult to measure. Without a reliable measuring tool it becomes difficult to pass judgment on what is too much and what is not enough.

One possible indicator of the adequacy of the United States' basic research effort might emerge from tracking the number of patents issued, on the grounds that this number in some manner measures the "worth of the research." *Statistical Abstract of the United States* lists the number of patents issued; Section 18, "Business Enterprise," in the 1977 edition indicates that 111,095 patents were filed in 1971 and 81,789 patents were issued. By 1976 these numbers had declined to 109,989 patents filed and 75,400 patents issued. This absolute decline in both patents filed and issued would seem to lend some support to those who feel that basic research is inadequate in the United States. As a matter of interest, more than twice as many patents were filed and issued to corporations than to individuals, indicating that over two-thirds of the creative effort in the United States is contained within the corporate framework, an important consideration in determining the appropriate marketing channels for R & D limited partnerships.[136]

When statistics became available for 1977, a survey by *Business Week* on the R & D spending of 624 companies, representing 90 percent of all the privately funded R & D performed by all United States companies, found that

> . . . *they spent more than $18 billion on R & D last year, a 16.4 percent jump over their 1976 expenditures. After being adjusted for inflation, the increase over 1976 shrinks to just above ten percent. Even though the figures suggest industry is now taking a more purposeful attitude toward new product and price development, many researchers warn that a business downturn will cut most R & D budgets quickly. . . .* [137]

Even though R & D expenditures did continue their climb in 1977, as noted above, concern was still being expressed that not enough was being done fast enough. As *Chemical Week* pointed out in an article appearing in the May 24, 1978 issue,

> *Government fears concerning lagging innovation in the U.S. have caused the Carter administration to undertake a major study of the role of the Federal Government in industrial R & D. The study will seek to ascertain the causes of decreasing R & D and make recommendations about what the Government can do to correct it. . . .*

It is interesting to note that a major incentive to encourage R & D spending is the R & D limited partnership described in this study and yet even five years after the *Snow* decision the government itself had not become aware of the implications of that decision.

Note this excerpt from an article that appeared in *Dun's Review* in September 1978 on this very topic:

> . . . *inflation in the U.S. has been worsened by the drop in productivity due to cutbacks in business spending for research and development. In 1963, the U.S. spent three percent of the GNP on R & D, while it now spends only 2.2 percent, and other nations have increased their R & D outlays. The Government has raised its R & D spending for 1978 by eleven percent and is studying the effects of regulation, taxes, trade and antitrust and procurement policies on R & D. Frank Press has been appointed to oversee Federal efforts in this direction. The Federal Government hopes to increase its part in research while allowing the private sector to handle development. To encourage business also to step up its R & D spending the following ideas are being considered: 1. The investment tax credit could cover R & D; 2. Patent periods could be extended; 3. Large government contractors would have mandatory minimum required R & D levels; 4. All regulatory agencies would have to assess the impact of the rules on innovation. . . .* [138]

Ignoring for the moment the usual arrogance of a government official when he says the government will "allow the private sector to handle development," the government is still missing the point that there are already adequate incentives for private companies to innovate. The problem lies in familiarizing the private sector with the advantages of the R & D limited partnership and then holding a consistent attitude toward the exploitation of these incentives long enough for their effect to be felt on the national economy.

It would appear from some information now available that research and development spending is still on the rise. *Chemical and Engineering News* carried an article in its January 15, 1979 issue indicating that 1979 R & D budgets were up 10 percent at United States chemical firms. The article said:

> . . . *by itself, the indicated industry-wide ten percent increase in world-wide R & D funding this year to $1.74 billion would not mark a boom. But coming after six straight years of significant increases in R & D support, including nine percent and eight percent increases in 1977 and 1978, the addition this year means a very strong situation for R & D at basic chemical companies. . . . For 1979, DuPont's R & D budget, by far the industry's largest, may top $400 million for the first time. This would be a one-year increase of seven percent, more than double the three percent gain in 1978.*
>
> *DuPont and other larger R & D backers heavily influence the chemical industry's total R & D spending. The R & D budgets at DuPont, Dow Chemical, Union Carbide, and Monsanto will account for more than sixty percent of the chemical industry's R & D spending this year.* [139]

There seems to be a conflict between what some authors are writing about R & D expenditures in the United States and what is actually happening.

The *Dun's* article quoted above talks about "cutbacks in business spending for research and development" when in fact R & D spending increased. It is true that it dropped when expressed as a percent of GNP, but the GNP is made up of all goods and services produced in the United States and not just those of private, profit-oriented companies. Those companies' R & D expenditures actually increased and are continuing to increase. It is perhaps a good sign that the government is increasing its expenditures for pure research for this is an area appropriate to government and universities. The appropriate way to encourage private investment in development expenditures, if any is needed, is through tax incentives. As David Packard, chairman and co-founder of the Hewlett-Packard Company, said in an editorial in the December 3, 1979, issue of *Business Week*, "If the Government will fix the tax structure and get out of our way, we'll take care of ourselves."[140] It is suggested that the government has already done so by not overruling *Snow*. It appears that if the United States is in fact falling behind the rest of the world in an absolute sense, a fact not clearly established, the situation is beginning to correct itself.

However, whether the United States is falling behind, holding its own, or surging ahead in the production of new and innovative products and processes, all the available literature agrees that R & D is needed by any nation wishing to raise its standard of living and to provide a decent and secure life for its citizens and that in the United States, R & D is a big industry in its own right and is growing at the present time at least as fast as the general economy. The hypothesis of this study requires, if it is to be sustained, that a demand exist for R & D. This review would suggest that the requirement is being met.

Research and Development in Japan

Much has been written concerning Japan's spectacular economic recovery from the shambles of World War II. Almost flawless economic growth has been sustained in that country for almost thirty years, propelling Japan from a relatively backward country, in the sense of Western industrialization, with a reputation of producing shoddy products to a leading industrialized nation with an enviable reputation of quality and integrity. As the Japanese will be the first to admit, this sustained economic drive was made possible by the importation of technology and by the lack of necessity, due to the "nuclear umbrella" provided by the United States, of devoting any significant internal resources to defense spending. All of this economic growth was sustained by a country that has, for all practical purposes, no natural resources under its direct control. The Japanese have learned how to compete in the Western world and are doing it with skill and dedication seldom witnessed. But how long can this drive be sustained? The answer will lie in Japan's ability to create and sustain an independent R & D effort, and herein some writers detect a flaw in Japan's industrial base. This section is included here to illustrate how the approach of Japan differs from that of the United States in this critical area.

This study, of course, is primarily concerned with the response of the United States to the obvious need for a sustained R & D effort, but it is usually profitable to study one's competitor and Japan will probably be the United States' major competitor during the next decade.

As early as 1971, Japan itself began to be aware that a basic problem existed in its economy. As Yujiro Koike, president of Matsushita Electrical Industrial Company, said in an article that appeared in the July 10, 1971 issue of *Business Week*: "There's nobody else to follow anymore." The article continued:

> *Koike's remark suggests Japan has caught up with the rest of the world technologically. But also, U.S. and European companies, nervous about Japanese competition, are making it tougher to buy their R & D results. . . . It is the first time since Japan began its industrialization a century ago that lack of research has mattered. Japan's recent industrial growth has been spectacular: Between 1960 and 1970, GNP rose from $43.5 billion to more than $196 billion while exports soared from $4 billion to more than $19 billion . . . by copying and licensing the work of others, Japanese industry was able to get the latest knowledge and to compete successfully with the world's industrial leader.*

The article went on to point out various reasons why Japan will have difficulties mounting an independent research effort. For instance,

> *. . . the Japanese will have to overcome a series of problems that include: a lack of research investment, traditions that inhibit the movement of good researchers from company to company and that stifle the flow of research information, student disruptions of universities' research projects and finally diversion of research talent into non-innovative technological chores in industry.*[141]

The article concluded with a quotation from United States Attaché Hiatt:

> *. . . there are limits to what they are likely to achieve in a rush. There are few good industry-related research institutes in Japan . . . whereas we've got dozens of them—and breakthroughs come from many, not just one.*[142]

That article was written in 1971. As someone once said, it does not pay to underestimate one's opponent. Hiatt seems to be doing just that.

In April 1972 an article appeared in the *Columbia Journal of World Business* entitled "Japan's Technology Now Challenges the West."

> *The success of Japan's export offensive is due in large part to the successful adaptation of Western technology. It has improved on this imported technology and is now exporting it back to the rest of the world. . . . Japan has succeeded in casting off the old stigma of being an exporter of "shoddy" manufactures*

and is now gaining a world-wide reputation as a manufacturer of high-quality products. . . . without the "technological backlog" provided by the West, the Japanese could not have modernized their industrial structure so quickly. This does not mean, however, that they idly borrowed and imitated Western industrial arts. The very process of adopting alien technology to different production and marketing milieus entails a great deal of ingenuity.[143]

The key to this "miracle" lies not only with the ability to adapt Western technology but with the unique role that government plays in Japan. As the article noted,

. . . the Government had a master plan to modernize the economy and to strengthen export-oriented industries. Technological acquisition was a means to this end.

One significant role played by the Government was that of a "countervailing power" protecting Japanese firms which were desperately in need of modern technology and, as a consequence, had weak bargaining power vis-à-vis Western firms. Undesirable competition among Japanese firms for the purchase of a given type of technology was discouraged under administrative guidelines.[144]

It appeared then, as now, that Japanese business and government are essentially on the same side rather than in an adversary relationship, as presently exists in the United States.

One of the factors favoring Japan as a buyer was the availability of alternative sources of supply. If the Japanese could not secure a given type of technology from, say, British firms, they easily managed to find alternative suppliers in other countries.[145]

Within the United States the situation was even more favorable for the Japanese.

Perhaps more important is the fact that there is much stronger interfirm competition in the United States for improving existing products and marketing new ones than in any other country. Hence, even if one company jealously guards industrial know-how, its competitors in this vast domestic market may easily supply to the Japanese a similar or even superior technology. . . .

In addition to the advantages of imported technology, there is almost

. . . a national obsession to prove to the world their capacity to create a prosperous economy . . . their desire to eradicate their stereotype image as producers of "shoddy" goods has been one of the most powerful forces motivating the Japanese to improve the qualities of their exports. Goods shipped overseas are, in general, far more carefully produced and inspected than goods sold at home. . . .[146]

Note the sense of pride here—again the feeling of national unity on the part of the Japanese. Unfortunately it is precisely this feeling which has been missing from the American scene for the past two decades.

Relative to R & D, Japan apparently took note of its shortcomings in "creating" the technology upon which its future depended:

There are several promising signs that for the first time in its industrial history Japan is indeed reaching the stage of being more a technological leader than a borrower. Perhaps the most important is the fact that in the early 1960's the Japanese realized that they could no longer depend entirely on Western sources for further technological development and began to invest heavily in their own R & D facilities and activities. Japan's R & D expenditure, expressed as a proportion of GNP, was 1.5 percent in 1969, still much lower than those in the U.S. (3.0 percent in 1967), the U.K. (2.4 percent in 1966), France (2.3 percent in 1967), and West Germany (2.1 percent in 1967). But Japan has been increasing R & D expenditure at a much faster rate than GNP, thereby improving the ratio. For example, the rate of increase in R & D expenditure was 14.8 percent, 24 percent, 26.6 percent and 21.5 percent for 1966, 1967, 1968 and 1969 respectively. . . . [147]

In brief, the Japanese are running fast to develop the independent research base they need to assume a leading role in the various "knowledge intensive" industries they have chosen to compete in. They seem to have a clear idea of what is required to successfully compete in world markets. Note in the following list two significant requirements for success—cooperation between government and industry, and a fierce desire to succeed. Both attitudes have been notably lacking in the United States in recent years.

To succeed in the above effort [to become a developed nation] a nation needs: (1) an educated populace, (2) discipline (especially labor discipline), (3) capital (but this is of lesser importance than the other points mentioned herein), (4) stability of the form and thrust of government, (5) a business oriented climate in government, (6) marketing know-how, (7) a fierce desire to succeed, both individually and as a nation, (8) its market thrust should be aimed at the developed nations. Japan had all of these but marketing know-how—and it acquired this rapidly. . . .

In addition, the Japanese have a broad strategic view to their industrialization efforts that somewhat precludes the necessity of always being first. As an example,

Most of the really major new technical concepts tend to be available for product development by almost anyone. It is the refinements that are protected by patents. Therefore it is not usually a major handicap not to discover the major new breakthroughs—they are almost always available for use at a reasonable cost; if there is a cost, it is the necessity for continuous innovation and refinement that many do not grasp or fully understand. [148]

. . . if Japan's universities continue to develop, if new knowledge is avidly sought and cherished, if industry and government continue to expand R & D and if the profession of science is well regarded and rewarded, then Japan has as much chance of coming up with Nobel and other prestigious honors for new scientific developments as the other fully developed nations.[149]

This does not sound like a strategy that would admit defeat. As one reads more and more about the Japanese, one gains increasing respect for them as competitors—honorable competitors. They intend to play the game to win, but to win by producing better products at a lower cost.

With regard to specific areas of interest to the Japanese, it seems to be their intention to concentrate on the so-called knowledge intensive industries. As an example,

. . . significant increase of R & D will be seen in the areas of "resource saving" and the "knowledge intensive" industries. The latter refers to such as the following in Japan: (1) R & D oriented industries such as computers, aircraft, industrial robots, fine chemicals, synthetic chemicals, etc. (2) assembly industries of advanced technology such as communications equipment, numerically controlled machines, pollution control equipment, educational equipment, etc. (3) "fashion" industries such as dresses and high-fashion clothing, interior accessories and commodities, audio electronic equipments, etc.[150]

In addition to having a basic strategy that appears to be capable of concentrating resources at the point needed, the Japanese have a basically different management "style" that tends to set them apart from their Western counterparts. Two key features of management policy that lead to the so-called Japanese style are (1) lifetime employment for nearly all white-collar and many blue-collar workers, and (2) payment of wages greatly dependent on age and length of service. The Japanese, as a result of the above characteristics of their system, have some advantages:

(1) they are not always fighting for maximum budget so as to be able to continue a product when it is in the decline phase of its life cycle or has encountered other obstacles most difficult to overcome since the salaries of the C.E.O. and his men will continue and they may end up with better assignments. (2) the decisions of management tend to be more the long-term view. In the U.S.A. especially the shorter term view tends to often surface because the executives tend to often move from company to company. (3) innovations and new products are more easily introduced to the firm. People are not afraid of new ideas, new products, and new systems because they will not be personally hurt by these changes. (4) Japanese were supposed to be robbed of an incentive drive, according to some Western "experts." Yet the opposite seems to be true, probably because (a) they want to see the company they will be with for the rest of their lives grow; (b) it is normal to try to beat competitors and (c) it is more fun to belong to a successful company—and also to maybe make more money.[151]

The above sounds like a winning concept. Most probably when the Japanese need new ideas to compete, they will be available. The impression one gets from reading about the Japanese business efforts is one of teamwork and harmony on a national scale. While it is obvious that there are problems, there seems to be a strong consensus within the country that a successful business community is a prerequisite for a successful country, a belief that is not shared by a large portion of the American population at the moment.

Correlation Between R & D Expenditures and Various Financial Ratios

While there appears to be widespread belief that R & D is good and lack of it is bad, there appears very little in the literature to suggest a method of determining how much is enough. So far as can be determined, a trial-and-error approach seems to be taken by most managements. Of course, because of the long time delay between expending the research money and realizing the return, it is not always easy to be certain whether it was the research expenditure that caused the increased profit or something else. One source was uncovered, however, which attempted to discover the correlates of R & D expenditure.

Klaus Brockhuff of the Battelle Institute in Frankfurt, Germany, published a paper in the *Management International Review* in 1970 entitled "Determinants of Research and Development Expenditure in Some Chemical Corporations in Germany." The purpose of the study was that

> . . . *first it should help to clarify the question whether different firms in one industry follow different policies in determining their R & D expenditures; the criterion used is the search for the policy which explains best the R & D expenditures in one firm or the other over a given interval of time. Second, it might serve as a basis of information for investigators who want to make a multi-national comparison of results.*[152]

Apparently one of the most difficult chores in preparing this paper was to find enough companies for which comparable financial data were available for a valid statistical analysis to be made. Only four such companies were found in Germany. Next, to achieve the best possible fit against the available data, several hypotheses were tried: (1) that firms should try to determine their R & D expenditure such that their long-range profits are maximized; (2) that firms might look at profits as a financial basis for their future expenditures, and especially their R & D expenditure, or, somewhat differently stated, that corporate policy should use estimates of future profits as a starting point for determining future R & D expenditure, where those profits are estimated from current and past profit figures; (3) that if the opinion is held that R & D ought to be financed by the commitment of internal funds only, then cash flow could be used as a determinant for R & D expenditure; and (4) that R & D expenditure depends on sales.

Unfortunately, none of the hypotheses was properly supported by the data on all of the companies at the same time, although one hypothesis or another matched one or two companies better than others. The best that can be said is,

> . . . thus far we have to conclude that sales generally explain R & D expenditure better than a finance variable.[153]

One would expect that with the vast amount of public data available in the United States, a proper correlation could be found. Its determination would be a useful guide for managements as they plan their companies' R & D programs.

This section of the literature review has established that R & D activities in the United States are considered essential to the economic health of industry and the country as a whole. The present magnitude of these expenditures is in excess of $40 billion per year and has been steadily increasing in absolute terms in recent years although the expenditures have shown a slight decline when expressed as a percentage of GNP. The government recently has expressed concern about the lack of sufficient growth in R & D activities and has initiated a study to determine what government can do to encourage greater effort in this field. Japan is seen as the principal competitor in many of the "knowledge intensive" fields and, despite some pessimism expressed as to its ability to respond to the challenge of innovative thinking without foreign support, the chances seem to be in favor of Japan's remaining a formidable competitor throughout the eighties.

A brief look at an attempt to correlate R & D expenditures with some significant financial ratios failed to produce useful information. This section has therefore established that a need exists in the United States for significant amounts of R & D expenditures and that this need will continue for the indefinite future. The next section will look into the profitability and cash flow positions of American industry to determine the desirability of channeling new funds into R & D activities in order to ease the corporate burden of limiting R & D activities to internally generated funds.

CORPORATE INCENTIVES TO COLLABORATE WITH AN R & D LIMITED PARTNERSHIP

As pointed out in the earlier section that investigated the taxation aspects of R & D limited partnerships, the availability of R & D deductions to individuals places the limited partnership in a more favorable situation relative to the cost of performing research and experimentation than a corporation, assuming that the individual limited partners are in a higher tax bracket than the corporation. However, to change the established behavior patterns, developed over many years, of any significant number of corporations, there must be compelling reasons to change, perhaps over and above the obviously improved utilization of their research dollars as outlined above.

The corporation must sense that a true need to change exists within its organization. As Robert B. Stone, General Motors' purchasing staff vice president, noted in a recent *Business Week* article,

> *The auto companies are tapping their suppliers' knowhow to reach govern-ment-mandated goals. We're finding out more and more that we don't have all the ideas. . . . "*

The article went on to say that

> *. . . such a statement would have been anathema in Detroit until recently because of the auto makers' deepseated, "not-invented-here" syndrome—their unwillingness to consider outsiders' suggestions.*[154]

Here it is suggested that government pressure for conformance to new performance standards is providing pressure in the auto industry for change. But do corporations in general feel pressure for financial assistance to per-form needed R & D work? Certainly the previous section of this chapter illustrated the need for R & D. Billions of dollars for R & D are funded by industry every year. It is obvious that somehow or other the funds are found. But are they enough or could the funds have been put to better use if a new or more efficient source of funds were available?

As pointed out in the introduction, the triple-pronged attack of inflation, foreign competition, and product and plant obsolescence appears to be threatening the liquidity of many United States corporations. The attitude and strategy of the Japanese toward R & D were reviewed earlier. This part of the literature review will investigate the effects of inflation and product obsolescence on United States corporations.

Inflation, Return of Equity, and Corporate Liquidity

Inflation appears to have become institutionalized in the United States and in many, if not all, other parts of the world as well. Whereas a few years ago the government talked of beating inflation, implying that it could be eliminated, it now talks only of reducing it. If the current inflation rate could be reduced to "only" 6 percent, it would be viewed as a major victory for the government and yet a sustained rate of inflation of 6 percent would reduce the value of the dollar by 50 percent in only 12 years. The fact that this erosion of the value of the dollar is also dangerously undermining the liquidity of all United States businesses is perhaps not so obvious, but un-fortunately true.

Mirjan Ivanetic wrote in the January–February 1975 issue of the *Harvard Business Review*:

> *In recent years, U.S. Corporations have consistently overspent their internally generated funds. All standard yardsticks to compute liquidity show steady*

declines in the 1964-1973 decade. The current ratio of all non-financial cor-
porations, which was as high as 2.29 in 1962, declined to 1.36.

Ivanetic cited two reasons he believed were causing this loss of liquidity to occur; the first was U.S. tax policy, "which favors debt over equity in a discriminatory way and to the detriment of economic soundness." Such policy has encouraged management to use leverage and at least part of the diminished liquidity can be attributed to management decisions to utilize leverage when it was available. Ivanetic pointed out that

Internally generated funds accounted for only 72 percent of all expenditures
of manufacturing corporations in the decade, the remainder coming from an
increase in nondebt, long-term liabilities (3%), new capital stock (4%) and
additional indebtedness (21%). . . . Total indebtedness of these corporations
grew from 16% of total assets in 1963 to 23% in 1973.

But inflation seems to be the principal cause and in this, of course, management has no option but to adapt the best it can. Ivanetic continued,

. . . the rate at which inflation is consuming funds, causing abnormal increases
in asset and liabilities, is forcing companies to add heftily to both sides of the
balance sheet. Inasmuch as the larger retained earnings and other liabilities
are insufficient to absorb the accelerated asset growth, corporations must
borrow more and more. . . . Receivables and inventories cannot be reduced
quickly enough to maintain liquidity. . . . Moreover, if nondebt liabilities and
equity do not grow at the same rate as current assets and new fixed assets,
the balance sheet can be balanced only by additional short- and long-term
borrowings. Cash and cash equivalents, the only remaining liquidity element,
become to a great degree a function of additional borrowing. . . . With real
profits suspect because of the inclusion of inflation-generated inventory profits,
with capitalization ratios decreasing and with liabilities mounting, borrowing
capacity is unfortunately also diminishing.[155]

The results of these developments are that many companies and even some entire industries can no longer obtain additional credit while others can "get only limited amounts and therefore have curtailed expenditure and rationed newly obtained funds." Ivanetic pointed out that during times when inflation was at a minimum and the equity market was strong, "reduction of cash and equivalents to the minimum was considered a sign of good management, while low liquidity and high leverage were supposed to generate maximum earnings." He suggested that the time had come to return to prudent financial management. Among other things, he suggested that the following should be considered:

Stability of earnings: The more cyclical a company's earnings, the more solid
its capital structure should be to enable it to survive adverse conditions. . . .
Cash flow requirements: Even a profitable company can encounter serious

cash flow problems; expansion, requiring additional working capital as well as fixed assets, is usually the cause.

Finally he concluded.

The need to strengthen our equity markets is well known. It is also obvious that inflation must be checked. Finally, realizing that we cannot live beyond our means, we must make certain funds allocations based on national needs. . . . This does not mean a planned economy, Russian style. By establishing priorities and accordingly shaping tax and other incentives, however, we could help the private sector channel investments into those areas of the economy that have been granted National priority.[156]

Interestingly, at the time this article was written the *Snow* decision had already been handed down and all federal priorities, following the Arab oil boycott in 1973–1974, had been directed toward resolving the energy "crisis." Assuming, as most do, that a concentrated effort in the field of additional research and development efforts would help to resolve the energy problems, all necessary tax incentives were in place at the time this article appeared. That was nine years ago.

While Ivanetic certainly recognized that a problem existed and correctly identified the causes, he failed to comprehend exactly why corporate liquidity could not be maintained during an inflationary period by simply raising prices enough to offset any decrease in liquidity caused by the necessity of financing the increased working capital that resulted from the "phantom" expansion forced on industry by inflation. Certainly new strategies were needed to cope with the prospects of continued high inflation.

Shortly after Ivanetic's article appeared in the *Harvard Business Review*, Allen H. Seed, in an article published in the March 1975 issue of *Management Review* entitled "Needed: Strategies to Improve Cash Flow," suggested that

. . . many business leaders view their enterprises as a portfolio of assets in natural business entities that constitute what we call "strategy centers." A strategy center is an area of business with an independent marketplace for goods or services for which one determines objectives and strategies for reaching such objectives. . . . [157]

Growth businesses require capital for introducing new products, penetrating new markets, and expanding capacity . . . the important point is that strategies be matched with the position of each business (or business unit) in its life cycle. A climate of business adversity and shortages of capital also suggests that strategies for each package of assets in the portfolio be reshaped to (1) improve returns in relation to risks, (2) balance funds generation with usage, and (3) insure the survival of the enterprise. . . . [158]

Seed went on to propose how a strategic evaluation might be developed and suggested that virtually every business can find new sources of funds to improve cash flow. He noted that new methods of financing are being developed every day, but was concerned that,

> *Partly because petrodollars are not available in the term debt money market, the gap between the availability of short- and long-term investment capital is widening. . . . Companies are trying several methods to improve cash flow in the short term: . . . redirecting research and development to eliminate high-risk projects that offer limited return, shifting resources away from projects requiring extensive fund commitments, and reducing overhead. . . .* [159]

Seed concluded by noting,

> *In short, the environment of capital scarcity that we are facing has three basic implications that apply to virtually every company: [1] it is just as important to manage the flow of funds as it is to manage the results shown on the income statement. [2] employed capital must earn more. [3] corporations should strive toward a position of capital self-sufficiency, to the extent practical. . . . All this requires imaginative, hardheaded management. But an organization's survival could depend on it.* [160]

While Seed recognized that changing economic environments require changing strategies, he did not directly address the problem as to why the environment is changing. What is it about inflation that causes capital shortages and loss of corporate liquidity? In May 1977, *Fortune* carried an article by Warren E. Buffett entitled "How Inflation Swindles the Equity Investor." While the article was written with the investor in mind rather than corporate management, the points made seem to get to the core of the problem of corporate liquidity in an inflationary economy:

> *It is no longer a secret that stocks and bonds do poorly in an inflationary environment. . . . But the reasons for the stock markets' problems in this period are still imperfectly understood. . . . For many years the conventional wisdom insisted that stocks were a hedge against inflation. The proposition was rooted in the fact that stocks are not claims against dollars, as bonds are, but represent ownership of companies with productive facilities. These, investors believed, would retain their value in real terms, let the politicians print money as they might. . . .* [161]

But it did not turn out that way and, according to Buffett, the reason lies in the fact that in many ways stocks are really very similar to bonds. He pointed out that in the three decades following World War II, the return on equity of either the Dow Jones Industrials or the Fortune 500 tended to keep coming back to a level of around 12 percent. He noted, "It shows no signs of exceeding that level significantly in inflationary years (or in years of stable prices, for that matter)." Of course, if the owners of the companies had purchased their interests at book value, their return would have been 12 percent also, so in a sense the stock can be thought of as an "equity coupon" returning 12 percent. As inflation has increased, the return on equity capital has not. During the period from, say, 1946 to 1966 earning a 12 percent return was very good, and part of this return was reinvested in the company to in turn earn 12 percent. As the rate of inflation began to pick up, the rate of 12 percent on relatively risky common stock began to look less advantageous, consequently less value was placed on the "equity" coupon of 12 percent and stock prices started to fall. Again, why during inflationary times did the return on equity not increase?

Buffett continued:

> *Must we really view that twelve percent equity coupon as immutable? Is there any law that says the corporate return on equity capital cannot adjust itself upward in response to a permanently higher average rate of inflation?*
>
> *There is no such law, of course. On the other hand, corporate America cannot increase earnings by desire or decree. To raise that return on equity, corporations would need at least one of the following: (1) an increase in turnover i.e., in the ratio between sales and total assets employed in the business; (2) cheaper leverage; (3) more leverage; (4) lower income taxes; (5) wider operating margins on sales. And that's it. There simply are no other ways to increase returns on common equity.*[162]

Buffett then went on to point out that to increase turnover, the receivables, inventory, or fixed assets would have to increase at a rate slower than inflation-induced sales increase. Receivables are likely to increase in direct proportion to sales and, in the long run, inventories can be slowed down a little with LIFO (last-in first-out); fixed assets will lag somewhat behind the sales increase at least until replacement of the physical facilities (at inflated prices) is required. But the effect is small, as Buffett noted:

> *. . . during the decade ending in 1975, despite generally accelerating inflation and the extensive use of LIFO accounting, the turnover ratio of the Fortune 500 went only from 1.18/1 to 1.29/1.*[163]

With regard to "cheaper leverage" this appears unlikely because in periods when inflation rates are high, borrowing becomes more expensive, not cheaper. With regard to "more leverage" Buffett felt this was unlikely.

> *Proof of that proposition can be seen in some other Fortune 500 statistics; in the twenty years ending in 1975, stockholders' equity as a percentage of total assets declined for the 500 from sixty-three percent to just under fifty percent. In other words, each dollar of equity capital now is leveraged much more heavily than it used to be.*

The prospects for lower corporate taxes also seemed unlikely to Buffett:

> *Investors in American corporations already own what might be thought of as a Class D stock. The Class A, B, and C stocks are represented by the income tax claims of the federal, state and municipal governments. . . . Whenever the*

Class A, B, or C "stockholders" vote themselves a larger share of the business, the portion remaining for Class D—that's the one held by the ordinary investor— declines.[164]

The last possible way of increasing return on equity then is to increase profit margins during times when inflation rates are high. Recent statistical evidence does not seem to inspire confidence that margins will actually widen in a period of inflation. As Buffett noted,

> *In the decade ending in 1965, a period of relatively low inflation, the universe of manufacturing companies reported on quarterly by the Federal Trade Commission had an average annual pretax margin on sales of 8.6 percent. In the decade ending in 1975 the average margin was eight percent. Margins were down, in other words, despite a very considerable increase in the inflation rate.*
>
> *If business was able to base its prices on replacement cost, margins would widen in inflationary periods. But the simple fact is that most large businesses, despite a widespread belief in their market power, just don't manage to pull it off. Replacement cost accounting almost always shows that corporate earnings have declined significantly in the past decade.*[165]

In short, there has been no demonstrable proof that even the major companies can increase their prices fast enough to offset the effects of inflation. The 12 percent return on equity, for whatever reason, seems likely to continue for some time. If it is further assumed that half of that 12 percent is paid out in dividends, then 6 percent remains to finance growth, either real or "phantom." In periods when inflation is greater than 6 percent, a loss of liquidity begins to occur. When inflation rates move into the double-digit rate, the loss of liquidity can be rapid. But if all available funds are going just to finance working capital increases required by higher sales levels brought about solely by inflationary price increases, where will the capital come from to purchase new capital equipment for expansion or even to replace worn-out equipment that was purchased years ago at much lower prices?
As Buffett noted,

> *. . . large gains in real capital, invested in modern production facilities, are required to produce large gains in economic well-being. Great labor availability, great consumer wants, and great government promises will lead to nothing but great frustration without continuous creation and employment of expensive new capital assets throughout industry. That's an equation understood by Russians as well as Rockefellers. And it's one that has been applied with stunning success in West Germany and Japan. High capital-accumulation rates have enabled those countries to achieve gains in living standards at rates far exceeding ours, even though we have enjoyed much the superior position in energy.*[166]

In short, inflation decreases corporate liquidity because increasing amounts of working capital are required to finance inflation-induced sales increases. Corporations seem unable to raise prices fast enough to generate the funds required to finance any real growth. So long as inflation continues, it can be expected that corporations increasingly will find themselves pressed for funds even if "record" profits are continually reported.

Dun's Review in June 1978 carried an article supporting this position. Entitled "All About Profit," the article noted that "both profit margins and the return on equity of manufacturing corporations have fluctuated within fairly distinct bands for decades. . . . " The maximum change in return on equity shown by *Dun's*, for instance, was between 10 percent and 15 percent for the twenty years from 1955 to 1975.[167]

What all of this says is that if 50 percent payout in dividends is to be maintained, a return on equity must be earned that is at least twice the inflation rate, just to supply the additional working capital required by inflationary sales increases. Funds for expansion must come from returns higher than that.

Profits finance growth; without profits, the industrial base of this country will wither and die; yet, as Financial World, in a July 15, 1976 article entitled "The Bottom Line Directory," pointed out,

> Perhaps no part of our private enterprise system has been so abused as "profits." They've been called everything, especially "dirty." . . . Sociologists decry them, ministers condemn them, and the labor movement in its public declarations treat them as ill-begotten. Polls confirm that most Americans feel some antipathy to business community, but especially mistrust business profits on a grand scale. . . . But it is from profits that expansion occurs. New products devised, more jobs created and economic stability fashioned . . . and it is from taxes on profits that a great portion of the services provided by goverment is financed.[168]

An interesting point not raised by this article is how this misconception of the role that profits play in the national economy became so widespread. Nor is any method of reversing public opinion on profits proposed. Yet the consequences of continued public opposition to financially strong United States businesses could very well cause major political upheavals in this country.

As the article noted,

> It is true, of course, that other nations exist without profits and the free market in their economic system. But these systems, both past and present, have gone hand-in-hand with an erosion of political liberties, and all Americans are quick to reaffirm their conviction in our basic political and economic freedoms.

> So not only is profit important to the investor and businessman, but we strongly suspect that if the economic system that has propelled this country into its primacy is to survive, the general public will have to recognize corporate profits as an integral and desirable part of that system.[169]

The *Bottom Line Directory* lists the top 500 companies by net earnings. In 1975 American Telephone and Telegraph was number 1, but its return on equity was only 10.2 percent. Assuming the inflation rate in the United States runs 12 percent per year, it is interesting to note that only four companies in the top 50, Dow Chemical, American Home Products, Merck and Co., and Pittston, earned twice that inflation rate.[170]

In 1976 only one company, American Home Products, exceeded twice that inflation rate. Interestingly, the four lowest, all earning less than 10 percent on equity (in the top 50 companies listed by profit) were Texaco, United States Steel, Pacific Tel and Tel, and Pacific Gas and Electric—two utilities, a steel company, and an oil company. With the exception of U.S. Steel, which the public seems to have no current feelings about, the other three all seem to be perceived by the public as overcharging for their services.

In 1977, Edmund A. Mennis, senior vice president of the Security Pacific National Bank, wrote, in summarizing his article "Perspectives on Industry Profits,"

> . . . *a moderate uptrend since 1970 in the return on assets before taxes has been caused more by an increase in turnover than by an improvement in margins. The use of leverage to improve the return on net worth peaked in 1974, and is expected to continue downward through 1977. For the future, improvements in turnover are presumably limited, and there is scant reason to expect gains in earnings before interest and taxes. With less resort to borrowing, and equity markets not strongly attractive, internal corporate financing may become increasingly important.*[171]

This position seems to support Buffett's position that no more rapid turnover, no increased leverage, no more leverage, no increased profit margins are likely to occur as inflation picks up steam.

In April 1978, *Citibank* carried an article entitled "Profits '77—Sales Were the Spur" in which the above positions were again reconfirmed. As the article stated,

> *The sixteen percent rise in after-tax corporate earnings last year was without doubt a good showing. But when adjusted for inflation factors and depreciation, the gains were more apparent than real. . . . Profit margins were generally under pressure, and there was little overall improvement in rates of return or net worth among non-financial firms. . . . There was an even greater acceleration in overhead costs per unit, and profit margins were squeezed accordingly. Thus, the entire rise in profits, on the average, came through the increase in dollar volume of sales.*[172]

Some evidence is beginning to appear that the inflation-induced squeeze on corporate liquidity is inducing changes in the behavior of corporate management. As noted in the introduction to this section, the auto companies, faced with not only inflation-induced liquidity problems but with essentially a government mandate to downsize all of their cars, are beginning to change their relationship with their suppliers. In the September 24, 1979 issue of *Business Week* there was an article entitled "Detroit's New Face Toward Its Suppliers" in which it was noted that

> . . . *auto makers have been uncharacteristically considerate in their dealings with the thousands of outside vendors that supply some $40 billion worth of parts each year.*[173]

The Ford Motor Company recently initiated a new program called the "Supplier Research Program" in which up to a thousand or more ideas that Ford feels will be needed for future models are listed and suppliers are encouraged to invest their funds in developing them. So far, there is no guarantee that the products, if developed, would be purchased, but that may become a possibility in the future. The article continued,

> *The new, longer term supply contract now being written will give suppliers some relief from this pressure. But to win such favored treatment from GM, Ford, or Chrysler a supplier must be able to claim something special, usually a technological edge over other suppliers.*[174]

In a personal conversation Gerald C. Scott, the features and supplier research manager at the Ford Motor Company, on September 24, 1979 commented that,

> *Ford must generate $25 billion in capital expenditures between now and 1985 to comply with government mandated automobile regulations. The limited R & D partnership may be a useful vehicle even for a company the size of the Ford Motor Company.*

Going from the very large to the very small company, an article in the December 3, 1979 *Business Week* stated:

> *An even more innovative money-raising scheme is that of Western Digital Corp. . . . Western needs $2.5 million to fund the research and development of six new semiconductor chips. Its Chairman, Charles W. Missler, is trying to finance that development by setting up tax-sheltered limited partnerships with outside investors. The idea, . . . required that investors put up $50,000 per unit. The investors will benefit from the tax shelter of financing new research as well as from royalty income on the sale of the chips, which will be manufactured and marketed by Western Digital. "This is our only feasible way to raise capital," says Missler, who figures the cost of such financing at around nine percent.*

> *Despite the widening range of innovative cash-raising strategies, hundreds of small companies are still going empty-handed. They either cannot afford to pay strangulating rates of interest or cannot find the funds. Period.*[175]

In summary, the literature seems to support the view that inflation causes a decline in liquidity of businesses, and this is in fact occurring as a result of the high and persistent inflation rates in the United States economy. The subsequent increased demand for funds by many corporations, both large and small, seems to be creating an open-mindedness on the part of corporate management to entertain new and imaginative solutions to their problems. Indications are that this motivation is high enough to overcome the very real problem of the N.I.H. (not-invented-here) syndrome which in the past has made it difficult for corporations to collaborate on a large scale with outsiders. This change in motivation coupled with the financial advantages of R & D limited partnerships accruing to all participants may indicate that the time is right for such a collaboration to take place on a large scale.

Product Obsolescence and the Product Life Cycle

The effect of the declining corporate liquidity brought about by inflation-induced sales increases is that fewer funds are available to develop replacement products for aging product lines. This problem compounds itself very quickly: not only must a manufacturer contend with competition, obsolete production equipment, and the introduction of replacement products by his competitor, but as the product reaches the end of its useful life, the profit margins decline, reducing the cash flow back to the corporation, thus further accelerating the problems. Once caught in this trap, it can be very difficult to escape unless some new source of funds, external to the product line in question, is made available.

As many people have observed over the years, products seem to have a life of their own. From initial introduction into the marketplace each product seems to follow a pattern of growth, maturity, and eventual decline that appears to be preordained or at least controlled by factors that are remarkably similar regardless of the product or marketplace. Joel Dean, in an article entitled "Pricing Policies for New Products" which appeared in the *Harvard Business Review,* is generally recognized as the originator of the term "product life cycle" to describe this phenomenon. As Edward S. Ojdana, Jr., wrote,

> *Dean's concept of the product life cycle differs somewhat from that which is generally accepted today. He saw the cycle as consisting of three elements or components that usually reach maturity at the same time: (1) the technical component (the product and its development); (2) the market component (adoption of the product by consumers); (3) the competitive component (relationships among suppliers of the product). . . . In the twenty-five years since Dean's original article appeared in the literature, the product life cycle concept has been generally recognized and accepted in a number of business oriented disciplines, particularly marketing. According to Buzzell, "Few (if any other) general theories have been so widely discussed or so generally accepted by both academic observers and by marketing practitioners."*[176]

While there is certainly not unanimity of opinion as to the exact name of each stage in this cycle, a reasonably composite view would be to recognize four stages in the life of a product: introduction, growth, maturity, and decline. Each of the stages has certain distinct characteristics even though the line between them is, for the most part, a little fuzzy. For example, as Ojdana pointed out, during the introduction stage prices are high, competition is almost nonexistent, total profits are negative or low, and unit production costs are high. As the product enters its growth stage, prices will soften, mass entry of competition will appear, total profits will peak, and unit production costs will be declining. As the mature stage is reached prices will stabilize; competition will be at a maximum, some will exit, and substitute products will appear; total profits will start to decline; and unit production costs will be stable and low. In the declining stages prices will be declining, there will be buy-outs and mergers among the competition, and the survivors will become specialists. Total profits will be falling but good opportunities for the specialist will be available. At this point unit production costs will start to increase.[177]

As noted above, profit margins are the key to liquidity. Ojdana described the behavior of profit margin as the product passes through the various stages of growth as becoming positive in the introductory stage; increasing rapidly during the growth stage; declining as the product reaches maturity; and, depending on whether the manufacturer becomes the sole remaining specialist or drops out because of a wish to employ his resources elsewhere or just because the competition is too intense, profit margins in the declining phases can either decline or remain high.

Here then is a basis of strategy. As the product reaches maturity, as indicated by peaking profit margins, a decision must be made: Either withdraw from the market while cash flow from the product line is still strong or be prepared to be the last survivor. Not many succeed at "being the last survivor," but for those who do, the marketplace is theirs. To reach a decision to leave a market when it is at its peak may be good strategy but it requires that another product line be available at the right time. This implies that a decision to develop such a product had been made sometime earlier. Such a decision required the expenditure of research and development funds. So long as these decisions are made in a timely fashion and the funds are available to execute the decision and bring the product to a sufficient stage of development in order to introduce it to the marketplace at about the time other major products are reaching maturity, a healthy continuation of the company's activities can be expected. However, once a point is reached where a major product line reaches maturity and starts its inevitable decline and no new products are in the wings ready to step on the "marketing stage," the only choice left to the company is to try to become the last survivor. As this product slips further and further into the decline stage, cash flow decreases and any hope of generating funds for the development of replacement products rests solely on whether the remaining competitors decide to withdraw. If two or more of the competitors are in the same position relative to a new product line, that is, if they have none, failure of both is likely unless a merger can be arranged in time.

Of course the assumptions above are based on the belief that the product life cycle is in fact a good decision model. As Ojdana pointed out, "product life cycle" theory would be a valuable tool in long-range planning if the theory were valid.

Long-range planning requires a set of hypotheses concerning the future, before specific plans can be made. Knowing what conditions are likely to prevail in the future allows decisions to be made concerning what actions should be taken to circumvent unfavorable futures and to exploit favorable futures. The product life cycle has been recommended by many writers as a basis for determining appropriate managerial actions or emphasis.

> *The functional emphasis required for successful product exploration—engineering and research, manufacturing, marketing, and financial control—changes from phase to phase in the cycle as shifts occur in the economies of profitability.*[178]

Ojdana was somewhat concerned about the inevitability of the life cycle. Is it not possible to do something to change it? He noted:

> *The inevitability of the product life cycle presents several conceptual problems relating to the direction of causation. The actions of an individual firm, reactions by its competitors, and the level of consumer acceptance will affect the shape of the firm's brand sales curve. At the brand level, many product and market characteristics are parameters controllable by the firm (advertising, price, etc.).*
>
> *At the product form and class level, the patterns of behavior over the life cycle reflect the sum of individual firms' actions. If a reasonably large number of firms have brands in the market, no individual firm may drastically affect the pattern of behavior over the life cycle of the product class or form. The behavior pattern is thus a result of competitive action, reaction, and market behavior. Under these conditions, the product life cycle could be viewed as an inevitable phenomena, but it is the product form or class life cycle and not the brand life cycle that is inevitable. . . .* [179]

At the end of a chapter that was concerned with examining the product life cycle as a descriptive, predictive, and decision model, Ojdana concluded:

> *. . . (1) the decline in average production cost hypothesized by product life cycle theory is probably the result of learning (i.e., experience gained from previous production) and not economies of scale, (2) price increases as well as price declines during the growth stage are consistent with economic theory. . . . (3) the increase in unit profits that is hypothesized to occur during the growth stage of the product life cycle is consistent with economic theory. . . . (4) entrance of firms into a market for a product as hypothesized by product life cycle theory is not consistent with economic theory unless barriers to entry*

are erected during the growth stage. This inconsistency may be the result of defining profits differently from economic profits. (5) the behavior of prices, profits and the exit of competitors during the decline stage appears to be consistent with economic theory.[180, 181]

It would appear from the work of Ojdana and others that the product life cycle theory demands that replacement products be available, and hence by inference, that a commitment of development funds be made before a key product line enters the declining stages of product life. This assumes that funds for the development must be generated by that product line. Failure to make such a commitment will lead to either failure of the firm or the necessity of being a sole survivor in the field, a decision not solely within the power of one particular company to make as other competitors may find themselves in the same situation. Needless to say, product obsolescence appears inevitable and early commitment of sufficient funds to develop replacement products is a fundamental strategy that must be followed if continued survival is desired. Inflation complicates this picture by forcing funds needed for new product development to be diverted to working capital to support inflation-induced sales increases.

The first part of this review, dealing with establishing corporate need for new sources of research and development funds, was concerned with the effects of inflation on liquidity, and the above section looked briefly at what was seen to be the inevitability of product obsolescence. The final part of this section will look at the problems of a company that is approaching bankruptcy. Is a company in this position in need of research and development funds, or is there a point reached where funds directed to this end would be wasted?

Pending Corporate Bankruptcy—Can the R & D Limited Partnership Play a Part in a Turn-Around Situation?

The first part of this question would seem to require that a point can be identified in the affairs of a company at which time bankruptcy can be predicted to be a reasonable outcome if present policies or conditions prevail. Studies in this field were quite prevalent, as might be expected, in the 1930's. A study at that time and several later ones concluded that failing firms exhibit significantly different ratio measurements than continuing entities. A comprehensive study covering over 900 firms and comparing discontinuing firms with continuing ones was published by the *New York Bureau of Economic Research* in 1942. The title of the study was "Financing Small Corporations" by Merwin.

Edward I. Altman, now Professor of Finance, New York University, published his thesis entitled "The Prediction of Corporate Bankruptcy: A Discriminant Analysis" in 1967. Altman developed a model that could be used for predicting corporate bankruptcy with remarkable accuracy. As an example, for predicting one year in advance, for 33 cases studied the model was 95 percent accurate; for predicting two years in advance it was still 72 percent accurate for 32 cases studied. After that time period the accuracy fell to too low a number to be useful.[182]

Altman's model uses five financial ratios: (1) working capital divided by total assets, (2) retained earnings divided by total assets, (3) earnings before interest and taxes divided by total assets, (4) market value equity divided by book value of total debt, and (5) sales divided by total assets. Each of these factors is calculated, multiplied by a weighting factor, and added together. The total is designated as the Z factor. If the Z factor is above 3, it is predicted that the company will not be forced into bankruptcy within the next two years; if the Z factor is less than 1.8, bankruptcy within two years is very likely; a number in between 1.8 and 3 is in a gray area where no predictions are made. No opinion is stated by Altman as to whether the trend of the Z factor is a leading indicator of potential problems, but the trend of at least one company has been observed, and while insufficient data have been gathered to allow a rigid statistical analysis to be made, at least superficially it would appear that even if the Z factor is above 3, a downward trend should be cause for concern.

The most interesting aspect of Altman's model, besides its predictive accuracy, is that four out of five of the denominators in the ratios used relate to total assets. In short, if total assets can be reduced without decreasing near-term sales, working capital, earnings before taxes or retained earnings in like proportions, the Z factor can be increased. If this reduction in total assets can produce any cash whatsover, this cash can be applied against total debt and reduce the one factor that does not have total assets in the denominator. Obviously selling off unneeded or underutilized assets can reduce total assets and so benefit four of the ratios, and funds received from these sales can reduce debt. Research and development activities, no matter how well directed, cannot affect the short-term sales, profits, working capital, or retained earnings favorably so that disposal of any assets tied up in R & D activities with the subsequent application of these funds to debt reduction will have a beneficial effect on all five of Altman's factors. These actions might very well save the company from bankruptcy, but if alternate means of continuing the development of new products are not found, eventual failure will only have been delayed. Such tactics, in conjunction with outside collaboration with an R & D limited partnership, could provide continuation of the needed product development while freeing up assets needed to get the company back on its feet.

This section has reviewed the literature pertaining to the need of corporations for outside funds to pursue research and development activities. The next section will review literature concerning a key element in R & D limited partnerships: the investor. Is the need of U.S. corporations for R & D activities great enough to offer high enough returns, in the form of the favorable tax aspects of such an investment to individuals, to attract enough investors to make the R & D effort worthwhile? The next part of the literature review will explore that question in some depth.

THE INVESTORS—HOW MANY THERE ARE, WHAT THEY WANT, AND HOW THEY FEEL ABOUT LIMITED PARTNERSHIPS

If one link of a chain can be said to be more important than another, then in the chain of events that could lead to the establishment of large numbers of R & D limited partnersips, surely the investors must be that link, for without their participation no activity is possible.

This section will look at the literature pertaining to investors and their behavior, particularly those investors who would be considered reasonable candidates for participation in business ventures of this nature.

"High Income" United States Taxpayers

In 1975 approximately one million tax returns were filed by individuals (or couples filing jointly) whose adjusted personal gross income exceeded the ceiling of the 49 percent federal income tax bracket. This number, of course, excluded those individuals who already had taken advantage of "tax shelter" investments to reduce their adjusted income enough to avoid that tax bracket. It is assumed for the moment that these are the persons who might be considered prime candidates for an R & D partnership investment, not only because of their normal attention to keeping their income as well as earning it, but because at that income level an R & D limited partnership can more efficiently utilize their funds than can any corporation. For corporations paying lower tax rates, a correspondingly lower individual rate would represent the switchover point. If the next lower income bracket of adjusted personal gross income rates is used ($30,000 to $49,000), the total number of taxpayers quadruples to approximately 4,000,000. If inflation continues at its present rate, that group automatically will be propelled into the 49 percent-plus bracket and find themselves suddenly blessed with the privilege of giving more than half of their income to the federal tax collector. Since prospects for a significant abatement of the inflationary spiral in which the United States finds itself seem rather remote, investments in tax shelters probably will experience major growth, albeit for strange and not particularly desirable reasons. Noting from the references cited in this review that the total industrially financed R & D performed in the United States has averaged a level of about $20 billion, an investment in 1975 of only $20,000 by each person (or couple filing jointly) who was in the 49 percent-plus tax bracket could have financed all of the R & D activity in the United States. If the next group of investors, those who will soon move into the 49 percent-plus tax bracket, is included, the average individual investment required drops to only $5,000. While it obviously is not practical to assume everyone in a given tax bracket would become an investor, it is interesting to note that Delorean's investors' minimum participation was $150,000. Robert Nichols, president of Intervest, an investment management firm in Los Angeles, said that $5,000 investors in tax shelters were extremely easy to locate.[183]

Profile of a Typical Active Investor

A profile of the typical "active investor" was developed by *The Wall Street Journal* in 1977.[184] As part of a survey conducted by Belknap Marketing Services of Greenwich, Connecticut, a questionnaire was mailed to 1,902 individuals who had been identified as "active" by at least one of three major brokerage firms who collaborated in the survey. Replies were received from 1,009 addresses, a response rate of 53 percent. The survey summarized the demographic characteristics of the active investor as follows:

> *While typically married males (88 percent males and 79 percent being married) ranging in age from under 25 to over 75 (with their median age being 55) these active investors tend to be well-educated (82 percent have attended college . . .) and they are employed in almost all business and industrial categories, . . . fully one-third of them are corporate officers, partners or owners . . . and their household income is relatively high, ranging from less than $10,000 (3 percent) to over $150,000 (9 percent) with a median of $48,600.*[185]

Several other statistics are of interest to this study: 75 percent of the persons responding had household incomes of $25,000 or higher (those over $30,000 are represented by the 4,000,000 returns discussed in the previous section); 79 percent of their holdings was being held for long-term gain (a characteristic of limited partnerships investments); their median portfolio value was $183,000 with an average of $389,000; dividend yield was listed by only 26 percent of the respondents as being "very important"; and *The Wall Street Journal* was listed as the primary source of investment information by a margin of six to one over the nearest competitor.[186] While all of the addressees were selected because of their regular and preponderant investment in common stocks and other securities handled primarily by major brokerage houses (no one listed holdings in limited partnerships), the profile drawn was of someone who should have been interested in a limited partnership investment, provided it was presented to him in an appropriate format.

In agreement with that concept was the copy in a Merrill Lynch advertisement appearing in the December 1979 issue of *Fortune*:[187]

> *Tax shelters are neither devious nor limited to the very rich. If you're in a 50 percent tax bracket, you should consider some of these. The phrase "tax shelter" conjures up images of byzantine legal arrangements and obscure foreign companies. It's a wrong impression. In fact, the phrase itself is misleading.*

At Merrill Lynch, we prefer to talk about tax investments.

We mean, simply, investments that can provide both a return on your capital and certain meaningful tax benefits. If the investment itself doesn't seem sound, we won't have anything to do with it.

Merrill Lynch specializes in three kinds of tax investments with particularly favorable risk/reward ratios: Oil and gas exploration, real estate equities, and the leasing of barges and boxcars.[188]

So far then, as a general statement, it appears that there are enough investors in relation to the R & D activities in the United States to materially affect the manner in which these activities are carried out, assuming that investment conditions are favorable and that investments of from $5,000 to $150,000 are not unreasonable for fairly large numbers of investors. Certainly Merrill Lynch seems aware that a market for such investments exists.

But what are the characteristics of an investment in a limited partnership from an investor's viewpoint, and what specific advantages or characteristics of this type of investment are of most interest to the investor?

Investor's View of Limited Partnerships

Matthews noted that:

The stereotype limited partner in the popular press would have him a doctor, lawyer, movie star, or sports superstar. To the degree that any members of these groups generate large annual incomes and face a huge tax "bite," this generalization might be described as fairly accurate.[189]

However, as noted above, more and more taxpayers are being forced into the high tax brackets, so that in time, if the trend is not reversed, everyone would seem to be a prime candidate. The image of the seeker of a tax shelter as a "tax dodger" is hardly appropriate. As Matthews remarked,

The limited partner need not be a "tax dodger" to find the limited partnership inviting. Take an example of a real estate offering wherein a recreational development is proposed. In today's market for diversion and relaxation, such investments offer returns as great as those in Wall Street stocks. For simple profit motivation, an investor might decide that his best chance to participate in expected profits is to invest in a limited partnership. As a limited partner, the investor will likely know where the development is to be made and will derive possible intangible benefits from watching and inspecting his investment as it takes shape. Stocks in large public companies are hard-pressed to match this attribute of limited partnerships.[190]

However, as Matthews continued,

Regardless of the advantage of a tax shelter for his hard-earned investment

dollars, the limited partner has committed his capital to a business venture for a lengthy period and is generally unable to liquidate his interests.[191]

. . . being locked-in as a limited partner may appear to be the product of an unequal bargaining position between the promoters and investors; however, the economic realities of the business ventures undertaken in the last few years by limited partnerships soften criticism of this common trait of investment fixity.[192]

It should also be noted that research and development types of limited partnership must also attempt to "lock in" the investment insofar as possible because, by the very nature of R & D activities, an invention "half-way" reduced to practice could be worthless and the withdrawal of funds part way through a project most probably would jeopardize the investments of all of the partners involved. However, as Matthews noted, this characteristic has been common to many limited partnership activities in the past.

The major advantages and disadvantages to the limited partners were listed by Matthews as the following:

(1) Tax shelter; (2) possible economic return on their investment; (3) investment without management responsibility; (4) limited liability; (5) a piece of the "action tango." . . .

Suffice it to say, that all limited partners this study has been able to contact have indicated the possibility of reducing their federal income tax bite as the major, if not sole, motivation for investing in a limited partnership. . . . The potential of economic return, together with the likelihood of using "soft dollars" for investment, is likely to rank as a major incentive for most limited partners. . . .[193]

It is a somewhat discouraging commentary on the profitability of the tax shelter ventures offered to date that, in the eyes of the investors, few if any of these ventures could have stood on their own feet without the associated tax benefits.

While the advantages of investment without management and limited liability require little comment so long as the partnership stands up to government challenges on those two issues, the "piece of the action tango" requires some elaboration. As Matthews noted,

Not to be discounted is what one spokesman for a cattle management group termed as "Schmaltz," i.e., the desire of investors to associate themselves with what they feel to be glamorous industries. This is evidenced in the Black Watch cattle breeding herds sold to "Wall Street Cowboys" during the late 1960's. A related investor motivation is the opportunity to "tango where the action's at." This nebulous concept refers mainly to the real or imagined desire of all investors to capture the newness of an innovation or approach before other investors overcrowd the industry or legislative response lowers the boom on another lucrative loophole. The excitement allowed the well-heeled city investor by participating in an oil exploration venture, or owning together with other "club" members a lot of cattle, is difficult if not impossible to measure quantitatively in assessing investor rationale for buying limited partnership interests. To discount this attraction of a limited partnership is most unrealistic, as any underwriter for such interests will likely admit.[194]

The underlying reasoning for an investor's decision to ascribe value to intangibles such as "Schmaltz" will become more apparent when some of the literature relating to decision theory is reviewed later in this section. Suffice it to say here that economic value plus intangibles add up to "utility" for an investor, and it is this value that he is apparently trying to maximize; no level of irrationality need be ascribed to an investor's actions in considering "intangibles" in investment decisions.

Matthews listed the following disadvantages to limited partners:

(1) High management fees to the general partner; (2) no control rights; (3) no ready market for their interests; (4) difficulty in guarding and/or remedying unfair management practices as self-dealing; (5) the possibility that unlimited liability might be imposed; (6) the collapsibility of promised shelter.[195]

Items (1) and (4) will of course not arise in dealings with ethical general partners. Items (5) and (6) can be avoided by setting up the partnership so that it is not gimmicky and not pressing the intent of the tax legislation that permitted the partnership in the first place. Item (2) is a critical part of the concept of limited partnerships. Without this "disadvantage," limited liability cannot be achieved. Item (3), the problem of no ready market for their interests, is keyed to the nature of the projects undertaken as well as to the lack of a market for these interests at present, even if the project itself was not restrictive by nature. Presumably if a sufficient number of limited partnerships' interests were available, a market could be established; the trading of such issues might either jeopardize the tax status because the partnership will appear to be a corporation or raise the necessity of registering the interests as securities. Neither of these alternatives would be beneficial to the partnership as a whole.

To determine more precisely why investors participated in limited partnerships, Matthews conducted a survey of the limited partners of a cattle-feeding fund by mailing a questionnaire to each of the 94 limited partners of the fund, accompanied by an introductory letter explaining the purpose of the inquiry. Thirty-nine completed questionnaires were returned.

Matthews explained the results of the survey as follows:

It was not surprising that almost all the limited partners responding became aware of the fund and its investment attraction through their brokers because most investments in registered offerings are channeled through professional broker organizations, whether stock investments or limited partnership interests. Indeed, several of the limited partners were brokers themselves . . . of the various responses to the question of what the limited partners viewed as the advantages of their investment in the fund, the most frequent response was tax shelter, accounting for nearly 80 percent of the responses. Although some limited partners did indicate an interest in the profit potential of their investments, the kingpin of the possible advantages was indisputably the prospect of deferring taxes, i.e., tax shelter. Given the prevailing enthusiasm of the investment community in attempting to sell tax shelter first and economic investments second, there is little reason to question the validity of these survey responses. . . . [196]

Among the disadvantages which the limited partners listed in their responses, restrictions on the transferability of their partnership interest were most frequently mentioned. Non-transferability, however, is one of the four characteristics that a limited partnership must have if it is to be taxed as a partnership instead of an "association," an event that would destroy all tax benefits to the investors. It must be assumed, then, that the investor's displeasure is directed to the IRS and not the fund management. Also mentioned was the inability to convert ordinary income into capital gains, a feature found in several other tax shelters as well as in the R & D limited partnership. [197]

Again and again in the literature the investors, and all other participants for that matter, have concentrated on the tax aspects, to the detriment of the underlying profitability of the venture. With regard to the return the respondents expected to get,

Nearly 50 percent indicated that they expected a return on equity invested in the range of 15-20 percent per annum with some expectations reaching as high as 25-40 percent per annum. [198]

So while they did not say profit was an important motivation in the original investment decision, at least half expected good to high returns on their investments.

In response to the question, what would they do if certain tax law changes were to cancel significant portions of the tax shelter treatment of the fund, 77 percent of the investors responded that they would "ride out their existing cattle fund investments but make no further fund investments in cattle feeding funds." [199]

With regard to questions concerning prior participation in limited partnerships, nearly 75 percent had invested in other limited partnerships; only 30 percent had invested in cattle feeding funds; the remaining investments were predominantly in real estate and oil drilling or exploration. [200]

In summary,

These investors were primarily seeking a tax benefit in the form of income deferral. . . . Their reaction [to tax reform denying income deferral] was clear and quick: if the tax environment is altered so that cattle feeding investments must depend solely upon economic profitability, the limited partner of this 1970 fund would find such ventures unattractive for further investment consideration. [201]

It would appear that projects offering sufficient profitability to attract investors while still retaining the tax shelter advantages available for correctly structured limited partnerships are somewhat rare. There would seem to be no inherent reason why this should be true, and indeed, the future continuity of these ventures may very well depend on discovering ways to so structure them or at least to avoid those projects from which profit is unlikely to be obtained even some time in the future.

In the present investment climate, however, Matthews pointed out what must be present in a project if a successful limited partnership is to be brought into being:

> . . . it would seem that the availability of deductible expenses during the start-up period of a business is a prime factor for potential adopters of the limited partnership. Furthermore, the deductible expenses generally must either be capable of being bunched at the end of a taxable year or be associated with start-up expenses. The substantial expenses incurred during the development stage might [must] be either immediately deductible as ordinary operating expenses or deductible as depreciation over the appropriate life of the asset if capital assets are being created. . . .
>
> . . . it cannot be denied that more than just deductible expenses are necessary for the success of a limited partnership offering. Nonetheless, the types of expenses—whether they are manipulable, their magnitude, and their recurrence—are definitely factors in the successful merchandising of a limited partnership in agriculture. . . .[202]

However, as Matthews noted, all of this is useless without sophisticated management:

> Management willing and able to cope with the complexities of large-scale financing activities is required.[203]

Besides competent management, ethical management is also required if limited partnerships are to remain viable entities whether for R & D activities or any other type of projects. Matthews wrote:

> While the clamor for tax reform against tax shelters is an obvious impediment, the abuse of the limited partnership by promoters and/or unscrupulous management is a less visible eroding factor. . . . [204]

Again Matthews noted that while tax benefits are mentioned most often as key to the investor's decision,

> . . . a helping hand for those seeking to curtail if not eliminate tax shelters . . . could arise from the failure of funds to earn reasonable profits for their investors. Even though limited partner investors sought out the funds for tax

shelter motivations, the profit incentive is still regarded relevant and necessary to their investment decisions. . . .

Failure of funds to generate satisfactory economic profits would have an obvious effect upon taxpayers seeking tax shelter opportunities. However, absent unprofitable times, the funds are expanding and new funds are being created. The throttle for growth would then seem primarily to be in the hand of Congress.[205]

Matthews' work was primarily related to limited partnerships in agriculture. The most frequent occurrence of limited partnerships has been in real estate. The typical characteristics of the real estate limited partnership investor were summed up by Wayne E. Etter and Donald R. Levi in their article "Investor Views of Real Estate and Limited Partnerships":

Syndications have become a significant force in the real estate market in recent years. The typical investor in such syndications: (1) is from 35–54 years old, (2) is most likely to have a principal occupation in business, sales, law or medicine, (3) has maintained an investment portfolio for several years and currently holds a diversified portfolio, and (4) has no close friendship or family ties with the syndication general partner. Investors prefer investments providing a rapid rate of capital appreciation rather than periodic cash return. The length of the holding period is relatively unimportant. They seek protection against inflation and taxes and prefer to rely on the advice of syndicator/brokers rather than their own knowledge. When asked to evaluate the potential for investment of common stocks, municipal bonds, and real estate syndications, the latter is clearly preferred.[206]

The profile of the typical real estate limited partnership investor does not differ significantly from that of the typical "active investor" surveyed by *The Wall Street Journal.*

Review of Decision Theory as Applied to Potential Investors

The above review is primarily concerned with what investors do and what they believe they are seeking when an investment decision is made. The underlying causes of why they do what they do and the determination of whether their future actions can be predicted are important if any reasonable estimate of the future potential of a somewhat different investment medium is to be made.

The field of academic pursuit known as decision theory is beyond the scope of this study, but even a cursory review of it may provide some indication of the direction in which further inquiry must go. Decision theory goes beyond trial-and-error or intuitive guesses as a basis for setting up new investment vehicles. Organizers of limited partnership ventures utilizing decision theory can maximize their chances of success prior to investing large amounts of "front-end" money only to find out that the concept did not sell.

The most comprehensive summary of the work done and being done in the field of decision theory was uncovered in *New Directions in Psychology II*, under the chapter heading "Emerging Technologies for Making Decisions," written by Ward Edwards, Harold Lindman, and Lawrence D. Phillips and published in 1973.

In the introduction, the authors describe as nonsense the concept that only man can make decisions and machines can only carry them out:

> *Unaided machines make decisions all of the time. Your automobile engine decides, with no intervention by you, when its engine is warm enough so that water should be permitted to circulate through the radiator. The point is that man knows best what effect he wants a decision-making machine to produce. . . . One indispensable human function in decision making then, is evaluation of the anticipated consequences of decisions.*[207]

In short, machines can be designed to repeatedly make correct decisions but the value system accompanying these decisions must be determined by the person designing the system. For instance,

> *If we knew in detail how heredity and environment have managed to shape a man's value system, we could design a machine to set his house thermostat for him, though we probably would not.*[208]

The primary reason to study decision making at some length is that

> *research and experience suggest the ego-deflating conclusion that men often make poor decisions.*
>
> *. . . decision making has interested its students for a long time, and mathematicians have developed many tools important in analyzing it. Among them are probability theory, utility theory, the theory of games, classical and Bayesian statistics, and operations research.*
>
> *Our conclusion will be that these technologies offer immense promise for improving the quality and speed of decision making, but that human beings will continue to be indispensable for certain functions for the forseeable future.*[209]

The authors point out that decision theorists distinguish between two classes of theories, normative and descriptive. A normative model or theory is a set of rules describing what people ought to do; a descriptive model of decision making predicts, or tries to predict, what a person will do.

The descriptions of what an investor does in relation to investments in limited partnerships are equivalent of descriptive models. A normative model of decision making will predict correctly the behavior of anyone who is willing and able to apply that model in making his own decisions.

The larger and more important the decision, the more likely is the decision-

*maker to calculate carefully the potential consequences of his act and so try
to make the normatively correct decision.*[210]

For the most part attempts to "build in" a value system to normative
systems have been abandoned. At best these systems are

> *. . . no more than sets of rules designed to ensure that acts will be coherent
> or internally consistent with one another in the pursuit of whatever goals the
> decision maker may happen to have. Nevertheless, this requirement of co-
> herence of internal consistency is a very strong one, so strong that no one
> seems able to satisfy it fully.*[211]

The implication here is that an investor who is making what is regarded
as a major investment decision, will attempt to make a normative correct
decision. An understanding of what that "correct decision" is will allow an
observer to at least understand what a person is striving for, even when the
goal is not achieved.

> *Every descriptive model in psychology actually contains two parts. One is a
> description of the environment and task facing the organism; the other is a
> description of the basic response tendencies that the organism brings to that
> environment and task. The interplay of these two kinds of descriptions produces
> the detailed predictions about the behavior of the organism in the situation.*
>
> *. . . It is relatively simple to add to these normative models rather trivial
> assumptions about the way that men behave in response to decision-making
> tasks, and come up with very sophisticated predictions about what men will
> actually do. This is especially so because men very often attempt to do the
> best they can in a decision-making task; that is, men attempt to behave as a
> normative model would prescribe.*[212]

One other distinction is made by the authors, in describing static versus
dynamic decision theory. A static theory applies when all of the relevant
information is supplied prior to making a decision, and based on that information, a decision is made. A dynamic theory, on the other hand, conceives
that a decision maker faces a sequence of decisions that may or may not all
seek the same goal. "Only the dynamic approach can hope to do justice to
the complexity of the real world."[213]

Everyone seems to feel that decisions should be made rationally, but a
clear definition of rationality that everyone answers to is almost impossible
to find. The authors list at least four criteria of rationality that they believe
all can accept, beginning with the principle of rationality called decidability.

> *Given any two outcomes, A & B, a decision maker should be able to tell
> whether he prefers A to B, or B to A, or whether he is indifferent about them.
> . . . The second uncontroversial principle of rationality is more important, both
> theoretically and empirically. It is called the principle of transitivity. . . . If*

you prefer outcome A to outcome B and outcome B to outcome C, it would be irrational of you to prefer outcome C to outcome A.[214]

. . . The third relatively uncontroversial principle of rationality is concerned with rules for determining preferences, rather than with consistency relations among preferences. The principle of dominance . . . is simple, sweeping and common to all conceptions of rationality. If for every possible state of the world act A produces at least as desirable an outcome as act B, and if for at least one state of the world the outcome of act A is definitely better than that of act B, you should never prefer act B to act A. . . . The fourth relatively uncontroversial principle, called the sure-thing principle, states that when you are making a choice between two possible actions, outcomes that do not depend on your choice should not influence your choice.[215]

One other concept must be introduced before the conclusion is drawn from the four criteria for rationality listed above: the notion of utility. Value can be expressed in rather absolute terms. As an example, one dollar is always one dollar; but one dollar may be worth a great deal more to a poor man than to a rich one. In other words, one dollar has a higher utility to one person than to another. It turns out that the concept of utility as applied to an outcome produces more consistent results than value.

Our conclusion, a controversial one that is coming to be accepted by most students of the theory of decision making, is that there is really only one candidate for the title of optima or rational strategy for making decisions. That is the strategy of choosing the act with the largest expected utility; more formally it is called the strategy of maximizing expected utility. We shall call it the EU strategy, or EU model, for short. To apply this model, you assign a numerical utility to each outcome and determine a numerical probability for each state. Then multiply the utility of the outcome of an act if a given state obtains by the probability of that state, and sum these products over the various states. Do this for each available act, and choose the act for which that sum is largest.[216]

One problem here will be taken up later, the notion that probability, like value, may be different for different people, hence a subjective probability used in the above EU model seems to best describe a person's decisions.

But first, there is a competitor to the EU model, known as the minimax principle.

A person applying the minimax principle acts as if, no matter what act he may choose, nature will subsequently turn out to be in that state which is least favorable for that act. The appropriate strategy under such conditions is to choose that act whose worst possible outcome is least unpleasant—in more concise language, to minimize the maximum loss (hence the name minimax). For decisions in which nature or chance is the "opponent," such a strategy is unduly pessimistic, and indeed it was not proposed primarily for "games against nature." In competitive situations in which the decision-maker faces a rational opponent, the strategy makes more sense. But in competitive games, also, the minimax strategy turns out to be too conservative; it gives up most possibilities of exploiting an opponent's mistakes. It is safe to say that a minimax businessman or poker player would soon go broke.[217]

Other models are possible, of course, but these two are sufficient for the purpose here. Rather than expand on the various types of models, a somewhat detailed look at probability would be more useful. As mentioned above, there are some problems with the notion of probability. Here are some mentioned by the authors:

In a very important sense, everyone agrees about what a probability is. It is a number between zero and one, inclusive. These numbers obey several laws, all derivable from the simple rule that the sum of the probabilities assigned to a mutually exclusive set of events one of which must happen, is one.[218]

The arguments arise not in a mathematical sense, but from the observations that should be used to relate these concepts to the real world. Three kinds of observations relate to these numbers:

(1) Relative frequencies: If a coin is flipped a large number of times, the difference between the number of heads and the number of tails increases with the number of flips. . . . but the ratio of the number of heads to the total number of flips, for a fair coin will be very likely indeed to be very close to 0.5. . . . From this viewpoint, the ratio of heads to total tosses for a finite number of tosses, while not a probability, is what is called an unbiased estimator . . . of that probability.[219]

This type of probability is normally encountered in various situations that seem to have a mathematical origin or at least can be reduced to a mathematical model of some sort. Yet this turns out to be a rather limited concept of probability. As the authors point out,

. . . using this conception of probability, most uncertainties that men experience cannot be described by means of probabilities. Uncertainty about matters of fact is one example: What is the probability that the eighth President of the United States had more than three children? We do not know whether he did or not and yet we would certainly accept an even-money bet that he did not, provided that its offeror were as ignorant as we. . . . The coin toss is the textbook example of relative frequencies. But how should the coin be tossed? The successive tosses should be under "substantially identical" conditions. But the conditions cannot be "absolutely identical," or the coin would come up the same way every time.[220]

Whereas before reading this reference it seemed "obvious" that a fairly flipped coin would come up equally heads or tails if flipped long enough, here is the disquieting thought that if one were to build a precision coin-flipping machine, it could very well come up heads every time. If it did, would the machine be viewed as "fixed"? And if so, how would one go about "unfixing it"? Obviously, it would be adjusted so that it would flip an even number of heads and tails. But then it would appear to be simply carrying out the desire of the machine "adjuster" to have an equal number of heads and tails rather than following some immutable law of nature.

(2) Symmetry and Necessary Views: Some mathematicians have attempted to treat probability as a branch of logic and have argued that at least some probabilities are logically necessary. Such views hinge on various versions of the notion that some partitions are sufficiently symmetric so that all elements of the partition should be considered equally likely. . . . There must be something of at least psychological importance in this idea, since one of our major industries is built around it. Every popular form of gambling except betting on contests of strength or skill depends on devices like shuffled cards, perfectly cubical dice, or symmetrically laid-out roulette wheels. All such devices use visible symmetry to support the idea that the symmetric elements are equally likely. . . . [221]

This concept seems obvious on the face of it, although a determination that some device is in fact symmetric would be, at best, a personal judgment. (Is the roulette wheel really symmetric when red has come up 33 times in a row at Monte Carlo?)

(3) The Personalistic View: You might be willing to say, "Heads on the next flip of this coin has probability 0.5" if and only if you would as soon guess heads as not, even if there were some important reward for being right. Your verbal statement of probability and your choices among gambles are devices whereby you can report your opinion about the coin. Such consistent opinions, we think, are the essence of probability. Your opinions about a coin can of course differ from your neighbor's. Hence the personal in the phrase "personal probability." Any probability should in principle be indexed with the name of the person, or people, whose opinion it describes: . . . However, not all opinions about uncertain events can be dealt with as probabilities; opinions, to be treatable as probabilities, must be consistent, which turns out to mean no more than that they must add up to one. [222]

This passage says, in essence, that one may believe and call it a probability, that a coin will come up heads three out of every four tosses, provided that one is also willing to believe that tails will come up one out of every four tosses.

Now to return to the expected utility (EU) model, that is, that persons attempt to maximize their expected utility. It can now be seen not only that value is not as useful as utility, but that observable probability is not as useful as personal or subjective probability in predicting decision strategies. If utility is used, and if the personal probabilities add up to 1, it

> . . . *has become customary to call that quantity a subjectively expected utility (SEU) and so to call the model the SEU maximization model, or SEU model. . . . However, descriptive versions of the SEU model also exist in which the probabilities are not required to add up to any specified constant.*[223]

A good deal of research effort has gone into the problem of how utility and subjective probability are measured, but that work is beyond the scope of this book. Suffice it to say that much work has been done and such measurements can be made, although controversial results are more often than not obtained.

From this brief summary it can be concluded that the investors mentioned in Matthews' report, who seemed to place considerable weight on the "Schmaltz" in the project or who wanted to be "where the action was," were not acting irrationally as seems to be implied. In fact the "personal utility" that they were maximizing may place great weight on being where the action is and not so much weight on a high rate of return on equity. Likewise, the almost universal desire for tax deferral, many times far outweighing what others might consider "good business judgment," is more than likely the result of receiving a high degree of "utility" from "beating the government" so that those investors are also maximizing the expected utility of their investment. The concept of subjective probabilities also explains why different people will view entirely differently the likelihood of a given project's succeeding.

For example, suppose that an investor is offered an interest in a project to develop a small car that will get one hundred miles to the gallon while carrying four people at fifty miles per hour. If the investor is totally ignorant of engineering principles but has been advised that the project is feasible by someone in whom he has confidence, he may rate it as having an even chance of success and be acting rationally. Next, an investor with considerable engineering experience in the automobile industry but who retired during the 1971 model year and has been out of touch since, may have a very strong opinion that such a project has practically no chance of success; 100:1 against it, he might say. He is acting rationally in view of his background. Yet a third investor might be approached who happens to be very much involved in a similar project and feels that a breakthrough in engine technology is just around the corner and hence that the project has a very good chance; better than even, he might say. All three potential investors are in fact acting rationally based on their backgrounds and experience. Who is right? As the project progresses and information is fed back to these persons, their opinions will probably change. But that brings up one last point that is of great interest to this subject.

A number of experiments have been performed in which subjects are asked to estimate probabilities of certain events occurring, after having been given a certain amount of information. All such experiments point to the fact that "men are conservative information processors."[224] In other words, they always will guess a lower probability that an event will occur than the information presented to them would indicate.

Why are men so conservative in these tasks? Many speculations can be proposed; some of them can be checked experimentally. One obvious hypothesis is simply that men are impressed by the fact that probabilities must lie between 0 and 1. As the data push their opinion up nearer and nearer to these limits, they become increasingly reluctant to change opinions in the face of further information, since they are getting closer and closer to the point at which their opinions cannot change any further. . . . A second kind of hypothesis about why people are conservative in posterior probability estimation is that they have no incentive to be anything else. . . . Whatever the merits or demerits of a built-in tendency to conservatism in information processing in daily life, such a tendency is clearly a hindrance to human effectiveness in information-processing systems. Such systems have no need for built-in, conservative, information-processing biases; they can provide much less automatic, more rational biases in rather different ways. Consequently, the finding of human conservatism raises some problems for the design of man–machine systems intended to perform information processing in a more or less optimal way.[225]

If in fact men are not able to extract all of the available information that is presented to them and as a result always make conservative estimates of events for which the information is pertinent, the clear need is for better systems to evaluate the information received rather than more information. The investor today is inundated with information. Without really making any effort, more information on a given project can be obtained than can ever be processed. Certainly all of the effort of the SEC under the Securities Act of 1933 is to direct more information to the potential investor. Yet it appears that much of this effort is now misdirected. What to do with the information so that the "subjective expectation utility" function can in fact be maximized would seem to take precedence over more and more information.

Out of all of this, Edwards concludes in another article that

All in all, the evidence favors rationality. Men seem to be able to maximize expected utility rather well, in a too-restricted range of laboratory tasks. . . . more detailed analysis of such experiments . . . indicates that substantial deviations from rationality seldom occur unless they cost little; when a lot is at stake and the task isn't too complex for comprehension, men behave in such a way as to maximize expected utility. . . .

. . . the conservatism phenomenon is a large, consistent deviation from optimal information-processing performance. Nevertheless, it is surprising to those newly looking at this area that men can do as well as they do at probability or odds estimation. . . .

Total rejection of the notion that men behave rationally is as inappropriate as total acceptance would be. On the whole, men do well, exactly how well they

do depends in detail on the situation they are in, what's at stake, how much information they have, and so on. . . . [126]

Another interesting aspect of probabilities is that men seem to prefer some probabilities to others for no explicable reason. As Robert Libby and Peter C. Fishburn noted:

Edwards . . . showed the pervasiveness of probability preferences (e.g., that for bets with the same positive expected return, subjects preferred bets involving a 0.5 probability of winning to all others) and noted that they cannot be accounted for by non-linear utility curves. Fryback, Goodman, and Edwards (1973) replicated this finding in a field experiment conducted in a Las Vegas casino. In his review article, Edwards . . . says that: "The results showed that two factors were most important in determining choices: general preferences or dislikes for risk-taking, and specific preferences among probabilities . . . subjects strongly preferred low probabilities of losing large amounts of money to high probabilities of losing small amounts of money—they just didn't like to lose. [227]

This information seems to indicate that business ventures that expect to attract investors ought to be structured so that the probability of success is perceived to be about 0.5 as opposed to longer odds or less probability. Of course another view could be derived from the apparent inability of men to extract all of the information that is possible from data presented to them; that is, for really impossible projects, the odds of failure will be conservatively estimated. This may account for many business failures that occur each year.

Another interesting aspect of human behavior that is applicable to the investor is that experimental research seems to support the proposition that given equal information, men will bargain to an equity position. Edwards performed a number of bargaining games and his conclusions were stated as follows:

The main finding from these studies of multi-person games seems to be that people import into bargaining situations a strong desire for equity. Equity-seeking is promoted by effective and free communication and seriously hindered or even prevented by severely restricted communication.

In the same chapter, Edwards also noted:

Furthermore, if one member of a bargaining pair knew the costs, prices, and profits of both, while the other knew only his own costs, prices, and profits, then the member with more information was at a disadvantage, because he more quickly arrived at the equitable offer and consequently was at a disadvantage in subsequent bargaining. [228]

This statement has enormous implications. Assuming equity is desired, the party with the most information should impart it to the other as quickly as possible. It would thus appear that full disclosure as required by the SEC actually works to the advantage of the promoters as they usually have more information about both sides than the investors.

Several studies of behavior and risk-taking decisions indicate what is known as a risky shift in group decision that persists even after the group has disbanded. What is meant here is that if an individual is asked to ascertain the subjective probability of any event occurring and is then placed in a group situation where a discussion of the event can occur, the group will come to a "riskier" conclusion than the individuals making up the group would have reached individually and that this "risky shift" persists.[229] The riskly shift phenomenon has interesting aspects relative to an unregistered offering of security interests in a limited partnership. Rule 146, in essence, requires a "due diligence" meeting of potential investors to give them an opportunity to question the promoters about any aspect of the project about which they feel a need for further information. Assuming that this meeting was so structured as to encourage group participation and that the promoters were in fact willing to bring all pertinent information "out on the table," the group as a whole would probably arrive at some estimation of the probability that the project would be a success. Assuming the discussion was carried on in good faith with competent participants, there is no reason that this estimate of the probability of success would not be a good one. However, the "risky shift" principle would indicate that the estimate, whatever it is, would be a riskier conclusion than any one of the group members would have made independently and that the tendency to assume a riskier position will persist after the meeting. In this sense the "due diligence" meeting will actually work to the benefit of the promoters, certainly not what the SEC had in mind. It should be pointed out that the conclusions reached by the group, assuming it has been provided with correct and complete information, certainly a prime responsibility of the promoters, are not necessarily wrong or overly optimistic. They simply will be more optimistic estimates than any of the members are likely to have made alone.

In addition, perceived risk was found to correlate to various personality traits.

The relationships between perceived risk and personality measures believed to influence information processing were examined using correlation analyses. Perceived risk measures were positively related to a number of anxiety measures and negatively related to self esteem and risk taking. No significant patterns of relationships were found between perceived risk and rigidity or between perceived risk and perceptual measures previously related to such traits as tolerance of ambiguity, ego control, and rigidity. The construct validity of psychophysical perceptual measures of the personality traits of anxiety and rigidity was not supported.[230]

Again, investors' perception of a project and their ability to process the information about that project will depend on their perception of it, which will depend on certain personality traits that are subject to measurement. However, in a real-world situation it may be difficult to determine ahead of time the required traits of a potential investor.

Summary

This section has reviewed various aspects of potential investors—what they expect, how they will evaluate information given to them, and various methods by which a project can be presented so as to have the best chance of succeeding. It would appear that futher study into decision theory could be well worth the extra time involved, to reduce the chances of failing to interest enough investors in a project after "front-end" money has already been spent in assembling and presenting a project to investors.

The last section of this chapter will review briefly some literature relating to the probability of success of various development projects.

ASSESSING THE RISKS OF POTENTIAL R & D LIMITED PARTNERSHIP PROJECTS

The key to the success of any business venture is to achieve a satisfactory risk–reward ratio. The trick of course is to know how to ascertain such a ratio in advance of committing funds to the project. In R & D limited partnerships, as described in this chapter, the reward portion of the ratio is enhanced when the individual taxpayer is in a higher tax bracket than the corporation. The advantage should be briefly reviewed at this point. Assume that the limited partner is in the 50 percent tax bracket and the corporation is in the 25 percent tax bracket. (State and local taxes have been ignored here because they are too varied to be treated with any degree of completeness by a review of this nature. In addition, the 25% R & D tax credit available under the Economic Recovery Tax Act of 1981 is not included in this discussion because no Revenue Rulings have yet been issued by the IRS nor has sufficient time elapsed to determine how the tax credit may eventually apply to future R & D partnerships, individuals, or corporations.) The partnership need expend only 50/75 or about 67 percent of the funds that the corporation must expend to achieve the same results, assuming, of course that each is equally efficient in the management of the funds. Assuming further that the risk–reward ratio for a given project was already acceptable to the corporation, the partnership should be in a position to offer at least as good a reward to its partners while sharing the tax savings, in some manner acceptable to both, between the corporation and the partnership. This sounds acceptable in principle but there are a number of pitfalls in the argument.

First, with regard to the introduction of a new product, the limited partnership will be concerned with only the portion of the effort that involves the R & D activities. A second factor is how the partnership will evaluate, to its own satisfaction, the various risks involved. In short, the partnership must guard against accepting from a corporation R & D projects that have an unreasonable level of risk involved and the partners must look to their own resources to determine the risk.

An earlier section of this literature review analyzed tax aspects of R & D limited partnerships and concluded that if R & D expenditures are in fact to be treated by the IRS as deductible expenses to the individual partners, the partnership must assume the risk of development. But what is that risk and how can it be minimized while still complying with the tax laws? This section of the literature review discusses published information that could assist in determining that risk.

Not a great deal has been published that really gets to the core of the problem, not because of lack of interest but simply because of the nature of the problem itself. Stated in its most nebulous form, the problem appears as follows: What is the probability that a given product idea can become a successful product?

From an overall view this is an extremely difficult queston to answer if for no other reason than an acceptable definition of "successful" seems to be lacking.

In addition, it is necessary to define at what point an idea is considered a new product idea; is it when an inventor cries, "Eureka," or is it after the idea has been "reduced to practice"? Further questions would involve whether certain industries have different levels of risk and if so whether the rewards are proportional or better than others. A more general question could be raised concerning risk–reward ratios. Is it true that higher risks imply higher rewards; or in other words, does the marketplace recognize risks and reward those who incur these risks at a higher level than those in more "riskless" endeavors? This question leads to another question: Is the marketplace perfect and can it in fact recognize various levels of risks? If it cannot, or if its perception of these risks differs from the true risks, if such "truth" exists, then there is no hope that a correct risk–reward ratio exists. It should then follow that some "risks" are better rewarded by the marketplace than others. This leads to the conclusion that one should seek out risks that the marketplace views as high and rewards accordingly but in fact are low. It would seem more than likely, particularly in view of the various decision theories reviewed in the previous section, that different people would have different subjective probabilities of success for any given project. Hence those planning to enter a market should choose those products for which the probabilities of success are viewed as high while the market views the probability of success as low.

Considering for the moment the overall question of the new product introduction from an inventor's viewpoint, C. Hilyard Barr commented,

. . . the probability of an inventor's placement ranged from one to two percent. The inventor's overall probability of success in the marketplace, also taking into account the probability of placement, gave a combined chance of 1:200.[231]

However, this assessment was viewed from an inventor's viewpoint. From a corporate viewpoint Barr noted, "The probability of an organization's pre-evaluated product being successful in the market ranged from 25 to 80 percent."[232] This statement certainly expressed a considerable difference and an implication that the organization's pre-evaluation process dramatically increased the probability of success. Still, though, by increasing the scope of the corporate effort from concept to market success, Barr noted that then the success ratio is about 1 percent. It would appear that a screening process that was rather effective was put to use by the organization to increase its success ratio so dramatically. Such a screening process was described by Barr. It indicates that of 100 new ideas generated from all sources, approximately 50 survive initial rough screening and 35 survive preliminary technical and economic screening. Of the ideas for which some product development work is done, only eight emerge as potential products that are submitted to market testing. Finally five products emerge for which commercialization is pursued and of these only two become profitable products.[233]

Another view of product risk cited by Barr was given by the Research Institute of America as follows:

The risks were ranked from the highest probability of success to the lowest as follows: 1. present market, present product (.75 probability of success), 2. present market, new product (.50 probability of success), 3. present product, new market (.25 probability of success), 4. new product, new market (.05 probability of success).[234]

From the above it is seen that the probability of success of new products is highly dependent on how broad the view is as to what constitutes the area of concern for which the risk is to be taken. Note that the introduction of a new product entails at least two broad categories of risk. First, will the idea really work; and second, assuming that it does work, can it be successfully marketed? Assuming that a corporation that intends to manufacture and market a product is considering collaborating with a limited partnership to perform the R & D activities required to prepare the product for production, what risks must be assumed by each? Certainly the corporation is better prepared to assume the risk that, once the product is developed, it can be sold. The partnership can meet the requirements of the tax laws as well as fulfill its primary responsibility by assuming only those risks associated with developing the product. This risk can further be separated into the conceptual idea· and the reduction of that idea to practice. The partnership is not an organization likely to originate ideas, so that the risk of "creating" an acceptable idea might better be assumed by others, including of course the corporation with which collaboration is planned. Certainly if the collaborating corporation initiates the idea, the "not-invented-here" syndrome is less likely to rear its ugly head, thus eliminating another hazard. It would appear, then that the proper role for the limited partnership in the introduction of new products to the marketplace is that of reducing someone else's conceptual idea to "practice" in the legal sense of the term. At that point all further risk would be assumed, in advance, by the collaborating corporation.

Using this strategy, the risks are reduced to those associated with the question, what is the probability that a given concept accepted as marketable by the partnership's "customer" can be reduced to practice in such a manner as to meet the customer's pre-specified requirements? This is the minimum risk that must be assumed by the partnership; unfortunately, ascertaining that probability is highly subjective.

Using the screening process described above by Barr, it would appear that if 35 products enter the development stage and eight acceptable products emerge, the probability is somewhat in excess of .25 but the reasons given for the elimination of products were not revealed. If the reason was failure to achieve desired specifications, this risk would be assumed by the partnership. Other reasons might be present, however, which would have the effect of decreasing the risk to the partnership. The partnership has one great advantage at this point over the corporation. In most instances, as it will be organized to develop only a single product, a staff can be assembled who are specialists in just that particular product. By engaging only the finest specialist in a particular field, the probability of success for that one product is considerably enhanced. By how much? The literature does not seem to provide an answer, but a case-by-case evaluation at the time by highly competent and perhaps impartial technical personnel would seem to provide the best possible answer to the question.

Another possible approach to reducing the partnership risk is by concentrating on those industries for which overall risk is a minimum. Such an approach was suggested by Haim Falk and James A. Heintz in their paper entitled "Assessing Industry Risk by Ratio Analysis." They stated:

> The purpose of this paper is to demonstrate a technique for scaling industries according to degree of risk. The scaling is based on particular industry characteristics as measured by industry financial ratios.
>
> In recent years a considerable amount of research has been performed examining the relationship between financial ratios and company risk. . . . In general researchers appear to have had considerable success in identifying a relationship between company financial ratios and risk.[235]

The problem with this approach is that there is not an obvious link between the risk of the industry and the risk involved in R & D activities. In other words this approach does not differentiate between the various risks involved and not all risks are associated with new product development.

Several references in the literature purported to provide financial criteria for managing R & D programs. As Mike C. Merz noted in his article entitled "Simple Financial Criteria for Planning R & D Projects,"

> *A simple basic rule, namely that the sales of a new product must recover more financial resources than those used to start it, can be applied in deciding which research and development projects should be measured by net income, depreciation and amortization, and general and administrative expenses. GE, Hewlett-Packard, IBM and Upjohn all use this resource recovery approach. To apply this rule, the new product sales potential is estimated, this figure is multiplied by the financial resource recovery rate, and estimates are made of how much must be spent to start the new product. If resources recovered are more than those spent, the R & D project is advantageous to the company. The R & D manager does not have to be a finance expert to use this method as he must only estimate sales, R & D costs, and capital expenditures. The simplicity of this approach makes it easily understood and applied.[236]*

The problem with this simple approach is that if costs and sales could be accurately estimated before a project were started, there would be no problem in the first place. It is precisely in the area of estimating total R & D costs to bring a new product up to certain specifications and then estimating the actual sales volume generated by a product with those specifications that trouble is likely to be encountered.

A system similar to the above but utilizing information feedback loops to reestimate the probabilities of success as the project progresses was proposed by A. J. Parker and E. Turban. They describe their system as follows:

> *A modified managerial economic analysis is presented for research and development type projects. The maximum expenditure justified (MEJ) formula is related to the classical managerial economic analysis based on present values through several practical modifications. A comparison of the MEJ and the projected research cost shows whether the project will be profitable. It also predicts the potential return from the research expenditure. The comparison tells, for any desired period, the probable profit of the project to the company. Since probabilities are included in the calculation of this profit, it is a projected figure with an allowance included for possible failures; with continued success at the various stages of research, the expected profit will, therefore, continue to rise. . . . [237]*

This method should be an improvement over the first, as the feedback feature would allow a decision to be made to withdraw from the project if certain progress was not being made. However, personal experience indicates that progress toward goals is almost always reported to a very high percentage of completion. At that point problems seem to develop, and driving the project through to its final stages of completion is often costly. By that time it is usually too late to back out.

In general then, it can be said that the proper risk for the R & D limited partnership to assume should be restricted to that of reducing someone else's idea to practice in accordance with a pre-agreed set of specifications and an assurance that the product will be purchased if such specifications are met. The risk to the partnership is then reduced to that of guaranteeing that performance specifications can be met and the risk of doing this can be reduced by employing a specialist to pre-evaluate the project and then the best specialist in the field to carry on the work. From a practical viewpoint, the wide range of projects available for R & D limited partnerships to undertake should provide an acceptable level of risk for almost any investor; in short, there should be something for everyone.

Summary

This chapter has covered all of the topics believed necessary for evaluation of the R & D limited partnership as a viable business entity, starting with a general background of limited partnerships and followed by a detailed review of the literature pertaining to R & D limited partnerships in particular. A review of two actual R & D limited partnerships was followed by a brief look at the need for R & D activities in the United States as well as the need of United States corporations for new sources of risk capital to assist in the updating and modernizing of their facilities and product lines. This was followed by a review of the literature relating to that all-important member of the team, the investor. Finally, an attempt was made to quantify the risks involved in ventures of this type.

The next chapter defines the methodology used to accept or reject the basic hypothesis of this book, namely that R & D limited partnerships will be formed involving American inventors, small businesses and corporations in need of financial assistance for new product development, and independent American investors.

Notes For Chapter 2

[2]"Statistics of Income, 1975," Department of the Treasury, Internal Revenue Service, Publication 438 (July, 1978).

[3]Stephen E. Roulac, *Real Estate Securities and Syndications* (Chicago: National Association of Real Estate Boards, 1973), p. 91.

[4]Stephan Frank Matthews, *The Limited Partnership as an Investment Vehicle in Agriculture* (Columbia: University of Missouri, 1974), p. 507.

[5]William Draper Lewis, "The Uniform Limited Partnership Act," *University of Pennsylvania Law Review* 720 (1917).

[6]See Commissioners' note to the ULPA, Eight Uniform Laws Annotated for 1922. For a discussion of this focus on limited liability, see E. Merrick Dodd, "The Evolution of Limited Liability in American Industry," *Harvard Law Review* (1948).

[7]Matthews, pp. 9–12.

[8]Roulac, p. 64.

[9]Don Augustine and Peter M. Fass, "The Liability of Limited Partners Having Certain Statutory Voting Rights Affecting the Basic Structure of the Partnership," 31 *Business Lawyer* 2087–2107 (July, 1976).

[10]Don Augustine and Peter M. Fass, *Private Real Estate Limited Partnerships—1979* (Practicing Law Institute), 810 Seventh Ave., New York, 1979, p. 15.

[11]Uniform Limited Partnership Act, Section 9; the text of ULPA is reproduced as Appendix A.

[12]Augustine and Fass, note 9, at 2084–2107.

[13]Frank L. Swan, *Tax Tactics, New Developments, and the Carter Administration Proposals* (Newport Beach, CA: Coopers & Lybrand, December 6, 1977), p. iv.

[14]"Tax Classification of Limited Partnerships—The IRS Bombards the Tax Shelter," 50 *New York University Law Review* 408 (May, 1977).

[15]Arthur Andersen & Co., *Tax Reform Act of 1976: Summary of Changes and Impact on Selected Businesses* (Chicago: Arthur Andersen & Co., 1976), p. 16.

[16]See note 14 at 410.

[17]See note 14 at 411.

[18]See note 14 at 412.

[19]See note 14 at 412, 413.

[20]See note 14 at 413.

[21]See note 14 at 415.

[22]See note 14 at 416.

[23]See note 14 at 417, 418.

[24]"Tax Classification of Limited Partnerships," 40 *Harvard Law Review* 745–762 (1977).

[25]See note 24 at 751, 752.

[26]See note 24 at 752, 753.

[27]See note 24 at 753, 754.

[28]Stefan Tucker, "How to Avoid the Major Limited Partnership Problems," 9 *The Practical Accountant* 67–70 (July–August, 1976).

[29]Robert N. Davies, "Tax Predictability in Limited Partnerships Financing—The Need for Certainty in Investment Decisions," 55 *Taxes* 749 (November, 1977).

[30]See note 14 at 411.

[31]Robert C. Livsry, "Limited Partnerships with a Sole Corporate General Partner: The Impact of Larson & Zuckman," 54 *Taxes* 139 (March, 1976).

[32]Bruce S. Lane, *The Tax Reform Act of 1976: Law and Explanation* (Chicago: Commerce Clearing House, Inc., 1978).

[33]"Tax Shelter: Use of Limited Partnerships," The Staff of the Joint Committee on Internal Revenue Taxation, September 13, 1975. Prepared for the use of the Committee on Ways and Means. P. 11.

[34]See note 33 at 12.

[35]Swan, Part 3, p. v.

[36]See note 15 at 2.

[37]See note 15 at 16.

[38]See note 15 at 16.

[39]See note 2 at 202.

[40]See note 15 at 71.

[41]See note 15 at 33.

[42]See note 15 at 49.

[43]See note 15 at 51.

[44]See note 15 at 60.

[45]See note 15 at 86, 87.

[46]*A Guide to SEC Corporate Filings* (Washington, D. C.: Disclosure Inc., 1978).

[47]Securities Act of 1933 As Amended, Section 2.

[48]Joseph C. Long, "Partnership, Limited Partnership and Joint Venture Interests as Securities," 37 *Missouri Law Review* 599, 600 (Fall, 1974).

[49]Rule 146—Securities Act of 1933; reproduced as Appendix E.

[50]See Appendix E, text of Rule, subsection (e)(1)(A).

[51]Telephone conversation with Robert Anestis, December 13, 1979.

[52]SEC, *Cost of Flotation of Registered Issues* (1971–1972) (Washington, D.C.: Securities and Exchange Commission, December 1974), p. 26.

[53]Matthews, p. 15.

[54]Matthews, p. 15.

[55]Nicholas G. Moore, Jay F. Ayers, and Frank R. Pope, "How Limited Partnerships Tax-Shelter the R & D of New Products or Technology," *Journal of Taxation* V49, pp. 138, 139, 141–144 (September, 1978).

[56]"Statistics of Income 1974: Business Income Tax Returns Partnerships," Department of the Treasury, Internal Revenue Service, Publication 438 (July, 1977), p. 17.

[57]Matthews, p. 2.

[58]*Snow v. Commissioner,* 416 U.S. 500 (1974). 1974 P-H Fed. Tax. at 1251. The text of the decision is reproduced as Appendix H.

[59]See note 58.

[60]See note 58.

[61]See note 58.

[62]Amy Rehm Hinderer, "Taxation—Research and Experimental Expenditures—Section 174, Distinguished from Section 162," 40 *Missouri Law Review* 688 (Fall, 1975). The text of the article is reproduced as Appendix I.

[63]See note 58.

[64]See note 58.

[65]"Federal Income Taxation," 36 *Ohio State Law Journal* 175 (Fall, 1975).

[66]See note 58.

[67]See note 58.

[68]John W. Lee, "Pre-Operating Expenses and Section 174: Will *Snow* Fall?" 27 *Tax Lawyer* 381 (Spring, 1974).

[69]Lee, p. 385.

[70]Lee, p. 382.

[71]Lee, p. 383.

[72]Lee, p. 384.

[73]Lee, p. 384.

[74]Lee, p. 385.

[75]Lee, p. 387.

[76]See note 62 at 688.

[77]See note 62 at 686.

[78]Lee, p. 405.

[79]Lee, p. 409.

[80]Lee, p. 409.

[81]Lee, p. 413.

[82]Lee, p. 415.

[83]See note 62 at 689.

[84]See note 62 at 690.

[85]See note 62 at 690.

[86]See note 62 at 691.

[87]Matthews, p. 220.

[88]See note 15 at 16.

[89]See note 58.

[90]Internal Revenue Code of 1954, Section 174, "Research and Experimental Expenditures." The text of the Section is reproduced as Appendix K.

[91]See note 90.

[92]See note 90.

[93]Internal Revenue Code of 1954, Section 1235, "Sale or Exchange of Patents." The text of the Section is reproduced as Appendix L.

[94]CCH Stand. Fed. Tax Rep., "Sale or Exchange of Patents—Section 1235," at 4744A.

[95]See note 94 at 4745.

[96]See note 93.

[97]See note 94 at 4745.

[98]See note 94 at 4744A.

[99]See note 93.

[100]See note 93.

[101]See note 94 at 4745.

[102]Robert W. Anestis and Alan H. Finegold, "The R & D Limited Partnership—A Flexible Response to the Invitation of Section 174," paper presented to Pittsburgh Tax Club, December 11, 1979. The text of the paper is reproduced as Appendix J.

[103]"Patents & Inventions." Vol. 3B *Mertens' Laws of Federal Income Taxation*, p. 965.

[104]"Early Report on *Snow* Decision," 50 *American Bar Association Journal* 1428–1430 (November, 1974).

[105]See note 62 at 690.

[106]"Election to Defer and Amortize R & D Expenses," 47 *CPA Journal* 42, 43 (May, 1977).

[107]"R & D Associates" (private file).

[108]Moore et al., pp. 138, 139, 141–144.

[109]Moore et al., p. 138.

[110]Moore et al., p. 140.

[111]Moore et al., p. 140.

[112]Moore et al., p. 140.

[113]Moore et al., p. 140.

[114]Moore et al., pp. 143, 144.

[115]"R & D Tax Shelters: High Payoffs for High Technology," Vol. I, No. 7, *NewTech* 10, 11 (September, 1979).

[116]"Use Partnerships to Finance R & D," *INC.* 46 (November, 1979).

[117]Moore et al., p. 142.

[118]Matthews, p. 74.

[119]Confidential Offering Memorandum, "R & D Associates," p. 29 (document is filed with other source information for this partnership).

[120]See note 62 at 690.

[121]Delorean Research Limited Partnership, *Private Placement Memorandum* No. 217 (March 23, 1978), p. 19.

[122]See note 121 at 117.

[123]Michel Domsch, "The Organization of Corporate R & D Planning," 11 *Long Range Planning* 67 (June, 1978).

[124]Domsch, p. 67.

[125]Domsch, pp. 67, 68.

[126]Robert F. Dee, "The Ship Called America," address to shareholders of Smith Kline Corp., October 1978, pp. 2, 3.

[127]"1974 Forecast for R & D," 16 *Industrial Research* 41 (January, 1974).

[128]See note 127.

[129]See note 127.

[130]"Is R & D Investment Being Short Changed?" 218 *Iron Age* 66 (November 22, 1976).

[131]See note 130.

[132]See note 130 at 66, 67.

[133]See note 130 at 67.

[134]See note 130 at at 66, 67.

[135]"R & D Spending Rise, But Worries Remain," 192 *Industry Week* 24 (January 3, 1977).

[136]*Statistical Abstract of the United States,* 1977, Section 18, "Business Enterprise," p. 557.

[137]"R & D Spending Patterns for 600 Companies," *Business Week* 58–77 (July 3, 1978).

[138]Ann M. Reilly, "A Big Boost for R & D?" 112 *Dun's Review* 770 (September, 1978).

[139]"1979 R & D Budgets Up 10% at Chemical Firms," *Chemical and Engineering News* 12, 13 (January 15, 1979).

[140]"Finance," *Business Week* 108 (December 3, 1979).

[141]"The Flaw in Japan's Boom," *Business Week* 42 (July 10, 1971).

[142]See note 141 at 43.

[143]Terutono Ozawa, "Japan's Technology Now Challenges the West," 7 *Columbia Journal of World Business* 41–49 (April, 1972).

[144]Ozawa, p. 43.

[145]Ozawa, p. 43.

[146]Ozawa, p. 47.

[147]Ozawa, p. 48.

[148]"R & D in Japan Revisited: The 1970 Decade," 12 *Management Internatinal Review* 32, 33 (1974).

[149]See note 148 at 34.

[150]See note 148 at 34.

[151]See note 148 at 37.

[152]Klaus Brockhuff, "Determinants of Research and Development Expenditure in Some Chemical Corporations in Germany," 10 *Management International Review* 71 (1970).

[153]Brockhuff, p. 81.

[154]"Detroit's New Face Toward Its Suppliers," *Business Week* 140–149 (September 24, 1979).

[155]Mirjan Ivanetic, "Borrowed Liquidity: Signal of Corporate Distress," 53 *Harvard Business Review* 7 (January–February, 1975).

[156]See note 155 at 8.

[157]Allen H. Seed, "Needed: Strategies to Improve Cash Flow," 64 *Management Review* 11 (March, 1975).

[158]Seed, pp. 15, 16.

[159]Seed, pp. 16, 17.

[160]Seed, p. 18.

[161]Warren E. Buffett, "How Inflation Swindles the Equity Investor," 95 *Fortune* 250 (May, 1977).

[162]Buffett, pp. 252, 253.

[163]Buffett, p. 253.

[164]Buffett, pp. 255, 256.

[165]Buffett, p. 256.

[166]Buffett, p. 264.

[167]"All About Profit," 111 *Dun's Review* 79 (June, 1978).

[168]"The Bottom Line Directory," *Financial World* 13 (July 15, 1976).

[169]See note 168 at 14.

[170]See note 168 at 15.

[171]Edmund A. Mennis, "Perspectives on Industry Profits," 12 *Business Economics* 84 (January, 1977).

[172]"Profits '77—Sales Were the Spur," *Citibank* 4 (April, 1978).

[173]See note 154 at 140.

[174]See note 154 at 145.

[175]See note 140 at 138.

[176]Edward S. Ojdana, Jr., *Dimensions of the Product Life Cycle*, D.B.A. Dissertation, University of Southern California, 1974, pp. 3–5.

[177]Ojdana, p. 26.

[178]Ojdana, p. 134.

[179]Ojdana, pp. 135, 136.

[180]Ojdana, pp. 138, 139.

[181]Ojdana, p. 139.

[182]Edward I. Altman, "The Prediction of Corporate Bankruptcy: A Discriminant Analysis," Ph.D. dissertation, University of California, Los Angeles, 1967.

[183]See note 121 at i; also, conversation with Robert Nichols, September 7, 1979.

[184]"Active Investors: A Survey of Active Investors," conducted for *The Wall Street Journal* by Belknap Marketing Services, Greenwich, CT (March, 1977), p. 9.

[185]See note 184.

[186]See note 184 at 39.

[187]Merrill Lynch advertisement, 100 *Fortune* 54 (December, 1979).

[188]See note 187.

[189]Matthews, p. 53.

[190]Matthews, p. 54.

[191]Matthews, p. 65.

[192]Matthews, p. 67.

[193]Matthews, p. 73.

[194]Matthews, pp. 74, 75.

[195]Matthews, p. 75.

[196]Matthews, pp. 219–221.

[197]Matthews, p. 222.

[198]Matthews, p. 222.

[199]Matthews, p. 226.

[200]Matthews, p. 227.

[201]Matthews, pp. 227, 228.

[202]Matthews, pp. 230–232.

[203]Matthews, p. 233.

[204]Matthews, p. 243.

[205]Matthews, pp. 271, 272.

[206]Wayne E. Etter and Donald R. Levi, "Investor Views of Real Estate and Limited Partnerships," 46 *Appraisal Journal* 112–121 (January, 1978).

[207]Ward Edwards, Harold Lindman and Lawrence D. Phillips, "Emerging Technologies for Making Decisions," *New Directions in Psychology II* (New York: Holt, Rinehart & Winston, 1965), p. 261.

[208]Edwards et al., p. 262.

[209]Edwards et al., pp. 262, 263.

[210]Edwards et al., p. 263.

[211]Edwards et al., p. 264.

[212]Edwards et al., p. 264.

[213]Edwards et al., p. 265.

[214]Edwards et al., p. 272.

[215]Edwards et al., pp. 273, 274.

[216]Edwards et al., pp. 277, 278.

[217]Edwards et al., p. 279.

[218]Edwards et al., p. 287.

[219]Edwards et al., p. 288.

[220]Edwards et al., p. 288.

[221]Edwards et al., p. 289.

[222]Edwards et al., p. 290.

[223]Edwards et al., p. 296.

[224]Edwards et al., p. 303.

[225]Edwards et al., pp. 306–311.

[226]*International Encyclopedia of the Social Sciences*, IV (New York: Macmillan, 1968), p. 41.

[227]Robert Libby and Peter C. Fishburn, 15 *Journal of Accounting Research* 280, 281 (Autumn, 1977).

[228]Amos Tversky and Ward Edwards, *Decision Making* (Baltimore, MD: Penguin Books, 1967), pp. 88, 89.

[229]Wayne E. Hensley, "Probability, Personality, Age and Risk Taking," 95 *Journal of Psychology* 139 (1977).

[230]Charles M. Schaninger, "Perceived Risk and Personality," 3 *Journal of Consumer Research*, 95 (September, 1976).

[231]C. Hilyard Barr, *Placement Problems of an Independent Product Developer* (Los Angeles: Pepperdine University, School of Business and Management, April, 1975), p. iii.

[232]Barr, p. iii.

[233]Barr, p. 21.

[234]Barr, p. 26.

[235]Haim Falk and James A. Heintz, "Assessing Industry Risk by Ratio Analysis," 50 *Accounting Review* 758 (October, 1975).

[236]Mike C. Merz, "Simple Financial Criteria for Planning R & D Projects," 27 *Managerial Planning* 13–16 (July/August, 1978).

[237]A. J. Parker and E. Turban, "Research & Development Projects," 20 *Engineering Economist* 173–186 (September, 1975).

CHAPTER THREE

Methodology

This chapter discusses briefly the background of events that led up to this research project, restates the research problem, and outlines the methodology developed to support or reject the major hypothesis.

Two broad areas of concern prompted the author to undertake this study. The first was this country's apparent loss of world leadership in technical innovation, which seems to have started in the mid-sixties and continues to this day. The initative for pushing back the leading edge of technology seems to have passed from America to Japan or perhaps Germany. The ability and willingness to advance the state of the art of most of the technologies vital to this country seem to have vanished. If they are, as we hope, just lying dormant, must they wait for another Pearl Harbor or a Sputnik to bring them to life?

The second area of concern was the difficulty that lone inventors and small businesses have in raising funds to bring new and innovative ideas to the marketplace. Long years of experience in this field have convinced the author that while funds can be obtained, in most cases control of the invention or idea is lost before any real benefit to the creative persons responsible for the idea has been received. The corporate world and the world of small business or the lone inventor are entirely different. Large corporations are able to concentrate huge resources in a given area when the need arises. This is vital to the mass production stages of most product marketing efforts. But corporations are notoriously weak when it comes to creativity. Contrary to the beliefs of many, creativity is basically a lonesome process. The kind of mind that is forever thinking of new and better ways to do things is not content to exist in the corporate world. The creative mind wants to be free, to change things, to move things around to its liking. The free, creative thinker is seldom happy in the corporate world which of necessity must be somewhat regimented. How then can the creative mind be encouraged to create and be supplied with the resources required, without losing the independent vitality that is so necessary to the creative process? In the author's experience, this has been, is, and will probably continue to be a problem.

The R & D limited partnership concept of funding new product development seems to offer great opportunity for diverting significant investment funds into critical technological areas while at the same time solving two major problems; funding corporate development programs, which have been weakened by continuing high inflation rates, and providing funds to inventors and small businesses to allow their inherent creative abilities to be better utilized without stifling them in the process of helping them.

A specific case in point, with regard to the first problem, has been the failure of this country, thus far, to respond adequately to the so-called energy crisis that began with the Arab oil embargo in 1973.

The use of "so-called" is not meant to imply that a crisis does not exist. It most certainly does. But the crisis has been brought about more by inept political maneuvers than by a universal shortage of energy. The world is full of potential sources of energy, but when the economic incentives imposed by the various governments in the world to utilize what is available to us are sufficiently distorted, a true crisis can occur. This is what has happened. Let us examine briefly the events that led up to the "energy crisis" and how they relate to this study.

In 1973, with the imposition of the Arab oil embargo, the United States suddenly and somewhat painfully was made aware of its excessive dependence on foreign energy sources. Gas lines formed, everyone complained. The government declared "Project Independence," designed to make America independent of foreign oil by 1980.

In what seemed like a totally unrelated event at the time, the Supreme Court on May 13, 1974, handed down a decision in *Snow* v. *Commissioner* allowing an individual to deduct research and development expenses from income earned from other sources, even though the research activity did not meet hitherto accepted standards of an "existing trade or business" mentioned in Section 162 of the Internal Revenue Code. Section 174, enacted in 1954 precisely to encourage research and experimentation activities in "small and starting businesses," would now control the taxation of such activities in the United States as apparently Congress had intended twenty years before. In 1976 Congress enacted the Tax Reform Act of 1976. The Act's primary purpose was to curb the use of tax shelters but it specifically excluded real estate partnerships and failed to take any action to reverse the decision of the Supreme Court in the *Snow* case. The subsequent Revenue Act of 1978 also supported, by negative implication, the *Snow* decision.

In the meantime, everyone suddenly seemed concerned with the lack of new investment in American industries. The rate of reinvestment in Germany and Japan had exceeded that of the United States for a number of years, and the results were beginning to become apparent as the ability of this country to compete in world markets weakened. Obviously the steel industry was in trouble because of antiquated facilities. Foreign steel was being imported into the Pittsburgh area to build bridges. The newest steel technology was to be found not in the United States but in Japan. Because Congress had kept price controls on most petroleum products, the profit incentive was missing from the domestic petroleum industry, resulting in little visible activity to implement "Project Independence" except the setting up of new and bigger government agencies to resolve what was becoming known as the "energy crisis." In 1978 President Carter set up a commission to study ways in which the government could encourage increased expenditures for research and development activities, believing, correctly, that increased R & D expenditures would help to reduce the country's dependence on foreign oil, which incidentally had increased to over 50 percent from 35 percent at the time of the Arab oil embargo in 1973. Apparently President Carter and the commission were unaware that incentives to increase R & D expenditures had been in place ever since the *Snow* decision in 1974.

Finally, in January 1979 the Shah of Iran was overthrown, causing the United States to lose not only one of its staunchest allies in the Middle East but about 5 percent of its oil supply as well. In addition, the failure of the Carter Administration to support the Shah when faced with the threat of a revolution invited the loss of Saudi Arabia's confidence in the Unites States' determination to support its friends in a crisis, thus risking the loss of over 40 percent of this country's oil imports. Loss of Saudi Arabian oil would not be just inconvenient; it would be a direct threat to national security. If the United States were the only major power involved in the Middle East perhaps the issue could be resolved amicably. But the U.S.S.R. could be a net importer of oil by 1983 and its only apparent source is the Middle East. Head-to-head competition with the U.S.S.R. over oil supplies could very well lead to World War III because of the vital issues at stake. Obviously events were beginning to get out of hand and still the domestic energy program sat stalled for lack of direction and leadership.

Out of the ever worsening world situation may come the realization that the government in the United States is simply not able to deal at this time with the political realities within the United States concerning energy, at least in as direct a fashion as many would like. Perhaps the government has done what was needed by supporting the *Snow* decision and it is now up to the private sector to learn to use the incentives for investment in R & D that are now in place.

The unfolding of these events and the obvious necessity to search for solutions to get the private sector moving led to the initiation of this research project. The problem posed was stated as follows: In light of the *Snow* v. *Commissioner* Supreme Court decision in 1974 and the obvious need for accelerated research and development efforts in the United States, could R & D limited partnerships be formed among American inventors, small businesses, corporations, and investors in such a fashion that all parties concerned could be adequately compensated in view of the risks and obligations required of each party? The question was not only could they be formed, but would they be formed in sufficient numbers to direct meaningful amounts of new risk capital into the most needed technological areas. As noted above, by not overruling the Supreme Court or passing additional legislation when it had an opportunity to do so in 1976, and 1981, Congress has tacitly given its blessing to the formation of R & D limited partnerships.

The problem was restated, for the purposes of this project, in the form of a hypothesis: R & D limited partnerships will be formed involving American inventors, small businesses and corporations in need of financial assistance for new product development, and independent high tax bracket American investors. Simply stated the questions examined were: Is there a need for such enterprises? Does this form of business venture meet that need? Can the risks be reduced to levels acceptable to enough investors to divert meaningful amounts of investment funds into vital technological projects?

The basic and exploratory nature of the work in this field to date suggests that inferential analysis and testing are most appropriate for accepting or rejecting the hypothesis. The nature of the data does not warrant the application of rigorous statistical analysis. Instead the bigger and broader issues of this research are considered to be most pertinent. Two basic lines of argument have been pursued. First, a comparison has been made between certain key characteristics of the R & D limited partnership and those of the most popular forms of tax shelters: the real estate limited partnership, the oil and gas limited partnership, and the agricultural limited partnership. If a preponderance of characteristics were found to be common to those three and the R & D limited partnership, it would be inferred that such partnerships will in fact be formed and the hypothesis can be supported. If material differences were found, this line of argument could not be used to support the hypothesis.

The second line of argument has entailed determining whether a need exists for financing R & D activities in the United States, whether this business form responds to that need, and whether the rewards for such an investment can be made high enough to attract meaningful numbers of investors. If the answers to all three of these questions are in the affirmative, then it can be inferred that such business formations will occur.

As this research is primarily exploratory, the principal research instruments employed were a literature search and an examination of existing limited partnerships combined with actual testing; that is, have any such partnerships been formed since the 1974 Supreme Court decision?

The limitations of such an approach stem from the fact that this is in effect an *ex post facto* exploratory effort. Inferential methods always contain the shortcoming that no "foolproof" support of a hypothesis can be made. However, in an extensive literature search the evidence supporting the hypothesis was so overwhelming that it would seem conclusions reached by this method are valid. Certainly the numerous questions left unanswered invite further search utilizing more rigorous and formalized approaches.

It should be noted, though, that regardless of the fact that national interests seem to support the organizing of R & D limited partnerships at this time, it was assumed that they would be formed only if the economic return to the investors was the compelling reason for the investment.

The expected utility of such an investment, arising only from a desire to "do something" about the energy problem or other technologies of vital concern to the country may very well be a major factor in many investors' decisions to participate in such ventures. It would be hoped, of course, that the free enterprise system is up to providing for the needs of the country in and by itself, utilizing the profit incentive alone. But it would be comforting to believe that, since the country's survival may very well be at stake, motivations other than maximizing return on investment will cause such investments to be made.

METHODOLOGY SUMMARY

The methodology applied in this study can be summarized in outline form:

1. From the literature search, generalized "key" characteristics of limited partnership tax shelters are determined.
2. A data base utilizing actual limited partnership prospectuses as a data source was established. (Fifteen such sources were utilized in this research.)
3. From the data base specific "key" characteristics were extracted.
4. Specific "key" characteristics of existing limited partnerships were compared with existing R & D limited partnerships (two were examined) and an "ideal" R & D partnership.
5. In advance it was determined that a preponderance of matching characteristics would lead to support for the hypothesis while an absence of common characteristics would lead to a rejection of the hypothesis.
6. In advance it was determined that positive responses to the following questions, as answered in the literature, would establish support for the hypothesis: Is there a need; does this business form satisfy that need; and can the risks be reduced to a low enough level to attract investors?

The next chapter presents the results obtained by applying the methodology discussed in this chapter and outlined above.

CHAPTER FOUR

Summary of Results

The first argument utilized to support or reject the hypothesis in this study involved matching key characteristics of existing limited partnerships with those of the new type of limited partnership. A preponderance of matching characteristics would indicate support for the hypothesis; lack of matching characteristics would indicate that, based on this argument, the hypothesis must be rejected. The second argument involved gathering support from the literature to establish whether a need for the financing of R & D projects in the United States exists; whether this form of business can answer that need; and whether the risks and rewards involved could attract a reasonable number of investors. If all three parts of the questions were answered in the affirmative, the hypothesis would be considered supported; if not, it was to be rejected, at least based on this argument.

This chapter describes the key characteristics and how they were derived, the data base used, and the results of matching these characteristics to the data base partnerships. The second line of argument mentioned above is then examined in detail. Finally, a summary is presented indicating not only what conclusions can be drawn from the data but those parts of the problem that seem to defy solution, at least within the scope of this project. The next chapter summarizes the project, elaborates somewhat on the discussion here, and makes recommendations for further research in this field.

The essential characteristics of various forms of limited partnerships evolve from three general groupings of persons or organizations associated with the venture: the group that supplies goods and services to the partnership, the partnership itself, and the group of persons or organizations that are the "customers" of the partnership. Within the partnership itself, a further subdivision between the limited partners and the general partners must be made. The two groups outside of the partnership are included because different types of partnerships have different relationships with their suppliers and customers, by the very nature of the types of business they are in. In many cases the type of business combined with the limited partnership form can produce an inherent advantage or disadvantage for a partnership as opposed to a corporation. As an example, if a supplier is providing goods or services that are deductible by their purchasers as ordinary expenses, these goods or services will be worth more to a partnership composed of high tax bracket investors than they would be to a corporation in a lower tax bracket, since the after-tax dollars spent would be less for the partnership than for the corporation. This application of the principle would give the partnership an advantage in the marketplace because the partnership could obviously pay more, if necessary, or conversely could receive more benefits for the same expenditures.

The key characteristics can be thought of as having positive and negative connotations. In other words, the possession of positive characteristics would be considered an advantage while the possession of negative characteristics would be considered a disadvantage. For the R & D limited partnership to compete with other business entities for investors' capital and for customers and supplier services, it should possess as many of the positive characteristics and as few of the negative characteristics of its competitors as possible. When applicable in the following pages, the key characteristics are sometimes referred to as advantages or disadvantages.

1. *Supplier characteristics.* The following supplier characteristics are considered important in determining the relative advantages of various forms of limited partnerships:

(A)   The goods or services supplied to the partnership are fully deductible at the time of delivery.

(B)   The goods or services supplied to the partnership are fully deductible at the time they are utilized.

(C)   The goods or services provided to the partnership must be capitalized and depreciated over some fixed and predetermined time period.

(D)   The goods and services provided to the partnership have no determinable life and cannot be deducted in any manner unless the project involved is abandoned and determined to be worthless.

2. *Partnership characteristics.*

(A)   Relative to the general partner, the following characteristics are viewed as important and are of a positive nature:

(1)   Unrestricted management control of business.

(2)   Availability of capital from limited partners.

(3)   Less interference from the investor class as compared to corporate shareholders with voting power.

(4)   Opportunity to apportion overhead from general partner's other business activities.

(5)   Less dilution of control compared to that exercised by large lenders such as banks and insurance companies.

(6)   Share of partnership profits that is greater than the proportion of the general partner's investment to that of the limited partners.

(7)   Receipt of income from management fees.

(8) Minimum capital contribution requirement.
(9) Opportunity to accomplish some personal goals that would be impossible without additional capital provided by limited partnership.
(10) Possibility of achieving personal prominence in some field of endeavor that would be impossible without the limited partnership's capital contribution.

(B) Relative to the general partner, the following characteristics are viewed as important but are of a negative nature:
(1) Possession of unlimited liability.
(2) Risk to "up-front" money in forming partnership; failure to successfully complete partnership will result in total loss of funds expended in promotional efforts.
(3) Necessity of dealing with the limited partners after the partnership is successfully launched; keeping investors informed, receiving visits from them, and answering the inevitable queries as to "how are we doing" are necessary components of managing a successful partnership.
(4) Necessity of keeping informed of legislative changes that could affect the tax status of the partnership and perhaps engaging in lobbying efforts to protect the investors' tax shelter.
(5) Requirement, in many cases, to maintain a minimum net worth.

(C) Relative to the limited partner the following characteristics are viewed as important and of a positive nature:
(1) Tax shelter opportunities.
(2) Possible economic return on investment.
(3) No management responsibility required.
(4) Limited liability to investor.
(5) Opportunity to participate in activities giving personal satisfaction to the investor—intangible perhaps, but certainly a very real factor in increasing the "utility" of the investment to the investor.
(6) Intangible benefit of "beating the tax collector" at least temporarily; adds to the "utility" of the investment for some investors.
(7) A feeling of receiving "more than fair" returns. In view of the personalistic view of probabilities, the subjective probabilities of success of a given project may be considerably higher for a particular investor than for the general partner.
(8) Nonmonetary returns. Based on Maslow's theory that people have five broad classes of needs—1) physiological, 2) safety, both physiological and psychological, 3) social or love, 4) self-esteem, and 5) self-actualization—and that they move to the next higher level as each is attained, it is quite possible that the investor is on a higher level than the general partner and hence ascribes greater utility to nonmonetary returns (self-

actualization?) than does the general partner, who may still be struggling at level 3 or 4. Hence a higher proportion of the profits relative to the contribution assigned to the general partner may seem quite reasonable to a limited partner simply because the profits play a small part in the total "utility" the limited partner expects to receive from the investment. Support for this "mini-hypothesis" can be found in the huge contributions to charitable and other nonprofit organizations for which the contributor receives no "value" in return so that 100 percent of the "expected utility" is made up of intangibles.

(9) Possibility of leveraging the investment: partnership losses, through nonrecourse debt acquisition, can exceed the investor's original contribution, at least in the early stages of a project; hence the investor actually is able to borrow, interest-free, from the government an amount in excess of the investment.

(10) Avoidance of tax preference items, particularly as related to the Tax Reform Act of 1976; if not avoided, they can at least be minimized.

(11) Deductions based on calendar year. First-year losses could be bunched up a year-end to allow investors to receive large deductions even if they enter the partnership toward the end of the year, when they have a clear idea of what their income for the year is going to be.

(D) Relative to the limited partner, the following characteristics are viewed as important but are of a negative nature:

(1) High management fees to the general partner (front-end loading).

(2) No control rights.

(3) No ready market for partnership interests.

(4) Difficulty in guarding against or remedying unfair management practices such as self-dealing.

(5) Possibility that unlimited liability might be imposed due to either legislative changes or general partner incompetence.

(6) Collapse of the tax shelter aspect of the investment due, again, to either legislative changes or general partner incompetence.

(7) Possible future tax liabilities when no cash flow is available due to failure of the partnership or recapture of excess depreciation.

3. *Customer characteristics.* The following characteristics relative to the purchaser of the goods or services offered by the partnership are considered important in determining the relative advantages of the various types of limited partnerships:

(A) Can the purchaser immediately deduct the expenses incurred in purchasing the goods or services offered by the partnership?

(B) Can the purchaser deduct the expenses incurred in purchasing the goods or services offered by the partnership at the time they are utilized?

(C) Must the purchaser capitalize the goods and services offered by the partnership and receive deductions through depreciation?

(D) Do the goods and services offered by the partnership have no ascertainable life, which prohibits them from being deducted at all until they are written off as worthless?

These 41 key characteristics will be used to determine whether the R & D limited partnership possesses a preponderance of the characteristics of well established and successful limited partnerships in operation today.

DATA BASE UTILIZED

To establish a data base to work from, fifteen existing limited partnerships were examined, including the two R & D limited partnerships reviewed in Chapter 2. A sixteenth partnership was designated as an "ideal" R & D limited partnership, that is, one that had every legally permissible key characteristic so that it could be used as a benchmark.

The following limited partnerships constituted the data base utilized:

Real Estate Limited Partnerships:

1. Carlyle Real Estate Limited Partnership—VIII (September 12, 1978)
2. JMB Income Properties Ltd—VI (November 16, 1978)
3. American Property Investors—IX (November 7, 1978)
4. Monteleone Property Limited (April 1, 1978)
5. Commercial Exchange Property, Ltd. (July 14, 1978)

Oil and Gas Partnerships:

6. Patrick Petroleum Company 1979 Drilling Program (June 6, 1979)
7. McCullough Oil/Gas Exploration–Development Program 1978/1979 (February 2, 1979)
8. Saxon Funds—1979 Program (February 1, 1979)
9. MGF 79 Ltd. Oil and Gas Drilling Partnership for 1979 (January 5, 1979)
10. Damson 1978 Natural Gas Exploration/Production Partnership (September 15, 1978)

Agricultural Limited Partnerships:

11. Western Trio Cattle Company (May 14, 1973)
12. Wheatheart Cattle Company (March 22, 1971)
13. Circle Four Land and Cattle Company (June 14, 1973)

R & D Limited Partnerships:

14. R & D Associates (November 15, 1977)
15. Delorean Research Limited Partnership (March 23, 1978)

COMPARISON OF KEY LIMITED PARTNERSHIP CHARACTERISTICS

The partnerships listed were examined to determine how many of the key characteristics, both positive and negative, each possessed. No attempt was made to "weigh" the resulting tally as no rational basis could be determined, at least within the scope of this project, for doing so.

It was found, upon examining the results, that for discussion purposes it made sense to divide the 41 key characteristics into four major categories. First are those characteristics dictated by the *appropriate tax laws* pertaining to the particular activities with which the partnership is involved.

The second category pertains to what might be called *bargaining factors*—characteristics that were determined at the time a deal was made between the general and limited partners. In general it was felt that the general partners had the upper hand in these negotiations as they were the ones preparing the agreements and marketing the shares, although it must be admitted that it appears to be a free market and those who are responsible for assembling the deals risk their own "up-front" money and are probably keenly aware of what will sell and what will not.

The third category is made up of those factors associated with nonmonetary items—*the intangibles*. It became apparent as this research progressed that intangible factors may very well be essential in determining the future of any particular business venture, yet these are precisely the factors that are most elusive. Determining the expected utility and subjective probability of a group of investors seems a formidable task when approaching it in a straightforward manner. By turning the problem on its head and using the method of John Von Neumann and O. Morgenstern (*Theory of Games*, 1944), the problem might be solved. "One could instead observe actual behavior and infer from it the utility function that gave rise to it, assuming that the behaver was in fact behaving rationally."

But this seems to imply a trial-and-error type of solution. In other words, set up an R & D partnership based on the best experience available and then see whether it sells. If it does, an implied subjective expected utility can be deduced. But this can be very expensive. This problem area and approach will be discussed again later in this chapter.

The fourth category consists of characteristics that are inherent in the limited partnership framework of conducting business, such as *limited liability* for the limited partners and *unlimited liability* for the general partners. Within this framework of four categories, the following results were obtained.

Obviously some of the characteristics were in more than one category, particularly since some limited partnership characteristics were required to be present in order for the partnership to avoid being classed as an association for tax purposes; when a conflict arose, the characteristic was put into what was felt was the dominant category.

One significant point should be noted here. Within each group of partnerships examined, the entities did not vary enough in characteristics to differentiate between them. In other words, all the real estate limited partnerships were essentially similar, all the oil and gas partnerships were similar, and so on. The one exception was the two R & D limited partnerships, which differed on several points. Since the more seasoned partnerships closely resembled one another in a given category, an indication that a free market has "leveled" the various participants in a fairly general manner may be implied. The two R & D partnerships, however, are venturing into new territory and hence are still feeling their way in the field. Perhaps Von Neumann's method of determining utility is in process here.

Category One—Tax Law Considerations

Fifteen of the 41 characteristics mentioned were judged to be dominated by tax law considerations. These included eight supplier and customer related characteristics, one requirement to keep up with the laws, the maintenance of net worth problem for the general partner, the entire tax shelter aspect of limited partnerships, the ability to leverage an investor's contribution through nonrecourse debt acquisition, the threat of loss of either the tax shelter or the limited liability aspects of the investment, and the possibility of incurring a tax liability without cash flow to cover it.

Evaluation of these 15 factors produced the following results (grouped by industry; differentiation between companies within a given industry was not significant):

Real Estate Limited Partnerships:
   1. Partnerships in this group have a significant advantage over the other three groups in being able to offer a high degree of leveraging. This advantage has been eliminated for all other groups by the Tax Reform Act of 1976.
   2. The leveraging advantage mentioned above was, in general, offset by the disadvantage of a possible tax liability occurring due either to the foreclosure or depreciation "recapture" at some time in the future.
   3. Accelerated depreciation became a tax preference item.

Oil and Gas Limited Partnerships:
   1. This group suffered by comparison with the others because depletion, intangible drilling costs, and accelerated depreciation had become, under certain circumstances, tax preference items.

2.   The ability to "bunch up" expenses at the end of the year has been virtually eliminated.

Agricultural Partnerships:
The main disadvantage this group suffered under revised tax laws was the loss of ability, in many instances, to "bunch-up" expenses at year end by prepaying feed and other consumable items.

R & D Partnerships:
1.   The principal disadvantage caused by the tax laws for R & D partnerships is the possibility that a developed product that was not patented would be sold to a customer who then would be unable to deduct any of the R & D expense unless the purchased item was declared worthless at some later date. This stems from the fact that "know-how" has no determinable life and hence it cannot be capitalized and depreciated and it is not a current expense item.
2.   The principal advantage that R & D partnerships seem to have over the other three is the possibility of "bunching-up expenses" by prepaying for an outside laboratory to perform development work under some circumstances.

Scores for this category of key characteristics (absence of a negative characteristics scores as one plus) are as follows:

Type of Limited Partnership	Number of Key Characteristics
Real estate	11 out of 15
Oil and gas	10 out of 15
Agriculture	12 out of 15
R & D	9 out of 15

Category Two—Bargaining Factors

The category of bargaining factors includes the ability of the general partners to share overhead expenses between the partnership and their other business activities, the division of the profits, the income received from fees by the general partners, the amounts of capital contributed by the general partners, whether the "up-front" money is provided by the general partners or shared with the limited partners, and the profit level of the entire enterprise. This category of characteristics cannot really be "scored" in any sense as every item is open to negotiation between the partners. There is no particular reason to believe any one type of business has an advantage over any other unless it can be proven that one entire industry is more profitable than another. Certainly despite the high rate of inflation that has occurred during the past few years, real estate has done remarkably well in most parts of the country. But there are really no comparable statistics for R & D activities where a "hard" bottom-line figure can be determined. This category will have to be rated as "unknown," at least as to whether the project hypothesis can be supported or must be rejected.

Category Three—The Intangibles

The category of intangibles includes the value to the general partners of being able to pursue personal goals and receive public recognition, the value to the limited partners of participating in desirable activities ("Schmaltz," if you will) and "beating the tax collector," the subjective probability evaluation by the limited partners on the possible success or failure of the venture, and whether the limited partners are somewhat higher on Maslow's scale of human needs and thereby receive more nonmonetary satisfaction from the venture than the general partners. Every reference cites these as major factors in the determination of whether an investment will be made; yet, except for Von Neumann's method, it seemed beyond the scope of this study to even determine a method of solving the problem, let alone solve it.

A purely subjective comment is appropriate here. The tremendously wide field of potential projects available to R & D partnerships would seem to be able to offer as many or more intangible benefits to the investor as real estate or agriculture and should be able to offer as many or more intangible benefits to the investor as real estate or agriculture and should be able to match the fascination that the oil and gas business has provided investors for years. It would seem unreasonable to maintain that R & D has less intangible value. No score is possible for this category, because all of these items were either "unknown" or "maybe."

Category Four—Basic Characteristics of Limited Partnerships

The only basic characteristic noted here that differed among the various groups was that in the real estate partnerships most of the general partners' income seemed to come from commissions earned on real estate bought and sold by the partnership and from management fees. In some cases the commissions earned were as high as 18 percent of the total money raised. This seemed to be such an obvious conflict of interest that the score sheet indicated a minus with respect to the limited partners' having to guard against the actions of the general partner. While the conflict of interest theme recurs throughout all of the partnerships examined, the real estate commission seemed to be an outstanding problem. Other than that, the groups were the same.

Type of Limited Partnership	Number of Key Characteristics
Real Estate	10 out of 11
Oil and Gas	11 out of 11
Agriculture	11 out of 11
R & D	11 out of 11

SUMMARY OF FIRST ARGUMENT (MATCHING OF KEY CHARACTERISTICS)

Categories one and four (tax laws and basic limited partnership characteristics) scored as follows:

Type of Limited Partnership	Number of Key Characteristics
Real Estate	21 out of 26
Oil and Gas	21 out of 26
Agriculture	23 out of 26
R&D	20 out of 26

In Category two (bargaining factors), while no score could be given, it appeared reasonable and within the limits of the scope of this study to place all four industrial categories on an even basis although admittedly the ability to bargain for the investor's dollar is dependent on overall industry profit levels and the R & D profit level as an industrial classification is not yet available. The industries that R & D activities support include all of the industrial categories and hence it seems reasonable to assume that R & D organizers are free to choose the most fertile ground on which to base future projects. Category three (the intangibles) is the most fascinating category and just begs for more research. As no methods are presently available that could determine in advance, with any degree of certainty, what subjective expected utility an unknown group of investors would place on an investment in a new venture, no predictions can be made except for those projects already in existence for which background experience is available. In these instances, an implied subjective expected utility can be ascertained and that is in fact what is done as new real estate or oil and gas partnerships are set up. Organizers of R & D partnerships will have to rely on intuition until a backlog of experience is developed. Certainly there is a wealth of information in the literature to assist the organizer's intuition. Early R & D partnerships may stand a better chance of success if projects are chosen that are within the more familiar fields of activities. It would then be possible to utilize available data on the value investors place on the intangibles.

In summary, of those characteristics that appear susceptible to measurement, the R & D partnerships possess a preponderance of the key characteristics chosen for comparison purposes and hence the hypothesis seems supported by this line of reasoning.

The second line of argument is that if a need for a service exists, if a given type of business organization can fill that need, and if the economic rewards for doing so are high enough, such a business organization will be created.

The need for R & D activities in the United States seems to be self-evident. Approximately $20 billion per year is currently being spent by United States industry and the amount is growing every year. The federal government spends at least an equal amount and a government study is now underway to determine ways in which the federal government can encourage industry to spend more. The cost of a barrel of oil increased over ten times in less than eight years and not only must alternate energy sources be developed within the United States, but the entire industrial base of the United States must be redesigned. Basic industries need to be modernized. The high cost of energy now and in the future has in effect made obsolete even up-to-date manufacturing and transportation facilities which were designed to utilize relatively low-cost energy sources. The simple statement that the entire transportation system in the United States is obsolete is self-evident but its implications are so profound as to be almost overwhelming. The automobile industry is attempting to cope with the twin problems of rising energy costs and excessive government regulations and two of the three major automobile companies are currently in serious financial difficulties because of these efforts. Other industries will soon follow. The need for increased R & D activity, in light of the current world situation, must be assumed to be self-evident.

The second part of the argument has to do with whether the R & D limited partnership business form can properly respond to the need for increased R & D activity in this country. Many points have been made throughout this discussion to say that it can. Because investors in R & D limited partnerships are generally in a higher tax bracket than corporations, the partnership can do the same amount of work for less expenditure of after-tax dollars. For example, assuming that the limited partners are in the 50 percent tax bracket and the corporations are in the 25 percent tax bracket, the R & D limited partnership could accomplish the same thing as the corporation, if the funds were channeled through the limited partnership (of course with the partnership assuming the technical risks involved), for only 67 percent of the expenditure of after-tax funds. Even assuming the limited partners sold the developed products back to the corporations for the same price that the corporations estimated the work would cost, the 50 percent investor could receive 80 cents (at current tax rates) after-tax income for each 50 cents of after-tax funds invested, assuming capital gains tax treatment was allowed. It would be reasonable to assume that for taking the risk a higher price and hence a greater profit could be obtained for performing the work. It would seem that the R & D limited partnership can fulfill the need.

This discussion seems to answer the third part of the basic argument: Can the odds be reduced to a level low enough to attract meaningful numbers of investors? The question though is not fully answered. What are the odds of success in such ventures, and how can they be reduced to a minimum? First it should be noted that the IRS required that the partnership assume the risk of developing the product or a tax deduction will be denied. Therefore it is not possible to structure a deal so that the corporation desiring the development work can guarantee no loss to the partnership, despite the favorable financial rewards noted above. However, two things should be noted. First, at least two major risks are involved with new product development, the marketing risk (Can it be sold?) and the technical risk (Will it work?). The partnership is not required under IRS rulings to assume the marketing risk, only the technical risk. A deal can be made, in advance, that if a product can be developed to meet a company's specifications, the company will buy the product. This type of agreement eliminates a major unknown in evaluating a project.

The second item to note is that product invention involves at least two steps: conceiving the idea and then reducing it to practice. The IRS also recognizes these two steps and the partnership is required only to assume the risk for one, the reduction to practice. Therefore the evaluation of risk for the partnership involves estimating the cost of reducing to practice an already conceived product for which there is a guaranteed market. This type of evaluation, if performed by a competent technical team, can be performed with a reasonably high degree of accuracy. No specific number can be given because the range of probable projects that might be encountered is so broad; but it would certainly seem to bracket the odds of successfully drilling an oil well, which incidentally was stated by one of the oil and gas limited partnerships examined to be about 0.5. Oil and gas limited partnerships are highly successful in the United States. If the odds of succeeding at an R & D project can reasonably be expected to be as good or better, then success for R & D partnerships would seem assured. Again, the preponderance of arguments would seem to support the hypothesis.

There is of course a tendency, by the time a research project is well underway, to want to support the hypothesis. At the risk of destroying the arguments already developed, it must again be pointed out that the behavioral aspects of the investor would seem to be the controlling factor here and the inference that these behavioral aspects will be favorable to the hypothesis in itself seems to be purely subjective. Some substance can be given to that inference by the fact that several R & D partnerships have been formed. However, the argument then really boils down to how many will be formed, not will they be formed. Apparently only time (or more research on another project) will tell.

The next chapter briefly summarizes the project and makes recommendations for future work in this field.

CHAPTER FIVE

Summary, Conclusions, and Recommendations

This chapter presents a brief summary of the material covered in earlier chapters and discusses conclusions reached based on an analysis of this material. The subject of research and development activities in the United States has broad and far-reaching implications. An attempt was made therefore to frame these conclusions in a somewhat broader context than the immediate subject matter would seem to support. Research and development limited partnerships will be formed in increasing numbers in the next few years; but whether the full potential for directing needed investment funds into appropriate channels will be realized depends on a number of factors, primarily those relating to utilizing the advantages of the R & D limited partnerships as Congress intended rather than circumventing this intent through legal gimmicks. Extensive attempts to circumvent Congressional intent most probably would have the effect of forcing tax law revisions that would destroy the widespread benefits that can accrue to the investment community as well as to the country as a whole. All can benefit if a few can be convinced to refrain from attempts to squeeze more from the tax benefits than was intended or to oversell the tax benefits in an attempt to promote the development of fundamentally unsound projects. Finally, recommendations for future research in this field will be made and some suggestions will be offered for building a firm foundation under this exciting and potentially highly influential business entity—the R & D limited partnership.

SUMMARY

Sufficient information has been gathered for a determination to be made that an R & D limited partnership is a viable enterprise. The basic references required to organize such a business venture have been provided. Chapter 1 set the basic framework, Chapter 2 reviewed at some length the literature in this field. While the coverage was rather extensive, no attempt was made to cover all of the various tax aspects, as that is an effort far beyond the scope of this book. It was felt that the essential elements of tax law pertaining to limited partners were well represented, but it should be noted that only federal tax laws were reviewed even in this limited sense. In many states, state and local tax liabilities are significant and a review of local laws is essential before a final decision is made to form a limited partnership.

Chapter 3 presented some background information indicating the significance of this project to the broad national problem of directing new investment capital into activities relating to the development of alternate energy sources, as well as the closely related field of developing a more energy-efficient industrial base. Since this study was basically exploratory in nature, inferential analysis and testing were appropriate; the data generated did not lend themselves to rigid statistical analysis. The original hypothesis, that R & D limited partnerships will be formed involving American inventors, small businesses and corporations in need of financial assistance for new product development, and independent high tax bracket American investors, would be supported if R & D limited partnerships were shown to possess a preponderance of key characteristics common to well-established limited partnerships such as are prevalent in real estate, oil and gas, and agricultural industries. Further support for the hypothesis would be provided if the literature indicated that there was a need for increased R & D activities in the United States and that American inventors, small businesses, and corporations were in fact in need of additional financing, that this form of business organization could fill that need, and that the risks involved could be reduced to such a level as to attract signficant numbers of investors.

The results of the study were presented in Chapter 4. Inferential support for the hypothesis was provided by both lines of arguments. Many questions remain to be answered; but based on the information presented in this report, there is a strong likelihood that R & D limited partnerships will proliferate in the years ahead.

CONCLUSIONS

The basic conclusion of this project is that R & D limited partnerships will be utilized as a profitable investment vehicle for high tax bracket investors and as a means for corporations to shift both the burden of risk involved with the "reduction to practice" of marketable inventions generated within the corporation and the associated expenses involved to another group of investors without diluting their present shareholders' interests. Inventors and small businesses, as they become more aware of the tremendous potential of the limited R & D partnerships to provide needed funds while maintaining control of their projects, will utilize this means of funding in increasing numbers. As a matter of fact, because it has few alternative methods of funding new projects, this group might even surpass the large corporate group in its usage of this new investment vehicle. Investors in the partnerships will be able to directly participate in projects of their own choosing while enjoying tax shelter benefits second only to real estate limited partnership investments. While real estate investments still allow an investor to "leverage" the tax base, a feature denied all other business activities under present tax law, a very real risk exists that a future tax liability could be incurred at a time when no funds from the project are available. Such a risk is not present in a well structured R & D limited partnership, offsetting to some degree the near-term advantage of "leveraged" investments.

Under present tax laws, an investor in the 50 percent federal income tax bracket who participates in a well-structured R & D limited partnership can effectively accomplish the same amount of development work as a corporation in the 25 percent bracket while expending only 67 percent of the after-tax dollars the corporation would have to expend. In addition, when the developed product is sold, the resulting income could be taxed at capital gains rates. Not only can the R & D limited partnership perform the development work more efficiently than the corporation, in terms of after-tax funds expended, but it can convert ordinary income of the investor into long-term capital gains, a highly desirable goal. For this reason alone, the conclusions reached here seem to stand on firm ground.

In addition, the conclusion is reached that the laws upon which the R & D limited partnership are based will remain in effect for a reasonable period of time and are not likely to be overturned by Congressional action, a Supreme Court reversal, or an attack by the Internal Revenue Service. To preserve this status, however, it is viewed as essential that organizers of these partnerships make every attempt to conform with the intent of Congress and not look for "gimmicky" structures to circumvent that intent. Thinly capitalized corporations used as general partners to avoid liability, while legal, are not in the best interest of the public and should be avoided. Poorly conceived development projects passed off to investors solely on the basis of their tax-shelter aspects also can bring public disfavor upon the industry. "Industry" is the correct term because the implications of this form of business venture are so broad that most certainly an "industry" will spring up devoted solely to organizing and managing R & D limited partnerships. The key to continued viability of such an industry is to assure that the ventures are in fact profitable, excluding the tax benefits, and are formed on legitimate and ethical foundations.

The fact that significant diversion of capital from one segment of industry can occur due to changes in the tax laws is also supported by the literature. Congress, in truth, has its hand on the throttle. It may very well be that through the *Snow* decision the government has done all that is necessary and maybe all that is possible to encourage private industry in this country to get on with solving the energy problem as well as the long-standing problem of updating many basic industrial processes. It should be recognized that in an age of instant communication, open government, and widespread participation in government by many pressure groups of various political persuasions, direct action by the government to "solve" the energy problem may be impossible. Every path open to the government to resolve such vital issues as assuring the country of an adequate energy supply tends to favor one group over another, for everyone is both a consumer and a producer, or so it is hoped. By providing incentive to private investors to attack these problems in a rather subtle and not fully understood manner, the government may very well have hit upon, perhaps unintentionally, a method of solution to national problems that seems to have eluded the country for many years. In this manner the private enterprise system can operate as it was intended, while public debates on how the government ought to solve the problem can continue unbated. No harm will be done by the debates, everyone will have a say, and private industry will proceed to solve the problems.

One last fact should be noted here. In a sense, tax shelters operate as if the government were granting a non-interest-bearing loan to the high-income taxpayer who invests in a suitable project. In theory, at least, all taxpayers could participate in such ventures and hence all tax revenues could be in effect "loaned" back to the taxpayers at no interest provided they invest in the correct projects. This is at least an indication of the power of the tax laws to direct investment into socially desirable channels with very little visible political action required. Direct action by the government, with all of the obvious pitfalls, makes good window dressing. The real power to accomplish needed activities rests in the subtler methods that are the subject of this book. The tools are available and the need is great. The sooner the R & D limited partnership is recognized as a key instrument in furthering the general welfare of the country while simultaneously rewarding investors for participating of their own free will in such ventures, the better off the country will be. Perhaps in ventures of this type an acceptable compromise between free enterprise and government control can be found.

RECOMMENDATIONS FOR FURTHER WORK IN THIS FIELD

This section lists eight recommended research projects and offers some suggestions for actions that could be taken to assure that the R & D limited partnership actually achieves what it now has the potential to achieve. The following research projects are recommended.

1. A study to determine whether a predictable relationship exists between R & D expenditures and profitability. This study should be done on an industry-by-industry basis. While there is general agreement that R & D is good and more is better, the causal relationship between profits and R & D eludes most managements. Trial and error and past experience represent

current managements' methods in setting R & D budgets. If the organizers of R & D limited partnerships are to be able to approach managements of major corporations on rational grounds, the availability of such data would be most helpful.

2. A study to determine the probability of success in reducing an idea to "practice." This is a key number in any attempt to estimate the return on investment to an investor in an R & D project. How accurate are predictions of costs in projects of this nature? Several management tools to make such predictions are available. The most well known of these is the PERT system developed by the United States Navy for estimating completion dates and costs of the first Polaris missile program. PERT's best application is for projects that have not been done before, a perfect definition of R & D activities. But what has been the success ratio of projects employing these methods? Has any study been made to determine the probability of success and the probable range of error with regard to both cost and time? The literature revealed none in the form useful to a potential investor.

3. A study to determine whether a correlation exists between failure to expend R & D funds and eventual bankruptcy. Again this must be done on an industry-by-industry basis so that information useful to corporate management and potential organizers of R & D limited partnerships is instantly available. It would seem that such a correlation, at least for some industries, must exist. But no publication of such a study was uncovered in the literature.

4. The correlation between subjective probabilities of success for various R & D projects and the potential investors' background. Not only must investors be located, but they must have sufficient confidence in the success of the project to be willing to let other participants in the project make money also. Their willingness to share the proceeds of the venture will vary with their evaluation of the chances of success of the project. It seems reasonable to believe that varying backgrounds of investors would cause different evaluations to be made on their part as to the chances of success of any given project. A study that could determine the subjective probabilities of success with investors from different backgrounds would permit an organizer to contact only those investors who would be most likely to believe in the project. This determination can obviously not be done by testing the subject for this would be impossible from a practical standpoint. But general information concerning potential investors, such as schooling, profession, and hobbies, is sometimes available. If from such information an estimate could be made of their likely belief in certain projects, an organizer would have a better chance of putting together an investment package acceptable to all parties.

5. A study to determine the relative utility of various R & D limited partnership investments to the investor. How much value is placed on "beating the tax collector" or "helping to solve the energy problems," and various

other intangibles? Can this be determined from easily attainable information about a potential investor? If so, this knowledge would be useful to an organizer of an R & D limited partnership for the same reason stated above.

   6. A longitudinal study of several partnerships in key industries would provide some statistical grounds for predicting success in new ventures. At present the only statistics available seem to be those provided by an organization that is promoting a new partnership. As most limited partnerships are not registered, very little operating information concerning them is available. Such a study could provide important insights into the strengths and weaknesses of R & D ventures. No studies of this nature were located in the literature.

   7. A study to determine a method of collecting statistics of limited partnerships in the United States. In general, limited partnerships that are not registered need only file a certificate with some specified office in their home state, usually the county recorder's office, and thereafter its only reporting requirement is to file an income statement with the IRS (and state income reports where applicable). While the IRS publishes income statistics for all reporting entities, its report does not differentiate between general and limited partnerships and is too general in nature to be useful for evaluation purposes. A listing of all state or county offices collecting limited partnership certificates would allow access to all limited partners because their names must be published with the certificate. The list would be a basis for collecting statistics but it appears to be a tedious task. (Appendix N hints at the magnitude of the proposed task.)

   8. A study to devise a system for collecting and classifying viable development projects by industry and by originator of the idea. Undoubtedly this is a sizable task, but it is from this reservoir of ideas that the projects needed by the R & D limited partnerships must come.

   The following action programs are recommended.

   1. A nonprofit trade association should be formed whose primary purpose would be to set standards of acceptable characteristics of limited partnerships in general. These standards would of course exceed statutory requirements and would be written to insure that the intent of Congressional action is incorporated into partnerships organized according to the standards. This organization is a necessity to protect the industry against adverse public reaction, which would more than likely result in punitive and sometimes unwise legislative actions. Self-policing of an industry is a necessity if persons working in the industry wish to avoid policing by someone else. Financial support for such an association could possibly come from the National Association of Securities Dealers (NASD), whose members handle most of the marketing of partnership interests at present, or from the investors themselves. This association could also act as a clearinghouse for information on the past performance of limited partnerships. It should be

considered to represent potential investors and should provide such services as they might require. The industry must have satisfied investors if it is to succeed. Properly handled, a "seal of approval" from this association would be a prerequisite to the sale of any interest in a limited partnership.

2. A nonprofit organization should be formed to act as a clearinghouse for all potential R & D projects, particularly those associated with the energy program. This organization should be set up to perform technical evaluations of projects presented to it. It should be prepared to issue a "seal of approval" for projects. Again this is to protect the industry from gaining a reputation for financing ill-conceived projects put together by promoters whose only purpose is to achieve near-term tax writeoffs without concern for the eventual profitability of the projects. Potential contributors to this organization could be industrial corporations who intend to submit projects for evaluation. Even though a potential for conflict of interests exists, this organization should be oriented to investors. If they have questions about a potential project, they can come to this organization for an opinion. Again, properly handled, a "seal of approval" from this organization would be necessary for an R & D project to be launched. This also would be a self-policing type of organization.

The above recommendations, both the research projects and the two action programs, will accelerate the adaptation of the R & D limited partnership by the investor community and by corporate management. But even without these recommendations, the R & D limited partnership working in collaboration with industry is going to be an integral part of the industrial scene in the United States during the eighties and perhaps longer if the integrity of the industry can be maintained at a high level. Profitable cooperation among industry, the public, and the government will be the key to success in the years ahead. A great opportunity to start such a program is now at hand.

The next chapter will discuss how an actual R & D partnership is organized, funded, and managed. It will use as an example Electronic Equipment Development Ltd., a partnership organized by the author following the completion of the research portion of this study.

CHAPTER SIX

A Practical Guide to Forming an R & D Limited Partnership

The Five Key Steps

INTRODUCTION

The first five chapters of this book reviewed in some detail the history of the R & D limited partnership as well as the key technical factors affecting the acceptance or rejection of this business form as a meaningful financial vehicle in the United States today. The conclusions reached were that not only will large numbers of these partnerships be formed, but the concept represents a powerful tool, if properly utilized, for diverting significant investments into industries essential to the economic growth of the country.

This study was undertaken for a variety of reasons, some of which were outlined in Chapter 3. Certainly the world economic and political situation would seem to demand that the United States regain the technological momentum which it seems to have lost through many years of concentrating on redistributing wealth rather than increasing it. That momentum cannot be regained without considerable investment in R & D activities. Other factors were also present in the decision to proceed with this study.

Inflation was continuing to take its toll among the small business community; replacing outdated equipment was becoming increasingly difficult while funds for meaningful development projects seemed to have disappeared altogether. The individual inventor was in even worse shape. Everything new seemed to be happening in Germany or Japan while venture capital firms here for all practical purposes had abandoned the lone inventor. The inventor's lot had never been an easy one but now it seemed to be getting worse. The R & D limited partnership seemed a possible answer to all of these problems and hence work on this project proceeded despite heavy workloads in other areas.

After the formal study was completed it seemed only natural, in light of the strong indications that here indeed was a true financial breakthrough for inventors and small businesses, to proceed with putting into practice what the study had indicated would be a successful approach to the problem of obtaining much needed funds for product development. Shortly thereafter, Electronic Equipment Development Ltd. (EED), an R & D limited partnership, was formed by the author for the specific purpose of assisting a small company in the development of much needed new electronic products. This partnership, which was successfully funded only a few months after the completion of the formal research project, is typical of what can be done with this new investment vehicle.

Since the completion of this study and its subsequent publication, there has been an increasing demand from inventors and business people for details concerning how an actual project is created. The most practical way to respond to the numerous inquiries that have been received is to trace the development of EED from its inception to the present time, tying together the theoretical portions as covered in the first part of this book with the practical considerations required for the formation and operation of a successful business.

This chapter outlines the five key steps required to form a business of this nature, using, as appropriate, the development of EED as an example. The five key steps to be discussed are: (1) choosing the project, (2) determining the basic business structure, (3) preparing the key documents, (4) marketing the offering, and (5) managing the business.

CHOOSING THE PROJECT

The underlying motive of anyone attempting to organize a business that will require investment by others must be to organize a successful business— successful in the sense that the investors' money is eventually returned with sufficient increase to warrant the time that the funds were held. In short, the organizers of such a business must manage the business so as to protect and enhance the investment of their partners to the best of their ability. The basic key to achieving this goal is to choose the correct projects to begin with. At best, new product development is a risky business. As pointed out in Chapter 2, only about one idea in 200 ever becomes a successful product, but these odds can be reduced by careful screening. For the same type product in the same marketplace, corporations can, by proper screening methods, increase their probability of success to 0.75 or better, as mentioned in Chapter 2.

The problem then is not so much whether a system exists for successfully choosing projects, but whether the creative people responsible for the new ideas are willing to discipline themselves to use it. Dr. Linus Pauling, Nobel Prize-winning chemist, was asked during a television interview what was the key to successful creativity. Dr. Pauling answered that a person must first have lots of ideas and then have a good screening process. Most creative people generate new ideas constantly; it seems to be their nature. The essential difference between the successful creators and the not so successful ones is the self-discipline required to screen out their own bad ideas before too much time or effort is expended on them. The key thought here is that they must screen out the bad ideas themselves, for as one of Dr. Paul MacCready's co-workers on the first successful man-powered airplane project noted, "It's tough working with a genius because he's so convincing even when he's wrong." Unfortunately, this is typical of many, if not all, creative people. They are so convinced of the virtues of their ideas that they are able to persuade others who may not have sufficient technical background to be able to properly evaluate the invention. This can be a virtue if the idea is a good one but a disaster if it is not.

A screening process is essential, then, whether the organizer of the partnership is the inventor, in which case the process must be self-imposed, or whether other persons' ideas are to be used, in which case the organizer either must be technically qualified for self-judgment or must hire the talent needed. In either case the screening process must consider at least the following questions.

1. Does a current need exist for the product?

If there is an invention graveyard somewhere, it must be full of great inventions for which no need existed. It is a difficult, expensive, and time-consuming task to generate a need in a marketplace when none is apparent. It can be done but only at high risk, and projects requiring extensive market development of this nature are inappropriate for the R & D limited partnership. The product under consideration must satisfy a perceived need either by offering a better way than present products or by using an entirely new approach. The former has risks associated with entering a market against an established competitor; in this instance the primary question that should be asked is whether a dominant market share can be expected to be obtained with the new product. If so and if the market is expanding, the risks are minimized. If the market is stagnant or contracting, it is unlikely that a dominant position could be obtained and the product should be eliminated from consideration. If a substitute product is considered, one that satisfies the same market but in a new and unusual way, there is reasonable hope if the market is expanding. In short, me-too type products are risky unless the resources are available to establish a dominant position quickly and the market is growing. An ingenious approach to a growing market may allow a strong position to be attained with considerably fewer resources than the me-too approach. In either case a thorough knowledge of the marketplace is a prerequisite to product evaluation. If no one needs it or thinks he needs it, the product represents a high risk.

Three major product lines were selected for inclusion in the EED limited partnership. Each of the products was chosen in response to current market needs. A high-speed welder was designed to replace existing but lower-speed machines; a computer graphics project was designed to perform tasks similar to those of higher-priced systems now being sold; and an electronic components handling system was designed to perform the same task now being performed manually on existing production lines. Assuming the technical specifications could be met within the time frame and budgetary limits proposed, there was no doubt that a current need for the products existed.

Considerable research into product strategy has been published by the Strategic Planning Institute, 955 Massachusetts Avenue, Cambridge, Massachusetts 02139. In particular the relationship among market share, market growth, and profitability has been established under the PIMS Program (Profit Impact of Market Strategies), an industrially supported activity sponsored by the Strategic Planning Institute (SPI). Publications are available from SPI outlining the strategic considerations of new product introduction. Any company can participate in the PIMS Program if it agrees to provide certain product strategy information which then becomes part of the data base used to evaluate various strategies.

2. How many products are to be included in the partnership?

There are several compelling arguments for including more than one product in a single R & D partnership. From the viewpoint of the organizers, the greatest risk in the venture occurs at the beginning, when they must bear the cost of the legal fees required to form the venture as well as devote perhaps two or three months of their time without any real assurance that the necessary funds will be forthcoming to repay them for their efforts. If more than one product is included in the overall project, a rather wide range of funds would be required depending on whether one, two, or perhaps three projects were actually pursued. If, for example, only one-third of the funds needed for all the projects were obtained from investors, the project could continue by developing only one of the products. The legal work and other front-end costs would then not have been wasted. Most state securities regulations will not permit organizers to proceed with a project unless sufficient funds are available at the outset to complete each project proposed. Multiple products within a given project allow this requirement to be satisfied when less than 100% of the proposed funds is obtained during the offering period. In addition, multiple products with varying degrees of risk allow a more balanced overall project to be offered to investors. Granted, this method reduces the maximum return to the investors if a high-risk/high-return product is a huge success because of dilution by the low-risk/low-return product, but as noted earlier in this book most persons seem to have a preference for success probabilities of around 0.5, that is, an even bet. It's not that they don't like to win, it's just that they hate to lose. Oil and gas promoters may not be familiar with Ward Edwards and decision theory, but they have discovered, perhaps by trial and error, that reducing the odds of failure appeals to large numbers of investors and so have tailored their offerings to satisfy this preference. Organizers of R & D limited partnerships would do well to follow the same practice.

The only negative factor involved with multiple products within a single partnership is the possibility of adverse tax consequences in the event that capital gains treatment under Section 1235 for some reason is disallowed. If a partnership had only one product and the product was sold in its entirety, the partnership could claim that the sale represented sale of a capital item under Section 1262, whereas if multiple products were present the IRS would probably challenge such a claim on the grounds that the partnership was in the business of selling inventions and that the various products developed were being held in inventory for sale.

In general, it seems to be a good rule that decisions should be based on good business judgment rather than on trying to obtain the most favorable tax treatment. The reduced risk to both the organizers and the investors resulting from the multiple product approach seems to far outweigh the possible risk of adverse tax consequences.

When EED was formed, it was decided to include three projects, each one estimated to cost about one-third of the total funds that were to be obtained through the private offering. The first project was the development of a new type of automatic high-speed welding machine. This represented a relatively low-risk project since the company that was performing the R & D work (GTI Corporation) had been in that same business for over 25 years and had previously developed a somewhat similar machine. The second project chosen was the development of a new type of computer graphics system. As this was a new product in a new market (see Chapter 2) the odds of success were low, probably not more than 0.05. But the payoff for success was high because this was a new product in a rapidly expanding market. This was the "exploratory well" of the project. The third product chosen was actually several products grouped under the general heading of an electronic components handling system. The company involved had been in that marketplace for some time but this was a new line of products, hence the probability of success seemed to be around 0.5 or about an even bet if the references cited are correct. The mixture chosen seemed to have about an even chance of success with a very high payoff if the graphics project was a success and a moderate payoff if only the welding machine was successful.

3. What is the present status of the invention or product?

The R & D limited partnership is useful for only a rather narrow but crucial segment of a complete new product development program. The partnership is not the appropriate business form for creating ideas; it is probably not the optimum form, due to unlimited liability, for manufacturing the product; and market development is not deductible under Section 174, hence writeoffs of expenses of this nature within the context of the R & D partnership would probably be disallowed. However, for reducing a preconceived idea to practice, the R & D limited partnership is exactly the right type of business structure. Therefore, in choosing appropriate products for a partnership of this type, the idea should be in sufficiently concrete form that patent applications, at least of a preliminary nature, could be filed even though the idea has not yet been reduced to practice. Some development work will probably have been done, models may have been built, but the idea has not yet been developed to the point where commercialization is possible.

All three projects included in EED had been conceptualized to the point where preliminary drawings had been made (the computer graphics "drawings" consisted of block diagrams indicating major functions the finished computer was expected to perform) but no detail drawings existed and no actual experiments had been performed. No patents had been filed at the time of forming the partnership although it might have been possible to do so.

4. How much time is involved in reducing the idea (or product) under consideration to practice?

Two factors seem to dictate that the time span should be as short as possible, probably two years or less. First, there are risks. The future is difficult to predict and the further in the future one tries to predict, the riskier the prediction becomes. Second, there are the investors. Most investors in ventures of this nature do their tax planning on a year-to-year basis. While this has nothing directly to do with the projects undertaken, certainly the progress of each project is reviewed by the investors at least on an annual basis. If the potential success or failure of a project has not been resolved by the second year, the investors can start to lose interest. Or, restating the problem, if the investors do not believe that they will be pretty certain of the success or failure of a project by the second year, they probably will be reluctant to make the investment at all.

All of the projects included in the EED partnership were expected to be completed within an 18-month period.

This restriction may be unnecessarily limiting; some very prominent projects have exceeded that time limit. Delorean's car project has extended well beyond five years. Still, long projects involve high risks and uncertainty, and high risks discourage investment.

In choosing between projects, a short time period to reduce the idea to practice should be given preference over a longer and less certain time period.

5. How much money is required?

For all practical purposes there is no limit to the amount of money that could be made available to a properly structured and well managed R & D limited partnership. Partnerships from $100,000 up to $50,000,000 have been formed in the past few years. The important questions are not how much is available but how much does a given product require to have reasonable assurance that the program can be carried to a successful conclusion and how large a project are the organizers prepared to manage? The first question can be answered by a variety of techniques; the second involves examining the background, experience, and psychological makeup of the persons intending to manage the project.

Many inventors and small businesses have the feeling that if they could just get their hands on enough money, their problems would be solved. Yet the management of large sums of money requires considerable skill if it is to be done well and involves the unavoidable risk of facing investors who have placed great confidence in the management and telling them that the project has failed. Some people are not up to taking the responsibility. Harry Truman was often quoted as saying, "If you don't like the heat, get out of the kitchen." Rest assured that if a project involving millions of dollars starts to get into difficulty, there is a lot of heat.

Assuming that those involved in putting together the project are prepared to take the heat that could result from a failure, the next problem is to determine the funds required for each project under consideration. At this point a business plan is needed. While a business plan can take many forms, fundamentally five questions need to be answered: (1) Where am I? (2) Where do I want to be? (3) What objectives flow from the difference between (1) and (2)? (4) What are the sources of funds and how are they to be applied? (5) What are the personnel requirements? (What talents are required, how many people are needed, and when are they needed?)

For a development project that extends over a relatively long period of time and has a clear end objective, probably the most convenient form that this plan could take would be either the PERT network or critical path method (CPM) chart. For readers not familiar with either PERT or CPM, a vast amount of literature is available—too much perhaps. Several references are listed at the end of this chapter, any one of which can serve as an introduction.[238] The PERT system was developed for use in the Navy Polaris missile program in the late fifties and has since been used extensively in the defense and construction industries. If properly applied the PERT system can rather accurately forecast project costs and time of completion. While not many have viewed a CPM network as a business plan, it is in fact just that. The main ingredient for success in applying these techniques is a sincere desire to arrive at the truth.

The system involves hard work and a lot of front-end decision making, which seems to unsettle those who like to "let things work themselves out." Things don't usually "work themselves out," at least not within the fixed budget and fixed time frame involved with the partnership concept.

Once committed, the budget is fixed and it is difficult and embarrassing to raise additional funds if the original budget is not kept. Additional time inevitably costs money so late completions can also be embarrassing. The discipline to utilize the management tools that are available must be maintained throughout the life of the project.

Here then is another basic criterion for choosing a project. Not only must the funds required be within the bounds of the management's ability and experience but those projects whose expected expenses can be more accurately determined must be favored over those with large areas of unknown or unpredictable expenses. Predictability is a worthwhile attribute.

6. Which marketplace should be chosen?

Considerable attention was given to investors and their motivations in Chapter 2. One of the essential motivating factors that causes investors to choose one investment over another is their personal desire to "be where it's at" ("Schmaltz"). In other words, certain investors have definite preferences for one particular type of endeavor over another. Time and again this factor has been listed as second only to the desire to forestall tax payments, among the leading motivations for investing in tax-shelter types of business ventures. Assuming the organizers give equal weight to two projects, the project with the most current public appeal will probably prove to be the preferred project. Oil ventures continue to be popular, a lot of people like real estate, and in the R & D field there seem to be large numbers of investors currently interested in participating in the development of solar energy.

Assuming a popular marketplace is chosen, its size should be ascertained. Large markets are better than small ones and growing ones are infinitely superior to shrinking ones. However, once the partnership has picked the general marketplace in which it will compete, the proper strategy is to narrow down that marketplace to such a size that the proposed product can have a fair chance of dominating a narrow segment of the larger and growing marketplace. This "salami" approach is a winning tactic that has been employed by the Japanese with spectacular success in recent years.

While the above tactics are statistically correct and usually lead to success, one factor must not be overlooked: the interest of the organizers. No matter how logical to approach to the marketplace, if in the end the persons responsible for managing the project are not completely dedicated, for their own reasons, to the product, it stands a good chance to fail. Management enthusiasm for the marketplace is a vital ingredient.

7. Who, specifically, is going to buy the product, assuming it is successfully reduced to practice?

It is one thing to make sweeping generalities about the large numbers of potential customers there are for a product, but it is quite another thing to specify names and price levels. A key factor here is whether the partnership is prepared to develop the product without strong assurances from someone that the product can in fact be sold at a sufficiently high price to warrant the expenditure of development funds. This subject was covered in some detail in Chapter 2 and it was suggested, somewhat obliquely, that a partnership or its organizers should try to locate a manufacturer that would agree to buy the product before the project was started, assuming it met predetermined technical specifications within a given time period. This was the approach taken when EED was formed. The technical risk was assumed by the partnership, that is, the risk that the product could be developed, within th time and budgetary limits imposed at the outset, to such a point that predetermined technical specifications were met. At that time GTI (an electronic manufacturer) would guarantee a certain minimum payment to the partnership, hence accepting the marketing portion of the risk.

Another consideration is whether the potential customer is another manufacturer or the ultimate customer. Industrial customers are usually more knowledgeable and more predictable but they judge the worth of a product as a certain margin above its cost. Since they are usually quite familiar with manufacturing costs, high profit margins are more difficult to maintain in this marketplace unless a strong patent position is attained. The ultimate consumer is less knowledgeable, less predictable, and generally willing to pay based on a more subjective judgment of the worth of the product. Hence profit margins can be higher but consumer acceptances of new products are difficult to predict with any degree of accuracy. All other things being equal, a cost-saving type of product sold into the industrial market represents a lower risk than consumer-type products.

Even if the plan of the partnership is to sell the entire rights to the developed product to another company to manufcture, as is the usual case, consideration of the ultimate customer is of prime importance to the partnership because the value of the proudct to a potential licensee will be directly related to the ease of marketing the end product.

8.   What facilities are required for the development work?

One factor in comparing one product to another is the type of facilities required for the successful development of each one. Because of the tax structure involved, it is not advantageous for the partnership to own equipment. Instead, it should attempt to lease everything required or have the use of equipment that is presently available in someone else's laboratory. If the product under consideration requires highly specialized equipment, high costs could be involved, placing that product at a disadvantage against a product that could be developed in a somewhat more normal commercial laboratory. The development program should be carefully planned in advance so that unexpected costs can be avoided if at all possible.

9.   What special technical skills are required for the development work?

The partnership essentially starts from scratch in its development program. It is important therefore that any special technical skills required that are not available from the organizers of the project be recognized early in the planning stages. Lack of direct knowledge of where the skills can be obtained, and at what costs, would be reason for rejection of a particular project.

10. What is the present and anticipated future patent position?

If patents can reasonably be expected to be obtained on a particular product the R & D partnership has a considerable advantage, although lack of possible patent protection does not necessarily eliminate the product from consideration. The advantages of patents are threefold: first, it is easier from a legal point of view to assign a patent from one person or entity to another than to assign know-how; secondly, the purchaser of the product from the partnership will be able to capitalize and amortize the purchase price of the product if a patent exists; and finally, the patent may very well provide meaningful protection in the marketplace. The only negative aspect of patents is their cost, particularly if foreign patents are required. In rare cases the disclosure required in a patent may be considered a disadvantage as it gives a potential competitor a clear target to design around. On balance, however, a strong patent position is easier to manage to the holder's advantage than a tightly kept trade secret or know-how position.

11. What facilities are required to produce the product in marketable quantities?

Eventually the product must be produced in quantity by someone. In weighing one product against another, it is an advantage if relatively normal production facilities are sufficient. The need for highly specialized facilities may narrow the list of potential manufacturers to such a point that effective bargaining becomes difficult.

In summary, the following checklist should be used to determine which products are to be included in the proposed partnership:

1. Does a current need exist for the product?
2. How many products are to be included in the partnership?
3. What is the present status of the invention or product?
4. How long will it take to reduce the invention or product to practice?
5. How much money is required?
6. Which marketplace should be chosen?
7. Who is going to buy the product (the end customer)?
8. What development facilities are required?
9. What special technical skills are required for the development work?
10. What is the present and anticipated future patent position?
11. What production facilities are required?

In practice, a product evaluation matrix is set up with the items on the checklist arrayed against the various products under consideration. With a 1–10 rating system, it is possible to list the products in order of their desirability.

DETERMINATION OF THE BASIC BUSINESS STRUCTURE

Once the products that are to be developed by the parternship have been determined, it is possible to proceed to the next key step in the formation of the partnership: determining the basic business structure. This basic structure involves more than the partnership itself. All of the various building blocks required from inception of the idea to final manufacturing and sale of the product to the end user must be placed in proper relationship to one another if a smoothly running and efficient project is to ensue. So many permutations are possible that it is not possible to enumerate all of them but only to illustrate the process involved. Each situation will probably be different if for no other reason than that each participant in ventures of this sort is an individual who has different ambitions, motives, backgrounds, and talents to contribute to the projects. The following questions should be of help in identifying the key elements.

1. Who is the inventor?

This sounds like a simple question. But great difficulties have ensued when this simple question has not been clearly answered early in the formation of the new business. Several people sometimes participate in the creation of a new idea or product and it is essential that everyone be clearly identified. The term "inventor" here is used in its legal sense: the true creator of the idea who, if patents are involved, would be listed on the patent. Once the inventor is identified it is essential to do two things: (1) If the organizer and the inventor are not the same person, a clear understanding of the terms under which the inventor will assign rights in the invention to the partnership must be agreed to and (2) the desires, ambitions, and long-term goals of the inventor must be ascertained at least to the best of the ability of the organizer. The purpose of the first item is of course clear, but the second item is sometimes overlooked, to the ultimate detriment of the project. Creative people think differently than other people. They see the world through different eyes, "march to a different drummer" if you will. Failure to take this into account has caused many projects to fail. Whatever organization ensues from this analysis must take into account the almost paranoid thinking of many inventors. Their defensive nature is not without cause. Many have been cheated and will probably be cheated again. Absolute fairness and strict adherence to any agreements made are necessities if the project is to be successful.

Incidentally, not everyone is truly qualified to handle or deal with creative people. If the organizers of the partnership are not prepared or qualified to deal with this type of personality, they should consider some other line of work for this is an essential skill in forming and managing R & D partnerships.

2. Who will be the general partner?

An essential question. The general partner has complete management control of the partnership and carries unlimited liability with regard to the business of the partnership. State laws vary, but normally the general partner must maintain a personal net worth between 5 and 15 percent of the money raised in the partnership, not including any net worth of the partnership itself. As noted in Chapter 2, a corporation can be a general partner but is subject to similar net worth provisions. Co-general partners are frequently used although division of responsibility can become a problem. The responsibility for the entire enterprise rests on the general partner, therefore business experience would seem to be a prerequisite.

Unfortunately at this point problems can immediately arise. An inventor who is also the organizer of the partnership will be reluctant to hand over control of the project to anyone else and indeed the initial reason for considering the R & D limited partnership may have been the desire of the inventor to maintain control of an invention. If this is the case then, like it or not, the inventor is going to have to do a little studying to gain at least an elementary understanding of management principles. Actually this chapter of the book was added primarily to assist inventors and small businesses who wish to retain control of their projects. The management tools required are available and can be learned by anyone truly dedicated to to learning. This chapter can only provide an outline of what is required.

The American Management Association in New York is probably one of the best organizations in the world for total dedication to teaching management principles to working persons. The AMA seminars cover all of the basic management functions and are given throughout the year in cities throughout the United States and in many foreign countries. In addition many business colleges give part-time M.B.A. courses that cover all the basic management principles. Any inventor determined to be the general partner in a partnership of any financial magnitude should acquire as much knowledge in this area as possible. Once acquired, it is never lost and becomes a valuable asset. A creative mind with a sound business background is a hard combination to beat. The determination of who is to become the general partner is second in importance only to knowing who is the inventor.

3. Who will actually perform the R & D activities?

Tax law does not require that the partnership actually perform the R & D work and in many instances this work is subcontracted to a commercial laboratory or a corporation specifically set up for that purpose. There is nothing wrong with the partnership's doing the work itself although most partnerships of this nature are operated purely as financial entities and try to avoid the complexities of acquiring facilities and dealing with employees.

Many commercial laboratories in this country have a surprising array of equipment available on a rental or lease basis. Assuming a suitable facility is already in existence, it is probably to the benefit of the partnership to utilize the facility rather than go to the expense of setting up an entirely new operation. However, there is a tendency to want to control everything first-hand and in many instances this tendency has resulted in new facilities being created solely for the project at hand. This is a key decision that must be made before the final business structure can be determined.

4.   How will the product be manufactured?

In general the product, once developed, is not manufactured by the partnership. All substantial rights are sold to an outside corporation which then proceeds to manufacture and sell the product. The partnership is paid a royalty, under the authority of a licensing agreement, based on sales of the product. There is nothing to prevent a partnership from manufacturing its own products but due to the unlimited liability aspect of limited partnerships, the general partner is usually not inclined to take on the added liability of a manufacturing operation. Also, if capital gains treatment is to be obtained under any of the IRS provisions, a sale of all substantial rights to the product must be made in an arm's-length transaction with another entity.

Assuming it is not prearranged, nothing can prevent the limited partners or the general partner from receiving an equity position in the manufacturing company in return for relinquishing their royalty rights. A manufacturing company may be inclined toward equity to preserve cash flow during the early stages of manufacturing a new product. Again, the decisions concerning the manufacture of the product must be made before the partnership is organized so that the entire structure can be reviewed prior to committing funds to the operation.

5.   What is the present patent position of the products that are to be developed?

The patent situation was discussed earlier. Once the product selection has been completed, a review of the patent situation must be made. The problem here is that IRC Section 1235 permits capital gains treatment of the sale of all substantial rights to an invention only if the creator and those who financed the reduction to practice of the invention are individuals, not employees or a corporation.

If the inventor's identity and status as an individual and not an employee have been determined and if the invention has not yet been "reduced to practice" and patents applications have already been filed, a simple assignment of the patent rights by the inventor to the partnership in return for funding the effort to reduce the idea to practice will probably secure capital gains treatment for the inventor and all individuals in the partnership when all substantial rights to the invention are sold. However, if the inventor is an employee at the time of creating the invention or becomes an employee during the process of reducing the idea to practice, and subsequent patents are filed, complications could arise. This is not to say that capital gains treatment could not still be obtained but the closer the business structure adheres to the ideal "model" envisioned when the statute was written, the more certain the tax treatment will be. In all cases, to receive capital gains treatment under Section 1235 the contractual arrangements between the inventor and the partnership must have occurred prior to the "reduction to practice" of the invention. This may occur before or after application for a patent but cannot occur later than the earliest time that commercial exploitation of the invention occurs.

The key items to look for are: (1) Has a patent been filed? (2) What was the status of the inventor at the time of filing, i.e., an individual or an employee? (3) What was the status of the invention, i.e., had it been reduced to practice in a legal sense? (4) What relationship exists among the inventor, the partners, and the organization chosen to manufacture and market the product? If the inventor owns more than 25% of the corporation acquiring the rights to the invention, the inventor and the partners will be denied capital gains treatment under paragraph (d) of Section 1235 but could obtain such treatment under other sections of the Code provided they held less than 80% of the stock in the acquiring corporation.

6. What are the long-term goals of the various participants?

Before the final structure is decided a careful look at the long-term goals and motivations of the various individuals who will participate in the venture is absolutely essential. Again, the key to a harmonious and successful project is the inventor. What does the inventor want? Does he want to run a manufacturing business with its never ending day-to-day frustrations or simply to see his invention successfully developed and marketed? Are profits from his invention solely for the purpose of continuing his creative work an escape from drudgery into something new and different? Is recognition the primary motive, or the acquisition of power? Does the inventor realize that the daily management of a successful and growing business is a full-time career which will in time crowd out the creative work that has probably been done in the past?

The problem here is that the attributes required for a successful, creative career are not necessarily the same as the attributes required of a successful manager. Good managers must have empathy with other people; they are "people persons." Creative minds have difficulty relating to people in a practical day-to-day sense. They are loners, spending most of their time in "another world" that they themselves create. Creative people usually require "closure"—that is, they want to solve problems. The day-to-day operation of a business never delivers closure. The same problems keep recurring. Resolving this inner conflict in an inventor who wants to control every aspect of an invention and yet is not committed to the management game is probably one of the most important factors in determining the correct business relationships in new-product projects, yet it is rarely addressed in a straightforward manner at the outset of a project. The R & D limited partnership offers the inventor the opportunity and legal framework to totally control an invention. It can be done but the more important question is should the inventor control everything and if not when should control be relinquished? This difficult question must be faced squarely and answered before the final relationship among all interested parties is fixed.

In general the motives of the other participants are easier to determine and of somewhat less importance than those of the inventor. Most investors are satisfied with reasonable protection for their investment and reasonable returns provided they are kept fully informed of the progress of the project and feel that the project is being managed in a professional manner. Few investors want any active control in the project as they generally have other business interests that occupy most of their time.

In summary, the following information is required to so arrange the various participants in the new venture that the resulting organization is correct from a legal standpoint, minimizes the tax burden, satisfies the inner motivations of the key persons involved, and can successfully reduce the invention to practice and bring it to the marketplace.

1. Who is the inventor (or inventors)?
2. Who will be the general partner?
3. Who will perform the R & D work?
4. How will the product be manufactured?
5. What is the present patent position?
6. What are the long-term goals of the key participants?

Using the above checklist, the EED project was structured as shown on charts 8 and 9 of Appendix O. Note that two stages are shown. Stage I represented that period of time during which the inventions were being developed. Stage II represented the time period during which payments were being received by the partnership from the sale of the successful products by GTI.

After the basic relationships have been established it becomes a somewhat easy matter to draw up a list of the legal documents that will be needed to launch the project. The next section of this chapter will discuss the documents that are required and the purpose of each. Appendix M contains a copy of each of the actual documents used to set up and operate EED.

PREPARING THE KEY DOCUMENTS

This section will discuss the legal documents required to set up, fund, and operate an R & D limited partnership that has a structure similar to that of EED, as shown on charts 8 and 9 of Appendix O. In no way is this discussion intended to replace the services of a competent lawyer. However, organizers who are familiar with what is required can make better use of their attorney's time and save a considerable amount of money in legal fees.

Five essential documents are required to operate the partnership in the form used by EED: (1) the partnership agreement, (2) the certificate of limited partnership, (3) the R & D contract, (4) the license agreement, and (5) the private placement memorandum. Each of these documents will be discussed separately to indicate its general purpose and any particular features that require special attention.

1. The partnership agreement

The corporate equivalent of the partnership agreement would probably be the articles of incorporation and the by-laws combined. The partnership agreement contains the total agreements that exist between the general partners and the limited partners and outlines the duties and responsibilities as well as the benefits to be received by each of the parties signing the agreement. As mentioned in Chapter 2, all of the states except Louisiana have adopted the Uniform Limited Partnership Act (Appendix A) as the official form of limited partnership agreement. No originality is required on the part of the lawyer in drafting this document. For the most part it is only necessary to fill in the blanks and note any particular exceptions taken by the state in which it is intended to register the partnership. There is no necessity to register the partnership in the state in which the organizer lives or intends to do business. The EED partnership was registered in Delaware and was required of course to comply with Delaware's law. The advantages to registering in Delaware are of a somewhat technical nature; primarily they involve the amount and kind of information required to be supplied concerning the limited partners. A comparison of the actual document filed for EED in Delaware (Appendix M) with the model document contained in Appendix A reveals that the two are essentially identical.

2. Certificate of limited partnership

This is the actual piece of paper that is filed with the appropriate state office and officially establishes the partnership as a legal entity. In California, this document is filed with the county recorder's office in the county that represents the principal place of business of the partnership. A list of the appropriate filing places in each of the states in contained in Appendix N. The certificate becomes a public document and at least one reason for filing in one state as opposed to another is the nature of the information required. The proper form of this certificate is contained in Section 2 (a) of the ULPA (Appendix A of this book) and the actual certificate filed by EED is contained in the Offering Memorandum (Appendix M) under Exhibit C.

3. The R & D contract

The R & D contract establishes the relationship between the partnership and the organization performing the actual R & D activities. There is nothing particularly unusual about this contract. Once the decision is made as to whether the partnership or an outside organization is going to perform the work, the contract can easily be drawn up. The EED structure was slightly inbred because the same organization (GTI) that was performing the R & D work eventually licensed the products. Therefore the license agreement is included in the R & D agreement. While there are perhaps many instances where this arrangement might be advantageous, there is not any particular reason why it must be so. What is essential is that the most appropriate organization perform the R & D to assure that the work is successful and that the most appropriate organization become the licensee to assure successful marketing of the product after it is developed. In this instance GTI served both purposes.

There is however one key feature of the contract that is somewhat unique and was considered critical to the prudent management of the partnership. Paragraphs 2.03 and 2.04 of the contract between EED and GTI require that GTI prepare a CPM (critical path method) chart for each project that is undertaken and that this chart then becomes part of the technical specifications. Failure to make satisfactory progress along the CPM chart would constitute a default and allow EED to withhold further payment. This clause was purposely included to allow the partnership to regain control of the project if preset schedules and budgets were not maintained. One of the primary causes of excessive losses occurring in development projects is the reluctance on the part of those performing the actual day-to-day work to admit that their work is going down a blind alley. Excessive schedule slippages and budget overruns generally signal trouble and it is essential that the general partner be able to withhold funds if trouble is suspected. A carefully prepared and monitored PERT or CPM network can serve as an excellent early warning system for the general partner.

4.   The license agreement

This agreement serves to establish the relationship between the manufacturing and marketing organization and the partnership. It is a fairly standard document; its key proviso is that if capital gains treatment of the income to the partnership is to be obtained all substantial interest must be transferred to the licensee under this agreement. The meaning of this is discussed at some length in Chapter 2 and in Appendix L.

5.   The private placement memorandum

Assuming that funds are needed for the project and that exemption from registration under the Securities Act of 1933 is to be claimed—that is, the offering is to be a private placement—a private placement memorandum is the document required to support exemption under any of the exemption rules. As Rule 146 is currently the most used exemption rule and in fact adequately covers most offerings that would be expected for R & D limited partnerships, it will be assumed that the offering must comply with that rule. (For recent changes in Rule 146, see Appendix T.)

This document is probably the most complex of the required documents. It includes all of the above documents as well as a vast amount of boilerplate that while seemingly meaningless is essential. The need for this document arises from Paragraph E in the text of rule 146 which requires that each offeree have access to or be provided with the same information as specified in Schedule A of the Act. As the Act (Securities and Exchange Act of 1933) is fundamentally a disclosure act, full disclosure of all pertinent information then becomes a requirement whether the offering is registered or not.

While it may be true that the offeree can obtain access to most of the information contained in a typical private placement memorandum, the burden of proof that the offeree did have the information rests with the offeror, hence the private placement memorandum must contain all information required under schedule A of the Act. This accounts for the large amount of what appears to be boilerplate and not directly relating to the project at hand. Beware, though, of cutting corners. The SEC means what it says and the rules must be followed to the letter. Certainly there are those who write sloppy private placement memorandums and get away with them but doing sloppy work has at least two disadvantages: (1) one might get caught; and (2) a prospective investor who is qualified to be an investor has seen many offerings and is able to quickly judge quality work. Investors are unlikely to have respect for the management of a venture that exhibits less than professional qualities in the offering phase of the project.

The private placement memorandum included in Appendix M was prepared for EED by the law firm of Kirkpatrick, Lockhart, Johnson and Hutchison in Pittsburgh. A prime example of a quality document, it can be used as a model with the following provisos: (1) laws are constantly changing, thus a current check must be made by any attorney preparing such a memorandum to assure that no significant changes have occurred; (2) the memorandum was offered in California, New York, and Florida in the form included in this book and in Pennsylvania with Exhibit D (projected cash flow) deleted; offerings in other states would require checking of appropriate state statutes to assure compliance; (3) direct plagiarism is not a sign of high professional standards, so considerable rewriting can be expected.

An opinion letter from the law firm that prepared the document is included. Most investors would want to see an opinion letter from a qualified law firm that at least covers most of the pertinent legal aspects of their investment. No reputable law firm is likely to write such a letter without a thorough review of this key document. However, there are many competent law firms that are not yet familiar with R & D limited partnerships. If organizers will take the time to study the model provided they will probably be able to assist their law firm in drawing up a quality document with less expenditure of time than if this model were not available.

Included in the model, as mentioned above, is a projected cash flow chart (Exhibit D) that was deleted from the Pennsylvania offering. Potential investors almost always refer to this section immediately. There is of course a strong temptation on the part of the organizers to present the best numbers possible, even to exaggerate a little. While it's probably true that only optimists start ventures, every effort should be made to present realistic numbers. Once in print, they last a long time and the reputation of the organizers rides on those numbers. While many things can and often do go wrong during a project, the numbers shown must represent the most accurate picture of projected results that can be obtained.

One other feature of the private placement memorandum prepared for EED is that the execution documents, that is, the forms the offeror expects the offeree to sign, were bound separately from the main document. This served two purposes. First, it was not necessary for the investors to tear out forms from their copies of the memorandum, thus preserving their copies intact; secondly, while many people connected with a project of this nature may be interested in reading the memorandum, only a very small number (and some state laws limit the number of offerees) are actually considered bona fide offerees. With separate execution documents, only the true offerees get those documents, thus providing a method of documenting which persons were receiving "information only" copies as compared to the actual offerees.

In summary, five key documents are required to organize and fund an R & D limited partnership structured in a manner similar to EED. They are: (1) the partnership agreement, (2) the certificate of limited partnership, (3) the R & D contract, (4) the license agreement, and (5) the private placement memorandum. When the documents have been prepared the next phase of the project—contacting investors—can begin. The next section of this chapter deals with that subject in some detail.

MARKETING THE OFFERING

This is probably the most critical phase of the project and the one most fraught with both psychological and legal dangers. The first decision to make is whether the offering will be marketed by the general partner or by an outside organization. While there are legal restrictions regarding who may sell securities, registration is usually not required for the general partner. Certainly, if a professional securities firm is available to sell the offering, the 8% or so it would charge is well worth the cost, particularly in view of the fact that the organizer doesn't have to pay the commissions anyway (the commissions are only payable if the offering is a success, in which case the funds will be available from the partnership). The problem is that many inventors and small businesses have no "track record" so no one will sell their offering without seeing their organization perform. This is a chicken-and-egg problem that can only be solved by a head-on attack. The general partner is going to have to sell the offering. It can be done. Here is how to do it.

As mentioned above, most R & D partnership offerings are unregistered and rely on Rule 146 in claiming exemption from registration under the

Securities Act of 1933. Rule 146 is discussed in some detail in Chapter 2, and a copy of the Rule itself is provided in Appendix E. A careful review of this material should be made prior to making any attempt to sell partnership units to anyone. There are severe restrictions on any form of general solicitation or advertising of the offering. A simple ad in a local newspaper, for instance, indicating that an offering is to be made or that funds are needed for a certain project could constitute a violation of Rule 146. Furthermore, no written communications are permitted with potential offerees unless the issuer has reasonable grounds to believe the potential offeree is qualified. How then is a private offering ever successfully completed unless the issuer has a large number of high tax bracket, knowledgeable friends? The answer is really very simple. In the course of preparing the offering, as outlined above, much outside help is required. All of the information that must be collected to properly assess the correct products to pursue, the information that must be gathered to determine the correct business structure (the second key event discussed in this chapter), the questions raised by a thorough study of this book prior to beginning the project, and the careful preparation of the five documents listed in the previous section of this chapter will bring the organizer into contact with many people. These people will become rather intimately involved in the project and, if the project appears to have potential and is being organized in a professional manner, they will begin to discuss it with their associates.

At this point it is well to realize that there is an acute shortage of high-quality investment opportunities in the general classifications of tax-advantageous situations. This may not be apparent to those needing investors but it is a fact. Not all offerings are made by honest people. Not all offerings are executed with enough care to receive the claimed tax benefits, not all offerings represent really achievable projects and finally, due to the restrictions of Rule 146 and the other exemption rules, it is difficult for a potential investor to hear about the good opportunities in time to participate. A large number of offerings are oversubscribed and many investors who wait too long to make a decision are left out. EED was oversubscribed and $100,000 had to be returned to disappointed investors. Note though that there is a shortage of only *quality* investment opportunities. There is lots of trash around and as a matter of fact near the end of the tax year that is about all that is available. The first secret of successfully selling an issue is to make every effort to produce a quality offering.

Now back to the first problem of how to locate potential offerees. Of all the groups with which one comes in contact while preparing an offering, the law firm and the accounting firm probably represent the greatest potential for contact with high tax bracket investors seeking shelters. If this is true (be assured that it is), it pays to deal with first-class, reputable law and accounting firms even if the cost is higher. The so-called big eight accounting firms have large numbers of wealthy individual clients as well as the more publicized corporate accounts and can, if they believe the proposed venture is properly conceived and well managed, arrange meetings with qualified investors. Once a small number of qualified investors are contacted, the problems of locating more becomes even easier: the investors themselves have friends who are also looking for suitable investments and, assuming the presentation is done well, personal recommendations from the first group of investors will provide a second and probably larger group to contact. As this point remember what the funeral directors and wedding consultants call the Rule of 200. Long experience has taught these two groups that most people know an average of 200 people; hence at weddings and funerals, when presumably everyone someone knows is invited, the average list of invitees is about 200. Assuming this to be true, and assuming that about 10 percent of a person's friends are in approximately the same income bracket, for each successful presentation to a qualified investor, a potential exists to contact 20 more. The pitfall here, of course, is that a bad presentation can also remove the same 20 persons from consideration. Bad recommendations can spread as fast as if not faster than good ones, so that it is essential that every effort be made to give a professional presentation every time.

How the information is presented to the potential investor is almost as important as the content of the offering. The presentation, that is, the form as well as the content, becomes of prime importance. The following paragraphs will offer some guidelines as to how this can be done in an effective manner.

First and foremost it must be understood that people retain very little of the information that is told to them. On the average the retention rate of information after 24 hours when that information is presented orally is only about 20 percent and that number is probably optimistic. However, by simultaneously presenting the information visually as well as orally the retention rate can be increased to about 75 percent, an enormous improvement. As most investors will want to consult with their attorneys and accountants before making any decision, it is essential that they retain enough of what is said for a long enough period to intelligently discuss the matter with their advisors. Therefore an audio-visual presentation is essential. Many books have been written and many seminars given on effective presentations so that only a summary of the subject will be presented here.

One of the most effective seminars was given several years ago by Richard J. Kulda, who summarized his presentation in a booklet called "Professional Eloquence." (Copies of this booklet can be obtained by writing to Professional Eloquence, 10845 Meads Avenue, Orange, CA 92669.) Of the various choices of visual presentations, such as slides, viewgraphs, or charts, straightforward, neatly prepared 20″ × 28″ charts are probably most effective, provided they can be transported without difficulty. It is essential that the charts be kept simple and uncluttered and that they be big enough so that everyone in the audience can see everything on the chart without undue effort. Presentations of this nature seem to be limited to an audience of from one to ten. Reasonably sized charts can contain enough information on each one so that the total number of charts can be limited to about 20 or less.

Assuming the method of presenting the information has been resolved, what information should be presented? The first ground rule is that only information already provided in the private placement memorandum should be given in the presentation. This is to insure that not only are no conflicting facts given, but when the private placement memorandum it taken away by the potential investor, it contains all of the information available.

Copies of the charts used by the author in the EED presentation are included in Appendix O. The originals of these charts are 20″ × 28″. They use white cards mounted on a blue background and have black letters about a half-inch high. The charts were professionally prepared and cost about $50.00 each in 1980. Not cheap, but the investment was returned many times over.

At this point two of the three essential tools are complete: the private placement memorandum and the audio-visual presentation. The third essential tool is the presenter. Appearance is of prime importance and the manner of the presentation is vital to a successful presentation. First, with regard to appearance, a conservative, neat, well-groomed look is important. Creative persons who feel that it's the idea that counts and hence their appearance is of secondary importance place themselves at a considerable disadvantage with this attitude. While jeans, tee shirts, jogging shoes, long hair, and a beard may be the "in" costume with the creative group this year, it is very seldom the "in" costume for potential investors. Like it or not, it's the "establishment" that invests most of the money in this country and one takes high risks by failing to conform to its standards of dress and manners. It must be remembered that in approaching an investor with the limited partnership concept, the general partner is asking that person to turn over a considerable sum of hard-earned money, and the investor loses almost all control of the funds the instant the subscription agreement is signed and the check delivered. If the investor doesn't have complete confidence in the ability and integrity of the general partner, the investment will never be made.

With regard to the manner in which the presentation should be given, an absolutely straightforward approach must be taken. Complete honesty is essential. If the investor is left with the slightest feeling that something is being withheld or if information is given that turns out to have been shaded slightly in favor of the presenter, the investment will probably not be made.

Most professionals in the presentation business advise their clients to practice presentations either in front of a mirror or with family or friends. Some people have no luck at all with this approach (including the author). Spontaneity is lost by practicing, but if stage fright is a problem, rehearsals do help.

Referring again to Rule 146, it should be noted that not only must the potential investor be provided all the information that would be required in a registration statement (paragraph E) but the Rule requires that the offeree be given the opportunity to "ask questions of, and receive answers from the issuer and to obtain any additional information necessary to verify the accuracy of the information given by the issuer." The presentation prepared above can now be used in a variety of ways to satisfy Rule 146 as well as to persuade a potential investor to become an actual investor.

The "normal" procedure if a brokerage house were handling the program would be for the salesperson to telephone selected clients and present an outline of the offering (this is sometimes printed up and mailed to qualified clients). If the client expresses interest over the telephone a copy of the private placement memorandum is mailed so that the client has an opportunity to read the material and consult with a lawyer and accountant. After some period of time and several phone calls, a "due diligence" meeting is called of all interested investors who have previously received the private placement memorandum. At this meeting the general partner would give the presentation discussed in the previous paragraph and would be available for questions. At this time, a decision is expected from the potential investors, the money is collected, and the offering closed.

However, if the general partner elects to sell the offering, as was presumed above, a somewhat different procedure seems to be more effective, albeit requiring more effort, while still complying with Rule 146. In this method, the general partner, after locating the potential investor, tries to arrange a personal meeting at which time the presentation is given on a one-to-one basis. The private placement memorandum is then left with the offeree. After the offeree has had a chance to read over the material and consult with advisors, follow-up phone calls are made to determine whether any further information is required. At this point, the offeree may ask that the presentation be repeated for the benefit of a lawyer or accountant. The presentation is then repeated, again affording all parties the opportunity to ask further questions.

These face-to-face presentations not only satisfy the requirements of Rule 146 but offer ample opportunity for the general partner and the limited partners to get to know each other a little better. While this may not be thought to be necessary, the general partner and the offeree are in fact considering going into business together and will be partners for a number of years. The somewhat impersonal approach that the brokerage houses tend to take seems to overlook the future relationship that is going to exist. The offerees are not "just investors" purchasing corporate shares on a stock exchange; they will become partners and rather close associates of the general partner. It would seem prudent to determine, insofar as possible, whether this is going to be a happy relationship before the investment is made.

In this approach no particular attempt is made to gather together all potential partners in one grand meeting at the end of the offering period. The face-to-face meetings and small gatherings seem to satisfy everyone. The "individualistic" process described appears to be highly effective but quite time-consuming. Incidentally, the presentations should be tape recorded if at all possible because the burden of proof that the investor was given all the information requested lies, as mentioned before, with the issuer, in this case the general partner.

The EED offering was handled, in the manner described, by the general partner. The first potential contact was made on August 21, 1980, and the offering was closed on October 14, 1980. The offering, as mentioned above, was oversubscribed by $100,000 and raised a net amount of $1,200,000, all units having been sold by the general partner.

One of the essential ingredients of the EED offering that seemed to contribute to its success was the lack of "front-end loading," as it is called in the trade. In other words there was an absolute minimum of expenses charged to the partnership during its formation. No sales commissions were paid since the general partner sold all of the units and did not charge the partnership a fee for this effort. There were no organizational charges or project development charges as they are sometimes called. The only major expense incurred was the legal fees involved in forming the partnership, developing the private placement memorandum, drawing up the R & D contract, and advising the general partner during the fund-raising efforts.

While the general partner is paid a modest management fee on a monthly basis during the life of the partnership, the only real profit the general partner can make occurs after the limited partners have recovered all of their original investment. In short, treating the limited partners in a fair and equitable manner by organizing the venture so that the general partner shares in the risks as well as the benefits seems to be a feature that is attractive to investors. Unfortunately, this feature is not typical of most limited partnership offerings of any type.

After the specified offering period has elapsed or all of the required funds have been collected, the offering should be officially closed. Up to this time the subscription agreements that have been collected have only been signed by the offerees and returned with the appropriate checks to the general partner. In general it is not advisable to accept these subscriptions on behalf of the partnership until the actual closing day, to give the general partner ample opportunity to examine the execution documents that were returned and to double-check on the qualifications of the offerees. It is absolutely essential that all potential investors be qualified under the Rule 146 guidelines and any state requirements. An impartial, qualified lawyer should review all documents prior to signing them and returning them to the new limited partners. This is best done all at once on the "closing day." At this time letters should be sent to all limited partners that have been accepted by the general partner informing them that their subscription has been accepted and that the partnership is now in business. If any of the subscription agreements are rejected, a cover letter informing the investor of this fact should be sent immediately. Samples of letters indicating acceptance or rejection are included in Appendix P.

It is difficult to send rejection letters. The irony of the situation is that after weeks of work trying to convince the offeree to invest, once the decision is made, some hard feelings can occur if the investment is ultimately rejected. In order to avoid any accusations of unfair discrimination, it is helpful to keep a time log of when the checks were received, although legally the

private placement memorandum should be so worded that the general partner
has absolute discretion to accept or reject any subscription.

Not only should a log be kept of when checks arrive but an accurate,
bound log book should be kept of all of the partners' activities relative to the
offering during the entire offering period. The log aids in following up on
calls to prospective investors, and if any questions are ever raised as to
whether the offering was in fact a private offering, the log book would serve
as an excellent defense. During the EED offering each copy of the private
placement memorandum was numbered if it was sent to an offeree and
lettered if it was sent to someone for information purposes only. A bound
log book with permanently numbered pages was kept in which each numbered or lettered copy of the memorandum was assigned a separate page.
Each time a phone call or a visit was made to a person holding a particular
copy, that fact and the subject of the conversation or visit were noted in the
log book. To those persons who did not become limited partners but who
had received an offering copy of the memorandum, a final letter was sent
asking that the memorandum and the execution documents be returned. The
log book tells the whole story when the project is completed and is a valuable
and necessary tool.

After the projects have been chosen, the necessary documents prepared,
the investors contacted, and the money received, the business has to be
managed. The next sections of this chapter will deal with some of the necessary details as well as with some management attitudes that lead to good
relationships among all of the participants in ventures of this nature.

MANAGING THE BUSINESS

Successfully managing a business of this nature involves two distinct problem
areas: the everyday mechanical details of the business, such as banking,
filing tax returns, paying bills, etc., and the relationships between the general
partner and the limited partners. Each of these areas will be discussed in a
separate section.

The Mechanics of the Business

The following is a minimum list of more or less mechanical chores that
must be performed in order to conduct the business of the partnership in an
orderly fashion.

1. *Filing the partnership certificate*
This is actually done in two steps. When the partnership agreement is
first drawn up and prior to contacting any investors, the partnership should
actually be brought into legal existence. To do this a "nominee" limited
partner is named who can sign the certificate along with the general partner.

This nominee has no obligations and disappears from the partnership when the "real" limited partners are accepted by the general partner. This first certificate can now be filed with the appropriate state office (see Appendix N) and the partnership will become a legal entity. The second step occurs after the offering is closed and the limited partners are known. Each of the limited partners now signs a new certificate along with the general partner and this final certificate is refiled with the same office as the first. That is all there is to it.

2. *Obtaining a taxpayer's identification number*

In order to file tax returns, open bank accounts, and perhaps for other reasons a taxpayer's identification number must be obtained from the IRS for the partnership. This is done by filing a copy of Form SS-4 with the appropriate office of the IRS. A copy of this form is included in Appendix Q. In due course the number will arrive. It is possible to open bank accounts without the number on a temporary basis if one is known at the bank, but the sooner the number is obtained, the more likely confusion with the IRS can be avoided.

3. *The escrow bank account*

Prior to soliciting anyone for funds, an escrow bank account should be opened. The offering memorandum usually provides that funds received prior to obtaining the minimum funds specified will be deposited in an escrow account and will be available for return to the subscriber in the event the minimum amount specified cannot be obtained. While the money thus deposited cannot be used to pay any bills, interest can and should be earned on these funds. EED earned approximately $10,000 interest while the offering was underway so the amount is not insignificant. (No risky investments though, just Treasury Notes or major bank certificates of deposit.) The general partner could be held personally responsible for loss of these funds. After the minimum amount has been received or the offering is closed this account can be closed.

4. *The general bank account*

At the same time the escrow account is opened, a general account should be opened. After the minimum amount is raised, the money can be transferred from the escrow account into the general account and the partnership is ready to do business.

5. *Maintaining books and records*

The partnership agreement will specify that the general partner keep accurate books and records and that these be available for inspection by the limited partners at any time upon reasonable notice. Unless the general partner just happens to be a CPA, it would be well to engage the services of a reputable accounting firm to maintain records. Even though a big eight firm may be used to prepare tax returns and perform other somewhat major accounting tasks, the day-to-day recordkeeping can very well be done by a smaller, less expensive accounting firm. Someone who can do a good job is all that is needed.

6. *Filing tax returns*

So far as the limited partners are concerned, filing the tax return correctly and on time is one of the most if not the most important task the partnership must do. Do it right and do it on time. One of the big eight firms can be a help here. Getting them to move rapidly isn't the easiest thing to do, but they know their profession and if they sign the tax return they will be prepared to defend their actions if called upon to do so. Partnerships are a little strange in the tax department as was noted in Chapter 2. They file tax returns but do not pay taxes. Attached to the partnership tax return are pages of forms comprising the K-1 form, which contains information about the individual partners. This is the form that the partners must file with their returns to indicate their share of the gains or losses of the partnership. They combine this information with their tax returns and then pay the net amount due. It is important that the limited partners get these forms early so that they know their individual tax liability as soon as possible. Good partnership management practice should be to get the K-1's to the limited partners no later than March 1st and earlier if possible. The accountants will complain, but it can be done.

7. *Managing the project*

Almost lost in all the details is the single most important responsibility of the general partner, that of managing the projects. The R & D contracts should be signed as soon as possible and whatever money is required to be transferred should be transferred as soon as possible. Appropriate PERT or CPM charts should be developed, critical paths established, and the work started. Constant monitoring of the key events, the critical path, monies spent, estimated budgets, and completion dates is essential. Serious budget or time slippages should be acted upon without delay. It seems to be some sort of basic law that late projects will run over budget. Any major time slippage should be viewed as an emergency as budget overruns are sure to follow. Projects that consistently fail to meet intermediate objectives should be dropped. Sending good money after bad is easy to do but almost always a mistake. General managers have to be tough; after all, they are the ones who will have to face the partners in the event the projects are not successful.

8. *Progress reports*

Two distinctly different types of report are necessary. The first are the financial reports generally required by the partnership agreement at least on an annual basis. Most investors prefer quarterly reports because this is the usual practice for public corporations. Regardless of their frequency the reports should include at a minimum a balance sheet, an income statement, and a source and application of funds statement. Short notes from the general partner and from the accounting firm preparing the report are standard procedure. None of these reports has to be audited but, for the protection of the general partner, it would seem good practice to have the annual report audited by one of the big eight firms.

The second category of reports has to do with the progress of the projects themselves. No project ever runs exactly as planned, but a straightforward statement of how things are going on a monthly basis tends to bring all of the partners together as a group and to defuse any potential problems over program slippages. An example of an EED monthly progress report to the limited partners is included in Appendix R.

The Relationship Between the General Partner and the Limited Partners

The limited partnership arrangement is a little strange in a way. The limited partners put up essentially all of the money and yet are precluded by statute, at the risk of losing their limited liability status, from participating in the management of the business. The general partner in effect operates in a role of sole owner of the business. It is of course relatively easy for a general partner to take advantage of this situation and operate the business solely for personal purposes, ignoring the limited partners altogether. However easy this might seem to be it is a decidedly shortsighted view. Not only is it discourteous but lack of sincere communication with the group that funded the business can lead to strained relations that cause serious problems at just the moment when good working relations are essential. In the opinion of the author the limited partners should be treated as equal partners and kept fully informed of all events concerning the business. Of course the general partner should avoid forcing limited partners into participating in management decisions that could jeopardize their limited liability; but keeping all of them fully informed is never a disadvantage. And besides, what about that next big project?

SUMMARY

This chapter has covered the five key steps required to organize, fund, and operate an R & D limited partnership. They are:

1. Choosing the project.
2. Determining the basic business structure.
3. Preparing the key documents.
4. Marketing the offering.
5. Managing the business.

Each of these key steps was explained in some detail and this information, combined with the somewhat more theoretical discussion in the first five chapters of the book, should permit inventors, small businesses, and larger corporations to take advantage of the tremendous opportunities afforded by this exciting new method of funding new product development. Certainly the problem of obtaining sufficient funds for development has been a long standing problem of new and starting businesses, a fact recognized by Congress over 25 years ago. Today, with inflation and interest rates hovering in the double digit range, new product development funds are even more difficult to obtain and even the largest corporations are beginning to feel the pinch. High on the list of national priorities is the need to "reindustrialize America." Reindustrialization begins with research and development activities. These activities cannot begin without proper funding. The investors are available and eagerly looking for good investments. Literally thousands of individual inventors and small businesses have the ideas and the country needs to regain its technical leadership of the world. The methods outlined in this book have been available since the Supreme Court decided in favor of Mr. Snow in 1974. So, what are we waiting for? Let's go for it.

Note for Chapter 6

[238] "Critical Path Scheduling," The Service Bureau Co., a division of Control Data Corp., copyright © 1978, Control Data Corp., in-house brochure; "IBM Job Analysis System (JAS)," First Ed. (December 1978), in-house brochure; Pert-O-Graph System, Halcomb Associates, 510 E. Maude Avenue, Sunnyvale, CA 94086, in-house brochure.

Bibliography

Books

Andersen, Arthur & Co. *Tax Reform Act of 1976: Summary of Changes and Impact on Selected Businesses.* 2nd ed. Chicago. Revised September, 1976.

Augustine, Don, and Peter M. Fass. *Private Real Estate Limited Partnerships—1979.* Real Estate Law & Practice, Course Handbook, Series No. 163. N 4-4336/N6-4329. Practicing Law Institute.

Commerce Clearing House, Inc. *California "Blue Sky" Laws.* Chicago.

———. *Capital Gains & Losses.* Special Rules. January 15, 1979, pp. 54,005, 54,007, 54,008.

———. *Internal Revenue Code.* IRC Sec. 1231 (a), 1231, 1235, 1221, 1222, 1223.

———. *Research Expenditures.* IRC Sec. 174.

———. *Sale or Exchange of Patents.* IRC Sec. 1235 & Capital Gains Discussion.

———. *Securities Act—Regulations.* Reg. 230. (Rule 146) Transactions by an Issue Deemed not to Involve any Public Official. November 13, 1978.

———. *Tax Reform Act of 1976: Law & Explanation.*

———. *Transactions Between Partner and Partnership.* IRC Sec. 707, pp. 45, 107, 45, 112.

A Guide to SEC Corporate Filings. Washington, D.C.: Disclosure Incorporated.

Hamilton, Robert W. *Cases on Corporations—Including Partnerships & Limited Partnerships.* St. Paul: West Publishing Co., 1976.

International Encyclopedia of the Social Sciences. New York: Macmillan, 1968, Vol. IV, pp. 34–62.

———. Vol. VIII, pp. 194–202.

Lane, Bruce S. *The Tax Reform Act of 1976—What it Means for Real Estate Limited Partnerships,* 1977.

New Directions in Psychology II. New York: Holt, Rinehart & Winston, Inc., 1965.

Prentice-Hall, Inc. *Gain From Sale of Depreciable Property Between Certain Related Taxpayers.* IRC Sec. 1239. 1974.

———. "Snow vs. Commissioner," *Federal Tax.* 1974.

———. *Tax Reform Act of 1976.* Report Bulletin 43. October 1, 1976.

———. *Trade on Business Expenses.* IRC Sec. 162. 1974.

Roulac, Stephen E. *Real Estate Securities and Syndications.* Chicago: National Association of Real Estate Boards, 1973.

Swan, Frank L. *Tax Tactics, New Developments and the Carter Administration Proposals.* Newport Beach, CA: Coopers & Lybrand, 1977.

Tversky, Amos, and Ward Edwards. *Decision Making.* Baltimore, MD: Penguin Books, 1967.

Magazines, Journals, and Periodicals

Augustine, Fass, Lester & Robinson. "The Liability of Limited Partners Having Certain Statutory Voting Rights Affecting the Basic Structure of the Partnership," *Business Lawyer,* XXXI (July, 1976), 2087–2107.

Ayers, Jay F., Nicholas G. Moore, and Frank R. Pope. "How Limited Partnerships Tax-Shelter the R & D of New Products or Technology," *Journal of Taxation,* XLIX, 3 (September, 1978), 138–139, 141–144.

Blum, Stuart H. "Investment Preferences and the Desire for Security: A Comparison of Men and Women," *Journal of Psychology,* XCIV (September, 1976), 87–91.

Boudreaux, Kenneth J. "Managerialism and Risk–Return Performance," *Southern Economic Journal,* XXXIX (January, 1973), 366–372.

Briedis, Irene, and Rolf O. Kroger. "Effects of Risk and Caution Norms on Group Decision Making," *Human Relations,* XXIII, 3, 181–190.

Brockhuff, Dr. Klaus. "Determinants of Research and Development Expenditure in Some Chemical Corporations in Germany," *Management International Review,* X, 4–5 (1970), 71–84.

Buffett, Warren E. "How Inflation Swindles the Equity Investor," *Fortune,* XCV, 6 (May, 1977), 250–254.

Caruthers, Donald S. "True Debt—Leveraging in Real Estate Limited Partnership Tax Shelters," *Journal of Real Estate Taxation,* IV, 1 (Fall, 1976), 5–23.

Domsch, Michel. "The Organization of Corporate R & D Planning," *Long Range Planning,* XI, 3 (June, 1978), 67–74.

Etter, Wayne E., and Donald R. Levi. "Investor Views of Real Estate and Limited Partnerships," *Appraisal Journal,* XLVI, 1 (January, 1978), 112–121.

Falk, Haim, and James A. Heintz. "Assessing Industry Risk by Ratio Analysis," *Accounting Review,* L (October, 1975), 758–779.

Fisher, I. N., and G. R. Hall. "Risk and Corporate Rates of Return," *Quarterly Journal of Economics,* LXXXIII (February, 1969), 79–92.

Hensley, Wayne E. "Probability, Personality, Age and Risk Taking," *Journal of Psychology,* XCV (1977), 139–145.

Kipp, E. M. "How to Construct an Effective Corporate R & D Budget," *Research Management,* XXI, 3 (May, 1978), 14–17.

Lee, John W. "Pre-Operating Expenses and Section 174: Will *Snow* Fall?" *Tax Lawyer,* XXVII, 3 (Spring, 1974), 381–416.

Long, Joseph C. "Partnership, Limited Partnership and Joint Venture Interests as Securities," *Missouri Law Review,* DXXXI, 4 (Fall, 1972), 599–600.

Mann, Lowell E. "Revenue Procedure 74-17 Diminishes Changes of Favorable Ruling on Limited Partnerships," *The Journal of Taxation,* XLII, 1 (January, 1975), 16–20.

Mennis, Edmund A. "Perspective on Industry Profits," *Business Economics,* XII, 1 (January, 1977), 84–94.

Morris, Ronald A. "Tax Notes—Organization of Limited Partnerships Hindered," *National Real Estate Investor,* XIX, 9, 37.

Ozawa, Terutono. "Japan's Technology Now Challenges the West," *Columbia Journal of World Business,* VII, 4 (April, 1972), 41–49.

Panken, A. J. and E. Turban. "Research & Development Projects," *Engineering Economist*, XX, 3 (September, 1975), 173–186.

Schaninger, Charles M. "Perceived Risk and Personality," *Journal of Consumer Research*, III (September, 1976), 95–100.

Seed, Allen H. "Needed: Strategies to Improve Cash Flow," *Management Review*, LXIV (March, 1975), 11–18.

Tucker, Stefan. "How to Avoid the Major Limited Partnership Problems," *The Practical Accountant*, IX (1976), 67–70.

Weil, Frank A. "Management's Drag on Productivity," *Business Week* (December 3, 1974), 14.

———

"All About Profit," *Dun's Review*, CXI, 3 (June, 1978), 79–81.

"An Analysis of Federal R & D Funding by Function," *National Science Foundation* (1969–1979), 78–320.

"A Big Boost for R & D," *Dun's Review*, CXII, 3 (September, 1978), 770.

"Borrowed Liquidity: Signal of Corporate Distress," *Harvard Business Review*, LIII, 7 (1975), 6–8.

"The Bottom Line Directory," *Financial World*, CVL (July 15, 1976), 13–16.

"Brighter Look for R & D," *Industrial Research*, XVIII (January, 1976), 54–55.

"Can Semi-Conductors Survive Big Business?" *Business Week* (December 3, 1979), 66–86.

"Carter Endorses R & D Amid Fiscal Belt Tightening," *Electronics Design*, XXV (December 6, 1978), 51.

"Chemical R & D: The Trend is Up," *Chemical Week*, CXXII, 15 (April 12, 1978), 36.

"The Corporate Profits Outlook Funding 1977," *Business Economics*, XII (January, 1977), 78–83.

"Cost of Research Index, 1920–1970," *Operations Research* (January–February, 1972), 1–18.

"Cyclical Behavior of Profit Margins," *Journal of Economic Issues*, XII, 2 (June 1978), 287–305.

"Detroit's New Face Toward Its Suppliers," *Business Week* (September 24, 1979), 140–149.

"Early Report on *Snow* Decision," *American Bar Association Journal*, LX, 11 (May 13, 1974), 1428, 1430.

"Economic Road Maps," *The Conference Board* (September, 1978).

"Election to Defer and Amortize R & D Expenses," *CPA Journal*, XLVII, 5 (May, 1977), 42–43.

"Energy Increase of 18 Percent Paces Industrial R & D Spending in 1975," *National Science Foundation* (October 27, 1976), 1–4.

"Federal Income Taxation," *Ohio State Law Journal*, XXXVI (Fall, 1975), 175–189.

"The Flaw in Japan's Boom," *Business Week* (July 10, 1971), 42–43.

"Forecast of R & D Spending in 1985," *Research Management*, XX (May, 1977), 3–4.

"$45.2 Billion for R & D," *Research/Development*, XXIX (January, 1978), 22–24.

"$42.7 Billion for R & D," *Research/Development*, XXVIII (January, 1977), 24–27.

"Funds for Performance on Basic Research, Applied Research & Development by Industry, 1971–1975," *Electronic Market Data Book—1977*, 126–127.

"How to Select Successful R & D Projects," *Management International Review*, LXVII, 12 (December, 1978), 25.

"How to Stay in Front," *Business Week* (December 3, 1979), 138.

"How 1200 Companies Performed in 1977, *Business Week* (March 20, 1978), 79–114.

"Impact on New External Values on Industrial R & D," *Research Management* (March, 1978), 29–33.

"Increased R & D Funding Seen in 1977," *Automotive News* (January 31, 1977), 88.

"Industrial R & D and Innovation," *National Science Foundation* (1977), 91–275.

"Industrial Research from 1975–2050," *Research Management,* XVII (November, 1974), 21–23.

"Industry's Cash Flow Still an Encouraging Sign," *Iron Age,* CCXX (September 19, 1977), 25.

"Inflation Ups the R & D Ante," *Business Week* (May 17, 1969), 78, 80.

"International Indications of Science & Technology," *National Science Foundation* (1977), 1–205.

"Is R & D Investment Being Short Changed?" *Iron Age,* CCXVIII (November 22, 1976), 66–67.

"Limited Increase in R & D," *Industrial Reseach,* XV (January, 1973), 73.

"Limited Partnerships—The IRS Attack on Tax Shelters," *The Ohio CPA,* XXXIV, 3 (Summer, 1975), 101–120.

"Limited Partnerships: Profits and Danger," *Commodities,* VII (March/April, 1978), 46.

"Limited Partnerships With a Sole Corporate General Partner: The Impact of Lanson & Zuckman," *Taxes,* LIV, 3 (March, 1976), 132–142.

"Managerialism and Risk–Return Performance: Reply," *Southern Economic Journal,* XL (January, 1974), 507–508.

"Managing R & D in Japan," *Management International Review,* XII, 1 (1972), 65–73.

"The Market Directed Product Development Process," *Research Management,* XX, 5 (September, 1977), 25–32.

"National Policy and Company R & D in Japan," *Research Management,* XVII (January, 1974), 27–33.

"National R & D Policies Study is Planned," *Research Management,* XXI, 3 (May, 1978), 2–4.

"1985 R & D Funding Projections," *National Science Foundation* (June, 1976), iii–25.

"1974 Forecast for R & D," *Industrial Research,* XVI, 1 (January, 1974), 36–41.

"1979 R & D Budgets Up 10% at Chemical Firms," *Chemical & Engineering News,* LVII, 3 (January 15, 1979), 12–13.

"No Proof That Federal R & D Boosts Economy," *Chemical & Engineering News,* LV, 47 (November 21, 1977), 23–24.

"Percentage Depletion Under the New At Risk Provisions," *Tax Advisor,* IX, 6 (June, 1978), 338–339.

"The Profits Are There For the Spending," *Business Week* (February 16, 1976), 23–24.

"Profits Decline to Record High—How's That Again?" *Iron Age,* XXII (April 17, 1978), 25–27.

"Profits '77—Sales Were the Spur," *Citibank* (April, 1978).

"Profits (1978) Will Hit $100 Billion," *Fortune,* XCVII (March 13, 1978), 12.

"The Prospective Payoff From R & D," *Dun's Review,* CIV (July, 1974), 91–93.

"R & D Expenditures to Rise 12.7% Next Year," *Chemical & Engineering News,* LIV, 51 (December 20, 1976), 6–7.

"R & D Funding in 1978 Predicted at $44 Billion," *Research Management,* XXI, 2 (March, 1978), 23.

"R & D Funding is Up 9% Reflecting Economic Recovery," *Chemical & Engineering News*, LV (October 24, 1977), 25–26.

"R & D Funding Seen Up 11.5% During 1976," *Chemical Marketing Reporter* (December 29, 1975), 4.

"R & D Funding to Rise 11% This Year," *Industrial Development*, CVL (January, 1976), 26–27.

"R & D Funding Will Increase in Real Dollars This Year," *Industrial Research* XX (January, 1978), 46–51.

"R & D in Japan. A Future That Will Challenge the U.S.," *Research Management*, XIV (January, 1971), 28–37.

"R & D in Japan Revisited: The 1970 Decade," *Management International Review*, XIV, 4–5 (1974), 31–38.

"R & D Renews its Focus on the New," *Chemical Week*, CXXII, 21 (May 24, 1978), 37–38.

"R & D Spending Patterns for 600 Companies," *Business Week* (July 3, 1978), 58–77.

"R & D Spending Rise, But Worries Remain," *Industry Week*, CXCII, 1 (January 3, 1977), 24.

"R & D Tax Policy," *Research Management*, XXI, 1 (January, 1978), 24–27.

"R & D Tax Shelters: High Payoffs for High Technology," *New Tech*, I, 7 (September, 1979), 10–11.

"Research and Development in Industry 1970," *National Science Foundation* (January, 1971), iii–110.

"Research and Development in Industry 1975," *National Science Foundation* (January, 1976), iii–92.

"Research and Development in Industry 1974," *National Science Foundation* (January, 1975), iii–83.

"Research and Development in Industry 1971," *National Science Foundation* (January, 1972), iii–78.

"Research and Development in Industry 1973," *National Science Foundation* (January, 1974, iii–76.

"Research and Development in Industry 1972," *National Science Foundation* (January, 1973), iii–84.

"Research and Development," *Management International Review*, LXVII, 12 (December, 1978), 36.

"Road Maps of Industry," *The Conference Board* (June, 1975).

"Survey of Indirect Costs in Industrial R & D," *Research Management*, XIII (March, 1970), 169–176.

"Tax Classification of Limited Partnerships," *Harvard Law Review*, XC (1975), 745–762.

"Tax Classification of Limited Partnerships: The IRS Bombards the Tax Shelter," *New York University Law Review*, LII, 2 (May, 1977), 408–441.

"Tax Exempt Organization and Limited Partnerships," *Taxes*, LIV, 6 (June, 1976), 334–344.

"Tax Predictability in Limited Partnerships Financing—The Need for Certainty in Investment Decisions," *Taxes*, LV, 11 (November, 1977), 745–753.

"Tax Reform—1978," *Journal of Real Estate Taxation*, V, 4 (Summer, 1978), 354–357.

"Taxation—Research and Experimental Expenditures—Section 174 distinguished from Section 162," *Missouri Law Review*, XL (Fall, 1975), 685–691.

"Technology and Jobs: The Vital Link is Weakening," *Dun's Review*, CX (July, 1977), 25, 28.

"$30 Billion for Research," *Industrial Research*, XIV (January, 1972), 50–53.

"$38.1 Billion for 1976 R & D," *Industrial Research*, XVIII (August, 1976), 13–14.

"$38.2 Billion for R & D," *Research/Development*, XXVII (January, 1976), 18–20.

"$35.4 Billion for R & D," *Research/Development*, XXVI (January, 1975), 18–20.

"$31 Billion for Research," *Industrial Research*, XV (January, 1973), 42–45.

"$28 Billion for Research," *Industrial Research*, XIII (January, 1971), 36–39.

"$27 Billion for Research," *Industrial Research*, XII (January, 1970), 46–49.

"23rd Annual McGraw-Hill Survey—Business' Plans for Research and Development Expenditure, 1978–81," Economics Department, McGraw-Hill Publications Company (May 22, 1978), 1–13.

"U.S. R & D Budgets are Looking Up: 14 Billion in 1975," *Chemical Marketing Reporter* (December 18, 1972), 40.

"U.S. R & D Spending Tops $40 Billion," *Industrial Research*, XIX (September, 1977), 78–79.

"U.S. R & D Will Get $40 Billion in 1977," *Industrial Research*, XIX (January, 1977), 52–54.

"Use Partnerships to Finance R & D," *INC.* (November, 1979), 46.

"Using R & D as a Guide to Corporate Profits," *Business Week* (May 24, 1978), 75.

"West Germany Boosts Research by One Fifth," *Nature*, CCLXXVII, 5696 (February 8, 1979), 423.

"What 600 Companies Spend for Research," *Business Week* (June 27, 1977), 62–84.

"When Will Research Pay Off in Profits," *Dun's Review*, C (October, 1972), 135.

"Where Private Industry Puts Its Research Money," *Business Week* (June 28, 1976), 62–84.

"Who Pays for New Project Development?" *Research Management*, XXI, 5 (September, 1978), 17–19.

"Why Profits May Be Better Than They Seem," *Business Week* (October 27, 1975), 28.

Daily Graphs (Summary of R & D Expenditures for New York Stock Exchange, American Stock Exchange, and Over-the Counter Companies).

Fortune (Merrill Lynch advertisement), C, 12 (December, 1979), 54.

International Encyclopedia of the Social Sciences, IX (1968), 581–585.

Journal of Accounting Research, XV (Autumn, 1977), 272–292.

New Research Centers, Issue No. 1 (June, 1979), 1–38.

Government Publications and Miscellaneous

Altman, Edward Ira. *Financial Ratios Discriminant Analysis and the Prediction of Corporate Bankruptcy*, New York University, School of Business, Reprint Series No. 79.

Altman, Edward Ira. *The Prediction of Corporate Bankruptcy: A Discriminant Analysis*, University of California, Los Angeles, 1967.

Barr, Hilyard C. *Placement Problems of an Independent Product Developer*, Los Angeles: Pepperdine University, School of Business and Management, (April, 1975), iii.

Dee, Robert F. "The Ship Called America" (speech) (October, 1978).

Matthews, Stephen Frank. *The Limited Partnership as an Investment Vehicle in Agriculture*. Columbia: University of Missouri, 1974.

Scott, Gerald C. (Conversation between Author & Scott; Technical Planning & Operations. Ford Motor Company, Dearborn, Michigan) (September 24, 1979).

Sigmund, Ojdana Edward Jr., D.B.A. Dissertation, *Dimensions of the Product Life Cycle*, University of Southern California, 1974.

"Distinction of Marketing—Technical Risks," (Confidential Offering Memorandum), 9, 31.

"A Survey of Active Investors," conducted for *The Wall Street Journal* (March, 1977).

Delorean Research Limited Partnership (Private Placement Memorandum), 117.

Directory of Companies Required to File Annual Reports with the Securities and Exchange Commission. June 30, 1977. Washington: U.S. Government Printing Office, 1977.

General Rules Under the Securities Act of 1933, Bowne & Co., Inc. (May, 1978).

Regulation "A" Under the Securities Act of 1933, Bowne and Co., Inc. (October, 1977).

Securities Act of 1933 As Amended (Public No. 22, 73rd Congress) (H.R. 5480), Bowne & Co., Inc.

Statistical Abstracts of the United States, 1977, Sec. 18, 557.

Department of the Treasury, IRS. *Statistics of Income, 1974: Business Income Tax Returns.* Publication 438 (7–77).

Department of the Treasury, IRS. *Statistics of Income, 1975: Business Income Tax Returns, Sole Partnerships*, 201.

Department of the Treasury, IRS. *Summary of Effects of T.R.A. 1976 on Tax Shelters: Preliminary Statistics of Income, 1976*, Publication 453 (10–78), 2.

Securities and Exchange Commission. Washington D.C. *Securities Act of 1933* Rule 24D (effective 3-15-75).

The Staff of the Joint Committee on Internal Revenue Taxation. *Tax Shelter: Use of Limited Partnerships, etc.* Prepared for the use of the Committee on Ways & Means. September 13, 1975. Washington: U.S. Government Printing Office, 1975.

In-House Publications

Critical Path Scheduling, The Service Bureau Company, a division of Control Data Corporation, Copyright © 1978, Control Data Corporation.

IBM Job Analysis System (JAS), First Edition, December, 1978.

Pert-O-Graph System, Halcomb Associates, 510 E. Maude Avenue, Sunnyvale, CA 94086.

Uniform Limited Partnership Act

(Adopted in every state except Louisiana)

Section 1. *(Limited Partnership Defined.)*

A limited partnership is a partnership formed by two or more persons under the provisions of Section 2, having as members one or more general partners and one or more limited partners. The limited partners as such shall not be bound by the obligations of the partnership.

Section 2. *(Formation.)*

(1) Two or more persons desiring to form a limited partnership shall
   (a) Sign and swear to a certificate, which shall state

   I.   The name of the partnership,
   II. The character of the business,
   III. The location of the principal place of business,
   IV. The name and place of residence of each member; general and limited partners being respectively designated,
   V.   The term for which the partnership is to exist,
   VI. The amount of cash and a description of and the agreed value of the other property contrubited by each limited partner,
   VII. The additional contributions, if any, agreed to be made by each limited partner and the times at which or events on the happening of which they shall be made,
   VIII. The time, if agreed upon, when the contribution of each limited partner is to be returned,
   IX. The share of the profits or the other compensation by way of income which each limited partner shall receive by reason of his contribution,
   X.   The right, if given, of a limited partner to substitute an assignee as contributor in his place, and the terms and conditions of the substitution,
   XI. The right, if given, of the partners to admit additional limited partners,
   XII. The right, if given, of one or more of the limited partners to priority over the other limited partners, as to contributions or as to compensation by way of income, and the nature of such priority,
   XIII. The right, if given, of the remaining general partner or partners to continue the business on the death, retirement or insanity of a general partner, and
   XIV. The right, if given, of a limited partner to demand and receive property other than cash in return for his contribution.

   (b) File for record the certificate in the office of (here designate the proper office).

(2) A limited partnership is formed if there has been substantial compliance in good faith with the requirements of paragraph (1).

Section 3.   *(Business Which May Be Carried On.)*

A limited partnership may carry on any business which a partnership without limited partners may carry on, except (here designate the business to be prohibited).

Section 4.   *(Character of Limited Partner's Contribution.)*

The contributions of a limited partner may be cash or other property, but not services.

Section 5.   *(A Name Not to Contain Surname of Limited Partner; Exceptions.)*

(1)   The surname of a limited partner shall not appear in the partnership name, unless
   (a) It is also the surname of a general partner, or
   (b) Prior to the time when the limited partner became such the business had been carried on under a name in which his surname appeared.
(2) A limited partner whose name appears in a partnership name contrary to the provisions of paragraph (1) is liable as a general partner to partnership creditors who extend credit to the partnership without actual knowledge that he is not a general partner.

Section 6.   *(Liability for False Statements in Certificate.)*

If the certificate contains a false statement, one who suffers loss by reliance on such statement may hold liable any party to the certificate who knew the statement to be false
   (a) At the time he signed the certificate, or
   (b) Subsequently, but within a sufficient time before the statement was relied upon to enable him to cancel or amend the certificate, or to file a petition for its cancellation or amendment as provided in Section 25(3).

Section 7.   *(Limited Partner Not Liable to Creditors.)*

A limited partner shall not become liable as a general partner unless, in addition to the exercise of his rights and powers as a limited partner, he takes part in the control of the business.

Section 8. (Admission of Additional Limited Partners.)

After the formation of a limited partnership, additional limited partners may be admitted upon filing an amendment to the original certificate in accordance with the requirements of Section 25.

Section 9. (Rights, Powers, and Liabilities of a General Partner.)

(1) A general partner shall have all the rights and powers and be subject to all the restrictions and liabilities of a partner in a partnership without limited partners, except that without the written consent or ratification of the specific act by all the limited partners, a general partner or all of the general partners have no authority to

(a) Do any act in contravention of the certificate,

(b) Do any act which would make it impossible to carry on the ordinary business of the partnership,

(c) Confess a judgment against the partnership,

(d) Possess partnership property, or assign their rights in specific partnership property, for other than a partnership purpose,

(e) Admit a person as a general partner,

(f) Admit a person as a limited partner, unless the right so to do is given in the certificate,

(g) Continue the business with partnership property on the death, retirement or insanity of a general partner, unless the right so to do is given in the certificate.

Section 10. (Rights of a Limited Partner.)

(1) A limited partner shall have the same rights as a general partner to

(a) Have the partnership books kept at the principal place of business of the partnership, and at all times to inspect and copy any of them,

(b) Have on demand true and full information of all things affecting the partnership, and a formal account of partnership affairs, whenever circumstances render it just and reasonable, and

(c) Have dissolution and winding up by decree of court.

(2) A limited partner shall have the right to receive a share of the profits or other compensation by way in income, and to the return of his contribution as provided in Sections 15 and 16.

Section 11. (Status of Person Erroneously Believing Himself a Limited Partner.)

A person who has contributed to the capital of a business conducted by a person or partnership erroneously believing that he has become a limited partner in a limited partnership, is not, by reason of his exercise of the rights of a limited partner, a general partner with the person or in the partnership carrying on the business, or bound by the obligations of such person or partnership; provided that on ascertaining the mistake he promptly renounces his interest in the profits of the business, or other compensation by way of income.

Section 12.   (One Person Both General and Limited Partner.)

(1) A person may be a general partner and a limited partner in the same partnership at the same time.

(2) A person who is a general, and also at the same time a limited partner, shall have all the rights and powers and be subject to all the restrictions of a general partner; except that, in respect to his contribution, he shall have the rights against the other members which he would have had if he were not also a general partner.

Section 13.   (Loans and Other Business Transactions with Limited Partner.)

(1) A limited partner also may loan money to and transact other business with the partnership, and, unless he is also a general partner, receive on account of resulting claims against the partnership, with general creditors, a pro rata share of the assets. No limited partner shall in respect to any such claim

    (a) Receive or hold as collateral security any partnership property, or

    (b) Receive from a general partner or the partnership any payment, conveyance, or release from liability, if at the time the assets of the partnership are not sufficient to discharge partnership liabilities to persons not claiming as general or limited partners,

(2) The receiving of collateral security, or a payment, conveyance, or release in violation of the provisions of paragraph (1) is fraud on the creditors or the partnership.

Section 14.   (Relation of Limited Partners Inter Se.)

Where there are several limited partners the members may agree that one or more of the limited partners shall have a priority over other limited partners as to the return of their contributions, as to their compensation by way of income, or as to any other matter. If such an agreement is made it shall be stated in the certificte, and in the absence of such a statement all the limited partners shall stand upon equal footing.

Section 15.   (Compensation of Limited Partner.)

A limited partner may receive from the partnership the share of the profits or the compensation by way of income stipulated for in the certificate; provided, that after such payment is made, whether from the property of the partnership or that of a general partner, the partnership assets are in excess of all liabilities of the partnership except liabilities to limited partners on account of their contributions and to general partners.

Section 16.   (Withdrawal or Reduction of Limited Partner's Contribution.)

(1) A limited partner shall not receive from a general partner or out of partnership property any part of his contribution until
  (a) All liabilities of the partnership, except liabilities to general partners and to limited partners on account of their contributions, have been paid or there remains property of the partnership sufficient to pay them,
  (b) The consent of all members is had, unless the return of the contribution may be rightfully demanded under the provisions of paragraph (2), and
  (c) The certificate is cancelled or so amended as to set forth the withdrawal or reduction.

(2) Subject to the provisions of paragraph (1) a limited partner may rightfully demand the return of his contribution
  (a) On the dissolution of a partnership, or
  (b) When the date specified in the certificate for its return has arrived, or
  . (c) After he has given six months' notice in writing to all other members, if no time is specified in the certificate either for the return of the contribution or for the dissolution or the partnership.

(3) In the absence of any statement in the certificate to the contrary or the consent of all members, a limited partner, irrespective of the nature of his contribution, has only the right to demand and receive cash in return for his contribution.

(4) A limited partner may have the partnership dissolved and its affairs wound up when
  (a) He rightfully but unsuccessfully demands the return of his contribution, or
  (b) The other liabilities of the partnership have not been paid, or the partnership property is insufficient for their payment as required by paragraph (1a) and the limited partner would otherwise by entitled to the return of his contribution.

Section 17.   (Liability of Limited Partner to Partnership.)

(1) A limited partner is liable to the partnership
  (a) For the difference between his contribution as actually made, and that stated in the certificate as having been made, or
  (b) For any unpaid contribution which he agreed in the certificate to make in the future at the time and on the conditions stated in the certificate.

(2) A limited partner holds as trustee for the partnership

(a) Specific property stated in the certificate as contributed by him, but which was not contributed or which has been wrongfully returned, and

(b) Money or other property wrongfully paid or conveyed to him on account of his contribution.

(3) The liabilities of a limited partner as set forth in this section can be waived or compromised only by the consent of all members; but a waiver or compromise shall not affect the right of a creditor of a partnership, who extended credit or whose claim arose after the filing and before a cancellation or amendment of the certificate, to enforce such liabilities.

(4) When a contributor has rightfully received the return in whole or in part of the capital of his contribution, he is nevertheless liable to the partnership for any sum, not in excess of such return with interest, necessary to discharge its liabilities to all creditors who extended credit or whose claims arose before such return.

Section 18.   (Nature of Limited Partner's Interest in Partnership.)

A limited partner's interest in the partnership is personal property.

Section 19.   (Assignment of Limited Partner's Interest.)

(1) A limited partner's interest is assignable.

(2) A substituted limited partner is a person admitted to all the rights of a limited partner who had died or has assigned his interest in a partnership.

(3) An assignee, who does not become a substituted limited partner, has no right to require any information or account of the partnership transaction or to inspect the partnership books; he is only entitled to receive the share of the profits or other compensation by way of income, or the return of his contribution, to which his assignor would otherwise be entitled.

(4) An assignee shall have the right to become a substituted limited partner if all the members (except the assignor) consent thereto or if the assignor, being thereunto empowered by the certificate, gives the assignee that right.

(5) An assignee becomes a substituted limited partner when the certificate is approriately amended in accordance with Section 25.

(6) The substituted limited partner has all the rights and powers, and is subject to all the restrictions and liabilities of his assignor, except those liabilities of which he was ignorant at the time he became a limited partner and which could not be ascertained from the certificate.

(7) The substitution of the assignee as a limited partner does not release the assignor from liability to the partnership under Sections 6 and 17.

Section 20.   (Effect of Retirement, Death or Insanity of a General Partner.)

The retirement, death or insanity of a general partner dissolves the partnership, unless the business is continued by the remaining general partners
  (a) Under a right so to do stated in the certificate, or
  (b) With the consent of all members.

Section 21.   (Death of Limited Partner.)

(1) On the death of a limited partner his executor or administrator shall have all the rights of a limited partner for the purpose of settling his estate, and such power as the deceased had to constitute his assignee a substituted limited partner.

(2) The estate of a deceased limited partner shall be liable for all his liabilities as a limited partner.

Section 22.   (Rights of Creditors of Limited Partner.)

(1) On due application to a court of competent jurisdiction by any judgment creditor of a limited partner, the court may charge the interest of the indebted limited partner, with payment of the unsatisfied amount of the judgment debt; and may appoint a receiver, and make all other orders, directions, and inquiries which the circumstances of the case may require.
   In those states where a creditor on beginning an action can attach debts due the defendant before he has obtained a judgment against the defendant it is recommended that paragraph (1) of this section read as follows:

> *On due application to a court of competent jurisdiction by any creditor or a limited partner, the court may charge the interest of the indebted limited partner with payment of the unsatisfied amount of such claim; and may appoint a receiver, and made all other orders, directions, and inquiries which the circumstances of the case may require.*

(2) The interest may be redeemed with the separate property of any general partner, but may not be redeemed with partnership property.

(3) The remedies conferred by paragraph (1) shall not be deemed exclusive of others which may exist.

(4) Nothing in this act shall be held to deprive a limited partner of his statutory exemption.

Section 23.   (Distribution of Assets.)

(1) In setting accounts after dissolution of the liabilities of the partnership shall be entitled to payment in the following order:

(a) Those to creditors, in the order of priority as provided by law, except those to limited partners on account of their contributions, and to general partners,

(b) Those to limited partners in respect to their share of the profits and other compensation by way of income on their contributions,

(c) Those to limited partners in respect to the capital of their contributions,

(d) Those to general partners other than for capital and profits,

(e) Those to general partners in respect to profits,

(f) Those to general partners in respect to capital.

(2) Subject to any statement in the certificate or to subsequent agreement, limited partners share in the partnership assets in respect to their claims for capital, and in respect to their claims for profits or for compensation by way of income on their contributions respectively, in proportion to the respective amounts of such claims.

Section 24.   (When Certificate Shall be Cancelled or Amended.)

(1) The certificate shall be cancelled when the partnership is dissolved or all limited partners cease to be such.

(2) A certificate shall be amended when

(a) There is a change in the name of the partnership or in the amount or character of the contribution of any limited partner,

(b) A person is substituted as a limited partner,

(c) An additional limited partner is admitted,

(d) A person is admitted as a general partner,

(e) A general partner retires, dies or becomes insane, and the business is continued under Section 20.

(f) There is a change in the character of the business of the partnership,

(g) There is a false or erroneous statement in the certificate,

(h) There is a change in the time as stated in the certificate for the dissolution of the partnership or for the return of a contribution,

(i) A time is fixed for the dissolution of the partnership, or the return of a contribution, no time having been specified in the certificate, or

(j) The members desire to make a change in any other statement in the certificate in order that it shall accurately represent the agreement between them.

Section 25.   (Requirements for Amendment and for Cancellation of Certificate.)

(1) The writing to amend a certificate shall

(a) Conform to the requirements of Section 2(1a) as far as necessary to set forth clearly the change in the certificate which it is desired to make, and

(b) Be signed and sworn to by all members, and an amendment substituting a limited partner or adding a limited or general partner shall be signed also by the member to be substituted or added, and when a limited partner is to substituted, the amendment shall also be signed by the assigning limited partner.

(2) The writing to cancel a certificate shall be signed by all members.

(3) A person desiring the cancellation or amendment of a certificate, if any person designated in paragraphs (1) and (2) as a person who must execute the writing refuses to do so, may petition the (here designate the proper court) to direct a cancellation or amendment thereof.

(4) If the court finds that the petitioner has a right to have the writing executed by a person who refuses to do so, it shall order the (here designate the responsible official in the office designated in Section 2) in the office where the certificate is recorded to record the cancellation or amendment of the certificate; and where the certificate is to be amended, the court shall also cause to filed for record in said office a certified copy of its decree setting forth the amendment.

(5) A certificate is amended or cancelled when there is filed for record in the office (here designate the office designated in Section 2) where the certificate is recorded

    (a) A writing in accordance with the provisions of paragraph (1), or (2) or

    (b) A certified copy of the order of court in accordance with the provisions of paragraph (4).

(6) After the certificate is duly amended in accordance with this section, the amended certificate shall there after be for all purposes the certificate provided for by this act.

Section 26. (Parties to Actions.)

A contributor, unless he is a general partner, is not a proper party to proceedings by or against a partnership, except where the object is to enforce a limited partner's right against or liability to the partnership.

Section 27. (Name of Act.)

This act may be cited as The Uniform Limited Partnership Act.

Section 28. (Rules of Construction.)

(1) The rule that statutes in derogation of the common law are to be strictly construed shall have no application to this act.

(2) This act shall be so interpreted and construed as to effect its general purpose to make uniform the law of those states which enact it.

(3) This act shall not be so construed as to impair the obligations of any

contract existing when the act goes into effect, nor to affect any action on proceedings begun or right accrued before this act takes effect.

Section 29.   (Rules for Cases Not Provided for in This Act.)

In any case not provided for in this act the rules of law and equity, including the law merchant, shall govern.

Section 30.[1]   (Provisions for Existing Limited Partnerships.)

(1) A limited partnership formed under any statute of this state prior to the adoption of this act, may become a limited partnership under this act by complying with the provisions of Section 2; provided the certificates sets forth

(a) The amount of the original contribution of each limited partner, and the time when the contribution was made, and

(b) That the property of the partnership exceeds the amount sufficient to discharge its liabilities to persons not claiming as general or limited partners by an amount greater than the sum of the contributions of its limited partners.

(2) A limited partnership formed under any statute of this state prior to the adoption of this act, until or unless it becomes a limited partnership under this act, shall continue to be governed by the provisions of (here insert proper reference to the existing limited partnership act or acts), except that such partnership shall not be renewed unless so provided in the original agreement.

Section 31.[1](Act (Acts) Repealed.)

Except as affecting existing limited partnerships to the extent set forth in Section 30, the act (acts) of (here designate the existing limited partnership act or acts) is (are) hereby repealed.

[1] Sections 30, 31, will be omitted in any state which has not a limited partnership act.

Revised Uniform Limited Partnership Act

Historical Note

The Revised Uniform Limited Partnership Act was approved by the National Conference of Commissioners on Uniform State Laws in 1976. It supersedes the original Uniform Limited Partnership Act approved by the Conference in 1916.

Commissioners' Prefatory Note

The Revised Uniform Limited Partnership Act adopted by the National Conference of Commissioners on Uniform State Laws in August, 1976, was intended to modernize the prior uniform law while retaining the special character of limited partnerships as compared with corporations. The draftsman of a limited partnership agreement has a degree of flexibility in defining the relations among partners that is not available in the corporate form. Moreover, the relationship among partners is consensual, and requires a degree of privity that forces the general partner to seek approval of the partners (sometimes unanimous approval) under circumstances that corporate management would find unthinkable. The limited partnership was not intended to be an alternative in all cases where corporate form is undesirable for tax or other reasons, and the new Act was not intended to make it so. The new Act clarifies many ambiguities and fills interstices in the prior uniform law by adding more detailed language and mechanics. In addition, some important substantive changes and additions have been made.

Article 1 provides a list of all the definitions used in the Act, integrates the use of limited partnership names with corporate names and provides for an office and agent for the service of process in the state of organization. All of these provisions are new. Article 2 collects in one place all provisions dealing with execution and filing of certificates of limited partnership and certificates of amendment and cancellation. Articles 1 and 2 reflects an important change in the statuatory scheme: recognition that the basic document in any partnership, including a limited partnership, is the partnership agreement. The certificate of limited partnership is not a constitutive document (except in the sense that it is a statutory prerequisite to creation of the limited partnership), and merely reflects matters as to which creditors should be put on notice.

Article 3 deals with the single most difficult issue facing lawyers who use the limited partnership form of organization: the powers and potential liabilities of limited partners. Section 303 lists a number of activities in which a limited partner may engage without being held to have so participated in the control of the business that he assumes the liability of a general partner. Moreover, it goes on to confine the liability of a limited partner who merely steps over the line of participation in control to persons who actually know of that participation in control. General liability for partnership debts is imposed only on those limited partners who are, in effect, "silent general partners." With that exception, the provisions of the new Act that impose liability on a limited partner who has somehow permitted third parties to be misled to their detriment as to the limited partner's true status confine that liability to those who have actually been misled. The provisions relating to general partners are collected in Article 4.

Article 5, the finance section makes some important changes from the prior uniform law. The contribution of services and promises to contribute cash, property or services are now explicitly permitted as contributions. And those who fail to perform promised services are required, in the absence of an agreement to the contrary, to pay the value of the services stated in the certificate of limited partnership.

A number of changes from the prior uniform law are made in Article 6, dealing with distributions from and the withdrawal of partners from the partnership. For example, Section 608 creates a statute of limitations on the right of a limited partnership to recover all or part of a contribution that has been returned to a limited partner, whether to satisfy creditors or otherwise.

The assignability of partnership interests is dealt with in considerable detail in Article 7. The provisions relating to dissolution appear in Article 8, which, among other things, imposes a new standard for seeking judicial dissolution of a limited partnership.

One of the thorniest questions for those who operate limited partnerships in more than one state of organization. Neither existing case law nor administrative practice make it clear whether the limited partners continue to possess their limited liability and which law governs the partnership. Article 9 deals with this problem by providing for registrations of foreign limited partnerships and specifying choice-by-law rules.

Finally, Article 10 of the new Act authorizes derivative actions to be brought by limited partners.

Caveat

At this time [May 1977], the provisions of this Act have not been ruled upon by the Internal Revenue Service. We advise any state or interested party to monitor the tax consequences carefully when considering it. Particularly, we suggest that a delayed effective date be inserted in any bills introduced. A substantially delayed effective date would permit an IRS ruling before that date with respect to an enactment, and would preclude any adverse consequences to those who might rely on the Act's provisions.

REVISED UNIFORM LIMITED PARTNERSHIP ACT (1976)

Article 1—General Provisions

Article 2—Formation: Certificate of Limited Partnership

Article 3—Limited Partners

Be it enacted. . .

Article 1

General Provisions

§101. [Definitions]

As used in this Act, unless the context otherwise requires:

(1) "Certificate of limited partnership" means the certificate referred to in Section 201, and the certificate as amended.

(2) "Contribution" means any cash, property, services rendered, or a promissory note or other binding obligation to contribute cash or property or to perform services, which a partner contributes to a limited partnership in his capacity as a partner.

(3) "Event of withdrawal of a general partner" means an event that causes a person to cease to be a general partner as provided in Section 402.

(4) "Foreign limited partnership" means a partnership formed under the laws of any State other than this State and having as partners one or more general partners and one or more limited partners.

(5) "General partner" means a person who has been admitted to a limited partnership as a general partner in accordance with the partnership agreement and named in the certificate of limited partnership as a general partner.

(6) "Limited partner" means a person who has been admitted to a limited partnership as a limited partner in accordance with the partnership agreement and named in the certificate of limited partnership as a limited partner.

(7) "Limited partnership" and "domestic limited partnership" means a partnership formed by 2 or more persons under the laws of this State and having one or more general partners and one or more limited partners.

(8) "Partner" means a limited or general partner.

(9) "Partnership agreement" means any valid agreement, written or oral, of the partners as to the affairs of a limited partnership and the conduct of its business.

(10) "Partnership interest" means a partner's share of the profits and losses of a limited partnership and the right to receive distributions of partnership assets.

(11) "Person" means a natural person, partnership, limited partnership (domestic or foreign), trust, estate, association, or corporation.

(12) "State" means a state, territory, or possession of the United States, the District of Columbia, or the Commonwealth of Puerto Rico.

Commissioners' Comment

The definitions in this section clarify a number of uncertainties in existing law and make certain changes.

Contribution: this definition makes it clear that a present contribution of services and a promise to make future payment of cash, contribution of property or performance of services are permissible forms for a contribution. Accordingly, the present services or promise must be accorded a value in the certificate or limited partnership (Section 201 (5)), and, in the case of a promise, that value may determine the liability of a partner who fails to honor his agreement (Section 502). Section 3 of the prior uniform law did not permit a limited partner's contribution to be in the form of services, although that inhibition did not apply to general partners.

Foreign limited partnership: the Act only deals with foreign limited partnerships formed under the laws of another "State" of the United States (see subdivision 12 of Section 101), and any adopting State that desires to deal by statute with the status of entities formed under the laws of foreign countries must make appropriate changes throughout the Act. The exclusion of such entities from the Act was not intended to suggest that their "limited partners" should not be accorded limited liability by the courts of a State adopting the Act. That question would be resolved by the choice-of-law rules of the forum State.

General partner: this definition recognizes the separate functions of the partnership agreement and the certficate of limited partnership. The partnership agreement establishes the basic grant of management power to the persons named as general partner; but because of the passive role played by the limited partners, the separate, formal step of embodying that grant of power in the certificate of limited partnership has been preserved to emphasize its importance.

Limited partner: as in the case of general partners, this definition provides for admission of limited partners through the partnership agreement and solemnization in the certificate of limited partnership is a prerequisite to limited partner status. Failure to file does not, however, mean that the participant is a general partner or that he has general liability. See Sections 202 (e) and 303.

Partnership agreement: the prior uniform law did not refer to the partnership agreement, assuming that all important matters affecting limited partners would be set forth in the certificate of limited partnership. Under modern practice, however, it has been common for the partners to enter into a comprehensive partnership agreement, only part of which was required to be included in the certificate of limited partnership. As reflected in Section 201, the certificate of limited partnership is confined principally to matters respecting the addition and withdrawal of partners and of capital, and other important issues are left to the partnership agreement.

Partnership interest: this definition is new and is intended to define what it is that is transferred when a partnership interest is assigned.

Library References

Partnership 349 et seq.
C.J.S. Partnership § 449 et seq.

§ 102. [*Name*]

The name of each limited partnership as set forth in its certificate of limited partnership:

(1) shall contain without abbreviation the words "limited partnership";

(2) may not contain the name of a limited partner unless (i) it is also the name of a general partner or the corporate name of a corporate general partner, or (ii) the business of the limited partnership had been carried on under that name before the admission of that limited partner;

(3) may not contain any word or phrase indicating or implying that it is organized other than for a purpose stated in its certificate or limited partnership;

(4) may not be the same as, or deceptively similar to, the name of any corporation or limited partnership organized under the laws of this State or licensed or registered as a foreign corporation or limited partnership in this State; and

(5) may not contain the following words [here insert prohibited words].

Commissioners' Comment

Subdivision (2) of Section 102 has been carried over from Section 5 of the prior uniform law with certain editorial changes. The remainder of Section 102 is new and primarily reflects the intention to integrate the registration of limited partnership names with that of corporate names. Accordingly, Section 201 provides for central, State-wide filling of certificates of limited partnership, and subdivisions (3), (4) and (5) of Section 102 contain standards to be applied by the filling officer in determining whether the certificate should be filed. Subdivision (1) requires that the proper name of a limited partnership contain the words "limited partnership" in full.

§ 103. [Reservation of Name]

(a) The exclusive right to use of a name may be reserved by:

(1) any person intending to organize a limited partnership under this Act and to adopt that name;

(2) any domestic limited partnership or any foreign limited partnership, registered in this State which, in either case, intends to adopt that name;

(3) any foreign limited partnership intending to register that name; and

(4) any person intending to organize a foreign limited partnership and intending to have it register in this State and adopt that name.

(b) The reservation shall be made by filing with the Secretary of State an application, executed by the applicant, to reserve a specified name. If the Secretary of State finds that the name is available for use by a domestic or foreign limited partnership, he shall reserve the name for the exclusive use of the applicant for a period of 120 days. Once having so reserved a name, the same applicant may not again reserve the same name until more than 60 days after the expiration of the last 120-day period for which that applicant reserved that name. The right to the exclusive use of a reserved name may be transferred to any other person by filing in the office of the Secretary of State a notice of the transfer, executed by the applicant for whom the name was reserved and specifying that name and address of the transferee.

Commissioners' Comment

Section 103 is new. The prior uniform law did not provide for registration of names.

§ 104. [*Specified Office and Agent*]

Each limited partnership shall continuously maintain in this State:

(1) an office, which may but need not be a place of business in this State, at which shall be kept the records required by Section 105 to be maintained; and

(2) an agent for service of process on the limited partnership, which agent must be an individual resident of this State, a domestic corporation, or a foreign corporation authorized to do business in this State.

Commissioners' Comment

Section 104 is new. It requires that a limited partnership have certain minimum contacts with its State of organization, i.e., an office at which the constitutive documents and basic financial information is kept and an agent for service of process.

§ 105. [*Records to be Kept*]

Each limited partnership shall keep at the office referred to in Section 104 (1) the following: (1) a current list of the full name and last known business address of each partner set forth in alphabetical order, (2) a copy of the certificate of limited partnership and all certificates of amendment thereto, together with executed copies of any powers of attorney pursuant to which any certificate has been executed, (3) copies of the limited partnership's federal, state, and local income tax returns and reports, if any, for the 3 most recent years, and (4) copies of any then effective written partnership agreements and of any financial statements of the limited partnership for the 3 most recent years. Those records are subject to inspection and copying at the reasonable request, and at the expense, of any partner during ordinary business hours.

Commissioners' Comment

Section 105 is new. In view of the passive nature of the limited partner's position, it has been widely felt that limited partners are entitled to access to certain basic documents, including the certificate of limited partnership and any partnership agreement. In view of the great diversity among limited partnerships, it was thought inappropriate to require a standard form of financial report, and Section 105 does no more than require retention of tax returns and any other financial statements that are prepared. The names and addresses of the partners are made available to the general public.

§106. [*Nature of Business*]

A limited partnership may carry on any business that a partnership without limited partners may carry on except [here designate prohibited activities].

Commissioners' Comment

Section 106 is identical to Section 3 of the prior uniform law. Many states require that certain regulated industries, such as banking, may be carried on only by entities organized persuant to special statutes, and it is contemplated that the prohibited activities would be confined to the matters covered by those statutes.

§ 107. [*Business Transactions of Partner with the Partnership*]

Except as provided in the partnership agreement, a partner may lend money to and transact other business with the limited partnership and, subject to other applicable law, has the same rights and obligations with respect thereto as a person who is not a partner.

Commissioners' Comment

Section 107 makes a number of important changes in Section 13 of the prior uniform law. Section 13, in effect, created a special fraudulent conveyance provision applicable to the making of secured loans by limited partners and the repayment by limited partnerships of loans from limited partners. Section 107 leaves that question to a State's general fraudulent conveyance statute. In addition, Section 107 eliminates the prohibition in former Section 13 against a general partner (as opposed to a limited partner) sharing pro rata with general creditors in the case of an unsecured loan. Of course, other doctrines developed under bankruptcy and insolvency laws may require the subordination of loans by partners under appropriate circumstances.

Article 2

Formation: Certificate of Limited Partnership

§ 201. [*Certificate of Limited Partnership*]

(a) In order to form a limited partnership two or more persons must execute a certificate of limited partnership. The certificate shall be filed in the office of the Secretary of State and set forth:

(1) the name of the limited partnership;

(2) the general character of its business;

(3) the address of the office and the name and address of the agent for service of process required to be maintained by Section 104;

(4) the name and the business address of each partner (specifying separately the general partners and limited partners);

(5) the amount of cash and a description and statement of the agreed value of the other property or services contributed by each partner and which each partner has agreed to contribute in the future;

(6) the times at which or events on the happening of which any additional contributions agreed to be made by each partner are to be made;

(7) any power of a limited partner to grant the right to become a limited partner to an assignee of any part of his partnership interest, and the terms and conditions of the power;

(8) if agreed upon, the time at which or the events on the happening of which a partner may terminate his membership in the limited partnership and the amount of, or the method of determining, the distribution to which he may be entitled respecting his partnership interest, and the terms and conditions of the termination and distribution;

(9) any right of a partner to receive distribution of property, including cash from the limited partnership;

(10) any right of a partner to receive, or of a general partner to make, distributions to a partner which include a return of all or any part of the partner's contribution;

(11) any time at which or events upon the happening of which the limited partnership is to be dissolved and its affairs wound up;

(12) any right of the remaining general partners to continue the business on the happening of an event of withdrawal of a general partner; and

(13) any other matters the partners determine to include therein.

(b) A limited partnership is formed at the time of the filing of the certificate of limited partnership in the office of the Secretary of State or at any later time specified in the certificate of limited partnership if, in either case, there has been substantial compliance with the requirements of this section.

Commissioners' Comment

The matters required to be set forth in the certificate of limited partnership are not different in kind from those required by Section 2 of the prior uniform law, although certain additions and deletions have been made and the description has been revised to conform with the rest of the Act. In general, the certificate is intended to serve two functions: first, to place creditors on notice of the facts concerning the capital of the partnership and the rules regarding additional contributions to and withdrawals from the partnership; second, to clearly delineate the time at which persons become general partners and limited partners. Subparagraph (b), which is based upon the prior uniform law, has been retained to make it clear that the existence of the limited partnership depends only upon the compliance with this section. Its continued existence is not dependent upon compliance with other provisions of this Act.

Library References

Partnership 354.
C.J.S. Partnership §§ 455, 458, 460.

§ 202. [*Amendment to Certificate*]

(a) A certificate of limited partnership is amended by filing a certificate of amendment thereto in the office of the Secretary of State. The certificate shall set forth:

(1) the name of the limited partnership;
(2) the date of filing of the certificate; and
(3) the amendment of the certificate.

(b) Within 30 days after the happening of any of the following events an amendment to a certificate of limited partnership reflecting the occurrence of the event or events shall be filed:

(1) a change in the amount or character of the contribution of any partner, or in any partner's obligation to make a contribution;
(2) the admission of a new partner;
(3) the withdrawal of a partner; or
(4) the continuation of the business under Section 801 after an event of withdrawal of a general partner.

(c) A general partner who becomes aware that any statement in a certificate of limited partnership was false when made or that any arrangements or other facts described have changed making the certificate inaccurate in any respect, shall promptly amend the certificate, but an amendment to show a change of address of a limited partner need be filed only once every 12 months.

(d) A certificate of limited partnership may be amended at any time for any proper purpose the general partners may determine.

(e) No person has any liability because an amendment to a certificate of limited partnership has not been filed to reflect the occurrence of any event referred to in subsection (b) of this Section if the amendment is filed within the 30-day period specified in subsection (b).

Commissioners' Comment

Section 202 makes substantial changes in Section 24 of the prior uniform law. Paragraph (b) lists the basic events—the addition or withdrawal of partners or capital or capital obligations—that are so central to the function of the certificate of limited partnership that they require prompt amendment. Paragraph (c) makes it clear, as it was not clear under subdivision (2) (g) of former Section 24, that the certificate of limited partnership is intended to be an accurate description of the facts to which it relates at all times and does not speak merely as of the date it is executed. Paragraph (e) provides a "safe harbor" against claims of creditors or others who assert that they have been misled by the failure to amend the certificate of limited partnership to reflect changes in any of the important facts refered to in paragraph (b); if the certificate of limited partnership is amended within 30 days of the occurrence or the event, no creditor or other person can recover for damages sustained during the interim. Additional protection is afforded by the provisions of Section 304.

§ 203. [Cancellation of Certificate]

A certificate of limited partnership shall be cancelled upon the dissolution and the commencement of winding up of the partnership or at any other time there are no limited partners. A certificate of cancellation shall be filed in the office of the Secretary of State and set forth:

(1) the name of the limited partnership;

(2) the date of filing of its certificate of limited partnership;

(3) the reason for filing the certificate of cancellation;

(4) the effective date (which shall be a date certain of cancellation if it is not to be effective upon the filing of the certificate; and

(5) any other information the general partners filing the certificate determine.

Commissioners' Comment

Section 203 changes Section 24 of the prior uniform law by making it clear that the certificate of cancellation should be filed upon the commencement of winding up of the limited partnership. Section 24 provided for cancellation "when the partnership is dissolved."

§ 204. [Execution of Certificates]

(a) Each certificate required by this Article to be filed in the office of the Secretary of State shall be executed in the following manner:

(1) an original certificate of limited partnership must be signed by all partners named therein;

(2) a certificate of amendment must be signed by at least one general partner and by each other partner designated in the certificate as a new partner or whose contribution is described as having been increased; and

(3) a certificate of cancellation must be signed by all general partners;

(b) Any person may sign a certificate by an attorney-in-fact, but a power of attorney to sign a certificate relating to the admission, or increased contribution, of a partner must be specifically describe the admission or increase.

(c) The execution of a certificate by a general partner constitutes an affirmation under the penalties of perjury that the facts stated therein are true.

Commissioners' Comments

Section 204 collects in one place the formal requirements for the execution of certificates which were set forth in Section 2 and 25 of the prior uniform law. Those sections required that each certificate be signed by all partners, and there developed an unnecessarily cumbersome practice of having each limited partner sign powers of attorney to authorize the general partners to execute certificates of amendment on their behalf. Section 204 insures that each partner must sign a certificate when he becomes a partner or when the certificates reflect any increase in his obligation to make contributions. Certificates of amendment are required to be signed by only one general partner and all general partners must sign certificates of cancellation. Section 204 prohibits blanket powers of attorney for the execution of certificates in many cases, since those conditions under which a partner is required to sign have been narrowed to circumstances of special importance to that partner. The former requirement that all certificates be sworn has been confined to statements by the general partners, recognizing that the limited partner's role is a limited one.

§ 205. [*Amendment or Cancellation by Judicial Act*]

If a person required by Section 204 to execute a certificate of amendment or cancellation fails or refuses to do so, any other partner, and any assignee of a partnership interest, who is adversely affected by the failure or refusal, may petition the [here designate the proper court] to direct the amendment or cancellation. If the court finds that the amendment or cancellation is proper and that any peron so designated has failed or refused to execute the certificate, it shall order the Secretary of State to record an appropriate certificate of amendment or cancellation.

Commissioners' Comment

Section 205 changes subdivisions (3) and (4) of Section 25 of the prior uniform law by confining the persons who have standing to seek judicial intervention to partners and to those assignees who are adversely affected by the failure or refusal of the appropriate persons to file a certificate of amendment or cancellation.

§ 206. [*Filing in Office of Secretary of State*]

(a) Two signed copies of the certificate of limited partnership and of any certificates of amendment or cancellation (or of any judicial decree of amendment or cancellation) shall be delivered to the Secretary of State. A person who executes a certificate as an agent or fiduciary need not exhibit evidence of his authority as a prerequisite to filing. Unless the Secretary of State finds that any certificate does not conform to law, upon receipt of all filing fees required by law he shall:

(1) endorse on each duplicate original the word "Filed" and the day, month, and year of the filing thereof;

(2) file one duplicate original in his office; and

(3) return the other duplicate original to the person who filed it or his representative.

(b) Upon the filing of a certificate of amendment (or judicial decree of amendment) in the office of the Secretary of State, the certificate of limited partnership shall be amended as set forth therein, and upon the effective date of a certificate of cancellation (or a judicial decree thereof), the certificate of limited partnership is cancelled.

Commissioners' Comment

Section 206 is new. In addition to providing mechanics for the central filing system, the second sentence of this section does away with the requirement, formerly imposed by some local filing officers, that persons who have executed certificates under a power of attorney exhibit executed copies of the power of attorney itself. Paragraph (b) changes subdivision (5) of Section 25 of the prior uniform law by providing that certificates of cancellation are effective upon their effective date under Section 203.

Library References

Partnership 354.
C.J.S. Partnership § 459.

§ 207. [Liability for False Statement in Certificate]

If any certificate of limited partnership or certificate of amendment or cancellation contains a false statement, one who suffers loss by reliance on the statement may recover damages for the loss from:

(1) any person who executes the certificate, or causes another to execute it on his behalf, and knew, and any general partner who knew or should have known, the statement to be false at the time the certificate was executed; and

(2) any general partner who thereafter knows or should have known that any arrangement or other fact described in the certificate has changed, making the statement inaccurate in any respect within a sufficient time before the statement was relied upon reasonable to have enabled that general partner to cancel or amend the certificate, or to file a petition for its cancellation or amendment under Section 205.

Commissioners' Comment

Section 207 changes Section 6 of the prior uniform law by providing explicitly for the liability of persons who sign a certificate as agent under a power of attorney and by confining the obligation to amend a certificate of limited partnership in light of future events to general partners.

§ 208. [Notice]

The fact that a certificate of limited partnership is on file in the office of the Secretary of State is notice that the partnership is a limited partnership and the persons designated therein as limited partners are limited partners, but it is not notice of any other fact.

Commissioners' Comment

Section 208 is new. By stating that the filing of a certificate of limited partnership only results in notice of the limited liability of the limited partners, it obviates the concern that third parties may be held to have notice of special provisions set forth in the certificate. While this section is designed to preserve the limited liability of limited partners, the notice provided is not intended to change any liability of a limited partner which may be created by his action or inaction under the law of estoppel, agency, fraud, or the like.

Library References

Partnership 357.
C.J.S. Partnership § 459.

§ 209. [*Delivery of Certificates to Limited Partners*]

Upon the return by the Secretary of State pursuant to Section 206 of a certificate marked "filed," the general partners shall promptly deliver or mail a copy of the certificate of limited partnership and each certificate to each limited partner unless the partnership agreement provides otherwise.

Commissioners' Comment

This section is new.

Article 3

Limited Partners

§ 301. [*Admission of Additional Limited Partners*]

(a) After the filing of a limited partnership's original certificate of limited partnership, a person may be admitted as an additional limited partner:

(1) in the case of a person acquiring a partnership interest directly from the limited partnership, upon the compliance with the partnership agreement or, if the partnership agreement does not so provide, upon the written consent of all partners; and

(2) in the case of an assignee of a partnership interest of a partner who has the power, as provided in Section 704, to grant the assignee the right to become a limited partner, upon the exercise of that power and compliance with any conditions limiting the grant or exercise of the power.

(b) In each case under subsection (a), the person acquiring the partnership interest becomes a limited partner only upon amendment of the certificate of limited partnership reflecting that fact.

Commissioners' Comment

Subdivision (1) of Section 301 (a) adds to Section 8 of the prior uniform law an explicit recognition of the fact that unanimous consent of all partners is required for admission of new limited partners unless the partnership agreement provides otherwise. Subdivision (2) is derived from Section 19 of the prior uniform law but abondons the former terminology of "substituted limited partner."

Library References

Partnership 363.
C.J.S. Partnership §§ 464, 474.

§ 302. [*Voting*]

Subject to Section 303, the partnership agreement may grant all or a specified group of the limited partners the right to vote (on a per capita or other basis) upon any matter.

Commissioners' Comment

Section 302 is new, and must be read together with subdivision (b) (5) of Section 303. Although the prior uniform law did not speak specifically of the voting powers of limited partners, it is not uncommon for partnership agreements to grant such power to limited partners. Section 302 is designed only to make it clear that the partnership agreement may grant such power to limited partners. If such powers are granted to limited partners beyond the "safe harbor" of Section 303 (b) (5), a court may hold that, under the circumstances, the limited partners have participated in "control of the business" within the meaning of Section 303 (a). Section 303(c) simply means that the exercise of powers beyond the ambit of Section 303 (b) is not ipso facto to be taken as taking part in the control of the business.

Library References

Partnership 366.
C.J.S. Partnership §§ 469 ET SEQ.

§ 303. [*Liability to Third Parties*]

(a) Except as provided in subsection (d), a limited partner is not liable for the obligations of a limited partnership unless he is also a general partner, he takes part in the control of the business. However, if the limited partners participation in the control of the business is not substantially the same as the exercise of the powers of a general partner, he is liable only to persons who transact business with the limited partnership with actual knowledge of his participation in control.

(b) A limited partner does not participate in the control of the business within the meaning of subsection (a) solely by doing one or more of the following:

(1) being a contractor for an agent or employee of the limited partnership or of a general partner;

(2) consulting with and advising a general partner with respect to the business of the limited partnership;

(3) acting as surety for the limited partnership;

(4) approving or disapproving an amendment to the partnership agreement; or

(5) voting on one or more of the following matters:

(i) the dissolution and winding up of the limited partnership;

(ii) the sale, exchange, lease, mortgage, pledge, or other transfer of all or substantially all of the assets of the limited partnership other than in the ordinary course of its business;

(iii) the incurrence of indebtedness by the limited partnership other than in the ordinary course of its business;

(iv) a change in the nature of the business or;

(v) the removal of a general partner.

(c) The enumeration in subsection (b) does not mean that the possession or exercise of any other powers by a limited partner constitutes participation by him in the business of the limited partnership.

(d) A limited partner who knowingly permits his name to be used in the name of the limited partnership, except under circumstances permitted by Section 102(2) (i), is liable to creditors who extend credit to the limited partnership without actual knowledge that the limited partner is not a general partner.

§ 304. [*Person Erroneously Believing Himself Limited Partner*]

(a) Except as provided in subsection (b), a person who makes a contribution to a business enterprise and erroneously but in good faith believes that he has become a limited partner in the enterprise is not a general partner in the enterprise and is not bound by its obligations by reasons of making the contribution, receiving distributions from the enterprise, or exercising any rights of a limited partner, if, on ascertaining the mistake, he:

(1) causes an appropriate certificate of limited partnership or a certificate of amendment to be executed and filed; or

(2) withdraws from future equity participation in the enterprise.

(b) A person who makes a contribution of the kind described in subsection (a) is liable as a general partner to any third party who transacts business with the enterprise (i) before the person withdraws and an appropriate certificate is filed to show withdrawal, or (ii) before an appropriate certificate is filed to show his status as a limited partner, and in the case of an amendment, after expiration of the 30-day period for filing an amendment relating to the person as a limited partner under Section 202, but in either case only if the third party actually believed in good faith that the person was a general partner at the time of the transaction.

Commissioners' Comment

Section 304 is derived from Section 11 of the prior uniform law. The "good faith" requirement has been added in the first sentence of Section 304(a). The provisions of subdivision (2) of Section 304(a) are intended to clarify an ambiguity in the prior law by providing that a person who chooses to withdraw from the enterprise in order to protect himself from liability is not required to renounce any of his then current interest in the enterprise so long as he has no further participation as an equity participant. Paragraph (b) preserves the liability of the equity participant prior to withdrawal (and after the time for appropriate amendment in the case of a limited partnership) to any third party who has transacted business with the person believing in good faith that he was a general partner.

Library References

Partnership 371.
C.J.S. Partnership § 476 et seq.

§ 305. [Information]

Each limited partner has the right to:

(1) inspect and copy any of the partnership records required to be maintained by Section 105; and

(2) obtain from the general partners from time to time upon reasonable demand (i) true and full information regarding the state of the business and financial condition of the limited partnership, (ii) promptly after becoming available, a copy of the limited partnership's federal, state, and local income tax returns for each year, and (iii) other information regarding the affairs of the limited partnership as is just and reasonable.

Commissioners' Comment

Section 305 changes and restates the rights of limited partners to information about partnership formerly provided by Section 10 of the prior uniform law.

Library References

Partnership 366.
C.J.S. Partnership § 469 et seq.

Article 4

General Partners

§ 401. [*Admission of Additional General Partners*]

After the filing of a limited partnership's original certificate of limited partnership, additional general partners may be admitted only with the specific written consent of each partner.

Commissioners' Comment

Section 401 is derived from Section 9 (1) (e) of the prior law and carries over the unwaivable requirements that all limited partners must consent to the admission of an additional general partner and that such consent must specifically identify the general partner involved.

Library References

Partnership 363.
C.J.S. Partnership §§ 464, 474.

§ 402. [*Events of Withdrawal*]

Except as approved by the specific written consent of all partners at the time, a person ceases to be a general partner of a limited partnership upon the happening of any of the following events:

(1) the general partner withdraws from the limited partnership as provided in Section 602;

(2) the general partner ceases to be a member of the limited partnership as provided in Section 702;

(3) the general partner is removed as a general partner in accordance with the partnership agreement;

(4) unless otherwise provided in the certificate of limited partnership, the general partner:

(i) makes an assignment for the benefit of creditors;

(ii) files a voluntary petition in bankruptcy;

(iii) is adjudicated a bankrupt or insolvent;

(iv) files a petition or answer seeking for himself any reorganization, arrangement, composition, readjustment, liquidation, dissolution, or similar relief under any statute, law, or regulation;

(v) files an answer or other pleading admitting or failing to contest the material allegations of a petition filed against him in any proceeding of this nature; or

(vi) seeks, consents to, or acquiesces in the appointment of a trustee, receiver, or liquidator of the general partner or of all or any substantial part of his properties;

(5) unless otherwise provided in the certificate of limited partnership, [120] days after the commencement of any proceeding against the general partner seeking reorganization, arrangement, composition, readjustment, liquidation, dissolution, or similar relief under any statute, law, or regulation, the proceeding has not been dismissed, or if within [90] days after the appointment without his consent or acquiescence of a trustee, receiver, or liquidator of the general partner or of all or of any substantial part of his properties, the appointment is not vacated or stayed, or within [90] days after the expiration of any such stay, the appointment is not vacated;

(6) in the case of a general partner who is a natural person,

(i) his death; or

(ii) the entry by a court of competent jurisdiction adjudicating him incompetent to manage his person or his estate;

(7) in the case of a general partner who is acting as a general partner by virtue of being a trustee, the termination of the trust (but not merely the substitution of a new trustee);

(8) in the case of a general partner that is a separate partnership, the dissolution and commencement of winding up of the separate partnerhsip;

(9) in the case of a general partner that is a corporation, the filing of a certificate of dissolution, or its equivalent, for the corporation or the revocation of its charter; or

(10) in the case of an estate, the distribution by the fiduciary of the estate's entire interest in the partnership.

Commissioners' Comment

Section 402 expands considerably the provisions of Section 20 of the prior uniform law which provided for dissolution in the event of the retirement, death or insanity of a general partner. Subdivisions (1), (2) and (3) recognize that the general partner's agency relationship is terminable at will, although it may result in a breach of the partnership agreement giving rise to an action for damages. Subdivisions (4) and (5) reflect a judgment that, unless the limited partners agree otherwise, they ought to have the power to rid themselves of a general partner who is in such dire financial straits that he is the subject of proceedings under the National Bankruptcy Act or a similar provision of law. Subdivisions (6) through (10) simply elaborate on the notion of death in the case of a general partner who is not a natural person. Of course, the addition of the words "and in the partnership agreement" was not intended to suggest that liabilities to third parties could be affected by provisions in the partnership agreement.

§ 403. [*General Powers and Liabilities*]

Except as provided in the Act or in the partnership agreement, a general partner of a limited partnership has the rights and powers and is subject to the restrictions and liabilities of a partner in a partnership without limited partners.

Commissioners' Comment

Section 403 is derived from Section 9 (1) of the prior uniform law.

Library References

Partnership 367 et seq.
C.J.S. Partnership §§ 475, 482.

§ 404. [*Contributions by a General Partner*]

A general partner of a limited partnership may make contributions to the partnership and share in the profits and losses of, and in distributions from, the limited partnership as a general partner. A general partner also may make contributions to and share in profits, losses, and distributions as a limited partner. A person who is both a general partner and a limited partner has the rights and powers, and is subject to the restriction and liabilities, or a general partner and, except as provided in the partnership agreement, also has the powers, and is subject to the restrictions, or a limited partner to the extent of his participation in the partnership as a limited partner.

Commissioners' Comment

Section 404 is derived from Section 12 of the prior uniform law and makes clear that the partnership agreement may provide that a general partner who is also a limited partner may exercise all of the powers of a limited partner.

Library References

Partnership 355.
C.J.S. Partnership § 456.

§ 405. [*Voting*]

The partnership agreement may grant to all or certain identified general partners the right to vote (on a per capita or any other basis), separately or with all or any class of the limited partners, on any matter.

Commissioners' Comment

Section 405 is new and is intended to make it clear that the Act does not require that the limited partners have any right to vote on matters as a separate class.

Library References

Partnership 366.
C.J.S. Partnership § 469 et seq.

Article 5

Finance

§ 501. [*Form of Contribution*]

The contribution of a partner may be in cash, property, or services rendered, or a promissory note or other obligation to contribute cash or property or to perform services.

Commissioners' Comment

As noted in the comment to Section 101, the explicit permission to make contributions of services expands Section 4 of the prior uniform law.

Library References

Partnership 355.
C.J.S. Partnership § 456.

§ 502. [*Liability for Contributions*]

(a) Except as provided in the certificate of limited partnership, a partner is obligated to the limited partnership to perform any promise to contribute cash or property or to perform services, even if he is unable to perform because of death, disability or any other reason. If a partner does not make the required contribution of property or services, he is obligated at the option of the limited partnership to contribute cash equal to that portion of the value (as stated in the certificate of limited partnership) of the stated contribution has not been made.

(b) Unless otherwise provided in the partnership agreement, the obligation of a partner to make a contribution or return money or other property paid of distributed in violation of this Act may be compromised only by consent of all the partners. Notwithstanding the compromise, a creditor of a limited partnership who extends credit, or whose claim arises, after the filing of the certificate of limited partnership or an amendment thereto which, in either case, reflects the obligations, and before the amendment or cancellation thereof to reflect the compromise, may enforce the original obligation.

Commissioners' Comment

Although Section 17(1) of the prior uniform law required a partner to fulfill his promise to make contributions, the addition of contributions in the form of a promise to render services means that a partner who is unable to perform those services because of disability as well as because of an intentional default is required to pay the cash value of the services unless the certificate of limited partnership provides otherwise. Subdivision (b) is derived from Section 17(3) of the prior uniform law.

§ 503. [*Sharing of Profits and Losses*]

The profits and losses of a limited partnership shall be allocated among the partners, and among classes of partners, in the manner provided in the partnership agreement. If the partnership agreement does not so provide, profits and losses shall be allocated on the basis of the value (as stated in the certificate of limited partnership) of the contributions made by each partner to the extent they have been received by the partnership and have not been returned.

Commissioners' Comment

Section 503 is new. The prior uniform law did not provide for the basis on which partners share profits and losses in the absence of agreement.

Library References

Partnership 366.
C.J.S. Partnership § 469 et seq.

§ 504. [*Sharing of Distribution*]

Distributions of cash or other assets of a limited partnership shall be allocated among the partners, and among classes of partners, in the manner provided in the partnership agreement. If the partnership agreement does not so provide, distributions shall be made on the basis of the value (as stated in the certificate of limited partnership) of the contributions made by each partner to the extent they have been received by the partnership and have not been returned.

Commissioners' Comment

Section 504 is new. The prior uniform law did not provide for the basis on which partners share distributions in the absence of agreement. This section also recognizes that partners may choose to share in distribution on a different basis than any share in profits and losses.

Library References

Partnership 364, 366.
C.J.S. Partnership § 469, et seq.

Article 6

Distributions and Withdrawal

§ 601. [*Interim Destributions*]

Except as provided in this Article, a partner is entitled to receive distributions from a limited partnership before his withdrawal from the limited partnership and before the dissolution and winding up thereof:

(1) to the extent and at the times or upon the happening of the events specified in the partnership agreement; and
(2) if any distribution constitutes a return of any part of his contribution under Section 608(b), to the extent and at the times or upon the happening of the events specified in the certificate of limited partnership.

Commissioners' Comment

Section 601 is new.

Library References

Partnership 364, 367, 376.
C.J.S. Partnership §§ 471, 475, 482, 488.

§ 602. [*Withdrawal of General Partner*]

A general partner may withdraw from a limited partnership at any time by giving written notice to the other partners, but if the withdrawal violated the partnership agreement, the limited partnership may recover form the withdrawing general partner damages for the breach of the partnership agreement and offset the damages against the amoung otherwise distributable to him.

Commissioners' Comment

Section 602 is new but is generally derived from Section 38 of the Uniform Partnership Act.

Library References

Partnership 363, 364.
C.J.S. Partnership §§ 464, 471, 474.

§ 603. [*Withdrawal of Limited Partner*]

A limited partner may withdraw from a limited partnership at the time or upon the happening of events specified in the certificate of limited partnership and in accordance with the partnership agreement. If the certificate does not specify the time or the events upon the happening of which a limited partner may withdraw or a definite time for the dissolution and winding up of the limited partnership, a limited partner may withdraw upon not less than 6 months' prior written notice to each general partner at his address on the books of the limited partnership at its office in this State.

Commissioners' Comment

Section 603 is derived from Section 16(c) of the prior uniform law.

Library References

Partnership 363, 364.
C.J.S. Partnership §§ 464, 471, 474.

§ 604. [*Distribution Upon Withdrawal*]

Except as provided in this Article, upon withdrawal any withdrawing partner is entitled to recieve any distribution to which he is entitled under the partnership agreement and, if not otherwise provided in the agreement, he is entitled to receive, within a reasonable time after withdrawal, the fair value of his interest in the limited partnership as of the date of withdrawal based upon his right to share in distribution from the limited partnership.

Commissioners' Comment

Section 604 is new. It fixes the distributive share of a withdrawing partner in the absence of an agreement among the partners.

Library References

Partnership 364, 367.
C.J.S. Partnership §§ 471, 475, 482.

§ 605. [*Distribution in Kind*]

Except as provided in the certificate of limited partnership, a partner, regardless of the nature of his contribution, has no right to demand and receive any distribution from a limited partnership in any form other than cash. Except as provided in the partnership agreement, a partner may not be compelled to accept a distribution of any asset in kind from a limited partnership to the extent that the percentage of the asset destributed to him exceeds a percentage of that asset which is equal to the percentage in which he shared in distribution from the limited partnership.

Commissioners' Comment

The first sentence of Section 605 is derived from Section 16(3) of the prior uniform law. The second sentence is new, and is intended to protect a limited partner (and the remaining partners) against a distribution in kind of more than his share of particular assets.

Library References

Partnership 364.
C.J.S. Partnership § 471.

§ 606. [*Right to Destribution*]

At the time a partner becomes entitled to receive a distribution, he has the status of, and is entitled to all remedies available to, a creditor of the limited partnership with respect to the distribution.

Commissioners' Comment

Section 606 is new and is intended to make it clear that the right of a partner to receive a distribution, as between the partners, is not subject to the equity risks of the enterprise. On the other hand, since partners entitled to distributions have creditor status, there did not seem to be a need for the extraordinary remedy of Section 16(4) (a) of the prior uniform law, which granted a limited partner the right to seek dissolution of the partnership if he was unsuccessful in demanding the return of his contribution. It is more appropriate for the partner to simply sue as an ordinary creditor and obtain a judgment.

Library References

Partnership 364, 367.
C.J.S. Partnership §§ 471, 475, 482.

§ 607. [*Limitations on Distribution*]

A partner may not receive a distribution from a limited partnership to the extent that, after giving effect to the distribution, all the liabilities of the limited partnership, other than liabilities to partners on account of their partnership interests, exceed the fair value of the partnership assets.

Commissioners' Comment

Section 607 is derived from Section 16(1) (a) of the prior uniform law.

§ 608. [*Liability Upon Return of Contribution*]

(a) If a partner has received the return of any part of his contribution without violation of the partnership agreement or this Act, he is liable to the limited partnership for a period of one year thereafter for the amount of the returned contribution, but only to the extent necessary to discharge the partnership during the period the contribution was held by the partnership, limited partnership's liabilities to creditors who extended credit to the limited.

(b) If a partner has received the return of any part of his contribution in violation of the partnership agreement or this Act, he is liable to the limited partnership for a period of 6 years thereafter for the amount of the contribution wrongfully returned.

(c) A partner receives a return of his contribution to the extent that a distribution to him reduces his shares of the fair value of the net assets of the limited partnership below the value (as set in the certificate of limited partnership) of his contribution which has not been distributed to him.

Commissioners' Comment

Paragraph (a) is derived from Section 17(4) of the prior uniform law, but the one-year statute of limitations has been added. Par-

agraph (b) is derived from Section 17(2) (b) of the prior uniform
law but, again, a statute of limitations has been added. Paragraph
(c) is new. The provisions of former Section 17(2) that referred
to the partner holding as "trustee any money or specific property
wrongfully returned to him" have been eliminated.

Article 7

Assignment of Partnership Interests

§ 701. [*Nature of Partnership Interest*]

A partnership interest is personal property.

Commissioners' Comment

This section is derived from Section 18 of the prior uniform
law.

Library References

Partnership 363.
C.J.S. Partnership §§ 471, 475, 482.

§ 702. [*Assignment of Partnership Interest*]

Except as provided in the partnership agreement, a partnership interest is
assignable in whole or in part. An assignment of a partnership interest does
not dissolve a limited partnership or entitle the assignee to become or to
exercise any rights of a partner. An assignment entitles the assignee to
receive, to the extent assigned, only the distribution to which the assignor
would be entitled. Except as provided in the partnership agreement, a partner
ceases to be a partner upon assignment of all his partnership interest.

Commissioners' Comment

Section 19(1) of the prior uniform law provided simply that "a
limited partner's interest is assignable," raising a question whether
any limitations on the right of assignment were permitted. While
the first sentence of Section 702 recognizes that the power to
assign may be restricted in the partnership agreement, there was
no intention to affect in any way the usual rules regarding re-
straints on alienation of personal property. The second and third
sentences of Section 702 are derived from Section 19 (3) of the
prior uniform law. The last sentence is new.

Library References

Partnership 363.
C.J.S. Partnership §§ 464, 474.

§ 703. [*Rights of Creditor*]

On application to a court of competent jurisdiction by any judgment creditor of a partner, the court may charge the partnership interest of the partner with payment of the unsatisfied amount of the judgment with interest. To the extent so charged, the judgment creditor has only the rights of an assignee of the parntership interest. This Act does not deprive any partner of the benefit of any exemption laws applicable to his partnership interest.

Commissioners' Comment

Section 703 is derived from Section 22 of the prior uniform law but has not carried some provisions that were thought to be superfluous. For example, references in Section 22(1) to specific remedies have been omitted, as has a prohibition in Section 22(2) against discharge of the lien with partnership property. Ordinary rules governing the remedies available to a creditor and the fiduciary obligations of general partners will determine those matters.

Library References

Partnership 371.
C.J.S. Partnership § 476 et seq.

§ 704. [*Right of Assignee to Become Limited Partner*]

(a) An assignee of a partnership interest, including an assignee of a general partner, may become a limited partner if and to the extent that (1) the assignor gives the assignee that right in accordance with authority described in the certificate of limited partnership, or (2) all other partners consent.

(b) An assignee who has become a limited partner has, to the extent assigned, the rights and powers, and is subject to the restrictions and liabilities, of a limited partner under the partnership agreement and this Act. An assignee who becomes a limited partner also is liable for the obligations of his assignor to make and return contributions as provided in Article 6. However, the assignee is not obligated for liabilities unknown to the assignee at the time he became a limited partner and which could not be ascertained from the certificate of limited partnership.

(c) If an assignee of a partnership interest becomes a limited partner, the assignor is not released from his liability to the limited partnership under Sections 207 and 502.

Commissioners' Comment

Section 704 is derived from Section 19 of the prior uniform law, but paragraph (b) defines more narrowly that Section 19 the obligations of the assignor that are automatically assumed by the assignee.

Partnership 363.
C.J.S. Partnership §§ 464, 474.

§ 705. [*Power of Estate of Deceased or Incompetent Partner*]

If a partner who is an individual dies or a court of competent jurisdiction adjudges him to be imcompetent to manage his person or his property, the partner's executory, administrator, guardian, conservator, or other legal representative may exercise all of the partner's rights for the purpose of settling his estate of administering his property including any power the partner had to give an assignee the right to become a limited partner. If a partner is a corporation, trust, or other entity and is dissolved or terminated, the powers of that partner may be exercised by its legal representative or successor.

Commissioners' Comment

Section 705 is derived from Section 21(1) of the prior uniform law. Former Section 21(2), making a deceased limited partner's estate liable for his liabilities as a limited partner was deleted as superfluous, with no intention of changing the liability of the estate.

Article 8

Dissolution

§ 801. [*Nonjudicial Dissolution*]

A limited partnership is dissolved and its affairs shall be wound up upon the happening of the first to occur of the following:

(1) at the time or upon the happening of events specified in the certificate of limited partnership;

(2) written consent of all partners;

(3) an event of withdrawal of a general partner unless at the time there is at least one other general partner and the certificate of limited partnership permits the business of the limited partnership to be carried on by the remaining general partner and that partner does so, but the limited partnership is not dissolved and is not required to be wound up by reason of any event of withdrawal if, within 90 days after the withdrawal, all partners agree in writing to continue the business of the limited partnership and to the appointment of one or more additional general partners if necessary or desired; or

(4) entry of a decree of judicial dissolution under Section 802.

Commissioners' Comment

Section 801 merely collects in one place all of the events causing dissolution. Paragraph (3) is derived from Section 9(1)(g) and 20 of the prior uniform law, but adds the 90-day grace period.

Library References

Partnership 376.
C.J.S. Partnership §§ 488, 489.

§ 803. [*Winding Up*]

Except as provided in the partnership agreement, the general partners who have not wrongfully dissolved a limited partnership or, if none, the limited partners, may wind up the limited partnership's affairs: but the [here designate the proper court] court may wind up the limited partnership's affairs upon application of any partner, his legal representative, or assignee.

Commissioners' Comment

Section 803 is new and is derived in part from Section 37 of the Uniform General Partnership Act.

§ 804. [*Distribution of Assets*]

Upon the winding up of a limited partnership, the assets shall be distributed as follows:

(1) to creditors, including partners who are creditors, to the extent otherwise permitted by law, in satisfaction of liabilities of the limited partnership other than liabilities for destributions to partners under Section 601 or 604;

(2) except as provided in the partnership agreement, to partners and former partners in satisfaction of liabilities for distributions under Section 601 or 604; and

(3) except as provided in the partnership agreement, to partners first for the return of their contributions and secondly respecting their partnership interests, in the proportions in which the partners share in distributions.

Commissioners' Comment

Section 804 revises Section 23 of the prior uniform law by providing that (1) to the extent partners are also creditors, other than in respect to their interests in the partnership, they share with other creditors, (2) once the partnership's obligation accrues, it must be paid before any other distributions of an "equity" nature are made, and (3) general and limited partners rank on the same level except as otherwise provided in the partnership agreement.

Article 9

Foreign Limited Partnerships

§ 901. [*Law Governing*]

Subject to the Constitution of this State, (1) the laws of the state under which a foreign limited partnership is organized govern its organization and internal affairs and the liability of its limited partners, and (2) a foreign limited partnership may not be denied registration by reason of any difference between those laws and the laws of this State.

Commissioners' Comment

Section 901 is new.

Library References

Partnership 350.
C.J.S. Partnership § 451.

§ 902. [*Registration*]

Before transacting business in this State, a foreign limited partnership shall register with the Secretary of State. In order to register, a foreign limited partnership shall submit to the Secretary of State, in duplicate, an application for registration as a foreign partnership, signed and sworn to by a general partner and setting forth:

(1) the name of the foreign limited partnership and, if different, the name under which it proposes to register and transact business in this State;

(2) the state and date of its formation;

(3) the general character of the business it proposes to transact in this State;

(4) the name and address of any agent for service of process on the foreign limited partnership whom the foreign limited partnership elects to appoint; the agent must be an individual resident of this State, a domestic corporation, or a foreign corporation having a place of business in, and authorized to do business in this State;

(5) a statement that the Secretary of State is appointed the agent of the foreign limited partnership for service of process if no agent has been appointed under paragraph (4) or, if appointed, the agent's authority has been revoked or if the agent cannot be found or served with the exercise of reasonable diligence;

(6) the address of the office required to be maintained in the State of its organization by the laws of that State or, if not so required, of the principle office of the foreign limited partnership; and

(7) if the certificate of limited partnership filed in the foreign limited partnership's state of organization is not required to include the names and business addresses of the partners, a list of the names and addresses.

Commissioners' Comment

Section 902 is new. It was thought that requiring a full copy of the certificate of limited partnership and all amendments thereto to be filed in each state in which the partnership does business would impose an unreasonable burden on interstate limited partnerships and that the information on file was sufficient to tell interested persons where they could write to obtain copies of these basic documents.

Library References

Partnership 354, 357.
C.J.S. Partnership §§ 455, 458, 459, 460.

§ 903. [Issuance of Registration]

(a) If the Secretary of State finds that an application for registration conforms to law and all requisite fees have been paid, he shall:

(1) endorse on the application the word "Filed," and the month, day, and year of the filing thereof;

(2) file in his office a duplicate original of the application; and

(3) issue a certificate of registration to transact business in this State.

(b) The certificate of registration, together with a duplicate original of the application, shall be returned to the person who filed the application or his representative.

Library References

Partnership 354, 357.
C.J.S. Partnership §§ 455, 458, 459, 460.

§ 904. [Name]

A foreign limited partnership may register with the Secretary of State under any name (whether or not it is the name under which it is registered in its state of organization) that includes without abbreviation the words "limited partnership" and that could be registered by a domestic limited partnership.

Section 904 is new.

Partnership 358.
C.J.S. Partnership § 462.

§ 905. [*Changes and Amendments*]

If any statement in the application for registration of a foreign limited partnership was false when made or any arrangements or other facts described have changed, making the application inaccurate in any respect, the foreign limited partnership shall promptly file in the office of the Secretary of State a certificate, signed and sworn to by a general partner, correcting such statement.

Section 905 is new.

Partnership 354.
C.J.S. Partnership §§ 455, 458, 460.

§ 906. [*Cancellation of Registration*]

A foreign limited partnership may cancel its registration by filing with the Secretary of State a certificate of cancellation signed and sworn to by a general partner. A cancellation does not terminate the authority of the Secretary of State to accept service of process on the foreign limited partnership with respect to [claims for relief] [causes of action] arising out of the transaction of business in this State.

Section 906 is new.

Partnership 354, 357.
C.J.S. Partnership §§ 455, 458, 459, 460.

§ 907. [*Transaction of Business Without Registration*]

(a) A foreign limited partnership transacting business in this State may not maintain any action, suit, or proceeding in any court of this State until it has registered in this State.

(b) The failure of a foreign limited partnership to register in this State does not impair the validity of any contract or act of the foreign limited partnership or prevent the foreign limited partnership from defending any action, suit, or proceeding in any court of this State.

(c) A limited partner of a foreign limited partnership is not liable as a general partner of the foreign limited partnership solely by reason of having transacted business in this State without registration.

(d) A foreign limited partnership, by transacting business in this State without registration, appoints the Secretary of State as its agent for service of process with respect to [claims for relief] [causes of action] arising out of the transaction of business in this State.

Commissioners' Comment

Section 907 is new.

Library References

Partnership 362.
C.J.S. Partnership §§ 461, 465.

§ 908. [Action by [Appropriate Official]]

The [appropriate official] may bring action to restrain a foreign limited partnership from transacting business in this State in violation of this Article.

Commissioners' Comment

Section 908 is new.

Library References

Injunction 89(5).
C.J.S. Injunctions §§ 133 to 135.

Article 10

Derivative Actions

§ 1001. [Right of Action]

A limited partner may bring an action in the right of a limited partnership to recover a judgment in its favor if general partners with authority to do so have refused to bring the action or if an effort to cause those general partners to bring the action is not likely to succeed.

Commissioners' Comment

Section 1001 is new.

§ 1002. [*Proper Plaintiff*]

In a derivative action, the plaintiff must be a partner at the time of bringing the action and (1) at the time of the transaction of which he complains or (2) his status as a partner and devolved upon him by operation of law or pursuant to the terms of the partnership agreement from a person who was a partner at the time of the transaction.

Commissioners' Comment

Section 1002 is new.

§ 1003. [*Pleading*]

In a derivative action, the complaint shall set forth with particularity the effort of the plaintiff to secure initiation of the action by a general partner or the reasons for not making the effort.

Commissioners' Comment

Section 1003 is new.

§ 1004. [*Expenses*]

If a derivative action is successful, in whole or in part, or if anything is received by the plaintiff as a result of a judgment, compromise, or settlement of an action or claim, the court may award the plaintiff reasonable expenses, including reasonable attorney's fees, and shall direct him to remit to the limited partnership the remainder of those proceeds received by him.

Commissioners' Comment

Section 1004 is new.

Article 11

Miscellaneous

§ 1101. [*Construction and Application*]

This act shall be so applied and construed to effectuate its general purpose to make uniform the law with respect to the subject of this Act among states enacting it.

§ 1102. [*Short Title*]

This Act may be cited as the Uniform Limited Partnership Act.

§ 1103. [*Severability*]

If any provision of this Act or its application to any person or circumstance is held invalid, the invalidity does not affect other provisions or applications of the Act which can be given effect without the invalid provision or application, and to this end the provisions of this Act are severable.

§ 1104. [*Effective Date, Extended Date and Repeal*]

Except as set forth below, the effective date of this Act is _____ and the following Acts [list prior limited partnership acts] are hereby repealed.

(1) The existing provisions for execution and filing of certificates of limited partnerships and amendments thereunder and cancellations thereof continue in effect until [specify time required to create central filing system], the extended effective date, and Sections 102, 103, 104, 105, 201, 202, 203, 204 and 206 are not effective until the extended effective date.

(2) Section 402, specifying the conditions under which a general partner ceases to be a member of a limited partnership, is not effective until the extended effective date, and the applicable provisions of existing law continue to govern until the extended effective date.

(3) Sections 501, 502 and 608 apply only to contributions and distributions made after the effective date of this Act.

(4) Section 704 applies only to assignments made after the effective date of this Act.

(5) Article 9, dealing with registration of foreign limited partnerships, is not effective until the extended effective date.

§ 1105. [*Rules for Cases Not Provided for in This Act*]

In any case not provided for in this Act the provisions of the Uniform Partnership Act govern.

APPENDIX C

California Blue Sky Laws

REGULATIONS

Subarticle 11.

Oil and Gas Interests

(¶8609)

260.140.120. Application. The rules in this subarticle shall govern the qualification of oil and gas programs in the form of limited partnerships (herein sometimes called "programs") and will be applied by analogy to oil and gas programs in other forms. While applications not conforming to the standards contained herein shall be looked upon with disfavor, where good cause is shown certain guidelines may be modified or waived by the Commissioner.

NOTE: Authority cited: Section 25610, Corporations Code. Reference 25140, Corporations Code.

History: 1. Repealer of Subarticle 11 (Sections 260.140.121–260.140.124), Article 4, and new Subarticle 11 (Sections 260.140.120–260.140.131.9), Article 4 filed 12–6–74; effective thirtieth day thereafter (Register 74, No. 49).

(¶8610)

260.140.121. Definitions. The following definitions are applicable to this subarticle.

(a) "Affiliate" means (1) any person directly or indirectly controlling, controlled by or under common control with another person, (2) a person owning or controlling 10% or more of the outstanding voting securities of such other person, (3) any officer or director of such other person and (4) if such other person is an officer or director, any company for which such person acts in any such capacity.

(b) "Area of Interest" means a geologically described region in which a program intends to conduct its oil and gas exploration activities. The area of interest of a program shall not include less than all of any known producing geologic structure, or oil or gas field which is contained in the description of such area of interest, except that if good cause is shown, the Commissioner may allow an area of interest to exclude any lands adjacent thereto which are within any inland body of water or the coastal waters of the United States or any state.

(c) "Assessment" means any additional amounts of capital which a participant may be called upon to furnish, voluntarily or mandatorily, beyond his subscription.

(d) "Capital Contribution" means the total investment, including the original investment, assessments and reinvested amounts, in a program by a participant or by all participants, as the case may be.

(e) "Cost," when used with respect to property in Section 260.140.127.1 means (1) the sum of the prices paid by the seller for such property; (2) title insurance or examination costs, brokers' commissions, filing fees, recording costs, transfer taxes, if any, and like charges in connection with the acquisition of such property; and (3) bonuses, rentals ad valorem taxes paid by the seller with respect to such property to the date of its transfer to the buyer, interest on funds used to acquire or maintain such property, and such portion of the seller's expenses for geological, geophysical, seismic, land engineering, drafting, accounting, legal and other like services allocated to the property in accordance with generally accepted accounting principles, except for expenses in connection with the drilling of wells which are not producers of sufficient quantities of oil or gas to make commercially reasonable their continued operations, and provided that such expenses shall have been incurred not more than 36 months prior to the purchase by the program. When used with respect to services, "cost" means the expense incurred by the seller in providing such services, determined in accordance with generally accepted accounting principles. As used elsewhere, "cost" means the price paid by the seller in an arm's-length transaction.

(f) "Net Worth" means the excess of total assets over total liabilities as determined in accordance with generally accepted accounting principles.

(g) "Oil and Gas Interest" means any oil or gas royalty or lease, or fractional interest therein, or certificate of interest or participation or investment contract relative to such royalties, leases or fractional interests, or any other interest or right which permits the exploration of, drilling for, or production of oil and gas or other related hydrocarbons or the receipt of such production or the proceeds thereof.

(h) "Overriding Royalty" means an interest severed out of the lessee's working interest entitling its owner to a fraction of production free of the expense of production.

(i) "Participant" means the holder of a unit.

(j) "Partnership Agreement" means the limited partnership agreement of a program.

(k) "Program" means a limited or general partnership, joint venture, unincorporated association or similar organization, formed, or to be formed, for the primary purpose of exploring for oil, gas and other hydrocarbon substances or investing in or holding any interests which permit the exploration for or production of oil or gas or the receipt of such production or the proceeds thereof.

(l) "Prospect" of a program means an area in which such program owns or intends to own one or more oil and gas interests, which is geographically defined on the basis of geological data by the sponsor of such program and which is reasonably anticipated by the sponsor to contain at least one reservoir. Such area shall be enlarged or contracted on the basis of geological data to define the productive limits of such reservoir and must include all of the territory encompassed by any such reservoir.

(m) "Prospectus" shall have the meaning given to that term by Section 2(10) of the Securities Act of 1933, as amended, including a preliminary prospectus; provided, however, that such term as used herein shall also include an offering circular as described in Rule 256 of the General Rules and Regulations under the Securities Act of 1933, as amended, or, in the case of an intra-state offering, any document by whatever name known, utilized for the purpose of offering and selling units.

(n) "Reservoir" means a separate structural or stratigraphic trap containing an accumulation of oil or gas.

(o) "Sponsor" means any person directly or indirectly instrumental in organizing a program or any person who will manage or participate in the management of a program, including the general partner(s) and any other person who, pursuant to a contract with the program, regularly performs or selects the person who performs 25% or more of the exploratory, developmental or producing activities of the program, or segment thereof. "Sponsor" does not include wholly independent third parties such as attorneys, accountants, and underwriters whose only compensation is for professional services rendered in connection with the offering of units.

(p) "Subscription" means the original committed investment (excluding assessments) to a program by a participant upon its formation.

(q) "Tangible Costs" means those costs which are generally accepted as capital expenditures pursuant to the provisions of the Internal Revenue Code.

(r) "Unit" means an interest in a program.

(s) "Working Interest" means the operating interest under an oil and gas interest which carries with it the obligation to bear a proportionate share of all costs thereon.

Sponsor's Requirements

(¶8611)

260.140.122.1. Experience. The general partner or its chief operating officers shall have at least three years relevant oil and gas experience demonstrating the knowledge and experience to carry out the stated program policies and to manage the program operations. Additionally, the general partner or any affiliate providing services to the program shall have had not less than four years relevant experience in the kind of service being rendered or otherwise must demonstrate sufficient knowledge and experience to perform the services proposed. If any managerial responsibility for the program is to be rendered by persons other than the general partner, then such persons must be identified in the prospectus, their experience must be similar to that required of a general partner and must be set out in the prospectus, and a contract setting forth the basis of their relationship with the program must be filed with and not disapproved by the Commissioner.

(¶8611A)

260.140.122.2. Net Worth. (a) The financial condition of the general partner must be commensurate with any financial obligations assumed by it. The general partner must specifically have a minimum aggregate net worth at all times at least equal to the greater of (1) $100,000 or (2) the lesser of $1,000,000 or 5% of the total subscriptions made by participants in all existing programs organized by the general partner, including the one being offered.

(b) In determining the general partner's net worth, the value of proven reserves, as determined by an independent petroleum engineer, of oil, gas and other minerals owned by a general partner may be used. Notes and accounts receivables from all programs, interests in all programs, and all contingent liabilities will be scrutinized carefully to determine the appropriateness of their inclusion in the net worth computation.

(c) If more than one person acts or serves as general partner of a program, the net worth requirements may be met by aggregating the net worth of any persons. In addition, the net worth of any guarantor of the general partner's obligations to or for the program may be included in the net worth computations, but only if the guarantor's liability is coextensive with that of the general partner.

(¶8611B)

260.140.122.3. Reports to Commissioner. The partnership agreement shall require that the sponsor file with the Commissioner, concurrently with their transmittal to participants, a copy of each report made pursuant to Section 260.140.128.3 of these rules.

Participant Suitability

(¶8612)

260.140.123.1. Suitability Standards. In view of the limited transferability, the relative lack of liquidity, the high risk of loss or the specific tax orientation of many oil and gas programs, suitability standards which are reasonably related to the risks to be undertaken, will be required for the participants, and they must be set forth in a writing to be executed by all participants. It will be the responsiblity of the sponsor and the persons selling units to see that units are sold only to participants meeting the applicable suitability standards.

We have been informed that the Securities Division will apply the same standards in judging the R & D Limited Partnership as in Oil and Gas Interests.

(¶8612A)

260.140.123.2. Presumptive Suitability Standards. (a) Unless circumstances warrant and the Commissioner allows another standard, suitability standards for participants shall be presumptively reasonable if all of the following criteria are met.

(1) the participant has a net worth of $200,000 or more (exclusive of home, furnishings and automobilies), or

(2) the participant has a net worth of $50,000 or more (exclusive of home, furnishings, and automobiles) and had during the last tax year, or estimates that he will have during the current tax year, "taxable income" as defined in Section 63 of the Internal Revenue Code of 1954, as amended, some portion of which was or will be subject to federal income tax at a rate of 50% of more, without regard to the investment in the program.

(b) In the case of programs engaged primarily in investing in income producing properties (production purchase programs) the Commissioner may allow lower suitability standards than those described in Subsection (a). Subject to a satisfactory showing as to the plan of business of the program and the value of properites acquired or proposed to be acquired, the following suitability standards will be deemed reasonable if:

(1) the participant has a net worth of $75,000 or more (exclusive of home, furnishings and automobiles), or

(2) the participant has a net worth of $25,000 or more (exclusive of home, furnishings and automobiles) and an annual income of $20,000 or more.

(c) In the case of qualification by coordination, the application for such qualification should be accompanied by an undertaking by the issuer and underwriter to the limit sales in California to an identified class meeting these standards, together with a statement of the method to be employed in meeting this requirement.

(¶8612B)

260.140.123.3. Sales to Appropriate Persons. (a) In addition to the objective standards of suitability set forth in Section 260.140.123.2, it will be the responsibility of the sponsor and each person selling units to make every reasonable effort to see that such securities are an appropriate investment for the participants.

(b) Persons selling units shall specifically ascertain by means of a writing that the offering is appropriate for each participant. In doing so, such persons must determine that each participant or his representative has the capacity to understand the fundamental aspects of the program.

(c) Persons selling units shall, also, ascertain by means of a writing that the participants understand (when applicable):

(1) the risks involved in the offering, including the speculative nature of the investment;

(2) the financial hazards involved in the offering, including the risk of losing their entire investment;

(3) the lack of liquidity of units;

(4) the restrictions on transferability of units;

(5) the background and qualifications of the sponsor and/or the manager or persons responsible for the offering; and

(6) the tax consequences of the investment.

(d) All of the requirements of this section may be satisfied by the use of the same writing filed with and not disapproved as to form by the Commissioner and properly executed by each participant.

(¶8612C)

260.140.123.4. Maintenance of Suitability Records. The sponsor shall maintain for a period of at least four years a record of the information obtained to indicate that a participant meets the suitability standards established in connection with the offer and sale of the program units. In addition, he must obtain a representation from each participant that he has purchased units for his own account or, in lieu of such representation, information indicating that the participants for whose account the purchase was made met such suitability standards. Such information may be obtained from the participant through inclusion of such statment in the writing described in Section 260.140.123.3. of these rules. If units are sold by a broker-dealer, the sponsor shall obtain a commitment from the broker-dealer to the effect that such broker-dealer will obtain and maintain in its files the record of information which otherwise would have been required of the sponsor.

(¶8612D)

260.140.123.5. Minimum Investment. (a) The participant is required to make a minimum subscription to the program of at least $5,000, except that in the case of an offering being made pursuant to Regulation B under the Securities Act of 1933, the minimum subscription for pre-completion costs may be $1,500, and except in the case of an offering consisting of a series of limited partnerships to be formed during a consecutive 12-month period, the minimum subscription may be $5,000 for the entire series.

(b) Subsequent transfers of such units shall be limited to no less than a minimum unit equivalent to an initial minimum subscription except for transfers, which do not require a Commissioner's consent pursuant to Section 260.141.11 of these rules.

(¶8612E)

260.140.123.6. Installment Payments. (a) Provisions for deferred payments on account of the purchase price of program units may be allowed when warranted by the investment objectives of the program, but in any event such arrangements shall be subject to the following conditions:

(1) Installment payments, subsequent to the initial payment required by the terms of the offering, shall be made in not more than 3 payments and the full amount of the purchase price shall be paid not later than 9 months after the date on which such programs commence operations.

(2) Selling commissions payable on the units shall be paid only as and when the allocable part of the purchase price is paid by the participant.

(3) Such installments shall be contractually binding obligations of the buyer whether or not a promissory note is taken.

(4) If a promissory note is taken, the program shall not sell or assign it at a discount.

(b) In the event of a default in the payment of any installment due on an installment sale, the participant's percentage interest in the program should not be subject to forfeiture, but may be subject to a reasonable penalty for failure of the participant to meet his commitment. Provisions which conform to the following will be considered reasonable:

(1) A proportionate reduction of the participant's percentage interest in the program based on the ratio of his unpaid capital contribution as to the total capital contribution of all participants in the program; or,

(2) A subordination of the defaulting participant's right to receive revenues from the program until those non-defaulting participants who have paid the defaulting participant's assessment have received an amount of revenues from all revenues of the program equal to 300% of the proportionate amount of the defaulted capital contribution which they paid.

(¶8613)

260.140.124. Selling Commissions, Selling Expenses and Offering Costs. (a) Selling expenses of programs are subject to Section 260.140.20 of these rules and should not exceed 15% of the initial subscriptions. Management fees or payments for so-called management services are considered as additional promotional compensation and ordinarily will not be permitted.

(b) Commissions payable on the sale of program units shall be paid in cash based solely on the amount of initial subscriptions. Payment of commissions in the form of overriding royalties, net profit interests or other interests in production ordinarily will not be approved, except that no objection will be raised to the payment of commissions in the form of working interests in property of the program, provided the amount does not exceed that purchasable by applying the aggregate cash commission allowable to the unit offering price.

(c) All items of compensation to underwriters or dealers, including but not limited to, selling commissions, expenses, rights of first refusal, consulting fees, finders' fees and all other items of compensation of any kind or description paid by the program, directly or indirectly, shall be taken into consideration in computing the amount of allowable selling commissions.

(d) As an alternative to the provisions of Subsection (a) above, a sponsor may elect to receive twelve and one-half percent (12 1/2%) of the initial subscriptions to a program (excluding assessments) provided (i) that all selling expenses are paid by the sponsor, and (ii) that the receipt by the sponsor of said twelve and one-half percent (12 1/2%) and the payment of all selling expenses by the sponsor shall be fully set forth in the prospectus. Selling expenses as used in this Subsection means the total underwriting and brokerage discounts and commissions (including fees of the underwriters' attorneys) paid in connection with the offering and all other expenses actually incurred in connection with the offer and sale of the units, including expenses for printing, engraving, mailing, salaries of employees while engaged in sales activity, charges of transfer agents, registrars, trustees, escrow holders, depositaries, and engineers and other experts, expenses of qualification of the sale of the securities under Federal and State laws, including taxes and fees, accountants' and attorneys' fees.

(¶8614)

260.140.125. Sponsor's Compensation. The total amount of compensation of all kinds to the sponsor should be reasonable in the light of nature of the exploration and development proposed, the nature of the services to be provided by the sponsor and the identity of the participants. A landowner's royalty or an overriding royalty or other interests paid to persons unconnected with the program as consideration for the acquisition of properties for the program shall not be deemed to be sponsor's compensation.

(¶8614A)

260.140.125.1. Compensation Arrangements. Any form of compensation arrangement that conforms to the following standards shall be considered presumptively reasonable for a sponsor who actively participates in obtaining a significant portion of a program's prospects and who assumes management responsibility for drilling, completing, equipping and operating a significant portion of the program's wells.

(a) Cost and Revenue Sharing. The sponsor may elect a compensation arrangement where he shares in revenue on a basis related to certain costs paid by him.

(1) Where the sponsor agrees to pay all tangible costs of the program but in any case at least 10% of the total program's capital contribution, even if the tangible costs otherwise payable are less than such 10%, his share of revenue will be determined by the following formula:

(A) If the agreement is to pay all tangible costs, but in any case a sum of not less than 10% of the capital contributions of the program, the sponsor is entitled to receive 35% of the program revenues;

(B) If the agreement is to pay all tangible costs, but in any case a sum of not less than 15% of the capital contributions of the program, the sponsor is entitled to receive 40% of program revenues; and

(C) The sponsor's revenue sharing may be increased in additional increments of 5%, for each additional 5% increase in the percentage of capital contribution agreed to be paid by him, up to a maximum of 50% of revenues, subject to the sponsor's agreement to pay in any case all tangible costs.

(2) As an alternative to Subdivision (1), the sponsor may elect to receive 15% of revenues and an additional percentage of revenues determined by computing the sponsor's tangible costs as compared to total costs associated with obtaining production, on a prospect basis, until such time as the sponsor shall have received from such additional percentage of revenues an amount equal to his tangible costs; after which, revenues shall be distributed as follows: 15% of revenues to the sponsor and 85% of revenues to the participants until the participants shall have received on a program basis a return of their capital contributions and then, 15% plus the additional percentage of revenues shall be paid to the sponsor and the remainder to the participants.

(3) The agreement to pay tangible costs should include tangible costs for development during the life of the program. If the sponsor should enter into farm-out or other arrangements through which he is relieved of his obligation to pay for tangible costs, then the sponsor's share of revenue authorized by Subdivision (1) or (2) of this Section shall be determined on an individual basis. Any such variation from the basic format described in either of said Subdivisions shall be fully disclosed in the application for qualification and must be approved in advance of the effectiveness of the qualification.

(4) In order to elect either of the sharing arrangements authorized by Subdivisions (1) and (2) hereof, the following conditions must be met:

(A) the sponsor has a net worth of $300,000 or 10% of the total contributions to the program by the participants, whichever is greater, and

(B) the sponsor is under a contractual obligation to pay his share of expenses as such expenses are paid by the program and to complete his minimum financial commitment to the program, by the end of the second fiscal year succeeding the fiscal year in which the program commenced operations.

(5) For the purposes of this Subsection (a) if a well is not abandoned within 90 days of completion, then it shall be deemed to be a commercial well insofar as the program is concerned and the sponsor may not recapture its tangible costs upon abandonment.

(b) Other Compensation Arrangements. In lieu of the compensation arrangements authorized by Subsection (a) hereof, the sponsor may take one of the following:

(1) A promotional interest in the form of a subordinated percentage of the working interest which does not exceed 33 1/3% of the working interest. A subordinated interest shall provide for the return from production to the investors of 100% of their capital contribution, determined on a prospect or total program basis, before the holder of any subordinated working interest may receive a share of revenues, and should provide that, when such promotional interest is entitled to receive distribution, it will bear costs in the same ratio as it participates in revenues; or,

(2) An overriding royalty of not more than 1/32 of the program's share of production, convertible to not more than a 20% working interest after the return from production to the investors of 100% of their capital contribution on a prospect or total program basis.

(c) (Equivalent Arrangements.) If substantiated by the sponsor, any interest or combination of interests substantially equivalent to the compensation arrangements set forth in Subsections (a) and (b) above may be approved.

(d) (Sharing Arrangements.) The sharing arrangements set forth in this Section 260.140.125 shall not be considered presumptively reasonable (1) for a sponsor who does not actively participate in obtaining a significant portion of the program's prospects and who does not assume management responsibility for drilling, completing, equipping and operating a significant portion of a program's wells, unless such sponsor shall satisfactorily demonstrate that his compensation together with the costs of procuring such services for the program from third parties does not exceed the permissible compensation to the sponsor set forth in this Section, (2) where any overriding royalty is taken in a program in which lease acquisition costs are anticipated to exceed 25% of capital contributions to a program, (3) in the case of sharing arrangements where the sponsor does not pay his share or category of the costs on a current basis or where properties or revenues of the participants are pledged to obtain loans for the sponsor, (4) in the case of sharing arrangements in which the sponsor pays all development costs and exploratory wells are drilled on prospects which cannot reasonably be expected to require developmental drilling if the exploratory drilling is successful, or (5) in the case of sharing arrangements where the sponsor cannot demonstrate a financial ability to pay for his share of costs.

(e) Compensation for Regulation B Sponsors. As an alternative to the sharing arrangements authorized by this Section 260.140.125.1, the sponsor of a Regulation B offering may elect to retain a working interest in the well or tract involved equal to a percentage of the aggregate drilling and completion costs of such well or tract paid by him, plus an additional percentage of 15%. To the extent that the sponsor intends to render drilling and related services under a "turn key" contract, the amount of profits in excess of 10% of the cost of providing such services will be considered in determining the reasonableness of the sponsor's aggregate promotional compensation.

Each sponsor of a Regulation B offering shall file with the Commissioner one copy of each of Forms 3-G and 1-G within 30 days after filing with Securities and Exchange Commission.

(f) Compensation for Production Purchase Programs. Compensation to sponsors of production purchase programs shall be limited as follows:

(1) Where a major portion of the sponsor's management and operating responsibilities are performed by third parties, the cost of which is paid by the program, the sponsor may take a 3% working interest convertible to not more than a 5% working interest after the return from production to the investors of 100% of their capital contribution, computed on a total program basis.

(2) Where the sponsor maintains the operating capabilities and technical staff so as to be in a position to, and in fact does provide the program with a major part of the mangement and operating responsibilities of the program, the sponsor may take a 10% working interest convertible to not more than a 15% working interest after the return from production to the investors of 100% of their capital contribution, computed on a total program basis.

The sponsor's interest in a program or in properties owned by a program shall bear a pro rata share of all costs, expenses and obligations of the program including but not limited to costs of operations, general and administrative expenses, debt service and any other items of expense chargeable to the operations of the program.

(¶8615)

260.140.126. Program Expenses. (a) All actual and necessary expenses incurred by the program directly may be paid by the sponsor out of capital contributions and out of program revenues.

(b) A sponsor may be reimbursed out of capital contributions and program revenues for all actual and necessary direct expenses paid or incurred by it in connection with its operation of a program, and for an allocable portion of its general and administrative expenses, computed on a cost basis determined by an independent public accountant or certified public accountant in accordance with generally accepted accounting principles. Administrative and similar services must be fully supportable as to the necessity thereof and the reasonableness of the amounts proposed to be charged. The prospectus or offering circular shall disclose in tabular form an estimate of all such expenses to be charged to the program showing separately direct expenses, general and administrative expenses (including a separate breakdown for salaries to officers, directors and other principals of the sponsor and any affiliate of the sponsor).

(c) Except as may be permitted by Section 260.140.127.1 of these rules, the sponsor may not be reimbursed for any expenses incurred prior to commencement of operations of the program or any indirect, general or administrative expenses relating to the sale of program units.

Transactions with Affiliates and Conflicts of Interest

(¶8616)

260.140.127.1 Sales and Purchases. (a) Neither the sponsor nor any affiliated person shall sell or lease any property to or purchase or lease any property from the program, directly or indirectly, except pursuant to transactions that are fair and reasonable to the participants of the program and then subject to the following conditions:

(1) In the case of a sale or lease to a program:

(A) The prospectus discloses the fact that the sponsor will sell or lease property to the program and whether or not the property will be sold from the sponsor's existing inventory.

(B) The property is sold or leased to the program at the cost of the sponsor, unless the seller has reasonable grounds to believe that cost is materially more than the fair market value of such property, in which case such sale should be made for a price not in excess of its fair market value.

(C) If the sponsor sells or leases any oil, gas or other mineral interests or property to the program, he must, at the same time, sell to the program an equal interest in all his other property in the same prospect. If the sponsor or any affiliate subsequently proposes to acquire an interest in a prospect in which the program possesses an interest or in a prospect abandoned by the program within one year preceding such proposed acquisition, the sponsor shall offer such interest to the program; and, if case or financing is not available to the program to enable it to consummate a purchase of an equivalent interest in such property, neither the sponsor nor any of its affiliates shall acquire such interest or property. The term "abandon" for the purpose of this subsection and of subsection (b) of Section 260.140.127.2 of these rules, shall means the termination, either voluntarily or by operation of the lease or otherwise, of all of the program's interest in the prospect. The provisions of this subdivision shall not apply after the lapse of 5 years from the date of formation of the program.

(D) A sale or lease of less than all of the ownership of the sponsor in any interest or property is prohibited unless the interest retained by the sponsor is a proportionate working interest, the respective obligations of the sponsor and the program are substantially the same after the sale of the interest by the sponsor and his interest in revenues does not exceed the amount proportionate to his retained working interest. The sponsor may not retain any overrides or other burdens and may not enter into any farmout arrangements with respect to his retained interest, except to non-affiliated third parties.

(2) In the case of a purchase or lease of nonproducing property from a program, the purchase is made at a price which the higher of the fair market value or the cost of such property.

(3) In the case of producing property, the sponsor shall not be given an exclusive right to purchase such property. A sale of producing property

or interest therein, except for the sale of production, must consist of a sale of all of the program's interest in the property and must be made at a price determined by an appraisal prepared by an independent petroleum engineer. A sale of production must be on terms comparable to and competitive with prices obtainable on the open market.

(b) The oil program shall not purchase properties from nor sell properties to any program in which its sponsor or any affiliated person has an interest. This Subsection shall not apply to transactions among oil programs for whom the same persons acts as sponsor by which property is transferred from one to another in exchange for the transferee's obligation to conduct drilling activities on such property or to joint ventures among such programs, provided that the respective obligations and revenue sharing of all parties to the transactions are substantially the same and provided further that the compensation arrangement or any other interest or right of the sponsor and any affiliated person of such sponsor is the same in each program, or, if different, the aggregage compensation of the sponsor does not exceed the lower of the compensation he would have received in any one of the programs.

(c) Any other provision of these rules notwithstanding, a sponsor may purchase property in its own name and hold title in trust for the benefit of the program, where necessary to facilitate the acquisition of such property or the business purposes of the programs.

(¶8616A)
260.140.127.2. Restricted and Prohibited Transactions. (a) Neither the sponsor nor any affiliate shall enter into any farmout or other agreement with the oil program where in consideration for services to be rendered, an interest in production is payable to such sponsor or affiliate.

(b) During the existence of a program and before it has ceased operations neither the sponsor nor any affiliate (excluding another program where the interest of the sponsor is identical to or less than his interest in the first program) shall acquire, retain, or drill for its own account any oil and gas interest on any prospect upon which such program possesses an interest, except for sales or lease transactions which comply with Subdivision (D) of Section 260.140.127.1(a)(1) of these rules. In the event the program abandons its interest in the prospect, this restriction shall continue until one year following the abandonment. If the geological limits of a prospect are enlarged to encompass any interest held by such sponsor or affiliate, such interest shall be sold to such program in accordance with the provisions of Subdivision (C) of Section 260.140.127.1(a)(1) of these rules and any net income previously received by the sponsor or affiliate shall be paid over to such program. If within this period, the sponsor acquires additional acreage or interest in a prospect of the program, he must sell such to the program and is prohibited from retaining any such interest, except as may be permitted by Section 260.140.127.1(a) of these rules.

(c) The sponsor shall not take any action with respect to the assets or property of the program which does not benefit exclusively the program, including among other things:

(1) the utilization of funds of the program as compensating balances for his own benefit, and

(2) future commitments of production.

(d) All benefits from marketing arrangements or other relationships affecting property of the sponsor and the program shall be fairly and equitably apportioned according to the respective interests of each.

(e) Any agreements or arrangements which bind the program must be fully disclosed in the prospectus.

(f) Anything to the contrary notwithstanding, a sponsor may never profit by drilling in contravention of his fiduciary obligation to the participants.

(g) Neither the sponsor nor any affiliate shall render to the program any oil field, equippage or drilling services nor sell or lease to the program any equipment or related supplies unless:

(1) such person is engaged, independently of the program and as an ordinary and ongoing business, in the business of rendering such services or selling or leasing such equipment and supplies predominantly to other persons in the oil and gas industry in addition to programs in which he has an interest, and

(2) the compensation, price or rental thereof is competitive with the compensation, price or rental of other persons engaged in the business of rendering comparable services or selling or leasing comparable equipment and supplies which could reasonably be made available to the program, provided that, if such person is not engaged in a business within the meaning of Subdivision (1), then such compensation, price or rental shall be the cost of such services, equipment or supplies to such person or the competitive rate whichever is less.

(h) With the exception of compensation authorized by Section 260.140.125.1 of these rules, all services for which the sponsor and any affiliated person is to receive compensation shall be embodied in a written contract which:

(1) Precisely describes the services to be rendered and all compensation to be paid.

(2) Provides, in substance, that any material change in the terms of such contract must be approved by the vote of the holders of a majority of the units of the program.

(i) No loans may be made by the program to the sponsor.

(j) On loans made available to the program by the sponsor, the sponsor may not receive interest in excess of the amounts which would be charged the program (without reference to the sponsor's financial abilities or guaranties) by unrelated banks on comparable loans for the same purpose and the sponsor shall not receive points or other financing charges or fees regardless of the amount.

(¶8616B)
260.140.127.3. Exchange of Units. The program may not acquire property in exchange for units.

(¶8616C)
260.140.127.4. Commingling of Funds. The funds of a program shall not be commingled with the funds of any other person.

(¶8616D)
260.140.127.5. Liability. Sponsors shall not attempt to pass on to limited partners the general liability imposed on them by law except that the partnership agreement may provide that a general partner (a) may be held harmless and be indemnified by the partnership for any liability or loss suffered by the general partner solely by virtue of his acting as general partner for the partnership in connection with its activities and (b) shall not be liable to the partnership for any loss suffered by it in connection with its activities, provided that if such loss or liability arises out of any action or inaction of the general partner, the general partner must have determined, in good faith, that such course of conduct was in the best interests of the partnership, and such course of conduct must not have constituted gross negligence or gross misconduct by the general partner; and, provided further, that such indemnification or agreement to hold harmless shall only be recoverable out of the assets of the partnership and not from the limited partners.

Participants' Rights and Obligations

(¶8617)
260.140.128.1. Meetings. Meetings of the participants may be called by the general partner(s) or by participants holding more than 10% of the then outstanding units for any matters for which the participants may vote as set forth in the limited partnership agreements or charter document. Such call for a meeting shall be deemed to have been made upon receipt by the general partner of a written request from holders of the requisite percentage of units stating the purpose(s) of the meeting. The general partner shall deposit in the United States mails within fifteen days after receipt of said request, written notice to all participants of the meeting and the purpose of such meeting, which shall be held on a date not less than thirty nor more than sixty days after the date of mailing of said notice, at a reasonable time and place.

(¶8617A)
260.140.128.2. Voting Rights of Limited Partners. (a) To the extent the law of the state of organization is not inconsistent, the limited partnership

agreement must provide that holders of a majority of the then outstanding units may, without the necessity for concurrence by the general partner, vote to (1) amend the limited partnership agreement or charter document, (2) dissolve the program, (3) remove the general partner and elect a new general partner, (4) approve or disapprove the sale of all or substantially all of the assets of the program, and (5) cancel any contract for services with the sponsor or any affiliate without penalty upon thirty days' notice. The agreement should provide a detailed provision for the substitution of a new general partner and a provision for the purchase of the removed general partner's interest, excluding any interest he may have as an investor, including the following:

(1) A method of valuation of the removed general partner's interest which is fair. Normally, valuation at the time of such removal by means of an appraisal, arbitration or agreement will be deemed fair.

(2) A method of payment for such interest which is fair and which protects the solvency and liquidity of the partnership. If immediate payment would impose a hardship upon the partnership, the provision should call for payment plus reasonable interest to be postponed to the time payment of his subordinated interest would have been made.

(¶8617B)

260.140.128.3. Annual and Periodic Reports. (a) The partnership agreement or charter document shall provide for the transmittal to each participant of an annual report within 90 days after the close of the fiscal year, and of a semiannual report within 60 days after the end of the first six months of its fiscal year, containing, except as otherwise indicated, at least the following information:

(1) Financial statements, including a balance sheet and statements of income, partners' equity and changes in financial position prepared in accordance with generally accepted accounting principles and accompanied by an auditor's report containing an opinion of an independent certified public accountant or independent public accountant, except that semiannual reports need not be audited.

(2) A description of each geological prospect in which the program owns an interest, including the cost, location, number of acres under lease and the interest owned therein by the program.

(3) A list of the wells drilled by such program (indicating whether each of such wells has or has not been completed), the costs incurred in or allocable to drilling each well and the additional estimated costs to complete each well.

(4) A summary itemization, by type and/or classification of the total fees and compensation paid by the program, or indirectly on behalf of the program, to the sponsor and affiliates of the sponsor. If compensation is

paid on a subordinated interest subject to Subsection (b)(1) of Section 260.140.125.1 of these rules, a reconciliation of all such payments to the conditions precedent and limitations thereto. The report should provide comparative data from which competitive prices may be determined, pursuant to Subsection (g)(2) of Section 260.140.127.2 of these rules.

(5) With respect to a program which compensates the sponsor in the manner permitted by Subsections (a)(1), (a)(2) and (e) of Section 260.140.125.1, (A) a schedule reflecting the total program costs, and where applicable, the costs pertaining to each prospect, the costs paid by the sponsor and the costs paid by the participants (B) the total program revenues, the revenues received or credited to the sponsor and the revenues received or credited to the participants and (C) a reconciliation of such expenses and revenues to the limitations prescribed by said Sections.

(6) Annually, beginning with the fiscal year succeeding the fiscal year in which the program commenced operations, a compution of the total oil and gas proven reserves of the program and dollar value thereof at then existing prices and of each participant's interest in such reserve value. The reserve compuations shall be based upon engineering reports prepared by qualified independent petroleum engineers. In addition, there shall be included an estimate of the time required for the extraction of such reserves with a statement that because of the time period required to extract such reserves the present value of revenues to be obtained in the future is less than if immediately receivable. In addition to the annual computation and estimate required by this Section, as soon as possible, and in no event more than 90 days after the occurrence of an event leading to a reduction of such reserves of the program of more than 10%, a computation and estimate conforming to the above requirements shall be sent to each participant.

(b) By March 15 of each year, the general partner must furnish a report to each participant containing such information as is pertinent for tax purposes.

(¶8617C)

260.140.128.4. Access to Program Records. (a) The general partner shall maintain a list of the names and addresses of all participants at the principal office of the partnership. Such list shall be made available for the review of any participant or his representative at reasonable times, and upon request either in person or by mail the general partner shall furnish a copy of such list to any participant or his representative for the cost of reproduction and mailing.

(b) The participants and/or their accredited representatives shall be permitted access to all records of the program, after adequate notice, at any reasonable time. The sponsor shall maintain and preserve during the term of the program and for four (4) years thereafter all accounts, books, and other relevant program documents. Notwithstanding the foregoing, the sponsor may keep logs, well reports and other drilling data confidential for a reasonable period of time.

(¶8617D)

260.140.128.5. Admission of Participants. (a) Admission of participants to the program shall be subject to the following:

(1) Admission of Original Participants. Upon the original sale of partnership units by the program, the purchasers should be admitted as limited partners not later than 15 days after the release from impound of the purchasers' funds to the program, and thereafter purchasers should be admitted into the program not later than the last day of the calendar month following the date their subscriptions were accepted by the program. Subscriptions shall be accepted or rejected by the program within 30 days of their receipt; if rejected, all subscription monies shall be returned to the subscriber forthwith.

(2) Admission of Substituted Limited Partners and Recognition of Assignees. The program shall amend the certificate of limited partnership at least once each calendar quarter to effect the substitution of substituted limited partners, although the sponsor may elect to do so more frequently. In the case of assignments, where the assignee does not become a substituted limited partner, the program shall recognize the assignment not later than the last day of the calendar month following receipt of notice of assignment and required documentation.

(¶8617E)

260.140.128.6. Redemption and Repurchase of Units. (a) Ordinarily, the program may not be mandatorily obligated to redeem or repurchase any of the units of the program, although the program need not be precluded from purchasing such outstanding units if the purchase does not impair the capital or the operations of the program. Notwithstanding the foregoing, the program may obligate itself to redeem units under terms which comply with Section 260.140.116.6. of these rules.

(b) Provisions in the partnership agreement or other documents which require the unit owner to sell his unit or give the program or any other person the right to repurchase such unit, irrespective of the desire of the owner to sell, will not be approved.

(¶8617F)

260.140.128.7. Transferability of Program Units. Restrictions on assignment of units will not be allowed. Restrictions on the substitution of a limited partner are generally disfavored and will be allowed only to the extent necessary to preserve the tax status of the partnership and any restriction must be supported by opinion of counsel as to its legal necessity.

(¶8617G)

260.140.128.8. Assessability and Defaults. (a) In appropriate cases there may be a provision for assessability; provided, however, that the maximum amount which may be assessed for a voluntary assessment shall not exceed 100% of the initial subscription and for a mandatory assessment shall not exceed 25% of the initial subscription, and provided further, that in no case shall the total of all assessments exceed 100% of the initial subscription. All such assessments shall be solely for the purpose of drilling or completing a development well or wells or for acquiring additional interests or leases in a prospect which has proven production. In such cases, the aggregate offering price of the units as set forth in the application for qualification shall include and show separately the basic unit offering price and the maximum amount of the assessment.

(b) In the event of a default in all or a portion of the payment of assessments, the participant's percentage interest in the program represented by his unit should not be subject to forfeiture, but may be subject to a reasonable penalty for the failure of the participant to meet his commitment. Provisions which conform to the following will be considered reasonable:

(1) For voluntary assessments.

(A) A proportionate reduction of the participant's percentage interest in revenues derived from future development based on the ration of his unpaid assessment to all capital contributions and assessments used for such future development, or

(B) A subordination of the defaulting participant's right to receive revenues from future development until those nondefaulting participants who have paid the defaulting participant's assessment have received an amount of revenues from revenues of the program from future development equal to 300% of the proportionate amount of the defaulted assessment which they paid.

(2) For mandatory assessments.

(A) A proportionate reduction of the participant's percentage interest in program revenues based on the ratio of his unpaid assessment to all capital contributions and assessments, or,

(B) A subordination of the defaulting participant's right to receive revenues from the program until those nondefaulting participant's assesssment have received an amount of revenues from all revenues of the program equal to 300% of the proportionate amount of the defaulted assessment which they paid.

(C) In order to make any assessment, the sponsor shall include with the call for such assessment a statement of the purpose and intended use of the proceeds from such assessment, a statement of the purpose and intended use of the proceeds from such assessment, a statement of the penalty to be imposed for failure of the participant to meet the assessment, and to the extent practicable, a summary of pertinent geological data on the relevant properties to which the assessments relate.

(¶8617H)

260.140.128.9. Program Policies. The partnership agreement or charter document should include a recital in reasonable detail of the policies and objectives to be followed by the program. This will include a statement of the extent to which the program intends to engage in acquiring producing properties, acquiring or drilling on unproven or unexplored properties or acquiring or drilling on proven or semiproven properties.

Sales Materials and Marketing Restrictions

(¶8618)

260.140.129.1. Sales Literature. Sales literature, including without limitation, books, pamphlets, movies, slides, article reprints, and television and radio commercials, sales presentations (including prepared presentations to prospective participants at group meetings) and all other advertising used in the offer or sale or units shall conform in all applicable respects to filing, disclosure and adequacy requirements currently imposed on the sale of corporate securities under these rules. When periodic or other reports furnished to participants in prior programs are furnished to prospective participants in a program not yet sold, such reports will be treated as sales literature subject to the above requirements.

(¶8618A)

260.140.129.2. Group Meetings. All advertisements of and oral or written invitations to "seminars" or other group meetings at which units are to be described, offered or sold shall clearly indicate that the purpose of such meeting is to offer such units for sale, the minimum purchase price thereof, the suitability standards to be employed, and the name of the person selling the units. No cash, merchandise or other item of value shall be offered as an inducement to any prospective participants to attend any such meeting. All written or prepared audio-visual presentations (including scripts prepared in advance for oral presentations) to be made at such meetings must be submitted to the Department within the prescribed review period. The provisions of this Section shall not apply to meetings consisting only of representatives of securities' broker-dealers.

Disclosure and Marketing Requirements

(¶8619)

260.140.130.1. Offerings Registered with the Securities and Exchange Commission ("SEC"). With respect to offerings registered with the Securities and Exchange Commission under the Securities Act of 1933, as amended, and qualified with the Commissioner by coordination, a prospectus which is part of a registration statement which has been declared effective by said

Commission shall be deemed to comply with all requirements as to form of this Rule; provided, however, that the Commissioner reserves the right to require additional disclosure of substance in his discretion.

(¶8619A)

260.140.130.2. Contents of Prospectus. (a) The following information shall be included in the prospectus of each program:

(1) Information on Cover Page. There should be set forth briefly on the cover page of the prospectus a summary which should include the following:

The title and general nature of the units being offered; the maximum aggregate amount of the offering; the minimum amount of net proceeds; the minimum subscription price; the period of the offering; the maximum amount of any sales or underwriting commissions to be paid (or if none, or if such commissions are paid by the sponsor), the nature of any sharing arrangement and fees; the estimated amount of organization and offering expenses, the estimated amount to be paid during the first twelve (12) months following commencement of operations for administrative and similar services.

(2) Definitions. Technical terms used in the prospectus should be defined either in a glossary or as they appear in the prospectus.

(3) Risk Factors. Participants should be advised in a carefully organized series of short, concise paragraphs, under subcaptions where appropriate, of the risks to be considered before marking an investment in the program. These paragraphs should include a cross-reference to further information in the prospectus. In particular, in those cases where the sponsor has elected the compensation arrangement described in Section 260.140.125.1(a) (Cost and Revenue Sharing), there should be set forth the fact that there is a conflict where the sponsor must decide whether to complete a well which is anticipated to have a marginal return since the tangible costs he would incur would not appear to warrant his investment, although completion of the well would be in the best interests of the participants.

(4) Business Experience. The business experience of the sponsor(s), including general partner(s), principal officers of a corporate general partner (chairman of the board, president, vice president, treasurer, secretary or any person having similar authority or performing like functions) and others responsible for the program, shall be prominently disclosed in the prospectus, such disclosure indicating their business experience for the past ten years. The lack of experience or limited experience of the sponsor, or other person supplying services to the program, shall be prominently disclosed in the prospectus.

(5) Compensation. All indirect and direct compensation which may be paid by the program to the sponsor or any affiliate of every type and from every source shall be summarized in the forepart of the prospectus.

(6) Use of Proceeds. State the purposes for which the net proceeds to the program are intended to be used for each such purpose. Also state the minimum aggregate amount necessary to initiate the program and the disposition of the funds raised if they are not sufficient for that purpose.

(7) Assessments. If provisions for assessments are provided, the method of assessment and the penalty for default shall be prominently set forth.

(8) Investment Objectives and Policies. Describe the investment objectives and policies of the program.

(9) Description of Oil and Gas Interests. State the location and describe the general character of all materially important oil and gas interests now held or presently intended to be acquired by the program.

(10) Performance. (A) The previous program experience of the sponsor and other relevant parties shall be disclosed in the prospectus for all programs during the past ten years which:

(i) Involved a public offering registered under State or Federal securities laws.

(ii) Involved a private or limited offering, the results of which are material to an informed investment decision by the participant.

(B) Information on previous programs shall include, but not be limited to, the following:

(i) Name of the program, including the type of legal entity and state of incorporation or organization.

(ii) The effective date of the offering, the date it commenced operations and the date of dissolution or termination or, if it is continuing.

(iii) The total amount of units, the gross amount of capital raised by the program, the number of participants, and the amount of investment of the sponsor, if applicable.

(iv) The drilling results of the program, including the number of gross and net wells drilled, both oil and gas, both exploratory and developmental, and both successful and unsuccessful.

(v) Total dollar amounts of federal tax deductible items passed on to participants.

(vi) Cash distribution to participants.

(vii) Compensation and fees to the sponsor, segregated as to type.

(viii) Disclosure of any development wells drilled which did not or have not returned the investment therein within four years.

(ix) Such additional or different disclosures of the success or failure of the programs as may be permitted or required by the Commissioner.

(C) All of the foregoing information shall be set forth on a cumulative basis for each program.

(D) The following caveat should be prominently featured in the presentation of the foregoing information: "It should not be assumed that participants in the offering covered by this prospectus will experience returns, if any, comparable to those experienced by investors in prior programs".

(E) Information required to be set forth in Subsection (A) above shall be supported in the application for qualification by an affidavit of the sponsor that the performance summary is a fair representation of the information contained in the audited financial statement or the Federal income tax returns of the program or in other reports or data of the program sponsor.

(11) Operating Data. Include appropriate data with respect to each property which is separately described in answer to paragraph (9) above.

(12) The Program.

(a) Date of formation.

(b) Place of formation.

(c) Sponsor.

(d) Address and telephone number of the program and the sponsor.

(e) Duration.

(f) Information called for in items (a) through (e) hereof shall be given for any other programs in which the program invests.

(13) Summary of Terms of the Program.

(a) Powers of the sponsor.

(b) Rights and liabilities of the participants.

(c) Allocation of costs and revenues.

(d) Termination and dissolution.

(e) Meetings and reports.

(f) Amendment of partnership agreement.

(g) Provision for additional assessments.

(h) Other pertinent matters.

(14) Federal Tax Consequences.

(a) A summary of an opinion of tax counsel acceptable to the Commissioner and/or a ruling from the IRS covering major state and federal tax questions relative to the program, which may be based on reasonable assumptions such as those described in Section 260.140.130.4 of these rules. To the extent the opinion of counsel or IRS ruling is based on the maintenance of or compliance with certain requirements or conditions by the sponsor(s), the prospectus shall to the extent practicable, contain representations that such requirements or conditions have been met and that the sponsors shall use their best efforts to continue to meet such requirements or conditions.

(b) Tax treatment of the program.

(c) Tax treatment of the participants.

(d) Allocation of intangible drilling deductions, depreciation, depletion allowances, etc.

(e) Method of allocation of losses or profits and cash distributions upon transfer of a unit or the rights to income or revenues.

(f) Any other pertinent information applicable to the tax shelter aspects of the investment.

(g) Possibility of requirement for filing tax returns with states in which prospects are located.

(15) Units.

    (a) Amount.

    (b) Minimum purchase.

    (c) Assessability.

    (d) Transferability.

    (e) Voting rights.

(16) Plan of Distribution.

    (a) Discounts and commissions.

    (b) Estimated fees and expenses paid or reimbursed by the program.

    (c) Indemnification and hold harmless provisions.

    (d) Terms of payment.

    (e) Identity of underwriter, managing dealer and/or principal selling agent.

    (f) Type of underwriting—best efforts or firm commitment.

    (g) Minimum and maximum sales.

    (h) Escrow provisions.

    (i) Material relationship of underwriter to the program, if any.

(17) Pending Legal Proceedings. Briefly describe any legal proceedings to which the program or the sponsor is a party which is material to the program and any material legal proceedings between sponsor and participants in any prior program of the sponsor. Also, describe any material legal proceedings to which any of the program's or sponsor's property is subject.

(18) Transactions with Affiliates. Describe fully any transactions and the dollar amount thereof which may be entered into between the program and the sponsor or any affiliate. Include a full description of the material terms of any agreement and the dollar amount thereof between the program and the sponsor or any affiliate. Where the sponsor sponsors other programs, describe the equitable principles which will apply in resolving any conflict between the programs. In the case where the program has been in existence, include all transactions and contracts of the program with the sponsor or any affiliate during the period of such existence.

(19) Interest of Affiliates in Program Property. If within the past five years the sponsor or any affiliate has been in the chain of title or had a beneficial interest in any property to be acquired by the program this fact must be disclosed.

(20) Interest of Counsel and Experts in the Sponsor or Program. Where counsel for the selling representatives or the sponsor are named in the prospectus as having passed upon the legality of the units being registered or upon other legal matters in connection with the registration or offering of such units, there should be disclosed in the prospectus the nature and amount of any direct or indirect material interests of any such counsel, other than legal fees to be received by such counsel, in the sponsor or any affiliate. Any such interest received or to be received in connection with the registration or offering of the units being registered, including the ownership or receipt by counsel, or by members of the firm participating in the matter, of securities of the sponsor, any affiliate of the program for services shall be disclosed. Employment by the sponsor, other then retainer is legal counsel, should be disclosed in the prospectus.

(21) Investment Company Act of 1940. Where beneficial interests of a program are to be sold, treatment under the Investment Company Act of 1940 must be disclosed.

(22) Financial Statements. As provided elsewhere in these rules.

(23) Additional Information. Any additional information which is material should be included.

(¶8619B)

260.140.130.3. Financial Information Required on Application. The sponsor or the program shall provide as an exhibit to the application or where indicated below shall provide as part of the prospectus, the following financial information and financial statements:

(a) Cash Flow Statement of Program. As part of the prospectus, if the program has been formed and owns assets, a cash flow statement, which may be unaudited, for the program for each of the last three fiscal years of the program (or for life of the program, if less) and unaudited statements for any interim period between the end of the latest fiscal year and the date of the balance sheet furnished, and for the corresponding interim period of the preceding years.

(b) Balance Sheet of Program. As part of the prospectus, a balance sheet of the program as of the end of its most recent fiscal year prepared in accordance with generally accepted accounting principles and accompanied by an auditor's report containing an unqualified opinion of an independent certified public accountant or independent public accountant, and an unaudited balance sheet as of a date not more than ninety days prior to the date of filing.

(c) Statements of Income, Partners' Equity, and Changes in Financial Position of Program. As part of the prospectus, if the program has been formed and owns assets, statements of income statements of partner's equity, and statements of changes in financial position for the program for each of the last three fiscal years of the program (or for the life of the program, if less), all of which statements shall be prepared in accordance with generally accepted accounting principles and accompanied by an auditor's report containing an unqualified opinion of an independent certified public accountant or independent public accountant, and unaudited statements for any interim period ending not more than ninety days prior to the date of filing an application.

(d) Balance Sheet of General Partner.

(1) Corporate General Partner. A balance sheet of any corporate general partners as of the end of their most recent fiscal year, prepared in accordance with generally accepted accounting principles and accompanied by an auditor's report containing an unqualified opinion of an independent certified public accountant or independent public accountant, and unaudited balance sheet as of a date not more than ninety days prior to the date of filing. Such statements shall be included in the prospectus.

(2) Other General Partners. A balance sheet for each noncorporate general partner (including individual partners or individual joint venturers of a sponsor) as of a time not more than ninety days prior to the date of filing an application; such balance sheet, which may be unaudited should conform to generally accepted accounting principles and shall be signed and sworn to by such general partners. A representation of the amount of such net worth must be included in the prospectus.

(e) Statements of Income for Corporate General Partners. A statement of income for the last fiscal year of any corporate general partner (or for the life of the corporate general partner, if less) prepared in accordance with generally accepted accounting principles and accompanied by an auditor's report containing an unqualified opinion of an independent certified public accountant or independent public accountant, and an unaudited statement for any interim period ending not more than ninety days prior to the date of filing an application. The inclusion of such statements in the prospectus shall be at the discretion of the Commissioner.

(f) Filing of Other Statements. Upon request by an applicant, the Commissioner may, where consistent with the protection of investors, permit the omission of one or more of the statements required under this Section and the filing, in substitution thereof, of appropriate statements verifying financial information having comparable relevance to an investor in determining whether he should invest in the program.

(¶8619C)

260.140.130.4. Opinions of Counsel. The application for qualification shall contain a favorable ruling from the IRS or an opinion of counsel to the effect that the program will be taxed as a "partnership" and not as an "association taxable as a corporation" for Federal and State income tax purposes. An opinion of counsel shall be in form satisfactory to the Commissioner and shall be unqualified except to the extent permitted by the Commissioner. However, an opinion of counsel may be based on reasonable assumptions, such as: (a) facts or proposed operations as set forth in the prospectus and organization documents; (b) the absence of future changes in applicable laws; (c) compliance with certain procedures such as the execution and delivery of certain documents and the filing of a certificate of limited partnership or an amended certificate and (d) the continued maintenance of or compliance with certain financial, ownership or other requirements by the sponsor or general partner. The Commissioner may request from counsel as supplemental information such supporting legal memoranda and an analysis as he shall deem appropriate under the circumstances. To the extent the opinion of counsel or IRS ruling is based on the maintenance of or compliance with certain requirements or conditions by the sponsor or general partner, the prospectus shall contain representations that such requirements or conditions will be met and the partnership agreement shall, to the extent practicable, contain provisions requiring such compliance. There shall be included also an opinion of counsel to the effect that the units being offered will be duly authorized or created and validly issued interests in the program, and that the liability of the participants will be limited to their respective capital contributions, except as set forth in the prospectus.

Miscellaneous Provisions

(¶8620)

260.140.131.1. Reinvestment of the Participants' Revenues. (a) No offering will be approved by the Commissioner that includes a provision which requires that the participant reinvest his share of distributable cash distributions.

(b) Subject to compliance with applicable securities laws, a program may make available to its participants a voluntary plan for systematic reinvestments in such program or in any other program. No sales commissions may be charged the participants, however, for effecting such reinvestment.

(¶8620A)

260.140.131.2. Minimum Program Capital. No offering shall be approved by the Commissioner if the minimum subscriptions necessary to activate the program are less than $500,000. Additionally, in those instances where it appears unlikely that the stated objectives of the program can be achieved with the minimum subscriptions, the Commissioner may require a greater amount or a reduction of the stated objectives of the program.

(¶8620B)

260.140.131.3. Impound Condition. (a) An impound condition as described in Section 260.141.20 et seq of these rules may be imposed as a condition to the qualification of the program units.

(b) In those instances where a formal impound is not required, a provision must be included in the prospectus to the effect that all funds (including sales commissions and monies destined for reimbursement of offering costs) must be deposited in a trust account in a bank for the benefit of the participants of the program, subject to release only when the minimum program subscriptions have been deposited. The prospectus must also provide that such funds without deduction are to be promptly returned to the participants in the event that the minimum program subscriptions have not been obtained within the time specified in the prospectus, but in no event more than 6 months after commencement of the offering. A copy of the instructions to the bank utilized must be filed with the Commissioner prior to the effectiveness of the qualification.

(¶8620C)

260.140.131.4. Legend Condition. A legend restricting transferability, in the form set forth in Section 260.141.11 of these rules, will normally be required as a condition to the qualification for sale of units and must be fully described and set forth in the prospectus and the documents evidencing the units.

(¶8620D)

260.140.131.5. Offers of Exchanges. (a) No sponsor or any affiliates shall make or cause to be made any offer to a participant to exchange his units for a security of any company, unless:

(1) such offer is made after the expiration of two years after such program commenced operations;

(2) such offer is made to all participants;

(3) such offer, if made by a third party to the sponsor or principal underwriter, or any affiliate of such sponsor or principal underwriter, is on a basis not more advantageous to such sponsor, principal underwriter or affiliate than to participants.

(4) the value of the security or other consideration offered is at least equivalent to the value of the units;

(5) the value of any reserves used in computing the exchange ratio is supported by an appraisal prepared by an independent petroleum engineer within 120 days of the date such exchange is to be made; the value of any undeveloped acreage used in computing the exchange ratio is at cost unless fair market value, as evidenced by supporting data, is higher; and the value of other assets used in computing the exchange ratio is based upon audited financial statements prepared in accordance with generally accepted accounting principles consistently applied; and

(6) the offer is made pursuant to a qualification first obtained and, unless exempt, by means of a Registration Statement meeting the requirements of the Securities Act of 1933, as amended.

For purposes of this Section, and "offer of exchange" includes any security of an oil program which is convertible into a security issued by the sponsor or another issuer.

(¶8620E)

260.140.131.6. Other Securities. The sale of units in a program together with shares, options to purchase shares or other securities issued by the sponsor or another issuer ordinarily will not be permitted, unless such other securities viewed separately satisfy the requirements otherwise applicable to an open qualification.

(¶8620F)

260.140.131.7. Investments in Other Programs. Investments in units of another limited partnership, in general partnerships or joint ventures shall be prohibited unless (a) there is no duplication of selling commissions, selling expenses, offering costs, and sponsor's compensation or other fees and costs and (b) in the case of investments in other limited partnerships, such other limited partnerships shall provide for their limited partners all of the rights and obligations required by these rules to be provided by the original program.

(¶8620G)

260.140.131.8. Limited Offerings. The Commissioner may approve any offering on a basis other than that permitted in these rules, if the class of investors is sufficiently limited. The Commissioner will take into consideration in reviewing such restricted or limited offerings, among other things, the identity of the investors, the suitability standards to be employed, the relationship of the investors, the knowledgeability of the investors, the legal, business, technical and accounting advice available to and utilized by the investors and any other factors deemed relevant.

(¶8620H)

260.140.131.9. Provisions of Partnership Agreement. The requirements and/or provisions of appropriate portions of the following sections shall be included in the partnership agreement or other character document: 260.140.122.3; 260.140.123.6; 260.140.125.1; 260.140.126; 260.140.127.1; 260.140.127.2; 260.140.127.3; 260.140.127.4; 260.140.127.5; 260.140.128.1; 260.140.128.2; 260.140.128.3; 260.140.128.4; 260.140.128.5; 260.140.128.6; 260.140.128.7; 260.140.128.8; 260.140.128.9; 260.140.131.1; 260.140.131.5 and 260.140.131.7.

APPENDIX D

Reference Materials Available from Los Angeles Office of the SEC

Reference Materials are available for public examination at the Los Angeles regional office of the Securities and Exchange Commission, 10960 Wilshire Boulevard, Los Angeles, California.

Code of Federal Regulations

Includes the rules and regulations under the various acts administered by the Commission.

Securities Act of 1933
Securities Exchange Act of 1934
Investment Company Act of 1940
Investment Advisers Act of 1940
Public Utility Holding Company Act
Trust Indenture Act of 1939
Securities Regulations Handbook

Includes guide for preparation of registration statements, Commission registration and reporting forms and Commission accounting regulations.

Microfiche Reports
SEC Docket

A weekly publication containing all Commission releases for that week.

SEC Digest

A daily publication including, among other matters:

1. *A summary of major Commission announcements, rulemaking actions, and court and administrative decisions.*
2. *A summary of registration statements filed under the Securities Act of 1933.*

3. *A listing of periodic corporate reports (8-K's) filed with the Commission under the Securities Exchange Act of 1934.*

4. *A summary of reports filed with the Commission pursuant to Section 13(d) of the Securities Exchange Act of 1934, disclosing the acquisition of more than 5% of the equity securities of publicly traded reporting companies.*

Official Summary of Securities Transactions and Holdings

A monthly publication summarizing trading activities of "insiders" in publicly traded reporting companies.

Statistical Bulletin

A monthly report that includes such matters as:

1. *Trading information for securities listed on the New York and American Stock Exchanges; and*

2. *Data on security offerings registered with the Commission.*

Directory of Companies Filing Annual Reports with the Securities Exchange Commission

An annual publication listing companies alphabetically and by industry classification filing annual reports with the Commission. The directory includes companies with securities listed on national securities exchanges, companies with securities traded over the counter which are registered under Section 12(g) of the Securities Exchange Act of 1934, and certain companies filing pursuant to Section 15(d) of the Securities Exchange Act of 1934 as a result of having securities registered under the Securities Act of 1933.

SEC Corporation Index for Active and Inactive Companies

These annual publications show, among other matters:

1. *Name and address of issuer of securities.*

2. *File number of issuer.*

3. *Branch in Division of Corporation Finance to which the issuer is assigned for examination and other processing.*

4. *Filing and reporting requirements of the issuer.*

5. *State in which the executive office of the issuer is located.*

Annual Report of the SEC

An annual publication of the Commission summarizing its major activities for that fiscal year.

Work of the Securities and Exchange Commission

An annual publication summarizing and explaining the responsibilities and activities of the Commission.

Forms and Rules—for filing with the Commission under the various federal securities laws. (See Attachment)
Litigation Releases

Releases summarizing the Commissions enforcement program are included in the "SEC Docket." The public reference room maintains separate copies of litigation releases for the period prior to February, 1973.

Broker-Dealer and Investment Adviser Directory

This annual directory lists all broker-dealers and investment advisers registered with the Commission.

Broker-Dealer and Investment Adviser—registration statements and certain financial reports filed with the Commission by such registered entities
Definition offering circulars for companies that have filed Regulation A offerings with the Los Angeles Regional Office and the San Francisco Branch Office
Commission Ruling on the Freedom of Information Act
Securities Violations Bulletins

A summary of violations under the securities laws. (This index is issued by the Commission to assist in the detection and suppression of fraud in connection with securities transactions.)

ATTACHMENT

Rules

144 (also interp.)
145/153a
146
147
237
240
Net Capital Rule Summary

Regulations

Regulation A

Regulation B
Regulation 14A & 14C
Regulation 13D & 14D
Security Credit Transaction—Regulations X, G, T, and U

Guides

Preparation of Registration Statements
Preparation of S-4 and S-5
Expedited Processing of Registration Statements
Preparation of N-8B-1

BD, IA, TA, CA, and Miscellaneous Forms

ADV	Investment Adviser Registration
ADVW	Investment Adviser Withdrawal
A	Recommendation for Referral of B-D to SIPC
B	SIPC Reporting Form
BD	Broker-Dealer Registration (incl. Instructions)
BDW	Broker-Dealer Withdrawal
X17A-1	Report Pursuant to Rule 16a-2 under the Securities Exchange Act of 1934
X17A-5	Broker-Dealer Report of Financial Condition
X17A-5	Addendum
X17A-5	Facing Page
X17A-10	Broker-Dealer Annual Income and Expense Report
X17A-11	Information Required Pursuant to Section 17 of the Exchange Act and Rule 17a-11
MSD	Municipal Securities Dealers Registration
TA-1	Transfer Agents Registration
CA-1	Clearing Agents Registration

Forms under the 1933, 1934 and 1940 Acts

S-1, S-14, S-16	Securities Act of 1933 Registration Forms. Amend. to S-1, S-7, S-10
Form 3	Initial statement of beneficial ownership of securities.
Form 4	Statement of changes in beneficial ownership of securities.
Form 144	Notice of proposed sale of securities pursuant to Rule 144.
Form 12B-25	Application for extension of time for furnishing information pursuant to Section 13 or 15(d).
Form 6-K	Report of foreign issuer pursuant to Rules 13a-6 and 15d-16 of the Securities Exchange Act of 1934.

Form 7-Q	Quarterly reports by real estate companies under Section 13 or 15(d) of Securities Exchange Act of 1934.
Form 8	Amendment to application for registration or report filed pursuant to Section 12, 13 or 15(d) of Securities Exchange Act of 1934.
Form 8-A	Registration of certain classes of securities pursuant to Section 12(b) or (g) of the Securities Exchange Act of 1934.
Form 8-B	Registration of Securities of certain successor issuers pursuant to Section 12(b) or (g) of Securities Exchange Act of 1934.
Form 10	General form for registration of securities pursuant to Section 12(b) or 12(g) of Securities Exchange Act of 1934.
Form 10-Q	General form for quarterly reports under Section 13 or 15(d) of Securities Exchange Act of 1934.
Form 10-K	General form of annual reports filed with the Commission.
Form 11-K	Annual reports of employee stock purchase, savings and similar plans.
Form 12	Registration of securities by issuers which file reports with certain other federal agencies.
Form 12-K	Annual reports by issuers which file reports with certain other federal agencies.
Form 16	Application for registration of voting trust certificates and underlying securities.
Form 16-K	Annual report for voting trust certificates and underlying securities.
Form 20-K	Annual reports of foreign private issuers filed pursuant to Section 13 and 15(d).
Form N-1Q	Quarterly report for registered management investment companies.
Form N-1R	Annual reports for registered management investment companies.
Form N-8A	Notification of registration for investment companies.
Form N-8B-1	Registration statement of management investment companies.

INFORMATIVE SEC CORPORATE REPORTS CONVENIENTLY AVAILABLE THROUGH DISCLOSURE

10-K	The annual report filed by most publicly held companies. Part I, financial section, must be filed within 90 days following the close of the company's fiscal year, while Part II schedules can be filed up to 120 days after fiscal-year closing. 10-K's contain extensive, certified financial data, descriptions of various

company activities and often attachments and exhibits describing lease, securities, management and other agreements and plans.

12-K　　　　The annual report filed by certain companies which file annual reports with the Federal Power Commission, Interstate Commerce Commission, and Federal Communications Commission.

10-Q　　　　The quarterly financial report filed by most companies. It is the quarterly update to 10-K financial information, but is not certified. It must be filed within 45 days of the close of the fiscal quarter.

7-Q　　　　The quarterly report filed by some 125 real estate companies which do not file the 10-Q. This report contains quarterly financial information for the first three quarters of the year.

8-K　　　　A report of unscheduled material events or corporate changes of interest to shareholders or to the SEC. Among the events reported by the 8-K are changes in securities, business, financial or corporate positions or assets.

10-C　　　　NASDAQ listed companies use this filing to report changes in name and amount of NASDAQ-listed securities. It is similar in some respects to the 8-K form.

Form 8　　　　The form used to amend or supplement applications or reports previously filed such as the 10-K, 10-Q and 8-K. Extensive financial statements, exhibits and other attachments are frequently appended to the one-page form. Form 8 filings are designated within the *Disclosure* system as amendments to the original filing form.

Proxy Statement　　　　The information statement provided to designated classes of stockholders for formulating a decision on corporate matters to be brought to a vote at a shareholders' meeting. Copies of the final form must be filed before or at time of submission to shareholders.

Registration Statement　　A series of statements filed with the SEC before a new issue of securities can be offered to the general public. The report provides certified financial data and other pertinent information. The registration is divided into two parts: Part I, the "Red Herring," which contains all information to be submitted to a

	prospective purchaser, and Part II, which includes supplementary financial information not required in the Prospectus.
Prospectus	Certified financial statements provided to prospective security purchasers. The information items of the Prospectus are the same as those required in Part I in the final form of the Registration.
N-1R	The annual report filed by registered management-investment companies. It contains primarily financial information, much of it certified, and must be filed within 120 days following the close of the fiscal year.
N-1Q	The quarterly report on the status and activity of the portfolios and holdings of registered management-investment companies. The report must be filed within 30 days of the close of each calendar quarter in which there was "portfolio activity."
15d-G	This report is filed by companies to notify the SEC of discontinuance of requirement to file. It is important to those tracking filings by specific companies.
ARS	Annual Report to Shareholders. This is not a required filing, but is often submitted to the SEC as supplementary information. It contains summary financial data and frequently extensive descriptions of company activities and plans.
Listing Applications	The statements submitted to national or regional exchanges in order that a specific security can be listed and hence leaded through the exchange. Currently listing applications are provided for NYSE and AMEX.

Rule 146—
Securities Act of 1933

Regulations

(¶ 5718B)

Reg. § 230.146 (Rule 146) Transactions by an Issuer Deemed Not to Involve Any Public Offering

Reg. § 230.146

Preliminary Notes

1. The Commission recognizes that no one rule can adequately cover all legitimate private offers and sales of securities. Transactions by an issuer which do not satisfy all of the conditions of this rule shall not raise any presumption that the exemption provided by Section 4(2) of the Act is not available for such transactions. Issuers wanting to rely on that exemption may do so by complying with administrative and judicial interpretations in effect at the time of the transactions. Attempted compliance with this rule does not act as an election; the issuer can also claim the availability of Section 4(2) outside the rule.

2. Nothing in this rule obviates the need for compliance with any applicable state law relating to the offer and sale of securities.

3. Section 5 of the Act requires that all securities offered by the use of mails or other channels of interstate commerce be registered with the Commission. Congress, however, provided certain exemptions in the Act from such registration provisions where there was no practical need for registration or where the public benefits of registration were too remote. Among these exemptions is that provided by Section 4(2) of the Act for transactions by an issuer not involving any public offering. The courts and the Commission have interpreted the Section 4(2) exemption to be available for offerings to persons who have access to the same kind of information that registration would provide and who are able to fend for themselves. The indefiniteness of such terms as "public offering," "access" and "fend for themselves" has led to uncertainties with respect to the availability of the Section 4(2) exemption. Rule 146 is designed to provide to the extent feasible, objective

standards upon which responsible businessmen may rely in raising capital under claim of the Section 4(2) exemption and also to deter reliance on that exemption for offerings of securities to persons who need the protections afforded by the registration process.

In order to obtain the protection of the rule, all its conditions must be satisfied and the issuer claiming the availability of the rule has the burden of establishing, in an appropriate forum, that it has satisfied them. The burden of proof applies with respect to each offeree as well as each purchaser. See "Lively v. Hirschfield," 440 F. 2d 631 (10th Cir. 1971). Broadly speaking, the conditions of the rule relate to limitations on the manner of the offering, the nature of the offerees, access to or furnishing of information, the number of purchasers, and limitations on disposition.

The term "offering" is not defined in the rule. The determination as to whether offers, offers to sell, offers for sale, or sales of securities are part of an offering (i.e., are deemed to be "integrated") depends on the particular facts and circumstances. See Securities Act Release No. 4552 (November 6, 1962) (¶ 2770). All offers, offers to sell, offers for sale, or sales which are part of an offering must meet all of the conditions of Rule 146 for the rule to be available. Release 33-4552 indicates that in determing whether offers and sales should be regarded as a part of a larger offering and thus should be integrated, the following factors should be considered:

General Rules

(a) Whether the offerings are part of a single plan of financing;

(b) Whether the offerings involve issuance of the same class of security;

(c) Whether the offerings are made at or about the same time;

(d) Whether the same type of consideration is to be received; and

(e) Whether the offerings are made for the same general purpose.

4. Rule 146 relates to transactions exempted from Section 5 by Section 4(2) of the Act. It does not provide an exemption from the anti-fraud provisions of the securities laws or the civil liability provisions of Section 12(2) of the Act or other provisions of the securities laws, including the Investment Company Act of 1940.

5. Clients of an investment adviser, customers of a broker or dealer, trusts administered by a bank trust department or persons with similar relationships shall be considered to be the "offerees" or "purchasers" for purposes of the rule regardless of the amount of discretion given to the inqestment adviser, broker or dealer, bank trust department or other person to act on behalf of the client, customer or trust.

6. The rule is available only to the issuer of the securities and is not available to affiliates or other persons for sales of the issuer's securities.

7. Finally, in view of the objectives of the rule and the purposes and policies underlying the Act, the rule is not available to any issuer with respect to any transactions which, although in technical compliance with the rule, are part of a plan or scheme to evade the registration provisions of the Act. In such cases registration pursuant to the Act is required.

Text of Rule

(a) Definitions. The following definitions shall apply for purposes of this rule.

(1) Offeree Representative. The term "offeree representative" shall mean any person or persons, each of whom the issuer and any person acting on its behalf, after making reasonable inquiry, have reasonable grounds to believe and believe satisfies all of the following conditions:

(i) Is not an affiliate, director, officer or other employee of the issuer, or beneficial owner of 10 percent or more of any class of the equity securities or 10 percent or more of the equity interest in the issuer, except where the offeree is:

(a) Related to such person by blood, marriage or adoption, no more remotely than as first cousin;

(b) Any trust or estate in which such person or any persons related to him as specified in paragraph (a)(1)(i)(a) or (c) of this section collectively have 100 percent of the beneficial interest (excluding contingent interests) or of which any such person serves as trustee, executor, or in any similar capacity; or

(c) Any corporation or other organization in which such person or any persons related to him as specified in paragraph (a)(1)(i)(a) or (b) of this section collectively are the beneficial owners of 100 percent of the equity securities (excluding directors' qualifying shares) or equity interests;

(ii) Has such knowledge and experience in financial and business matters that he, either alone, or together with other offeree representatives or the offeree, is capable of evaluating the merits and risks of the prospective investment;

(iii) Is acknowledged by the offeree, in writing, during the course of the transaction, to be his offeree representative in connection with, evaluating the merits and risks of the prospective investment; and

(iv) Discloses to the offeree, in writing, prior to the acknowledgement specified in paragraph (a)(1)(iii) of this section, any material relationship between such person or its affiliates and the issuer or its affiliates, which then exist or is mutually understood to be contemplated or which has existed at any time during the previous two years, and any compensation received or to be received as a result of such relationship.

Note 1: Persons acting as offeree representatives should consider the applicability of the registration and anti-fraud provisions relating to brokers and dealers under the Securities Exchange Act of 1934 and relating to investment advisers under the Investment Advisers Act of 1940.

Note 2: The acknowledgement required by paragraph (a)(1)(iii) of this section and the disclosure required by paragraph (a)(1)(iv) of this section must be made with specific reference to each prospective investment. Advance blanket acknowledgement, such as for "all securities transactions" or "all private placements," is not sufficient.

Note 3: Disclosure of any material relationships between the offeree representative and its affiliates and the issuer or its affiliates does not relieve the offeree representative of its obligation to act in the interest of the offeree.

(2) Issuer. The definition of the term "issuer" in Section 2(4) of the Act shall apply, provided that notwithstanding that definition, in the case of a proceeding under the Bankruptcy Act, the trustee, receiver, or debtor in possession shall be deemed to be the issuer in an offering for purposes of a plan of reorganization or arrangement, if the securities offered are to be issued pursuant to the plan, whether or not other like securities are offered under the plan in exchange for securities of, or claims against, the debtor.

(3) Affiliate. The term "affiliate" of a person means a person that directly or indirectly through one or more intermediaries, controls, or is controlled by, or is under common control with such person.

(4) Material. The term "material" when used to modify "relationship" means any relationship that a reasonable investor might consider important in the making of the decision whether to acknowledge a person as his offeree representative.

(b) Conditions to Be Met. Transactions by an issuer involving the offer, offer to sell, offer for sale or sale of securities of the issuer that are part of an offering that is made in accordance with all the conditions of this rule shall be deemed to be transactions not involving any public offering within the meaning of Section 4(2) of the Act.

(1) For purposes of this rule only, an offering shall be deemed not to include offers, offers to sell, offers for sale or sales of securities of the issuer pursuant to the exemptions provided by Section 3 or Section 4(2) of the Act or pursuant to a registration statement filed under the Act, that take place prior to the six-month period immediately preceding or after the six-month period immediately following any offers, offers for sale or sales pursuant to this rule, provided that there are during neither of said six-month periods any offers, offers for sale or sales of securities by or for the issuer of the same or similar class as those offered, offered for sale or sold pursuant to the rule.

Note: In the event that securities of the same or similar class as those offered pursuant to the rule are offered, offered for sale or sold less than six months prior to or subsequent to any offer, offer for sale or sale pursuant to the rule, see Preliminary Note 3 hereof as to which offers, offers to sell, offers for sale or sales may be deemed to be part of the offering.

(2) Transactions by an issuer which do not satisfy all of the conditions of this rule shall not raise any presumption that the exemption provided by Section 4(2) of the Act is not available for such transactions. (Amended in Release No. 33-5975 (¶81,708), September 8, 1978, 43 F. R. 41194.)

(c) Limitation on Manner of Offering. Neither the issuer nor any person acting on its behalf shall offer, offer to sell, offer for sale, or sell the securities by means of any form of general solicitation or general advertising, including but not limited to, the following:

(1) Any advertisement, article, notice or other communication published in any newspaper, magazine or similar medium or broadcast over television or radio;

(2) Any seminar or meeting, except that if paragraph (d)(1) of this section is satisfied as to each person invited to or attending such seminar or meeting, and, as to persons qualifying only under paragraph (d)(1)(ii) of this section, such persons are accompanied by their offeree representative(s); then such seminar or meeting shall be deemed not to be a form of general solicitation or general advertising; and

(3) Any letter, circular, notice or other written communication, except that if paragraph (d)(1) of this section is satisfied as to each person to whom the communication is directed, such communication shall be deemed not to be a form of general solicitation or general advertising.

(d) Nature of offerees. The issuer and any person acting on its behalf who offer, offer to sell, offer for sale or sell the securities shall have reasonable grounds to believe and shall believe:

(1) Immediately prior to making any offer, either:

(i) That the offeree has such knowledge and experience in financial and business matters that he is capable of evaluating the merits and risks of the prospective investment, or

(ii) That the offeree is a person who is able to bear the economic risk of the investment; and

(2) Immediately prior to making any sale, after making reasonable inquiry, either:

(i) That the offeree has such knowledge and experience in financial and business matters that he is capable of evaluating the merits and risks of the prospective investment, or

(ii) That the offeree and his offeree representative(s) together have such knowledge and experience in financial and business matters that they are capable of evaluating the merits and risks of the prospective investment and that the offeree is able to bear the economic risk of the investment.

(e) Access to or Furnishing of Information.

Note: Access can only exist by reason of the offeree's position with respect to the issuer. Position means an employment or family relationship or economic bargaining power that enables the offeree to obtain information from the issuer in order to evaluate the merits and risks of the prospective investment.

(1) Either

(i) Each offeree shall have access during the course of the transaction and prior to the sale to the same kind of information that is specified in Schedule A of the Act, to the extent that the issuer possesses such information or can acquire it without unreasonable effort or expense; or

(ii) Each offeree or his offeree representative(s), or both, shall have been furnished during the course of the transaction and prior to sale, by the issuer or any person acting on its behalf, the same kind of information that is specified in Schedule A of the Act, to the extent that the issuer possesses such information or can acquire it without unreasonable effort or expense. This condition shall be deemed to be satisfied as to an offeree if the offeree or his offeree representative is furnished with information, either in the form of documents actually filed with the Commission or otherwise, as follows:

(a) In the case of an issuer that is subject to the reporting requirements of Section 13 or 15(d) of the Securities Exchange Act of 1934:

(1) The information contained in the annual report required to be filed under the Exchange Act or a registration statement on Form S-1 under the Act or on Form 10 under the Exchange Act, whichever filing is the most recent required to be filed, and the information contained in any definitive proxy statement required to be filed pursuant to Section 14 of the Exchange Act and in any reports or documents required to be filed by the issuer pursuant to Section 13(a) or 15(d) of the Exchange Act, since the filing of such annual report or registration statement, and

(2) A brief description of the securities being offered, the use of the proceeds from the offering, and any material changes in the issuer's affairs which are not disclosed in the documents furnished;

(b) In the case of all other issuers, the information that would be required to be included in a registration statement filed under the Act on the form which the issuer would be entitled to use, provided, however, that:

A. the issuer may omit details or employ condensation of information if, under the circumstances, the omitted information is not material, or the condensation of information does not render the statements made misleading.

Note: The issuer would have the burden of proof to show that, under the circumstances, the omitted information is not material and that any condensation does not render the statements made misleading.

B. if the issuer does not have the audited financial statements required by such form and cannot obtain them without unreasonable effort or expense, such financial statements may be furnished on an unaudited basis, provided that if such unaudited financial statements are not available and cannot be obtained without unreasonable effort or expense, the financial statements required by Regulation A under the Act may be furnished.

C. if the financial schedules required by Part II of the registration statement have not been prepared, they need not be furnished.

(c) Notwithstanding paragraph (e)(1)(ii)(a) and (b) of this section exhibits required to be held with the Commission as part of a registration statement or report need not be furnished to each offeree or offeree representative if the contents of the exhibits are identified and such exhibits are available pursuant to paragraph (e)(2) of this section; (Amended in Release No. 33-5975 (¶ 81,708), September 8, 1978, 43 F. R. 41194.)

(d) If the aggregate sales price of all securities offered in reliance upon this rule does not exceed $1,500,000, the information requirements of paragraph 1 of Regulation A under Section 3(b) of the Act; and (Amended in Release No. 33-5975 (¶ 81,708), September 8, 1978, 43 F. R. 41194.)

(2) The issuer shall make available, during the course of the transaction and prior to sale, to each offeree or his offeree representative(s) or both, the opportunity to ask questions of, and receive answers from, the issuer or any person acting on its behalf concerning the terms and conditions of the offering and to obtain any additional information, to the extent the issuer possesses such information or can acquire it without unreasonable effort or expense, necessary to verify the accuracy of the information obtained pursuant to paragraph (e)(1) of this section; and

(3) The issuer or any person acting on its behalf shall disclose to each offeree, in writing, prior to sale:

(i) Any material relationship between his offeree representative(s) or its affiliates and the issuer or its affiliates, which then exists or mutually is understood to be contemplated or which has existed at any time during the previous two years, and any compensation received or to be received as a result of such relationship;

(ii) That a purchaser of the securities must bear the economic risk of the investment for an indefinite period of time because the securities have not been registered under the Act and, therefore, cannot be sold unless they are subsequently registered under the Act or an exemption from such registration is available; and

(iii) The limitations on disposition of the securities set forth in paragraph (h)(2),(3), and (4) of this section.

Note: Information need not be provided and opportunity to obtain additional information need not be continued to be provided to any offeree or offeree representative who, during the course of the transaction, indicates that he is not interested in purchasing the securities offered, or to whom the issuer or any person acting on its behalf has determined not to sell the securities.

(f) Business Combinations.

(1) The term "business combination" shall mean any transaction of the type specified in paragraph (a) of Rule 145 under the Act and any transaction involving the acquisition by one issuer, in exchange solely for all or a part of its own or its parent's voting stock, of stock of another issuer if, immediately after the acquisition, the acquiring issuer has control of the other issuer (whether or not it had control before the acquisition).

(2) All the conditions of this rule except paragraph (d) and paragraph (h)(4) of this section shall apply to business combinations.

Note: Notwithstanding the absence of a written agreement pursuant to paragraph (h)(4), any securities acquired in an offering pursuant to paragraph (f) are restricted and may not be resold without registration under the Act or an exemption therefrom.

(3) For purposes of paragraph (f) only, the issuer and any person acting on its behalf, after making reasonable inquiry, shall have reasonable grounds to believe, and shall believe, at the time that any plan for a business combination is submitted to security holders for their approval, or in the case of an exchange, immediately prior to the sale, that each offeree either alone or with his offeree representative(s) has such knowledge and experience in financial and business matters that he is or they are capable of evaluating the merits and risks of the prospective investment.

(4) In addition to information required by paragraphs (e) and (f)(2), the issuer shall provide, in writing, to each offeree at the time the plan is submitted to security holders, or in the case of an exchange, during the course of the transaction and prior to the sale, information about any terms or arrangements of the proposed transaction relating to any security holder that are not identical to those relating to all other security holders.

(g) Number of Purchasers.

(1) The issuer shall have reasonable grounds to believe, and after making reasonable inquiry, shall believe, that there are no more than thirty-five purchasers of the securities of the issuer from the issuer in any offering pursuant to the rule.

Note: See paragraph (b)(1) of this section, the note thereto and the Preliminary Notes as to what may or may not constitute an offering pursuant to the rule.

(2) For purposes of computing the number of purchasers for paragraph (g)(1) of this section only:

(i) The following purchasers shall be excluded:

(a) Any relative or spouse of a purchaser and any relative of such spouse, who has the same home as such purchaser; and

(b) Any trust or estate in which a purchaser or any of the persons related to him as specified in paragraph (g)(2)(i)(a) or (c) of this section collectively have 100 percent of the beneficial interest (excluding contingent interests);

(c) Any corporation or other organization of which a purchaser or any of the persons related to him as specified in subdivision (g)(2)(i)(a) or (b) collectively are the beneficial owners of all the equity securities (excluding directors' qualifying shares) or equity interest; and

(d) Any person who purchases or agrees in writing to purchase for cash in a single payment or installments, securities of the issuer in the aggregate amount of $150,000 or more.

Note: The issuer has to satisfy all the other provisions of the rule with respect to all purchases whether or not they are included in computing the number of purchasers under Subdivision (g)(2)(i).

(ii) There shall be counted as one purchaser any corporation, partnership, association, joint stock company, trust or unincorporated organization, except that if such entity was organized for the specific purpose of acquiring the securities offered, each beneficial owner of equity interests or equity securities in such entity shall count as a separate purchaser.

Note: See Preliminary Note 5 as to other persons who are considered to be purchasers.

(h) Limitations on Disposition. The issuer and any person acting on its behalf shall exercise reasonable care to assure that the purchasers of the securities in the offering are not underwriters within the meaning of section 2(11) of the Act. Such reasonable care shall include, but not necessarily be limited to, the following:

(1) Making reasonable inquiry to determine if the purchaser is acquiring the securities for his own account or on behalf of other persons;

(2) Placing a legend on the certificate or other document evidencing the securities stating that the securities have not been registered under the Act and setting forth or referring to the restrictions on transferability and sale of the securities;

(3) Issuing stop transfer instructions to the issuer's transfer agent, if any, with respect to the securities, or, if the issuer transfers its own securities, making a notation in the appropriate records of the issuer; and

(4) Obtaining from the purchaser a signed written agreement that the securities will not be sold without registration under the Act or exemption therefrom.

Note: Paragraph (h)(4) of this section does not apply to business combinations as described in paragraph (f) of this section. Notwithstanding the absence of a written agreement, the securities are restricted and may not be resolved without registration under the Act or an exemption therefrom. The issuer for its own protection should consider, however, obtaining such written agreement even in business combinations.

(i) Report of Offering. At the time of the first sale of securities in any offering effected in reliance on this rule the issuer shall file three copies of a report on Form 146 with the Commission at the Commission's Regional Office for the region in which the issuer's principal business operations are conducted or proposed to be conducted in the United States. The copies of such report with respect to an issuer having or proposing to have its principal business operations outside the United States shall be filed with the Regional Office for the region in which the offering is primarily conducted or proposed to be conducted. No report need be filed for any offering or offerings in reliance on Rule 146 the proceeds of which total, cumulatively, less then $50,000 during any twelve-month period. If any material change occurs in the facts set forth on the report on Form 146 filed with the Commission, the person who filed the statement shall promptly file with the Commission, at the Regional Office of the Commission in which the original report on Form 146 was filed, three copies of an amended Form 146 disclosing such change. (Adopted in Release No. 33-5912 (¶ 81,524), effective May 3, 1978, 43 F. R. 10550.)

(Adopted in Release No. 33-5487 (¶2710), effective June 10, 1974, 39 F. R. 15261; amended in Release No. 33-5912 (¶81,524), effective May 3, 1978, 43 F. R. 10550; Release No. 33-5975 (¶81,708), September 8, 1978, 43 F. R. 41194.)

(Compilation reference: ¶2709.)

FORM 146

U. S. SECURITIES AND EXCHANGE COMMISSION
WASHINGTON, D.C. 20549
REPORT OF OFFERING IN RELIANCE
UPON RULE 146

SEC USE ONLY

Serial: Region

ATTENTION: Transmit for filing 3 copies of this form ☐
If this is an amended report check . . . . ☐

29-

---

1 NAME OF ISSUER

ADDRESS OF ISSUER	STREET	CITY	STATE	ZIP

AREA CODE–TELEPHONE NO.	ISSUER'S STATE *(or other jurisdiction)* OF INCORPORATION OR ORGANIZATION	DATE OF INCORPORATION OR ORGANIZATION:	SEC USE ONLY

1B TYPE OF BUSINESS: *(check one)*
☐ OIL/GAS   ☐ REAL ESTATE   ☐ OTHER *(specify):*

1C FULL NAME OF CHIEF EXECUTIVE OFFICER, GENERAL PARTNER(S), PROMOTER(S) AND CONTROLLING PERSON(S).

NAME: *(last, first, middle)*

INSTRUCTION: If the General Partner(s), Promoter(s) or Controlling Person(s) is *(are)* not a natural person(s), so state and provide similar information for a natural person(s) having primary responsibility for the affairs of the issuer.

1D NAMES AND ADDRESSES OF ALL ORGANIZERS, PROMOTERS AND SPONSORS OF, AND OF ALL OFFEREE REPRESENTATIVES *[as that term is defined in Rule 146(a)(1)]* INVOLVED IN, THE OFFERING REPORTED ON THIS FORM, INDICATING THE CAPACITY IN WHICH THEY ACTED.

NAME 1		CAPACITY		SEC USE
ADDRESS 1	STREET	CITY	STATE	ZIP
NAME 2		CAPACITY		SEC USE
ADDRESS 2	STREET	CITY	STATE	ZIP
NAME 3		CAPACITY		SEC USE
ADDRESS 3	STREET	CITY	STATE	ZIP
NAME 4		CAPACITY		SEC USE
ADDRESS 4	STREET	CITY	STATE	ZIP
NAME 5		CAPACITY		SEC USE
ADDRESS 5	STREET	CITY	STATE	ZIP

SEC 1686 (12-81)

2 TITLE OF THE CLASS OF SECURITIES SOLD OR TO BE SOLD IN THIS OFFERING . . . _____
AGGREGATE DOLLAR AMOUNT OF SALES TO DATE AND SALES TO BE MADE IN THE
FUTURE IN THIS OFFERING . . . .$ _____

INSTRUCTION: As to any securities sold or to be sold other than for cash or partly for cash and partly for other consideration state the nature of the transaction and the source and aggregate amount of consideration received or to be received by the issuer.

3 INDICATE BY CHECKMARK WHETHER THE ISSUER HAS MADE ANY PREVIOUS FILINGS WITH THE SECURITIES
AND EXCHANGE COMMISSION UNDER:

Number

- RULE 146 *(If so, specify number of filings)* . . . . [_____] . . . ☐ YES ☐ NO
- THE SECURITIES ACT OF 1933 AS AN ISSUER OF SECURITIES . . . . ☐ YES ☐ NO
- THE SECURITIES EXCHANGE ACT OF 1934 AS AN ISSUER OF SECURITIES . . . . . ☐ YES ☐ NO

ATTENTION: Pursuant to the requirements of Rule 146 under the Securities Act of 1933, the issuer has duly caused this report to be signed on its behalf by the undersigned officer or person acting in a similar capacity.

DATE OF REPORT _____   _____
                                                    (ISSUER)

                            (SIGNATURE)   _____

INSTRUCTION: Print the name and title of the signing representative under his signature. At least one copy of the report shall be manually signed. Any copies not manually signed shall bear typed or printed signatures.

─────────── **ATTENTION** ───────────
Intentional misstatements or omissions of facts constitute federal criminal violations (SEE 18 U.S.C. 1001).

ADDRESSES OF COMMISSION REGIONAL OFFICES

Securities and Exchange Commission
Atlanta Regional Office
1375 Peachtree Street, N.W.
Atlanta, Georgia 30309

Securities and Exchange Commission
Denver Regional Office
Suite 700
410 Seventeenth Street
Denver, Colorado 80202

Securities and Exchange Commission
New York Regional Office
26 Federal Plaza
New York, New York 10007

Securities and Exchange Commission
Boston Regional Office
150 Causeway Street
Boston, Massachusetts 02114

Securities and Exchange Commission
Fort Worth Regional Office
503 U. S. Court House
10th and Lamar Streets
Fort Worth, Texas 76102

Securities and Exchange Commission
Seattle Regional Office
3040 Federal Building
915 Second Avenue
Seattle, Washington 98174

Securities and Exchange Commission
Chicago Regional Office
Everett McKinley Dirksen Bldg.
219 South Dearbon Street
Chicago, Illinois

Securities and Exchange Commission
Los Angeles Regional Office
10960 Wilshire Boulevard
Los Angeles, California 90024

Securities and Exchange Commission
Washington Regional Office
Ballston Center Tower 3
4015 Wilson Boulevard
Arlington, Virginia 22203

Rule 147—
Securities Act of 1933

¶ 5718C

Reg. §230.147 (Rule 147) "Part of an Issue."

"Person Resident," and "Doing Business Within" for Purposes of Section 3(a)(11)

Reg. §230.147

Preliminary Notes

1. This rule shall not raise any presumption that the exemption provided by Section 3(a)(11) of the Act is not available for transactions by an issuer which do not satisfy all of the provisions of the rule.

2. Nothing in this rule obviates the need for compliance with any state law relating to the offer and sale of securities.

3. Section 5 of the Act requires that all securities offered by the use of the mails or by any means or instruments of transportation or communication in interstate commerce be registered with the Commission. Congress, however, provided certain exemptions in the Act from such registration provisions, where there was not practical need for registration or where the benefits of registration were too remote. Among those exemptions is that provided by Section 3(a)(11) of the Act for transactions in "any security which is a part of an issue offered and sold only to persons resident within a single State or Territory, where the issuer of such security is a person resident and doing business within . . . such State or Territory." The legislative history of that Section suggests that the exemption was intended to apply only to issues genuinely local in character, which in reality represent local financing by local industries, carried out through local investment. Rule 147 is intended to provide more objective standards upon which responsible local businessmen intending to raise local sources may rely in claiming the Section 3(a)(11) exemption.

All of the terms and conditions of the rule must be satisfied in order for the rule to be available. These are: (i) that the issuer be a resident of and doing business within the state or territory in which all offers and sales are made; and (ii) that no part of the issue be offered or sold to nonresidents within the period of time specified in the rule. For purposes of the rule the definition of "issuer" in Section 2(4) of the Act shall apply.

All offers, offers to sell, offers for sale, and sales which are part of the same issue must meet all of the conditions of Rule 147 for the rule to be available. The determination whether offers, offers to sell, offers for sale and sales of securities are part of the same issue (i.e., are deemed to be "integrated") will continue to be a question of fact and will depend on the particular circumstances. See Securities Act of 1933 Release No. 4434 (December 6, 1961). Release 33-4434 indicated that in determining whether offers and sales should be regarded as part of the same issue and thus should be integrated any one or more of the following factors may be determinative:

(i)   Are the offerings part of a single plan of financing;
(ii) Do the offerings involve issuance of the same class of securities;
(iii) Are the offerings made at or about the same time;
(iv) Is the same type of consideration to be received; and
(v)   Are the offerings made for the same general purpose.

Subparagraph (b)(2) of the rule, however, is designed to provide certainty to the extent feasible by identifying certain types of offers and sales of securities which will be deemed not part of an issuer, for purposes of the rule only.

Persons claiming the availability of the rule have the burden of proving that they have satisfied all of its provisions. However, the rule does not establish exclusive standards for complying with the Section 3 (a)(11) exemption. The exemption would also be available if the issue satisfied the standards set forth in relevant administrative and judicial interpretations at the time of the offering but the issuer would have the burden of proving the availability of the exemption. Rule 147 relates to transactions exempted from the registration requirements of Section 5 by the Act by Section 3(a)(11). Neither the rule nor Section 3(a)(11) provides an exemption from the registration requirements of Section 12(g) of the Securities Exchange Act of 1934, the anti-fraud provisions of the federal securities laws, the civil liability provisions of Section 12(2) of the Act or other provisions of the federal securities laws.

Finally, in view of the objectives of the rule and the purposes and policies underlying the Act, the rule shall not be available to any person with respect to any offering which, although in technical compliance with the rule, is part of a plan or scheme by such person to make interstate offers or sales of securities. In such cases registration pursuant to the Act is required.

4.   The rule provides an exemption for offers and sales by the issuer only. It is not available for offers or sales of securities by other persons. Section 3(a)(11) of the Act has been interpreted to permit offers and sales by persons controlling the issuer, if the exemption provided by that Section would have been available to the issuer at the time of the offering. See Securities Act Release No. 4434 (December 6, 1961). Controlling persons

who want to offer or sell securities pursuant to Section 3(a)(11) may continue to do so in accordance with applicable judicial and administrative interpretations.

(a) Transactions Covered. Offers, offers to sell, offers for sale and sales by an issuer of its securities made in accordance with all of the terms and conditions of this rule shall be deemed to be part of an issue offered and sold only to persons resident and doing business within such state or territory, within the meaning of Section 3(a)(11) of the Act.

(b) Part of an Issue.

(1) For purposes of this rule, all securities of the issuer which are part of an issue shall be offered, offered for sale or sold in accordance with all of the terms and conditions of this rule.

(2) For purposes of this rule only, an issue shall be deemed not to include offers, offers to sell, offers for sale or sales of securities of the issuer pursuant to the exemptions provided by Section 3 or Section 4(2) of the Act or pursuant to a registration statement filed under the Act, that take place prior to the six month period immediately preceding or after the six month period immediately following any offers, offers for sales or sales pursuant to this rule, provided that, there are during either of said six month periods no offers, offers for sale or sales of securities by or for the issuer of the same or similar class as those offered, offered for sale or sold pursuant to the rule.

> *Note:* In the event that securities of the same or similar class as those offered pursuant to the rule are offered, offered for sale or sold less than six months prior to or subsequent to any offer, offer for sale or sale pursuant to this rule, see Preliminary Note 3 hereof, as to which offers, offers to sell, offers for sale, or sales are part of an issue.

(c) Nature of the Issuer. The issuer of the securities shall at the time of any offers and the sales be a person resident and doing business within the state or territory in which all of the offers, offers to sell, offers for sale and sales are made.

(1) The issuer shall be deemed to be a resident of the state or territory in which:

(i) It is incorporated or organized, if a corporation, limited partnership, trust or other form of business organization that is organized under state or territorial law;

(ii) Its principal office is located, if a general partnership or other form of business organization that is not organized under any state or territorial law;

(iii) His principal residence is located, if an individual.

(2) The issuer shall be deemed to be doing business within a state or territory if:

(i) The issuer derived at least 80% of its gross revenues and those of its subsidiaries on a consolidated basis

(A) For its most recent fiscal year, if the first offer of any part of the issue is made during the first six months of the issuer's current fiscal year; or

(B) For the first six months of its current fiscal year or during the twelve month fiscal period ending with such six month period, if the first offer of any part of the issue is made during the last six months of the issuer's current fiscal year from the operation of a business or of real property located in or from the rendering of services within such state or territory; provided, however, that this provisions does not apply to any issuer which has not had gross revenues in excess of $5,000 from the sale of products or services or other conduct of its business for its most recent twelve month fiscal period;

(ii) The issuer had at the end of its most recent semi-annual fiscal period prior to the first offer of any part of the issue, at least 80 percent of its assets and those of its subsidiaries on a consolidated basis located within such state or territory;

(iii) The issuer intends to use and uses at least 80% of the net proceeds to the issuer from sales made pursuant to this rule in connection with the operation of a business or of real property, the purchase of real property located in, or the rendering of services within such state or territory; and

(iv) The principal office of the issuer is located within such state or territory.

(d) Offerees and Purchasers: Person Resident. Offers, offers to sell, offers for sale and sales of securities that are part of an issue shall be made only to persons resident within the state or territory of which the issuer is a resident. For purposes of determining the residence of offerees and purchasers:

(1) A corporation, partnership, trust or other form of business organization shall be deemed to be a resident of a state or territory if, at the time of the offer and sale to it, it has its principal office within such state or territory.

(2) An individual shall be deemed to be a resident of a state or territory if such individual has, at the time of the offer and sale to him, his principal residence in the state or territory.

(3) A corporation, partnership, trust or other form of business organization which is organized for the specific purpose of acquiring part of an issue offered pursuant to this rule shall be deemed not to be a resident of a state or territory unless all of the beneficial owners of such organization are residents of such state or territory.

(e) Limitation of Resales. During the period in which securities that are part of an issue are being offered and sold by the issuer, and for a period of nine months from the date of the last sale by the issuer of such securities, all resales of any part of the issue, by an person, shall be made only to persons resident within such state or territory.

Note 1: In the case of convertible securities resales of either the convertible security, or if it is converted, the underlying security, could be made during the period described in paragraph (e) only to persons resident within such state or territory. For purposes of this rule a conversion in reliance on Section 3(a)(9) of the Act does not begin a new period.

Note 2: Dealers must satisfy the requirements of Rule 15(c)2-11 under the Securities Exchange Act of 1934 prior to publishing any quotation for a security, or submitting any quotation for publication, in any quotation medium.

(f) Precautions Against Interstate Offers and Sales.

(1) The issuer shall, in connection with any securities sold by it pursuant to this rule:

(i) Place a legend on the certificate or other document evidencing the security stating that the securities have not been registered under the Act and setting forth the limitations on resale contained in paragraph (e);

(ii) Issue stop transfer instructions to the issuer's transfer agent, if any, with respect to the securities, or, if the issuer transfers its own securities, make a notation in the appropriate records of the issuer; and

(iii) Obtain a written representation from each purchaser as to his residence.

(2) The issuer shall, in connection with the issuance of new certificates for any of the securities that are part of the same issue that are presented for transfer during the time period specified in paragraph (e), take steps required by subsections (f)(1)(i) and (ii).

(e) The issuer shall, in connection with any offers, offers to sell, offers for sale or sales by it pursuant to this rule, disclose, in writing, the limitations on resale contained in paragraph (e) and the provisions of subsections (f)(1)(i) and (ii) and subparagraph (f)(2).

(Adopted in Release No. 33-5450 (¶2340), effective for offerings commenced on or after March 1, 1974, 39 R.R. 2353.)

Rule 240—
Securities Act of 1933

Release No. 5560/January 24, 1975

NOTICE OF ADOPTION OF RULE 240 UNDER THE SECURITIES ACT OF 1933—"EXEMPTION OF CERTAIN LIMITED OFFERS AND SALES BY CLOSELY HELD ISSUERS"; NOTICE OF ADOPTION OF FORM 240; AND NOTICE OF ADOPTION OF AMENDMENT TO RULE 144 UNDER SUCH ACT

(EFFECTIVE DATE: MARCH 15, 1975)

The Securities and Exchange Commission today announced the adoption of Rule 240 and related Form 240 under the Securities Act of 1933 ("Act"), "Exemption of Certain Limited Offers and Sales by Closely Held Issuers," which provides an exemption from registration for limited offers and sales of small dollar amounts of securities by an issuer that before and after the transaction pursuant to the rule has a limited number (100) of beneficial owners of its securities. The purpose of the rule is to provide an exemption from the registration but not the anti-fraud or other provisions of the Act for offers and sales that take place in the raising of capital by small businesses where, because of the small size and the limited character of the offering, the public benefits of registration are too remote. The rule is available for issuers only; it is not available for resales of securities by affiliates of the issuer or other persons. Generally speaking, Form 240 is a notice to be filed not more than once in each calendar year, with the Commission's Regional Office for the region in which the issuer's principal business operations are conducted reporting that a sale has been made in reliance on the rule. In connection with adoption of Rule 240 and Form 240, the Commission also adopted an amendment to Rule 144 under the Act which specifies that securities sold pursuant to Rule 240 would be deemed to be "restricted securities'' for the purpose of Rule 144 and could, therefore, be resold pursuant to its provisions.

The Commission proposed Rule 240, Form 240 and the amendment to Rule 144 for comment in June 1974 (Securities Act Release No. 5499, June 3, 1974) and received approximately thirty letters of comment thereon. Most commentators supported the concept of the proposed rule, but suggested certain modifications. The rule as adopted differs in several ways form that proposed. Among the revisions are the deletion of the prohibition on use of the rule by limited partnerships; the addition of a prohibition on use of the rule by investment companies registered or required to be registered under the Investment Company Act of 1940; the elimination of the limitation on the number of purchasers (but not the number of beneficial owners); the increase in the limitation on the number of beneficial owners from fifty to one hundred; the change in the period for calculating the aggregate amount that can be sold in reliance on the rule from a consecutive twelve month period to the twelve months preceding each sale; and the broadening of the exclusions in calculating such aggregate amount. These and other revisions from the proposed rule are discussed under the appropriate paragraph in the synopsis of the rule that follows. The Commission finds that these changes have already generally been the subject of comment or are technical in nature and that republication for comment is not required under the Administrative Procedure Act.

RULE 240 AND FORM 240

This release contains a general discussion of the background, purpose and general effect of the rule to assist in a better understanding of its provisions. A brief synopsis of each paragraph in the rule is also included. However, attention is directed to the rule itself for a more complete understanding.

Background and Purpose

Congress, in enacting the federal securities laws, created a continuous disclosure system designed to protect investors and to assure the maintenance of fair and honest securities markets. The Commission, in administering the implementing these laws, has sought to coordinate this disclosure system with the exemptive provisions provided by such laws. Rule 240 is a further effort in this direction.

The legislative history of the Securities Act of 1933 indicates that the main concern of Congress was to provide full and fair disclosure in connection with the offer and sale of securities. Congress recognized, however, that there were certain situations in which the protections afforded by the registration provisions of the Act were not necessary. Concerning those specified exemptions from the Act, the House Report stated that "The Act carefully exempts from its application certain types of . . . securities transactions where there is no practical need for its application or where the public benefits are too remote."[1]

Section 3(b) of the Act provides that the Commission may by rules, and subject to such terms and conditions as it may prescribe, "add any class of securities to the securities exempted as provided in this section (Section 3 of the Act), if it finds that the enforcement of this title with respect to such securities is not necessary in the public interest and for the protection of investors by reason of the small amount involved or the limited character of the public offering." The Commission believes that offers and sales of securities by an issuer pursuant to the rule are of such limited character and of such small amount that enforcement of the registration provisions of the Act with respect to such transactions are not necessary in the public interest or for the protection of investors. Notwithstanding the exemption from registration, however, the anti-fraud provisions of the federal securities laws, and the state securities laws, continue to apply to such transactions.

General Description

In summary, the rule provides that offers and sales of securities of the issuer by the issuer are exempt from registration if all the conditions of the rule are met. These conditions impose limitations on the manner of offering, the number of beneficial owners and the aggregate sales price of securities of the issuer, and resales of the securities. Other conditions prohibit payments for solicitation of buyers or in connection with sales and require the filing of a notice of sales. The conditions are intended to assure that the offering is one in which the dollar amount involved is small and the offering is limited in character.

The rule is only available to issuers of securities other than investment companies registered or required to registered under the Investment Company Act of 1940 and is not available to affiliates of the issuer or other persons for sale of the issuer's securities. The rule provides an exemption for the issuer transaction only, not for the securities themselves. Persons who acquire securities from issuers in a transaction complying with the rule acquire securities that are unregistered and that are deemed to have the same status as if such securities were acquired in a transaction exempt from registration under Section 4(2) of the Act; such securities can only be reoffered or resold if registered or, if available, pursuant to an exemption from the registration provisions of the Act such as Section 4(1) of the Act or Rule 237 thereunder. In this connection, the amendment to Rule 144 makes Rule 144 available for resales or securities acquired pursuant to Rule 240, provided that all the conditions of Rule 144 are met.

Synopsis of the Provisions of Rule 240

Preliminary Notes

The first preliminary note reminds issuers that Rule 240 provides an exemption from registration only, and not from the anti-fraud or other provisions of the federal securities laws. The second note reminds issuers that state law also applies to transactions under the rule and that the rule does not relieve the issuer from compliance to such law. A new third note has been added to make it clear that purported reliance on the rule is not an election and that the issuer can rely on any exemption that is otherwise available for transaction. The fourth note makes it clear that the rule is available to issuers only and is a transactional exemption, and is not available for resales of securities. The fifth note restates the Commission's position as with respect to Rules 144, 146 and 147, that the rule is not available to any issuer with respect to any transations which, although in technical compliance with the rule, are part of a plan or scheme to evade the registration provisions of the Act. For example, if an issuer liquidates and forms a new corporation for purposes of repeated use of the rule, the exemption provided by the rule would be unavailable. In such cases, registration pursuant to the Act is required.

A new sixth note outlines the relationship of offers and sales pursuant to the rule to offers and sales in reliance upon other exemptions. In determining the availability of such other exemptions, offers and sales pursuant to the rule must be given due consideration when applying the traditional integration guidelines set forth in Securities Act Release No. 4552. For example, while a transaction may be exempt pursuant to Rule 240, the same transaction may be part of a larger issue of securities and affect, for exampel the availability of an exemption under Regulation A, Section 3(a)(11) or Section 4(2) for other transactions which are part of such larger issue.

Rule 240(a): Definitions

Securities of the Issuer: Rule 240(a)(1).   The term "securities of the issuer" is defined for purposes of the rule to mean all securities of the issuer and its affiliates. Thus, securities of all classes of the issuer, as well as securities of affiliated corporations or other entities, would be considered in applying the conditions of the rule. The definition has been expanded from that proposed to make explicit that securities issued by partnerships with the same or affiliated general partners and fractional undivided interests in oil or gas rights created by the same or affiliated persons would be included within the meaning of the term "securities of the issuer."

Affiliate: Rule 240(a)(2).   The term "affiliate" or "affiliated" with a person is defined to be a person that directly or indirectly through one or more intermediaries, controls, or is controlled by, or is under common control with such person.

Executive Officer: Rule 240(a)(3). A definition of "executive officer" identical to that in the proxy rules and in form 10-K has been added since that term is used in paragraph (e) in indentifying persons whose transactions are excludable from the calculation of the aggregate sales price of securities sold if such transactions are made in reliance on an exemption other than the rule.

Deletion of Proposed Rule 240(a)(3): Definition of Predecessor. The definition of the term "predecessor" has been deleted since the term no longer appears in the rule. The Commission believes that the inclusion of predecessors in calculating the aggregate sales price and number of beneficial owners would be unduly restrictive in view of the purpose of the rule and the other conditions on the availability of the rule. However, if, for example, an issuer liquidates and forms a new corporation for the purpose of repeated use of the rule, the exemption provided by the rule would be unavailable. (See preliminary note 5.)

Promoter: Rule 240(a)(4).

A definition of "promoter" based on that in Rule 251 of Regulation A under the Act has been added to the rule since the term "promoter" is now used in paragraph (e) in identifying persons whose transactions are excludable from the calculation of the aggregate sales price of securities sold if such transactions are made in reliance on an exemption other than the rule.

Deletion of Proposed Rule 240(b): Use of the Rule

Paragraph (b) of the rule as proposed provided that the rule would not be available for the offer or sale of interests in limited partnerships, whether such offers or sales were made prior or subsequent to the formation of the partnership. The Commission has decided that it should not single out this one form of business organization, and therefore has revised the rule to make it available to all issuers of securities other than investment companies registered or required to be registered under the Investment Company Act of 1940. However, the rule makes it clear, in its definition of "securities of the issuer," that interests in partnerships with the same or affiliated general partners and that fractional undivided interests in oil or gas rights created by the same or affiliated persons would be considered to be securities of the same issuer. All sales by such partnerships or entities would therefore be aggregated in determining the amount sold and all purchasers of interests in these partnerships or entities must be considered in calculating the number of beneficial owners. This is intended to avoid repeated use of the rule by the same or related persons for a series of offerings.

Rule 240(b): Conditions to be Met

This paragraph provides that transactions by issuer involving the offer or sale of its securities in accordance with all the terms and conditions of the rule will be exempt from the registration provisions of the Act provided, however, that the issuer is not an investment company registered or required to be registered under the Investment Company Act of 1940. The rule has been made unavailable to such investment companies in light of the similar restrictions in Regulation A under the Act and on the availability to investment companies of Section 3(a)(11) of the Act. A note has been added to this paragraph to indicate that each individual transaction effected in reliance on the rule must meet all the terms and conditions of the rule; the availability of the rule will not be affected by other transactions effected in reliance on the rule but which do not meet all its terms and conditions. However, all such transactions must be considered in determining the availability of the exemptions for other offers or sales of unregistered securities. (See preliminary note 6.) A second note has been added to emphasize that the rule is available only to issuers for offers and sales of their securities.

Rule 240(c): Limitation on Manner of Offering

The rule provides that the securities shall not be offered or sold by any means of general advertising or general solicitation. Offers and sales in reliance on the rule cannot be made through newspapers, advertisements or other means of general advertising. Where such means are used, an exemption cannot be justified on the basis of the "limited character" of the offering pursuant to the rule.

Rule 240(d): Prohibition of Remuneration Paid for Solicitation or for Sales

The rule also provides that no commission or similar remuneration may be paid for solicitation of prospective buyers or in connection with sales of securities. This provision is based on similar ones in certain state securities statutes and is intended to assure that securities are not offered or sold using high pressure tactics or otherwise through organized securities distribution media.

Rule 240(e): Limitation on Aggregate Sales Price

In order to assure that only a limited dollar amount of securities is sold, the rule provides that the aggregate sales price of all sales of securities of the issuer as defined in subparagraph (a)(1) of the rule in reliance on the rule or otherwise without registration under the Act within the preceding twelve months shall not exceed $100,000. Three notes have been added to this paragraph to explain and illustrate the calculation of the aggregate sales price.

The rule specifically excludes from the computation of the dollar amount the following: (1) all securities of the issuer registered or exempt from registration under the Act is such securities were sold prior to the effective date of the rule; and (2) the following securities if sold in reliance on an exemption other than the rule: (i) nonconvertible notes or similar evidences of indebtedness (1) representing a purchase money mortgage or (2) issued to banks, savings institutions, trust companies, insurance companies, investment companies registed under the Investment Company Act of 1940, Small Business Investment Companies or Minority Enterprise Small Business Investment Companies licensed by the U.S. Small Business Administration, or pension or profit sharing trusts, and (ii) securities sold to promoters, directors, executive officers, or full-time employees of the issuer. It should be noted that the persons described in subparagraph (e)(2)(ii), but not the institutional lenders described in subparagraph (e)(2)(i), count as beneficial owners even in the event that the securities sold to such persons are not includable in calculating the aggregate sales price of securities of the issuer. In addition, nonconvertible notes must be included in the computation of the aggregate sales price when such notes have been issued with warrants or other rights enabling the purchaser to acquire an equity interest in the issuer.

The rule, as proposed, included a limitation on the aggregate dollar amount of securities that could be sold within any consecutive twelve month period. Upon reconsideration of this limitation, the Commission has determined that reliance on a consecutive twelve month period is unnecessarily confusing and it has therefore changed the calculation period to the twelve months preceding each sale.

Deletion of Proposed Rule 240(f): Number of Purchasers

The proposed rule contained a limitation on the number of persons who could purchase securities (other than registered securities) from the issuer, its predecessors or any affiliated issuers in a twelve month period in order to assure the limited character of any offering. As proposed, the rule limited the number of such purchasers to twenty-five in any consecutive twelve month period, with special provisions for computing the number of purchasers. The Commission has determined that the limitation on the number of purchasers in a twelve month period is not necessary in the context of the rule because of the overall limitation on the number (100) of beneficial owners of securities of the issuer as that term is defined in subparagraph (a)(1) of the rule. Accordingly, the Commission has deleted the limitation on the number of purchasers.

Rule 240(f): Limitation on the Number of Beneficial Owners

The rule provides that both immediately before and after any transaction in reliance on the rule, the issuer shall, after reasonable inquiry, have reasonable grounds to believe, and shall believe that the securities of the issuer as defined in subparagraph (a)(1) of the rule are beneficially owned by 100 or fewer persons. As proposed, the rule was limited to issuers with 50 or fewer beneficial owners and contained no provisions for a reasonable inquiry or for reasonable grounds for the issuer's belief concerning the number of beneficial owners of its securities. Upon reconsideration of this limitation, the Commission has determined that a limit of 100 beneficial owners would be consistent with the purposes of the rule and of Section 3(b) of the Act.

The rule contains special provisions for computing the number of beneficial owners where family relationships are involved or where the purchaser is a corporation or trust. In addition, banks and other institutional-type lenders described in subparagraph (e)(2)(i), that purchase or hold only nonconvertible notes or similar evidences of indebtedness of the issuer would be excluded. The purpose of this condition is to make the rule available only where the public interest in registration appears remote due to the limited number of beneficial owners involved. Notes to this paragraph of the rule have been added to remind issuers that purchasers of nonconvertible notes with warrants attached and persons described in subparagraph (e)(2)(ii) count in computing the number of beneficial owners.

Rule 240(g): Limitation on Resale

The condition relating to resale has been revised to make clear that the securities acquired pursuant to the rule are unregistered securities and that they are deemed to have the same status as if they were securities acquired in a transaction pursuant to Section 4(2) under the Act.

The rule requires the issuer to exercise reasonable care to assure that purchasers are not acting as underwriters, which reasonable care includes at least making reasonable inquiry to determine if the purchaser is buying for himself or others, informing the purchaser of the restrictions on resale,[2] and legending of the certificates.

In connection with such restrictions, the Commission is amending Rule 144 to include within the definition of "restricted securities" those securities acquired from the issuer in a transaction in reliance on Rule 240 under the Act or which were issued by an issuer in a transaction in reliance on Rule 240 and were acquired in a transaction or chain of transactions not involving any public offering. Thus, Rule 144 would be available for resales or securities acquired pursuant to Rule 240.

Rule 240(h): Notice of Sales

The rule requires that during each calendar year, an issuer which sells securities in reliance on the rule must file a notice on Form 240 with the Commission's Regional Office for the region in which the issuer's principal business operations are conducted within ten days after the close of the first month in which a sale in reliance on the rule is made. As proposed, the form would have had to be filed prior to the first sale. The Commission has concluded that issuers may have found it difficult to comply with an advance filing requirement and that a filing after the first sale would be satisfactory. Although many commentators objected to the filing requirement, the Commission believes that the filing requirement is presently justified in light of the experimental nature of the rule and the creation of a new exemption.

It should be noted, however, that the exemption provided by the rule will be available for the first $100,000 of the securities of the issuer sold by the issuer if the sale of such securities complied with all the conditions of the rule other than the notice requirement. However, the exemption provided by the rule will not be available for any subsequent sale of securities by such issuer unless such issuer files: (a) prior to such subsequent sale in reliance on this rule a notice on Form 240 covering the prior sale of all securities for which reliance on this rule is claimed; and (b) a notice on Form 240 covering such subsequent sale.

Form 240

Form 240 is a notice to be filed with the Commission's Regional Office for the region in which the issuer's principal business operations are conducted reporting that a sale(s) has been made pursuant to the rule. The Form is brief and requires information about the issuer, its officers, directors, principal stockholders and promoters, the aggregate sales price of unregistered securities, and the number of beneficial owners. It need only be filed once in each calendar year, within ten days after the close of the month in which the first sale(s) is made in reliance on the rule. The Form will be publicly available immediately in the regional office at which it is filed.

OPERATION OF RULE 240

The rule will operate prospectively only since there is now no similar exemption under Section 3(b). The staff will issue interpretative letters to assist persons in complying with the rule but will not issue no-action letters dealing with Rule 240. As to resale of securities, the staff will continue its present policy of not issuing no-action letters in Section 4(1) situations with respect to securities acquired on or after April 14, 1972, as set forth in the release accompanying the adoption of Rule 144 (Securities Act Release No. 5223, January 11, 1972).

In view of the objectives and policies underlying the Act, the rule is not available to any issuer with respect to any transaction which, although in technical compliance with the provisions of the rule, is part of a plan or scheme to evade the registration provisions of the Act. In such cases, registration is required.

Rule 240 relates only to transactions exempted by the rule from the registration provisions of the Act. It does not provided an exemption from the anti-fraud or other provisions of the federal securities laws or from provisions of state securities laws.

The rule is available only to the issuer of the securities and not to affiliates or other persons proposing to resell securities of the issuer. Such resale must be made in compliance with the registration provisions of the Act unless an exemption from such provisions is available. Also, the rule does not relieve issuers of their obligations under relevant state laws.

The Commission hereby adopts Rule 240 and Form 240 pursuant to Sections 3(b) and 19(a) of the Act, as amended, and amends Rule 144 under the Act pursuant to Sections 4(1) and 19(a) of The Act. The Commission finds that republication for comment of Rule 240, Form 240 and the amendment to Rule 144 is not necessary under the Administrative Procedure Act because the revisions made from the rule, form and amendment, as proposed, have already been the subject of public comment or are technical in nature. The text of Rule 240, Form 240 and of the amendment to Rule 144 is attached hereto. These actions are effective on and after March 15, 1975.

By the Commission

GEORGE A. FITZSIMMONS
Secretary

RULE 240—Preliminary Notes

1. Rule 240 relates to transactions exempted only from Section 5 of the Act by Section 3(b) of the act. It does not provide an exemption from the anti-fraud provisions of the federal securities laws or from civil liability provisions of Section 12(2) of the Act or other provisions of the federal securities laws.
2. Nothing in this rule obviates the need for compliance with any applicable state law relating to the offer and sale of securities.
3. Purported reliance on this rule does not act as an election; the issuer can also claim the availability of any other applicable exemption.
4. The rule is available only to the issuer of the securities and is not available to affiliates or other persons for resales of the issuer's securities. The rule provides an exemption only for the transactions in

which the securities are offered or sold by the issuer, not for the securities themselves. The securities acquired in a transaction effected in reliance on the rule are unregistered securities and are deemed to have the same status as if they were acquired in a transaction pursuant to Section 4(2) of the Act.

5. In view of the objectives of the rule and the purpose and policies underlying the Act, the rule is not available to any issuer with respect to any transactions which, although in technical compliance with the rule, are part of a plan or scheme to evade the registration provisions of the Act. In such cases registration pursuant to the Act is required.

6. While a transaction may be exempt pursuant to Rule 240, the same transaction may be part of a larger issue of securities and may affect the availability of a different exemption for other transactions which are a part of such larger issue. See Securities Act Release No. 4552 (November 6, 1962) concerning the integration of transactions.

(a) *Definitions*. For purposes of the rule only, the following definitions shall apply.

(1) *Securities of the Issuer*. The term "securities of the issuer" shall include all securities issued by the issuer and by any affiliate of the issuer. Securities issued by partnerships with the same or affiliated general partners and fractional undivided interests in oil or gas rights created by the same or affiliated persons shall be deemd to be included as "securities of the issuer."

(2) *Affiliate*. The term "affiliate" of or "affiliated" with a person means a person that directly or indirectly through one or more intermediaries, controls, or is controlled by, or is under common control with such person.

(3) *Executive Officer*. The term "executive officer" means the president, secretary, treasurer, any vice president in charge of a principal business (such as sales, administration or finance) and any other person who performs similar policymaking functions for the issuer.

(4) *Promoter*. The term "promoter" includes: (i) any person who, acting alone or in conjunction with one or more persons, directly or indirectly takes the initiative in founding and organizing the business or enterprise of an issuer; or (ii) any person who, in connection with the founding or organizing of the business or enterprise of the issuer, directly or indirectly receives in consideration of services or property, 10 percent or more of the proceeds from the sale of any class of securities. However, a person who receives such securities or proceeds either solely as underwriting commissions or solely in consideration of property shall not be deemed a promoter within the meaning of this paragraph if such person does not otherwise take part in founding and organizing the enterprise.

Note: Commissions may not be paid or given for soliciting buyers or in connection with sales of securities pursuant to the rule. See paragraph (d).

(b) *Conditions to be Met.* Transactions by an issuer involving the offer and sale of its securities in accordance with all the terms and conditions of this rule shall be exempt only from the provisions of Section 5 of the Act pursuant to Section 3(b) of the Act; provided, however, that the issuer is not an investment company registered or required to be registered under the Investment Company Act of 1940.

Note 1: Each individual transaction effected in reliance on the rule must meet all the terms and conditions of the rule; the availability of the rule will not be affected by other transactions effected in reliance upon the rule but which do not meet all its terms and conditions.

Note 2: This rule is available only for offers and sales by issuers of their securities. See Preliminary Note 4.

(c) *Limitation on Manner of Offering.* The securities shall not be offered, offered for sale or sold in reliance on this rule by any means of general advertising or general solicitation.

(d) *Prohibition of Remuneration Paid for Solicitation or for Sales.* No commission or similar remuneration shall be paid or given directly or indirectly for soliciting any prospective buyer or in connection with sales of the securities in reliance on this rule.

(e) *Limitation on Aggregate Sales Price.* The aggregate sale price of all sales of securities of the issuer as defined in subparagraph (a)(1) in reliance on this rule or otherwise without registration under the Act within twelve months preceding the point in time immediately after the last such sale shall not exceed $100,000.

Note 1: The calculation of the aggregate sales price may be illustated as follows. If an issuer sold $50,000 of its securities on June 1, 1975, in reliance on the rule, and an additional $25,000 on September 1, 1975, the issuer would be permitted to sell only $25,000 more until June 1, 1976 since until that date the issuer must count both prior sales toward the $100,000 limit. However, if the issuer made its third sale on June 1, 1976, the issuer could sell $75,000 of its securities since the June 1, 1975 sale would not be within the preceding twelve months.

Note 2: If a transaction relying on the rule fails to meet the limitation on the aggregate sales price, it does not affect the availability of the rule for the other transactions considered in applying such limitation. For example, if the issuer in the prior note made its third sale on May 31, 1976, in the amount of $30,000, the rule would not be available for that sale; but the exemption for the prior two sales would be unaffected.

Note 3: The calculation of the aggregate sales price would include all consideration received for the issuance of securities of the issuer, including cash, services, property, notes, or other consideration.

For purposes of computing the dollar amount of securities sold, the following shall be excluded:

(1) All securities of the issuer registered or exempt from registration under the Act, if such securities were sold prior to the effective date of this rule.

(2) The following securities if sold in reliance on an exemption from registration other than this rule:

(i) Nonconvertible notes or similar evidences or indebtedness (1) representing a purchase money mortgage or (2) issued to a bank, savings institution, trust company, insurance company, investment company registered under the Investment Company Act of 1940, Small Business Investment Company or Minority Enterprise Small Business Investment Company licensed by the U.S. Small Business Administration, or pension or profit sharing trust; or

Note: The exclusion set forth in this subparagraph does not apply to arrangements where nonconvertible notes are issued with warrants or other rights enabling the purchaser to acquire an equity interest in the issuer.

(ii) Securities sold to any promoter, director, executive officer, or full-time employee.

Note: It should be noted that this subparagraph (ii) only provides an exclusion for the computation of the aggregate dollar amount of securities sold; persons named in this subparagraph are not excluded from the computation of the number of beneficial owners in paragraph (f).

(f) *Limitation on Number of Beneficial Owners.* Both immediately before and immediately after any transaction in reliance on this rule, the issuer shall, after reasonable inquiry, have reasonable grounds to believe, and shall believe, that the securities of the issuer as defined in subparagraph (a)(1) are beneficially owned by 100 or fewer persons. For purposes of this provision:

(1) the following shall be deemed the same and not a separate beneficial owner:

(i) Any relative or spouse of a beneficial owner and any relative of such spouse, who has the same home as such beneficial owner:

(ii) Any trust or estate in which a beneficial owner or any of the persons related to him as specified in subparagraphs (f)(1)(i) or (iii) collectively have 100 percent of the beneficial interest (excluding contingent interests); and

(iii) Any corporation or other organization of which a beneficial owner or any of the persons related to him as specified in subparagraphs (f)(1)(i) or (ii) collectively are the beneficial owners of all of the equity securities (excluding directors' qualifying shares) or equity interests;

(2) There shall be counted as one beneficial owner any corporation or other organization, except that if such entity was organized for the specific purpose of acquiring the securities offered, each beneficial owner of equity interest or equity securities in such entity shall count as a separate beneficial owner; and

(3) There shall be excluded from the computation any owner of only a purchase money mortgage and any bank, savings institution, trust company, insurance company, investment company registered under the Investment Company Act of 1940, Small Business Investment Company or Minority Enterprise Small Business Investment Company licensed by the U.S. Small Business Administration, or pension or profit sharing trust which purchases or holds only nonconvertible notes or similar evidences of indebtedness of the issuer.

Note 1: The exclusion set forth in this subparagraph does not apply to arrangements where nonconvertible notes are issued with warrants or other rights enabling the purchaser to acquire an equity interest in the issuer.

Note 2: It should be noted that subparagraph (e)(2)(ii) only provides an exclusion for the computation of the aggregate dollar amount of securities sold; persons named in that subparagraph are not excluded from the computation of the number of beneficial owners.

(g) *Limitation on Resale.* In determining the availability of an exemption from registration for resale of securities acquired in a transaction effected in reliance on this rule, such securities shall be deemed to have the same status as if they had been acquired in a transaction pursuant to Section 4(2) of the Act and they cannot be resold without registration under the Act or exemption therefrom. The issuer shall exercise reasonable care to assure that the purchasers of the securities are not underwriters within the meaning of Section 2(11) of the Act, which reasonable care shall include, but not necessarily be limited to:

(1) making reasonable inquiry to determine if the purchaser is acquiring the securities for his own account or on behalf of other persons;

(2) informing the purchaser of the restrictions on resale; and

(3) placing a legend on the certificate or other document evidencing the securities stating that the securities have not been registered under the Act and setting forth or referring to the restrictions on transferability and sale of the securities.

(h) *Filing of Notice of Sales*

(1) During each calendar year, within ten days after the close of the first month in which a sale in reliance on this rule is made, the issuer

shall file with the Regional Office of the Commission for the region in which the issuer's principal business operations are conducted three copies of a notice on Form 240 which shall be signed by a duly authorized officer of the issuer or by a person acting in a similar capacity for a noncorporate issuer.

(2) Notwithstanding the foregoing, the exemption provided by this rule will be available for the first $100,000 of the securities of the issuer as defined in subparagraph (a)(1) sold by the issuer if the sale of such securities complied with all the conditions of this rule other than the notice requirement. However, the exemption provided by this rule will not be available for any subsequent sale of securities by such issuer unless such issuer files: (a) prior to such subsequent sale in reliance on this rule, a notice on Form 240 covering the prior sale of all securities for which reliance on this rule is claimed; and (b) a notice of form 240 covering such subsequent sale.

Text of Amendment to Rule 144 [Addition in Italics]

(a)(3) The term "restricted securities" means securities acquired directly or indirectly from the issuer thereof, or from an affiliate of such issuer, in a transaction or chain of transactions not involving any public offering *or from the issuer in a transaction in reliance on Rule 240 under the Act or which were issued by an issuer in a transaction in reliance on Rule 240 and were acquired in a transaction or chain of transactions not involving any public offering.*

FORM 240—Notice of Sales of Securities Pursuant to Rule 240

(To be filed with the Regional Office of the Securities and Exchange Commission for the region in which the issuer's principal business operations are conducted not more than 10 days after the close of the first month during the calendar year in which a sale is made in reliance on the rule.)

1. Name, address and telephone number (including area code) of the issuer of the securities sold;
2. Names (in full) of the executive officers, directors and promoters of the issuer (or of persons serving in similar capacities for noncorporate issuers) and of any persons beneficially owning 10 percent or more of the equity securities of, or equity interest in, the issuer;
3. Title of class of securities sold;
4. Aggregate sales price of unregistered securities sold within the preceding twelve months, computed in accordance with paragraph (e) of the rule;

Note: Sales prior to March 15, 1975, need not be reported.

5.   Number of persons who are beneficial owners of securities of the issuer as of the date of filing this Notice, computed in accordance with paragraph (f) of this rule.

Pursuant to the requirements of Rule 240 under the Securities Act of 1933, the issuer has duly caused this Notice to be signed on its behalf by the undersigned duly authorized officer or person acting in a similar capacity.

Date of Notice _____   Issuer _____

_____

(Officer)

Instruction. Print the name and title of the signing representative under his signature. At least one copy of the Notice shall be manually signed. Any copies not manually signed shall bear typed or printed signatures.

Attention: Intentional misstatements or omissions of facts constitute Federal criminal violations (see 18 U.S.C. 1001).

Edwin A. Snow et ux, Petitioners v. Commissioner

Edwin A. Snow et ux, Petitioners v. Commissioner of Internal Revenue, Respondent. U.S. Supreme Court, No. 73-641, May 13, 1974. Sixth Circuit, 32 AFTR 2d 73-5400 reversed. Year 1966. Decision for taxpayer.

1. OTHER ITEMIZED DEDUCTIONS—Research and experimental expenditures. Limited partner allowed deduction for his share of partnership's loss for tax year even though loss created by research and experimental expenditures for year in which no finished product available for marketing. Congressional intent in Sec. 174 was to put small and growing businesses on equal footing with well established concerns that had large research staffs. The expenditures were in connection with the partnership's business of developing a trash burner. Fact the trash burner wasn't marketable and no marketing activities had taken place in the year expenses were currently deducted was immaterial. Sec. 174 enacted to encourage search for new products. Preparatory and development costs were currently deductible. Reference: 1974 P-H Fed. ¶16,209 (17).

Syllabus

Certiorari To The United States Court Of Appeals For The Sixth Circuit
Petitioner Edwin A. Snow, who had advanced part of the capital in a partnership formed in 1966 to develop a special-purpose incinerator and had become a limited partner, was disallowed a deduction under §174 (a) (1) of the Internal Revenue Code of 1954, on his individual income tax return for that year for his pro rata share of the partnership's operating loss. Though there were no sales in 1966, expectations were high and the inventor-partner was giving about a third of his time to the project, an outside engineering firm doing the shopwork. The Tax Court and the Court of Appeals both upheld disallowance of the deduction, which §174 (a) (1) provides for "ex-

perimental expenditures which are paid or incurred by (the taxpayer) during the taxable year in connection with this trade or business as expenses which are not chargeable to capital account." Held: It was error to disallow the deduction, which was "in connection with" petitioner's trade or business, and the disallowance was contrary to the broad legislative objective of the Congress when it enacted §174 to provide an economic incentive, especially for small and growing businesses, to engage in the search for new products and new inventions. Pp. 2–4. 482 F.2d 1029, reversed.

DOUGLAS, J., delivered the opinion of the Court, in which all Members joined except STEWART, J., who took no part in the consideration or decision of the case.

Mr. Justice DOUGLAS delivered the opinion of the Court.

(1) Section 174 (a) (1) of the Internal Revenue Code of 1954, 26 USC §174, allows a taxpayer to take as a deduction "experimental expenditures which are paid or incurred by him during the taxable year in connection with his trade or business as expenses which are not chargeable to capital account." Petitioner was disallowed as a deduction his distributive share of the net operating loss of a partnership, Burns Investment Company, for the taxable year 1966. The U.S. Tax Court sustained the Commissioner, 58 TC 585. The Court of Appeals affirmed, 482 F.2d 1029 (32 AFTR 2d 73-5400) (CA6 1973). The case is here on a writ of certiorari because of an apparent conflict between the Court of Appeals for the Sixth Circuit with that of the Fourth Circuit in Cleveland v. Commissioner, 297 F.2d 169 (8 AFTR 2d 5989) (CA4 1961).

Petitioner was a limited partner in Burns, having contributed $10,000 for a four-percent interest in Burns. The general partner was one Trott who had previously formed two other limited partnerships, one called Echo to develop a telephone answering device and the other Courier, to develop an electronic tape recorder. Petitioner had become a limited partner in each of these other limited partnerships.[1]

Burns was formed to develop "a special purpose incinerator for the consumer and industrial markets." Trott was the inventor and had conceived of this idea in 1964 and between then and 1966 had made a number of prototypes. His patent counsel had told him in 1965 that several features of the burner were in his view patentable but in 1966 advised him that the incinerator as a whole had not been sufficiently "reduced to practice" in order to develop it into a marketable product. At that point Trott formed Burns, petitioner putting up part of the capital. Thereafter various models of the burner were built and tested.

During 1966 Burns reported no sales of the incinerator or any other product but expectations were high; and Trott was giving about one-third of his time to the project, an outside engineering firm doing the shopwork.[2]

Trott obtained a patent on the incinerator in 1970 and it is currently being produced and marketed under the name Trash-Away.[3]

Section 174 was enacted in 1954 to dilute some of the conception of "ordinary and necessary" business expenses under §162 (then §23 (a) of the Act) adumbrated by Justice Frankfurter in a concurring opinion in Deputy v. DuPont, 308 U.S. 488, 499 (23 AFTR 808) (1940), where he said the section in question (old §23 (a)) "involves holding one's self out to others as engaged in the selling of goods or services." The words "trade or business" appear, however, in about 60 different sections of the 1954 Act.[4] Those other sections are not helpful here because Congress wrote into §174 "in connection with" and §162 is more narrowly written than is §174, allowing "a deduction" of "ordinary and necessary expenses paid or incurred . . . in carrying on any trade or business." That and other sections are not helpful here.

The legislative history makes fairly clear the reasons. Established firms with ongoing business had continuous programs of research quite unlike "small or pioneering business enterprises."[5] Mr. Reid of New York, Chairman of the House Committee on Ways and Means, made the point even more explicit when he addressed the House on the bill:[6]

"Present law contains no statutory provisions dealing with the deduction of these expenses. The result has been confusion and uncertainty. Very often, under present law, small businesses which are developing new products and do not have established research departments are not allowed to deduct their expenses despite the fact that their large and well-established competitors can obtain the deduction. . . . This provision will greatly stimulate the search for new products and the new inventions upon which the future economic and military strength of a Nation depends. It will be particularly valuable to small and growing businesses."

Congress may at times in its wisdom discriminate taxwise between various kinds of business, between old and upcoming business and the like. But we would defeat the congressional purpose somewhat to equalize the tax benefits of the ongoing companies and those that are upcoming and about to reach the market by perpetuating the discrimination created below and urged upon us here.

We read §174, as did the Fourth Circuit Court of Appeals in Cleveland, "to encourage expenditure for research and experimentation." 297 F.2d. at 173. That incentive is embedded in §174 because of "in connection with," making irrelevant whether petitioners were rich or poor.

We are invited to explore the treatment of "hobby-losses" under §183. But that is far afield of the present inquiry for it is clear that in this case under §174 the profit motive was the sole drive of the venture. Reversed.

Mr. Justice STEWART took no part in the consideration or decision of this case.

---

[1] Both Echo and Courier claimed research and development expenses in 1965 and 1966; and they were not challenged by the Commissioner, apparently because their products were in a more advanced stage of development and were available for sale or licensing.

[2] Treas. Reg. §1.174–2 (2) provides: "The provisions of this section apply not only to costs paid or incurred by the taxpayer for research or experimentation undertaken directly by him

but also to expenditures paid or incurred for research and experimentation caused in his behalf by another person or organization such as, . . . an engineering company or similar contractor. . . ."

[3] Prior to 1970 Burns was incorporated and it produces and markets Trash-Away, petitioner being its Chairman of the Board.

[4] Saunders, Trade or Business, Its Meaning Under the Internal Revenue Code, So. Cal. 12th Inst. on Fed. Tax. 693 (1960).

[5] Hearings on H. R. 8300, 83d Cong., 2d Sess., Pt. I, p. 105.

[6] 100 Cong. Rec. 3425 (1954).

APPENDIX I

Taxation—Research and Experimental Expenditures— Section 174, Distinguished from Section 162

SNOW V. COMMISSIONER[1]

Petitioner Snow, employed full time as an executive of a large corporation, was a partner in Burns Investment Company, a limited partnership formed to develop a trash burning device for commercial and industrial use. In 1966, the first year of the company's existence, the general partner and inventor worked on but did not perfect a marketable device, and the partnership received no income. Burns reported a net operating loss for the year, claiming expenses of over $36,000 for research and development by reason of section 174 (a) (1) of the Internal Revenue Code of 1954.[2] Snow sought to claim his pro rata share of this deduction on his personal income tax return. The Commissioner determined that the deduction was not allowable and asserted a deficiency of over $6,000. The Tax Court[3] held for the Commissioner, and the Court of Appeals for the Sixth Circuit[4] affirmed. The Supreme Court reversed, holding that the deduction was proper.

Section 174 first appeared in the Internal Revenue Code of 1954. The 1939 Code contained no comparable provision,[5] to be deductible, research and development expenses had to come under section 23 (a) (1) of the 1939 Code, which was substantially the same as section 162 (a) of the present Code.[6] The expenses had to be characterized as "ordinary and necessary" and had to be incurred "in carrying on any trade or business." Under section 174, a taxpayer has a choice.[7] He may deduct research expenditures as an expense,[8] or he may capitalize them.[9]

The exact nature of these research and experimentation expenditures was not explained by Congress in the committee reports, nor was it defined in the Code itself.[10] Such expenses are described in the Regulations as those costs incurred in the laboratory sense.[11] The category may include expenses incidental to the development of a pilot model and can relate to either a general research program or one aimed at a particular product.[12] The actual research can be performed by a laboratory on behalf of the taxpayer.[13]

The opposing results reached by the Tax Court and the court of appeals, holding for the Commissioner, and the Supreme Court, for the taxpayer, reflect a basic ideological conflict on how to interpret section 174. The Code does not define the term "trade or business." A precise definition, adequate for all situations, may be impossible.[14] The traditional elements considered in determining the existence of a trade or business have been a profit motive[15] and an enterprise characterized by regularity of activities and the production of income.[16] The presence or absence of income, in itself, is not decisive.[17]

Older cases failed to distinguish between use of the term "trade or business" in section 174 and in section 162. Some courts denied section 174 deductions when unable to find the existence of a trade or a business as the term has been defined in cases arising under 162.[18] Once the courts following that narrow interpretation determined that there was no trade or business, the logical result was to rule that expenses incurred for research could not have been "in connection with" a trade or business. In *John F. Koons*,[19] the taxpayer bought an invention and paid a laboratory to make it marketable. The Tax Court denied a section 174 deduction of the amount paid the laboratory, holding that the expenses incurred for research were in anticipation of organizing a business and not in connection with an existing business.[20] A number of cases have followed the reasoning of the *Koons* case in first finding the absence of a going business, so that research expenditures were only preliminary to a potential business, and, therefore, nondeductible.[21]

The Tax Court in *Snow* cited *Koons* and its progeny and found that the expenses incurred were merely in preparation of entering a trade or business.[22] The Court of Appeals for the Sixth Circuit upheld the denial of a deduction, saying that a partnership without a marketable product was not engaged in a trade or business,[23] and that Snow himself was not engaged in the business of inventing merely because he had advanced funds to Burns and two other research enterprises.[24]

In the past, once a court found an existing trade or business under the test for section 162, it was typically more liberal in allowing the deductions under section 174 (a) (1). For example, in *Best Universal Lock Co.*,[25] a corporation whose regular line of business was the development of locks sought a section 174 deduction for expenditures made in research for the design of a new air compressor. The court allowed the deduction, saying that section 174 extended to expenses incurred in developing a new product unrelated to the past line of goods. In this respect one might observe the absence of any substantive difference between the kind of expenditures made by a business in its initial stage and those made by an ongoing business which undertakes the development of a new item unrelated to its regular line of goods.

Cleveland v. Commissioner,[26] cited by the Supreme Court[27] as being in conflict with the court of appeals' determination in *Snow*, may have been a judicial recognition of the lack of any such substantive difference. Cleveland was an attorney who advanced sums to an inventor, Kerla, under a trust agreement. According to this agreement, Kerla did not have to refund the money, but had to devote his time solely to the experimentation; the two men were to share equally in the anticipated proceeds. The Court of Appeals for the Fourth Circuit found that this agreement, though not using such terms, made the two men partners or equal participants in a joint venture.[28] Therefore, Cleveland had entered the inventing business and could claim the section 174 deduction. The court did not change the previous interpretation of the section, since it first looked for an existing business, and then to whether the expenses were incurred in connection with that business. But the practical result was that a partner's advances for research were deductible under section 174, even though no product was marketed that year.

In a surprisingly brief opinion, the Supreme Court held that Snow's advances to Burns qualified for expense treatment under section 174 (a) (1). It rejected the Commissioner's argument that the use of the term "trade or business" in section 174 should carry with it the restrictive interpretation arising under 162.[29] The Court stated that this decision was required if it were to carry out the intent of the legislature.[30] In support of this view, the Court emphasized the distinction between the prefatory phrases "in connection with" in section 174 and "in carrying on" from section 162, and quoted a statement made in 1954 by the Chairman of the House Ways and Means Committee, which concluded with: "(Section 174) will be particularly valuable to small and growing businesses."[31] The Court stated that this section was enacted to allow small businesses the same tax advantage as that previously enjoyed only by larger businesses with established research departments.[32]

Persuasive arguments can be made that Congress did not intend such a result. The Treasury Regulations for section 162 use the phrases "connected with or pertaining to" and "in connection with" as the apparent equivalent of the statutory language, "in carrying on."[33] In other sections of the Code where the term "trade or business" has appeared, legislators, courts, and the Commissioner have relied on the interpretations of the term as developed under section 162.[34] Under section 166, which distinguishes between business and non-business bad debts, defining the latter as "a debt other than . . . a debt created . . . in connection with a taxpayer's trade or business . . . ,"[35] the Supreme Court held that the meaning of trade or business as there used is identical to its established meaning under section 162.[36] The language in section 212, which allows a deduction to investors for certain income-producing expenditures, was also held not to broaden the traditional meaning of trade or business[37] under section 162.[38] It would seem that if Congress, which is presumed to be aware of such decisions, had intended section 174 to be broader than section 162, it would have used words such as "any profit-seeking activity" rather than "trade or business."

As alluded to by the court of appeals, a decision in favor of Snow makes possible a tax shelter for persons in high income brackets.[39] Such a taxpayer will be able to take a current deduction for sums advanced to an inventor-partnership, rather than proceeding with its manufacture whereby the proceeds would be ordinary income, may sell the invention to an established manufacturer; the amount received from the sale would then be taxed at the more favorable capital gains rate. In this way a taxpayer who advances funds to a limited partnership which is developing only one product will be in a more advantageous tax position than either a large business with an established research department or a taxpayer who invests in a corporation that is totally devoted to research.[40] One probable consequence of *Snow* will be to enhance the use of the limited partnership as a one-shot investment medium for new product development.

In *Snow* v. *Commissioner*, the Supreme Court held that the wording in section 174 makes more expenses deductible from present income than those considered "ordinary and necessary" under section 162,[41] and thereby initiated a new approach toward section 174 claims. So long as *Snow* is followed courts should no longer look first to whether a "trade or business," as interpreted under section 162, exists before deciding whether there are any deductible research expenses incurred "in connection with" a trade or business. The application of section 174 should depend upon the substance of the expenditures or the purpose for them, rather than upon the stage of advancement of the business when the expenditures are made. Therefore, if an expense is of the same type that a large business would attribute to its research department, then it will probably be eligible for a deduction under section 174, even though the taxpayer might not be engaged in a "trade or business" as defined in cases arising solely under section 162.

Reprinted from 40 *Missouri Law Review* 688 (Fall, 1975).

AMY REHM HINDERER

[1] 94 S. Ct. 18–6 (1974).

[2] Int. Rev. Code of 1954, § 1974 (a) (1), provides:
"A taxpayer may treat research or experimental expenditures which are paid or incurred by him during the taxable year in connection with his trade or business as expenses which are not chargeable to capital account. The expenditures so treated shall be allowed as a deduction."

[3] 58 T.C. 585 (1972).

[4] 482 F.2d 1029 (6th Cir. 1973).

[5] For an analysis of the uncertainties which existed with respect to research expenditures under 1939 Code, see Halperin, *Research Expenditures: Amortizable Bond Premiums: Corporate*

Contributions, in *Federal Tax Forum, How to Work with the Internal Revenue Code of 1954,* at 403–14 (1954).

[6] Int. Rev. Code of 1954, § 162 (a), provides in part: "There shall be allowed as a deduction all the ordinary and necessary expenses paid or incurred during the taxable year in carrying on any trade or business. . . . "

[7] Treas. Reg. § 1.174–1 (1968).

[8] Int. Rev. Code of 1954, § 174 (a) (1); Treas. Reg. § 1.174–3 (1968).

[9] Int. Rev. Code of 1954, § 174 (b). When no other method of amortization is practicable, the expenditures may be written off over a period of not less than sixty months, beginning with the month in which benefits are first realized. Treas. Reg. § 1.174–4 (1968).

[10] This accounts for part of the difficulty in determining the extent of the coverage that section 174 is to have. See Swanson, *Tax Treatment of Research and Experimental Expenditures,* 34 Taxes 541, 543 (1956).

[11] Treas. Reg. § 1.174–2 (a) (1) (1968).

[12] Id.

[13] Id., Treas. Reg. § 1.174–2 (a) (2). But the taxpayer is only covered by section 174 if the expenditures are of the type that would have been deductible if undertaken directly by himself. Swanson, supra note 10, at 544.

[14] "There is . . . no ultimate definition (of trade or business) because the deductibility is dependent on the examination of all the facts and activities of the taxpayer in each case." 4 A J. Mertens, *Law of Federal Income Taxation,* ch. 25, at 33 (1972).

[15] I.e., as opposed to self-satisfaction. Joe H. Cunningham, 27 CCH Tax Ct. Mem. 1219 (1968) (electrical engineer unable to deduct expenses incurred in researching mathematical formulas because seeking professional recognition, not profit).

[16] Richmond Television Corp. v. United States, 345 F.2d 901, 907 (4th Cir. 1965) (" . . . not engaged in carrying on any trade or business within the intendment of section 162 (a) until such time as the business has begun to function as a going concern and performed those activities for which it was organized"); Lamont v. Commissioner, 339 F.2d 377, 380 (2d Cir. 1965); Hirsch v. Commissioner, 315 F.2d 731, 736 (9th Cir. 1963); Miller v. Commissioner, 102 F.2d 476, 479 (9th Cir. 1939); Smith v. United States, 85 F. Supp. 838, 840 (W.D. Tenn. 1948); Wooten v. United States, 41 F. Supp. 496, 497 (N.D. Tex. 1941); Atkins v. United States, 14 F. Supp. 288, 290 (Ct. Cl. 1936).

[17] Johan A. Louw, 30 CCH Tax Ct. Mem. 1421 (1971).

[18] Stanton v. Commissioner, 399 F.2d 326 (5th Cir. 1968); Mayrath v. Commissioner, 357 F.2d 209 (5th Cir. 1966); John F. Koons, 35 T.C. 1092 (1961); Industrial Research Products, Inc., 40 T.C. 578 (1963) ("Merely working on inventions during the year in question with no activity of offering them for sale or license" held "insufficient to show engagement in an inventing business"); Myron E. Cherry, 26 CCH Tax Ct. Mem. 557 (1967); Charles H. Shafer, 23 CCH Tax Ct. Mem. 921 (1964); William S. Scull II, 23 CCH Tax Ct. Mem. 1353 (1964).

[19] 35 T.C. 1092 (1961).

[20] "Expenditures made in investigating a potential new trade or business, or preparatory to entering into such business, do not . . . qualify for the application of section 174 (a) (1)." Id. at 1101.

[21] Cases cited note 18 supra.

[22] 58 T.C. at 597.

[23] 482 F.2d at 1032. The court of appeals cited Justice Frankfurter's concurring opinion in Deputy v. DuPont, 308 U.S. 488, 499 (1940), for the accepted definition of a trade or business: "(C)arrying on any trade or business . . . involves holding one's self out to others as engaged in the selling of goods or services." 482 F.2d at 1031.

[24] Id. at 1033.

[25] 45 T.C. 1 (1965), see Rev. Rul. 71–162, 1971–1 Cum. Bull 97; cf. Kenneth Reiner, 24 CCH

Tax Ct. Mem. 1005 (1965). Courts have sometimes found the regularity of a taxpayer's research activities and revenue therefrom to be sufficient to justify a claim of being engaged in the business of inventing so that expenses are deductible under section 174. See, e.g., Johan A. Louw, 30 CCH Tax Ct. Mem. 1421 (1971).

[26] 297 F.2d 169 (4th Cir. 1961).

[27] 94 S. Ct. at 1877.

[28] 297 F.2d at 173 (emphasis added).

[29] 94 S. Ct. at 1878.

[30] Id.

[31] Id., quoting from 100 CONG. REC. 3425 (1954) (remarks of Congressman Reid).

[32] Id.

[33] Treas. Reg. § § 1.162–1 (a) (1960) ("connected with or pertaining to") and 1.162–17 (a) (1960) ("in connection with"). See H. R. REP. No. 2333, 77th Cong., 2d Sess. 75(1942) (terms used as equivalent by House Ways and Means Committee).

[34] See e.g., Morton Frank, 20 T.C. 511, 513–14 (1953), where the Tax Court held traveling expenses incurred in searching for a business to buy were not deductible under section 23 (a) (1) of the 1939 Code, the predecessor of section 162 (a) (2), because not "in the pursuit of a trade or business." The court spoke of expenses incurred "in connection with" a trade as equivalent to those incurred "in carrying on" a trade or business.

See Treas. Reg. § § 1.355–1, 1.355–4 (1960), which deal with the active business requirement of section 355, the provision for allowing tax-free separation of two or more existing businesses formerly operated by a single corporation; Treas. Reg. § 1.355–1 (d), ex. 5 (1960) (activities of research department of a wood products manufacturing corporation do not constitute a trade or business).

[35] INT. REV. CODE OF 1954, § 166 (d) (2) (emphasis added).

[36] Whipple v. Commissioner, 373 U.S. 193, 201–03 (1963); see Generes v. Commissioner, 405 U.S. 93, 103–04 (1972); Mark S. Campbell, 31 CCH Tax Ct. Mem. 371 (1972); Wallace L. Hirsch, 30 CCH Tax Ct. Mem. 1008 (1971); Leonard S. Krause, 26 CCH Tax Ct. Mem. 358 (1967).

[37] See Higgins v. Commissioner, 312 U.S. 212 (1941) (investing held not a trade or business).

[38] Trust of Bingham v. Commissioner, 325 U.S. 365, 373–74 (1945); McDonald v. Commissioner, 323 U.S. 57, 62 (1944); cf. United States v. Gilmore, 372 U.S. 39 (1963).

[39] 482 F.2d at 1031. The court of appeals found two competing interests: the desire to encourage research versus the desire to discourage tax shelters by strictly interpreting tax laws. See J. CHOMMIE, FEDERAL INCOME TAXATION 80 (1973) (normal approach toward deductions is one of strict construction against the taxpayer).

[40] A large business with a research department may take the current deduction authorized by section 174, but the proceeds it gets from the developed product are taxed as ordinary income. A stockholder who invests in a corporation with substantial research activities gets no current deduction under section 174, although any return ultimately realized on his investment is a capital gain, not ordinary income.

[41] The Supreme Court did not narrowly define the bounds of these other expenses. Snow, however, had attempted to analyze them in his brief. He contended that a normal business has three stages: (1) the investigatory stage, which consists of an evaluation of the prospective business; (2) the pre-operating stage, which includes all basic elements of the business, except that no product has yet been offered for sale; and (3) the carrying on stage, which covers the accepted concept of an active "trade or business." Snow's position, perhaps tacitly accepted by the Court, was that section 174 applies to the second as well as the third stage. Reply Brief for Petitioners at 18–19, Snow v. Commissioner, 94 S. Ct. 1876 (1974).

The R & D Limited Partnership— A Flexible Response to the Invitation of Section 174

I. *THE BASIS FOR CURRENT DEDUCTIBILITY; §174 AND THE SNOW CASE*

A. §174 (a)

1. Under §174 (a), a taxpayer may elect to deduct currently research or experimental expenditures paid or incurred by him in connection with his trade or business.

    a. Treas. Reg. §1.174–2 (a) (1) defines "research or experimental expenditures" as expenditures representing research and development costs in the experimental or laboratory sense.

    b. The term includes all such costs incident to the development of an experimental or pilot model, a plant process, a formula, an invention or an improvement of any of the above, and also encompasses the costs, including attorney's fees, of obtaining a patent.

2. Tax Shelter Implications of §174 (a)

    a. Meaning of "trade or business"

        1) In *Snow v. Commissioner*, 416 U.S. 500 (1974), the Supreme Court, reversing the Sixth Circuit Court of Appeals, held that a limited partner-investor was entitled to deduct his share of the partnership's R&D expenditures even though the partnership had not yet offered a product for sale in the year of deduction.

2) The Court premised its holding on the underlying Congressional purpose in enacting §174 to make the same tax benefits available to companies starting up as were available to larger, on-going entities. It therefore rejected the IRS position that §174 was to be interpreted under the §162 cases, which had held that expenses incurred prior to the sale of a company's first product were merely preparatory to commencing business and were not incurred "in carrying on" such business within the meaning of §162.

b. Limits of *Snow*: How active must the partnership be?

1) Although the taxpayer in *Snow* was a high-bracket investor seeking to shelter other income, the general partner was the inventor and the partnership itself played an active role in performing at least some of its research and development work.

2) Treas. Reg. §1.174–2 (a) (2) provides that §174 (a) applies to R&D expenses paid or incurred for R&D carried on in the taxpayer's behalf by another person or organization. Treas. Reg. §174–2 (a)(3) allows such a deduction only if the taxpayer bears the economic risks associated with the R&D; for example, no deduction will be permitted if the taxpayer purchases a prototype built by another under a performance guarantee.

3) Thus, it appears that as long as the partnership bears the economic risks of R&D conducted by another entity, *Snow* will apply and the costs of such R&D will be available to shelter the partners' other income.

c. Expenditures allocable to land or depreciable property

1) A taxpayer may not deduct amount allocable to the acquisition or improvement of land or depreciable or depletable property, even if such property is used for R&D. Treas. Reg. §1.174–2 (b).

2) Treas. Reg. §1.174–2 (b) (4) provides the following example: where a taxpayer expends $30,000 to develop a new machine, $10,000 of which represents the actual costs of material and labor, he may only deduct the $20,000 attributable to R&D.

3. §174 (b)

a. If a taxpayer elects not to deduct R&D expenses currently, he may elect to amortize such expenses.

b. Under §174 (b), research or experimental expenditures not currently deducted and not chargeable to depreciable or depletable property may be amortized over a period selected by the taxpayer of not less than 60 months, beginning with the month the taxpayer first realizes benefits from such expenditures.

4. Method of making §174 election

a. Under Treas. Reg. §1.174–3 (b), a taxpayer may elect to deduct his §174 expenses simply by claiming such a deduction on his tax return in the first year such expenses are paid or incurred.

b. If a taxpayer fails to deduct such expenses in the first year they are paid or incurred, he must obtain the Commissioner's consent in order to deduct R&D in subsequent years.

c. Under Treas. Reg. §1.174–3 (b) (3), a change of method requires the Commissioner's consent.

d. An election under §174 (b) is made by attaching a statement to the tax return for the first taxable year in which the amortization of R&D costs is applicable. Treas. Reg. §1.174–4 (b).

II. DISPOSITION OF COMMERCIAL INTELLECTUAL PROPERTY

A. Patents

1. §1235

a. Permits royalties on qualifying patent transfers by a "holder" of the patent to be treated as long-term capital gain income without regard to either the transferor's holding period or the fact that he may be in the business of transferring patents.

b. §1235 (b) defines "holder" as the individual whose efforts created the patent, or an individual who financed the inventor's efforts in exchange for an interest in the invention prior to its being reduced to practice.

1) Reduction to practice occurs when the invention has been tested and operated successfully, and not later than the earliest time the invention is commercially exploited. This may be either before or after a patent application has been filed.

2) A "holder" must be an individual; although a partnership as such does not qualify, each partner may qualify as a holder if, for example, one partner is the inventor and the remaining partners financed the inventor's efforts in exchange for interests in the partnership prior to the invention's being reduced to practice.

3) An investor does not qualify as a holder if he is the inventor's employer or related to the inventor. §1235 (d) defines a "related person," by reference to §267 (b) and (c), as including the spouse, ancestors and lineal descendants of the inventor and a corporation at least 25% of which is owned by the inventor; attribution rules apply in determining ownership. Although a controlled partnership is not listed in §267 (b), §707 (b) converts to ordinary income any gain realized on a transfer of property that does not

constitute a "capital asset" under §1221 by an individual to an 80% controlled partnership or between two commonly controlled partnerships; *see also Burde v. Commissioner,* 43 T.C. 252 (1964), in which §1235 (d) as well as §707 (b) was held to preclude capital gain on a transfer by an inventor and two individuals to a partnership comprised of the inventor and the wives of the other two individuals.

c.   §1235 applies only when a holder transfers all substantial rights in the patent. Thus, a transfer must consist of the exclusive right to make, use and sell the invention covered by the patent for the remaining life of the patent in order to qualify under §1235.

1)   Treas. Reg. §1.1235–2 (b) (1) defines all "substantial rights" as all rights which are of value at the time the rights to the patent are transferred.

2)   The Regulations list the following grants as not conferring all substantial rights:

(a)   a grant limited geographically within the country of issuance;

(b)   a grant limited in duration by the terms of the agreement to a period less than the remaining life of the patent;

(c)   a grant restricted to certain fields of use which constitute less than all the rights existing and having value at the time of the grant;

(d)   a grant giving the grantee rights to less than all the claims or inventions covered by the patent which exist and have value at the time of the grant.

3)   If a transferor retains the right to terminate the transfer at will, all substantial rights will not have been granted.

4)   Retention of the right to prohibit sublicensing or assignment and the failure to convey the right to use or to sell may or may not be substantial, depending on the circumstances. For example, failure to grant the right to "use" is insignificant if such right is meaningless or has no value at the time of the grant. *Bell Intercontinental Corp. v. United States,* 381 F.2d 1004, 1018 (Ct. Cl. 1967).

5)   The transferor's retention of title or other rights in the nature of a security interest for the purpose of securing payment or performance does not destroy an otherwise valid §1235 transfer.

Prepared and presented by Robert W. Anestis & Alan H. Finegold, Law Firm of Kirkpatrick, Lockhart, Johnson & Hutchison, Pittsburgh, PA. Delivered at the Pittsburgh Tax Club, December 11, 1979.

2. Patent Transfers Outside §1235

a. The IRS has held that a patent transfer failing to meet the technical requirements of §1235 may qualify for capital gains treatment under the general capital gains provisions of the Code. *Rev. Rul. 69–482,* 1969–2 C.B. 164; *c.f. Myron C. Poole,* 46 T.C. 392 (1966) *acq. on another issue,* 1966–2 C.B. 6, in which the Tax Court held that §1235 was the exclusive means by which a "holder" described in §1235 (a) was entitled to capital gains treatment on a patent transfer. The IRS specifically stated in *Rev. Rul. 69–482, supra,* that it would not follow the *Poole* case on this point. Although the Tax Court has not disavowed *Poole,* it has also not relied upon it to deny capital gains treatment in any subsequent case.

b. For a patent transfer outside of §1235 to qualify as a capital transaction, it must either be an outright fixed price sale or, if the payments are contingent on use, the rights granted must comprise all substantial rights in the patent within the meaning of the §1235 Regulations. *Rev. Rul. 69–482, supra.*

c. To qualify for long-term capital gains treatment outside of §1235, the transferor must have held the patent or the invention it covers for at least one year, and cannot be in the business of transferring patents. The holding period has been held to begin upon actual reduction to practice as defined above. *Burde v. Commissioner, supra.*

d. §483 imputes interest on deferred license payments in transactions not "described in §1235 (a)." See §483 (f) (4). Courts have held that a patent transfer by a corporation or by an individual who is neither the inventor nor an investor who acquired his interest prior to reduction to practice is not described in §1235 (a), since a corporation or such an individual cannot be a "holder" within the meaning of §1235 (b). Interest is therefore imputed to a corporation's or such an individual's capital gain royalty receipts; *Marcella Busse v. United States,* 76–2 USTC ¶9716 (Ct. Cl. 1976). However, courts have held that interest will not be imputed to capital gain royalties received by a "holder" outside of §1235, even if the transfer failed to qualify because e.g. it was to a related party; such a transfer is "described in §1235 (a)" even though it is not governed by §1235. *Goldman v. United States,* 74–2 USTC ¶9723 (E.D. La. 1974); *Curtis T. Busse,* 58 T.C. 389 (1972), aff'd., 479 F.2d 1147 (7th Cir. 1973). It should be noted that the IRS takes the position that any transfer outside of §1235 that qualifies for capital gains treatment is subject to §483. *Rev. Rul. 72–138,* 1972–1 C.B. 140.

3. Successive Transfers

a. Depending on the circumstances, a license granting all the rights then held in a patent by the grantor may produce capital gain royalties. In

MacDonald v. Commissioner, 55 T.C. 840 (1971), acq., 1973–1 C.B. 2, the court held that a taxpayer who held exclusive rights subject to an outstanding nonexclusive license was entitled to capital gains treatment under §1231 on a transfer of all the rights he held. *See also Rev. Rul. 78–328,* IRB 1978-36, 26, in which it was similarly held that a transfer of all rights the transferor had ever held in a patent, although less than all then existing rights, qualified for capital gains treatment.

b. Treas. Reg. §1235-2 (b) (1) implies that a preexisting license will preclude capital gains treatment under §1235; in defining "all substantial rights," it adds the parenthetical phrase "whether or not then held by the grantor." The IRS reinforced this interpretation in *Rev. Rul. 78–328, supra,* in which it stated that "no inference should be drawn from the Service's acquiescence in *MacDonald* that the regulations under §1235 are not controlling for purposes of §1235." Thus, it appears that if there is a preexisting license, a transferor must qualify under the general capital gains provisions—i.e., by having the requisite holding period and not being a dealer in patents in addition to effecting a transfer of all substantial rights in the patent—in order for royalties to be taxed as capital gains.

4. Tax Effects to Licensee

a. A patent licensee can deduct license payments regardless of whether the license results in capital gains or ordinary income in the hands of the licensor. Treas. Reg. §1.167(a)–3, 1.167(a)–6(a).

1) Because a patent has a determinable useful life, capital gains royalty payments have been held to represent a reasonable estimate of ratable depreciation charges over the life of the licensed patent. *Associated Patentees, Inc.,* 4 T.C. 979 (1954), *acq.,* 1959– 2 C.B. 3; *Rev. Rul. 67–136,* 1967–1 C.B. 58.

2) If a licensee under a capital gains license subsequently sells or assigns his rights, he will be subject to depreciation recapture under §1245. *Newton Insert Co. v. Commissioner,* 61 T.C. 570 (1974); *Allied Tube & Conduit Corp.,* 34 TCM 1218 (1975).

3) Ordinary income license royalties, like rent or any other royalties for the use of business-related property, represent ordinary and necessary business deductions. §162 (a) (3); *Differential Steel Car. Co.,* 16 T.C. 413 (1951), *acq.,* 1951–2 C.B. 2. Unlike depreciation deductions, §162 (a) deductions are not subject to recapture if the patent rights are sold.

5. Related Party Transactions

a. Although §1235 (d) precludes the use of §1235 by a taxpayer who sells a patent to a controlled corporation, significant tax benefits remain available in the context of related party patent transfers.

b. Capital gains.

1) As noted above, gain on a transfer of all substantial rights in a patent will constitute capital or §1231 gain outside of §1235 if the transferor has the requisite holding period and is not in the business of selling patents. Additional obstacles to capital gain treatment include the following: §707 (b); §1239; IRS challenge on the ground that a transfer to a related party cannot effect a divestiture of all substantial rights.

(a) The issue of whether a transferor is in the business of selling patents has rarely been raised since the enactment of §1235, and in the few cases in which it has been raised, the taxpayer has often prevailed. *See, e.g., PPG Industries, Inc.*, 55 T.C. 928, 1017 (1971), wherein the court held that a corporation which ordinarily licensed technology under ordinary income type licenses, but which had entered into only a single sale of technology prior to the capital gains license at issue, was not in the business of holding technology for sale to customers in the ordinary course of its business.

(b) §707 (b), as held in *Burde*, applies either directly or through §1235 (d) to a patent transfer by an individual to an 80% controlled partnership or between controlled partnerships; it does not apply, however, to a transfer by a partnership to a corporation controlled by the same interests.

(c) §1239 (a) converts to ordinary income any gain received on the sale of depreciable property to a "related person." §1239 (b) defines "related persons" as a husband and wife, an individual and 80% (in value) controlled corporation, and two commonly controlled corporations.

(1) §1239 has been held inapplicable to the transfer of a patent application prior to the receipt of a notice of allowance of important claims; a patent application as to which no such notice has been received is not a depreciable asset because it has no determinable useful life. Thus, in both *Davis v. Commissioner*, 491 F.2d 709 (6th Cir. 1974), *aff'g.*, 31 TCM 1155 (1972) and *Lan Jen Chu v. Commissioner,* 486 F.2d 696 (1st Cir. 1973), *aff'g.*, 58 T.C. 598 (1978), taxpayers were held entitled to capital gain treatment on royalties received on such transfers; note that a controlled corporation to which a patent application is transferred is entitled to take depreciation deductions for royalty payments if and when the payments are granted.

(2) §1239 does not apply to a transfer by a partnership to a corporation controlled by the partners, as long as no individual partner owns 80% in value of the corporation.

(d) The IRS has not succeeded in its occasional attempts to challenge the capital gain nature of royalties received from controlled entities on the ground that no actual divestiture of ownership has occurred. *See, e.g., Magee-Hale Park-O-Meter Co. v. Commissioner,* 15 TCM 254 (1956), wherein patent royalties were held to be deductible to the corporation under §167 and taxed as capital gain to the shareholders, one of whom was the inventor; *see also, Ross v. United States,* 1975–1 USTC ¶9183 (W.D. Wash. 1974); *United States Mineral Products Co. v. Commissioner,* 52 T.C. 177 (1969).

c. Deductible royalties

   1) As noted above, royalty payments are deductible regardless of whether they are made under a capital gains or ordinary income-type license. Thus, payments made by a controlled corporation to shareholder-licensors represent a method to bail earnings out of the corporation as deductible royalties rather than as non-deductible dividends.

   2) This may constitute a significant benefit even if the royalties do not qualify for capital gains treatment in the hands of the shareholders.

d. Sublicensing

   1) A capital gain license between related parties offers the possibility of transmuting a large percentage of ordinary income royalties received from sublicensees into capital gains.

   2) For example, if a partnership enters into a capital gain license with a related corporation (without running afoul of the §1239 80% rule), the license may provide as part of the consideration that the corporation remit to the partnership, e.g., 70 or 80% of any royalties it receives upon sublicensing. If a sublicense entered into by the corporation were nonexclusive, the sublicense royalties would constitute ordinary income to the corporation. The payments made to the partnership with respect to such sublicense would be deductible under §167 as a ratable charge against the corporation's "cost" for the patent. The 70 or 80% of the sublicense royalties received by the partnership would constitute capital gain in the hands of the partners since the royalties would be received under a capital gains license from the partnership to the corporation. *See Allied Tube & Conduit Corp. v. Commissioner, supra.*

B. Know-How

1. Fixed price sales

a. A fixed price sale of know-how produces capital gain, provided that the know-how can be characterized as a capital asset in the hands of the seller.

b. In general, know-how must be secret and protectible to be considered a capital asset. See, e.g., *Rev. Rul. 64–56,* 1964–1 C.B. 133, *amp'fd., Rev. Rul. 71–564,* 1971–2 C.B. 179; *United States Mineral Products Co.,* 52 T.C. 177, 197–98, (1969).

2. Capital gain licenses

a. A know-how license with royalty payments contingent on use will, like a patent license, produce capital gain if all substantial rights are transferred. *United States Mineral Products Co., supra.*

b. The most important property right in know-how is the right to prevent unauthorized disclosure. *E.J. DuPont de Nemours & Co. v. United States,* 288 F.2d 904 (Ct. Cl. 1961).

c. A know-how capital gains license must be perpetual or must last until the know-how becomes public knowledge and loses its protectibility under the laws of the country in which it is licensed. *PPG Industries, Inc.,* 55 T.C. 928, 1014–15 (1971).

d. For long-term capital gains treatment, a licensor must have held the know-how for at least one year prior to transfer; thus, the license should state that the initial grant is of know-how developed prior to a specific date. A grant of subsequently developed know-how need not allow for a sufficient holding period if the subsequent developments clearly relate back to the initial grant. *See Heil Co.,* 38 T.C. 989 (1962); *see also Kronner v. United States,* 110 F. Supp. 730 (Ct. Cl. 1953), in which the Court held that know-how transferred incident to patents took on the nature of the patents; a holding period for after-acquired know-how was held unnecessary, since the patent license would have precluded the licensor and third parties from using the know-how.

e. The licensee under a capital gains license is not entitled to deduct his license payments, either currently or through amortization, because know-how generally does not have a reasonably determinable useful life. *See Edward W. Reid,* 50 T.C. 33 (1968), in which deductibility was upheld on the ground that a know-how license granting exclusivity to everyone but the seller constituted an ordinary income-type license; *see also Yates Industries, Inc.,* 58 T.C. 961, 973–74 (1972), in which a lump-sum payment for trade secrets was held non-deductible on the ground that trade secrets have no ascertainable useful life.

f. A capital gains licensee is entitled to deduct know-how payments if the know-how becomes worthless and is abandoned.

3. Ordinary income licenses

a. A nonexclusive know-how license or a license for a provably shorter term than the estimated life of the know-how, or one limited to a particular territory or field of use will produce ordinary income to the licensor. *See Pickren v. United States,* 378 F.2d 595 (5th Cir. 1967), in which a 25-year license for know-how with value of indefinite duration was held to produce ordinary income.

b.   The licensee under an ordinary income license is entitled to deduct his royalty payments as ordinary and necessary business expenses. *Edward W. Reid, supra*; *Photocircuits Corp. v. United States*, 74–2 USTC ¶9558 (Ct. Cl. 1974).

4.   Use of an option in conjunction with the transfer of patents and know-how

a.   A prospective licensee will often desire to acquire an option to become an exclusive licensee in order to evaluate the marketability of the licensor's technology during the option period. Such an arrangement can have tax benefits for the licensor.

b.   If the option payment received by the licensor is to be applied against the capital gain royalties in the event the option is exercised, the licensee will not recognize the option payment as income until the taxable year when the option is either exercised or lapses. If the option is exercised, the initial option payment will be treated as capital gain; if the option is permitted to lapse, the payment will then be taxable as ordinary income. *Rev. Rul. 57–40*, 1957–1 C.B. 266; *Virginia Iron Coal & Coke Co. v. Commissioner*, 90 F.2d 919 (4th Cir. 1938); *The Dill Co.*, 33 T.C. 196 (1959); *Carl E, Koch*, 67 T.C. 71 (1976).

C. Trademarks

1.   Outright sales

a.   A trademark constitutes property within the meaning of §1221, and its outright sale for a fixed sum will produce capital gain. *Rev. Rul. 55–644*, 1955–2 C.B. 299. For trademark law reasons, a trademark is rarely sold except in conjunction with a sale of the goodwill associated with it.

b.   A trademark has no readily ascertainable useful life, so the purchaser will not be entitled to deduct or amortize the price. *See Rev. Rul. 55–644, supra*.

2.   Trademark licenses

a.   Under §1253, the transfer of a franchise, trademark or trade name results in ordinary income if the transferor retains "any significant power, right or continuing interest."

    1)   §1253 (b) (F) lists as a significant power the right to payment contingent on use or productivity.

    2)   For trademark law reasons, a transferor is required to retain quality control rights, and thus virtually any payments under a trademark license as opposed to a sale of the trademark incident to a transfer of the entire business will constitute ordinary income.

b. A trademark licensee can deduct ordinary income royalties as a business expense. §1253 (d) (1); §162 (a); *Leisure Dynamics, Inc. v. Commissioner,* 74–1 USTC ¶9328 (8th Cir. 1974); *Strickland v. United States,* 352 F.2d 1016 (6th Cir. 1965).

D. Foreign Licensing by U.S. Licensors

1. In the absence of a treaty exemption, license payments from a foreign licensee to a domestic licensor who has no permanent establishment in the foreign country will generally be subject to withholding tax.

2. Applicable tax treaties must be examined to determine the availability of an exemption and the rate of tax.

a. For example, although the U.S.–Canada Tax Treaty exempts capital gains from withholding, contingent payments for the use of a patent are subject to Canadian withholding even though such payments may be made under a license which would qualify under the IRC as a capital gains license. *See* Canadian Interpretation Bulletin No. IT-303 (1976), CCH 5 Canadian Tax Reporter ¶52,308.

b. The rate of withholding under the U.S.–Canada Tax Treaty for royalties paid for the use of patents, trademarks or know-how is 15%. U.S.–Canada Tax Treaty, Arts. II and XI.

c. Many U.S. Tax Treaties exempt gross royalties on commercial intellectual property. *See, e.g.,* U.S. Tax Treaties with: Austria, Art. VIII; Art. VIII; Norway, Art. 10; United Kingdom, Art. 12; Switzerland, Art. VIII; Sweden, Art. VI.

3. In general, amounts withheld as a payment of foreign income or profits taxes are creditable against U.S. taxes. IRC §§901–05.

a. A turnover or excise-type tax payable to a foreign country is not creditable. *See, e.g., Rev. Rul. 56–635,* 1956–2 C.B. 501 (German turnover tax).

b. In general, the foreign tax credit may not exceed the same proportion of U.S. tax that a licensor's taxable income from foreign sources bears to his taxable income from all sources for such taxable year. IRC §904.

4. Related Party Transactions

a. §1249 converts gain on the sale by a United States person of a patent or know-how to a foreign corporation controlled by it to ordinary income. Control is defined as direct or indirect ownership of more than 50% of the voting stock.

b. Under §482, the IRS can reallocate amounts deemed to be deductible license payments between controlled parties as non-deductible dividends, if the license payments do not reflect a legitimate arm's length charge. Most U.S. tax treaties contain provisions similar in nature and scope to §482.

Appendix K

Research Expenditures— Section 174

SECTION 174. RESEARCH AND EXPERIMENTAL EXPENDITURES

(Sec. 174 (a))

(a) TREATMENT AS EXPENSES.—

(1) IN GENERAL.—A taxpayer may treat research or experimental expenditures which are paid or incurred by him during the taxable year in connection with his trade or business as expenses which are not chargeable to capital account. The expenditures so treated shall be allowed as a deduction.

(2) WHEN METHOD MAY BE ADOPTED.—

(A) WITHOUT CONSENT.—A taxpayer may, without the consent of the Secretary or his delegate, adopt the method provided in this subsection for his first taxable year—

(i) which begins after December 31, 1953, and ends after August 16, 1954, and

(ii) for which expenditures described in paragraph (1) are paid or incurred.

(B) WITH CONSENT.—A taxpayer may, with the consent of the Secretary, adopt at any time the method provided in this subsection.

(3) SCOPE.—The method adopted under this subsection shall apply to all expenditures described in paragraph (1). The method adopted shall be adhered to in computing taxable income for the taxable year and for all subsequent taxable years unless, with the approval of the Secretary, a change to a different method is authorized with respect to part or all of such expenditures.

Source: New.

Amendments:

P.L. 94-455,
§§1901 (a) (30),
1906 (b) (13) (A)

P.L. 94-455,
§§1901 (a) (30),
1906 (b) (13) (A):
Amended Code Sec. 174 (a)
as follows:

§1901 (a) (29) substituted "August 16, 1954," for "the date on which this title is enacted" in Code Sec. 174 (a) (2) (A) (i). Effective for taxable years beginning after December 31, 1976. §1906 (b) (13) (A) amended 1954 Code by substituting "Secretary" for "Secretary or his delegate" each place it appeared. Effective February 1, 1977.

(Sec. 174 (b))

(b) AMORTIZATION OF CERTAIN RESEARCH AND EXPERIMENTAL EXPENDITURES.—

(1) IN GENERAL.—At the election of the taxpayer, made in accordance with regulations prescribed by the Secretary, research or experimental expenditures which are—

(A) paid or incurred by the taxpayer in connection with his trade or business,

(B) not treated as expenses under subsection (a), and

(C) chargeable to capital account but not chargeable to property of a character which is subject to the allowance under section 167 (relating to allowance for depreciation, etc.) or section 611 (relating to allowance for depletion),

may be treated as deferred expenses. In computing taxable income, such deferred expenses shall be allowed as a deduction ratably over such period of not less than 60 months as may be selected by the taxpayer (beginning with the month in which the taxpayer first realizes benefits from such expenditures). Such deferred expenses are expenditures properly chargeable to capital account for purposes of section 1016 (a) (1) (relating to adjustments to basis of property).

(2) TIME FOR AND SCOPE OF ELECTION.—The election provided by paragraph (1) may be made for any taxable year beginning after December 31, 1953, but only if made not later than the time prescribed by law for filing the return for such taxable year (including extensions thereof). The method so elected, and the period selected by the taxpayer, shall be adhered to in computing taxable income for the taxable year for which the election is made and for all subsequent taxable years unless, with the approval of the Secretary, a change to a different method (or to a different period) is authorized with respect to part or all of such expenditures. The election shall not apply

to any expenditure paid or incurred during any taxable year before the taxable year for which the taxpayer makes the election.
Source: New.

Amendments:

Sec. as amended
effective:
2-1-77

P.L. 94-455, §1906 (b) (13)
(A) . . .
P.L. 94-455, §1906 (b) (13)
(A):
  Amended 1954 Code by
substituting "Secretary" for
"Secretary or his delegate"
each place it appeared. Ef-
fective February 1, 1977.

(Sec. 174 (c))
(c) LAND AND OTHER PROPERTY.—This section shall not apply to any expenditure for the acquisition or improvement of land, or for the acquisition or improvement of property to be used in connection with the research or experimentation and of a character which is subject to the allowance under section 167 (relating to allowance for depreciation, etc.) or section 611 (relating to allowance for depletion); but for purposes of this section allowances under section 167, and allowances under section 611, shall be considered as expenditures.
Source: New.

(Sec. 174 (d))
(d) EXPLORATION EXPENDITURES.—This section shall not apply to any expenditure paid or incurred for the purpose of ascertaining the existence, location, extent, or quality of any deposit of ore or other mineral (including oil and gas).
Source: New.

(Sec. 174 (e))
(e) CROSS REFERENCE.—For adjustments to basis of property for amounts allowed as deductions as deferred expenses under subsection (b), see section 1016 (a) (14).
Source: New.

Sale or Exchange of Patents— Section 1235

SECTION 1235. SALE OR EXCHANGE OF PATENTS.

(Sec. 1235 (a))

(a) GENERAL.—A transfer (other than by gift, inheritance, or devise) of property consisting of all substantial rights to a patent, or an undivided interest therein which includes a part of all such rights, by any holder shall be considered the sale or exchange of a capital asset held for more than 6 months (9 months for taxable years beginning in 1977; 1 year for taxable years beginning after December 31, 1977), regardless of whether or not payments in consideration of such transfer are—

(1) payable periodically over a period generally coterminous with the transferee's use of the patent, or

(2) contingent on the productivity, use, or disposition of the property transferred.

Source: New.

Amendments:

P.L. 94-455, §1402
(b) (1) (V), (b) (2)

Sec. as amended effective:

P.L. 94-455, §1402 (b) (2), amended Code Sec. 1235 (a) by substituting "1 year" for "9 months." Effective with respect to taxable years beginning after December 31, 1977.

P.L. 94-455, §1402 (b) (1)
(V), (b) (2):
P.L. 94-455, §1402 (b) (1) (V), amended Code Sec. 1235 (a) by substituting "9 months" for "6 months." Effective with respect to taxable years beginning in 1977.

[Sec. 1235 (b)]

(b) "HOLDER" DEFINED.—For purposes of this section, the term "holder" means—

(1) any individual whose efforts created such property or

(2) any other individual who has acquired his interest in such property in exchange for consideration in money or money's worth paid to such creator prior to actual reduction to practice of the invention covered by the patent, if such individual is neither—

(A) the employer of such a creator, nor

(B) related to such creator (within the meaning of subsection (d)).

Source: New.

[Sec. 1235 (c)]

(c) EFFECTIVE DATE.—This section shall be applicable with regard to any amounts received, or payments made, pursuant to a transfer described in subsection (a) in any taxable year to which this subtitle applies, regardless of the taxable year in which such transfer occurred.

Source: New.

[Sec. 1235 (d)]

(d) RELATED PERSONS.—Subsection (a) shall not apply to any transfer, directly or indirectly, between persons specified within any one of the paragraphs of section 267 (b); except that, in applying section 267 (b) and (c) for purposes of this section—

(1) the phrase "25 percent or more" shall be substituted for the phrase "more than 50 percent" each place it appears in section 267 (b), and

(2) paragraph (4) of section 267 (c) shall be treated as providing that the family of an individual shall include only his spouse, ancestors, and lineal descendants.

Source: New.

Amendments:	Sec. as amended effective:
P.L. 85-866, §54 (a) . . .	"(d) Related Persons.—Subsection (a) shall not apply to any sale or exchange between an individual and any other related person (as defined in section 267 (b)), except brothers and sisters, whether by the whole or half blood."
P.L. 85-866, §54 (a): Amended Sec. 1235 (d) to read as above. Prior to amendment, Sec. 1235 (d) read as follows:	Effective for taxable years ending after September 2, 1958, but only for transfers after that date.

[Sec. 1235 (e)]

(e) CROSS REFERENCE.—For special rule relating to nonresident aliens, see section 871 (a).

Source: New.

Appendix M

Private Placement Memorandum

ELECTRONIC EQUIPMENT DEVELOPMENT LTD.

(A Delaware Limited Partnership)

$1,200,000

TWENTY-FOUR LIMITED PARTNERSHIP UNITS
$50,000 PER UNIT

This memorandum is reproduced here for informational usage only. The offering was closed on October 14, 1980.

Dated: August 11, 1980

Name of Offeree

ELECTRONIC EQUIPMENT DEVELOPMENT LTD.
(A Delaware Limited Partnership)

$1,200,000

Limited Partnership Interests
Offered in
24 Units of $50,000 Each
Minimum Purchase: One Unit

This is an offering of limited partnership interests in a Delaware limited partnership which will engage in the business of research and development and licensing or otherwise arranging for the manufacturing and marketing of various types of electronic equipment.

THIS OFFERING INVOLVES A HIGH DEGREE OF RISK. These limited partnership Units will be offered on a very limited basis to substantial and experienced investors only. This investment contains certain risks more fully described under the caption "Risk Factors" herein and is not suitable for an investor who does not meet the requirements as set forth herein. The Units are for investment only.

Unless extended, this offering will terminate on October 1, 1980. In no event will this offering extend beyond October 31, 1980. The General Partner reserves the right, in his sole discretion, to accept subscriptions for a minimum of $350,000.

	Offering Price	Selling Commission	Proceeds to the Partnership[2]
Per Interest	$ 50,000	$ —	$ 50,000
Total Minimum	350,000	—	350,000
Total Maximum	1,200,000	68,000[1]	1,132,000[1]

[1] Reflects the payment of an estimated selling commission of 8 percent with respect to the sale of 17 Units. Presently, no selling or placement agent has been retained. However, one or more persons who may be registered broker-dealers may be engaged to act on a "best efforts" basis if the General Partner determines, in his sole discretion, that raising all or a portion of the necessary capital funds for the Partnership would best be accomplished in this manner. The General Partner will not receive any selling commission in connection with his efforts to sell Units on behalf of the Partnership. See "Terms of Offering—Plan of Distribution."

[2] Before deducting expenses payable by the Partnership in connection with its formation and the sale of Partnership Units described herein. See "Use of Proceeds."

THE UNITS HAVE NOT BEEN REGISTERED UNDER EITHER THE SECURITIES ACT OF 1933, AS AMENDED, OR ANY STATE SECURITIES LAWS AND HAVE NOT BEEN APPROVED OR DISAPPROVED BY THE SECURITIES AND EXCHANGE COMMISSION OR ANY STATE SECURITIES AGENCIES. ANY REPRESENTATION TO THE CONTRARY IS UNLAWFUL. WITH RESPECT TO FEDERAL SECURITIES LAWS, THE UNITS ARE OFFERED PURSUANT TO AN EXEMPTION FROM THE REGISTRATION TO A LIMITED NUMBER OF PERSONS WHO ARE ACQUIRING SUCH INTERESTS FOR INVESTMENT PURPOSES AND NOT WITH A VIEW TO RESALE OR DISTRIBUTION.

EACH PENNSYLVANIA SUBSCRIBER WILL HAVE THE RIGHT TO WITHDRAW HIS SUBSCRIPTION AND HAVE HIS PAYMENT AND SUBSCRIPTION DOCUMENTS RETURNED WITHOUT INCURRING ANY LIABILITY TO THE GENERAL PARTNER, THE PARTNERSHIP, OR ANY OTHER PERSON WITHIN TWO BUSINESS DAYS AFTER HE HAS DELIVERED HIS EXECUTED SUBSCRIPTION AGREEMENT AND THE PURCHASE PRICE OR THE FIRST INSTALLMENT THEREOF. TO ACCOMPLISH THIS WITHDRAWAL, THE SUBSCRIBER NEED ONLY SEND A LETTER OR TELEGRAM TO THE GENERAL PARTNER INDICATING HIS INTENTION TO WITHDRAW. THE LETTER OR TELEGRAM SHOULD BE SENT AND POSTMARKED PRIOR TO THE END OF THE AFOREMENTIONED SECOND BUSINESS DAY. IF THE SUBSCRIBER SENDS A LETTER, IT IS PRUDENT TO SEND IT BY CERTIFIED MAIL, RETURN RECEIPT REQUESTED, TO INSURE THAT IT IS RECEIVED AND ALSO TO EVIDENCE THE TIME WHEN IT WAS MAILED. SHOULD THE SUBSCRIBER MAKE THE REQUEST ORALLY, HE SHOULD ASK

FOR WRITTEN CONFIRMATION THAT THE REQUEST HAS BEEN RECEIVED.

THIS MEMORANDUM DOES NOT CONSTITUTE AN OFFER TO SELL OR A SOLICITATION OF AN OFFER TO BUY BY ANYONE IN ANY STATE IN WHICH SUCH OFFER OR SOLICITATION IS NOT AUTHORIZED OR IN WHICH THE PERSON MAKING SUCH OFFER OR SOLICITATION IS NOT QUALIFIED TO DO SO, OR TO ANY PERSON TO WHOM IT IS UNLAWFUL TO MAKE SUCH AN OFFER OR SOLICITATION.

ANY DISTRIBUTION OF THIS MEMORANDUM TO ANY PERSON OTHER THAN THE OFFEREE NAMED ABOVE, IN WHOLE OR IN PART, OR THE DIVULGENCE OF ANY OF ITS CONTENTS, IS UN-AUTHORIZED.

THIS MEMORANDUM IS SUBMITTED ONLY IN CONNECTION WITH THE OFFERING OF THESE UNITS AND MAY NOT BE RE-PRODUCED OR USED DURING THIS OFFERING FOR ANY OTHER PURPOSE.

EXCEPT AS AUTHORIZED UNDER "TERMS OF THE OFFERING — ACCESS TO INFORMATION," NO DEALER, SALESMAN OR OTHER PERSON HAS BEEN AUTHORIZED IN CONNECTION WITH THIS OFFERING TO GIVE ANY INFORMATION OR MAKE ANY REP-RESENTATIONS OTHER THAN THOSE CONTAINED IN THIS MEM-ORANDUM AND, IF GIVEN OR MADE, SUCH INFORMATION OR REPRESENTATIONS SHOULD NOT BE RELIED UPON.

THE STATEMENTS IN THIS MEMORANDUM ARE MADE AS OF THE DATE HEREOF, UNLESS ANOTHER TIME IS SPECIFIED, AND NEITHER THE DELIVERY OF THIS MEMORANDUM NOR ANY SALE HEREUNDER SHALL CREATE, UNDER ANY CIRCUMSTANCE, AN IMPLICATION THAT THERE HAS BEEN NO CHANGE IN THE FACTS HEREIN SET FORTH SINCE THE DATE HEREOF.

OFFEREES ARE NOT TO CONSTRUE THE CONTENTS OF THIS MEMORANDUM AS LEGAL OR TAX ADVICE. EACH OFFEREE SHOULD CONSULT HIS OWN COUNSEL, ACCOUNTANT OR BUSI-NESS ADVISER, RESPECTIVELY, AS TO LEGAL, TAX AND RE-LATED MATTERS CONCERNING HIS PURCHASE OF THE UNITS HEREUNDER.

THE DELIVERY OF THIS MEMORANDUM SHALL CONSTITUTE AN OFFER TO A PROSPECTIVE PURCHASER ONLY AFTER HIS

COMPLETION OF A QUESTIONNAIRE AND ITS REVIEW AND AP-
PROVAL BY THE GENERAL PARTNER AND THEN ONLY WHEN
SUCH PURCHASER HAS BEEN NOTIFIED IN WRITING BY THE
GENERAL PARTNER THAT SUCH PURCHASER HAS BEEN AC-
CEPTED AND APPROVED AS A PERSON WHO MEETS THE SUIT-
ABILITY STANDARDS ADOPTED FOR THIS OFFERING. A PRO-
SPECTIVE PURCHASER, BY ACCEPTING DELIVERY OF THIS
MEMORANDUM, AGREES TO RETURN THIS MEMORANDUM AND
ALL RELATED DOCUMENTS TO THE GENERAL PARTNER IF THE
PROSPECTIVE PURCHASER IS NOT APPROVED BY THE GENERAL
PARTNER OR IF THE PROSPECTIVE PURCHASER DOES NOT AGREE
TO PURCHASE ANY OF THE UNITS OFFERED HEREBY.

TABLE OF CONTENTS

Exhibits

INTRODUCTION

This Private Placement Memorandum summarizes the terms of an offering to investors by Electronic Equipment Development Ltd., a Delaware Limited Partnership (the "Partnership") organized by James K. LaFleur (the "General Partner") under the Uniform Limited Partnership Act of Delaware. A copy of the Limited Partnership Agreement dated as of August 11, 1980 (the "Partnership Agreement") is attached as Exhibit A hereto. The General Partner has organized the Partnership for the purpose of raising capital and sponsoring research projects with the objective of developing various types of electronic equipment.

The Partnership has entered into a Research and Development Agreement dated as of August 11, 1980 with GTI Corporation ("GTI") (the "Research and Development Agreement") by which it has acquired all GTI's rights in research projects relating to three areas of electronic equipment development described under "Business of the Partnership—Research Projects." GTI has agreed to provide research and experimentation services to the Partnership with respect to the research projects which can be funded with the proceeds of this Offering. See "Use of Proceeds" for information concerning minimum and maximum funding plans. A copy of the Research and Development Agreement is attached as Exhibit B hereto.

If the research results in developing products meeting the technical specifications established by the Partnership and GTI with respect to each particular research project, then the Partnership has agreed with GTI to permit GTI to exploit commercially such technically successful projects. With respect to each such project, GTI is obligated to enter into a license agreement with the Partnership in the form of license agreement attached as an exhibit to the Research and Development Agreement. See "Business of the Partnership—Manufacturing and Marketing Arrangements." In addition, the Partnership intends to file patent applications with respect to all such projects which are patentable; it is presently contemplated that the General Partner will be the inventor or joint inventor with respect to all or most of the projects described herein.

The purchase of Units offered hereby involves a high degree of risk, and investors satisfying the suitability requirements described under "Terms of the Offering—Suitability Standards" should consider the following summary of the risks inherent in this Offering as well as the specific risk factors described under "Risk Factors."

The introduction of a new product to the marketplace involves two broad categories of risks. The first is of a technical nature—can the proposed product be developed to perform its intended function within the budgetary limits imposed on the project. Not everything can be achieved with even unlimited funds, while real budget limitations still further reduce that which can be accomplished. See "Risk Factors—Research and Development Risks."

The second broad area of risks involves the marketplace itself. That is, assuming the product performs up to expectations from a technical viewpoint, can it be sold in sufficient quantitites and at a sufficiently high price to realize the financial goals set at the outset of the project. Here such factors as market timing, external events beyond the control of the producer, competition and skill of the marketing organization are of key importance to the success of the venture. See "Risk Factors—Risks in Commercial Exploitation."

Three major groups of participants are involved in this undertaking: 1) GTI, 2) the Limited Partners, and 3) the General Partner. Each participant shares in these risks in what it is felt is the most appropriate manner and is similarly rewarded if those risks assumed by the respective participant are successfully overcome. The following is a summary of how each of the three participating groups or individuals is related to the two broad areas of risk-taking mentioned above and how each is rewarded if the appropriate risk is successfully overcome.

GTI Corporation

GTI has been a public corporation since 1960. During the entire period of time from then until today it has participated in the competitive marketplaces represented by projects described under "Business of the Partnership—Research and Development Projects" as the High Speed Welder and Marking and Handling Equipment. While the project described therein as Computer Graphics System is in a new field, GTI has done business with many of the large potential customers for the proposed Computer Graphics System for many years. In short, GTI believes that it knows its marketplace and as such is the best prepared of the three groups of participants to assume the risk of the marketplace. Accordingly, under the form of license agreement, GTI as licensee agrees to pay to the Partnership minimum royalty payments essentially equal to the limited partners' original investment allocable to a particular project within four years (on or before October 31, 1984) for each project for which all technical goals, as defined by a technical specification mutually agreed to at the outset of the project and as modified, have been satisfied. The benefits to GTI for assuming this risk are as follows:

1. GTI will acquire several new products meeting all required technical specifications which GTI's own market research indicates have highly satisfactory long term prospects in the marketplace in which it competes.
2. No "up-front" funds are required to be advanced by GTI; for those projects that are technically successful the required minimum royalty payments do not have to be paid until October 31, 1984, and such minimum payments may prove unnecessary if sufficient sales are made in earlier years to cause such projects to be self-supporting.
3. The Research and Development Agreement permits GTI to build up

its research and development capability without using its own funds. In addition, a fee is earned on the research activities equal to eight percent of the costs incurred.

The Limited Partners

The Limited Partners assume the technical risks of the projects. While GTI will be performing the actual research and development work, it is doing so on a "best efforts" basis only, and no assurances can be given that such efforts will be successful. The rewards to the Limited Partners for assuming these risks are as follows:

1. Regardless of whether any of the projects is technically successful, a large percentage of the total funds invested will result in Federal tax deductions (see "Income Tax Aspects" elsewhere in this Memorandum).
2. For each project that is technically successful, GTI agrees to pay to the Partnership, at a minimum, a return equal to its original investment allocable to that particular project.
3. Depending on the market success of any particular project, the Limited Partners could realize a total return equal to a maximum of three times their original investment in the High Speed Welder and Marking and Handling Equipment projects if these projects are fully funded and are wholly successful, and up to twenty times their original investment in the Computer Graphics System project if that project is wholly successful and the maximum cumulative royalties are paid with respect thereto.
4. The General Partner will take all steps which he feels are prudent to increase the likelihood that royalties received by the Partnership will be taxable as long-term capital gain; however, substantial questions of fact and law may affect such characterization (see "Income Tax Aspects").

The General Partner

The General Partner obtains no return unless both the technical risks and the marketing risks are overcome, since the minimum royalty to be paid by GTI is only sufficient to return the Limited Partner's original investment allocated to technically successful projects. Until all of the Limited Partner's investment is returned, the General Partner only receives 1% of the Partnership's income, which is a normal amount. Thereafter, he will receive 25% of such income. On the other hand, his original financial investment is minimal. Assuming all projects are both technically successful and are sufficiently successful in the marketplace to assure that maximum cumulative royalties are paid, the return to the General Partner will be substantial. See

Exhibit D attached hereto which sets forth the allocation between the General Partner and the Limited Partners of cash flow under different assumptions.

In any event, the General Partner will receive a management fee of $20,000 per year and reimbursement from the Partnership of a pro rata portion of his office expenses. A portion of such costs are to be satisfied out of the original proceeds of this offering, as set forth under "Use of Proceeds."

SUMMARY OF THE PARTNERSHIP AND OFFERING DATA

State of Organization	Delaware
General Partner	James K. LaFleur, Toluca Lake, California
Fees to the General Partner	Annual management fee of $20,000 payable in monthly installments commencing with the release of funds from escrow
Limited Partners	Investors who subscribe for and purchase the Units offered hereby
Partnership Business and Objectives	The sponsorship of research to be conducted by GTI concerning the development of various types of electronic equipment, the possible application for and obtaining of patent rights relating thereto, and the commercial exploitation of the commercial applications, if any, of the results of such research. See "Business of the Partnership," page 345
Research and Development Agreement	Sponsorship of research projects to be conducted by GTI over a period ending December 31, 1982 (which may be extended up to an additional 12 months) on a cost (plus eight percent fee) basis. After completion of this Offering, the Partnership will prepay 80% of the estimated research and development costs (including related fee) of the projects which are to be funded hereunder. After such prepayment has been expended the Partnership will pay to GTI all subsequent direct research costs plus a fee equal to eight per-

cent of the original cost estimates. The Partnership and GTI have also agreed that GTI and the Partnership shall enter into one or more license agreements (in substantially the form attached to the Research and Development Agreement) with respect to all research projects which result in products satisfying technical and other specifications established by GTI and the Partnership. The form of license agreement provides for the payment of a royalty based on net sales of such product, subject to the Partnership's receiving a minimum royalty and a maximum cumulative royalty for each such product covered by the license agreement. See "Business of the Partnership—Research and Development Agreement" and "Manufacturing and Marketing Arrangements," pages 345 and 352

Research Objectives

See "Business of the Partnership—Research Projects," page 349

Interests of the General Partner and Limited Partners

25% interest in distributions and tax effects to General Partner and 75% thereof to Limited Partners after Limited Partners receive an amount equal to 100% of their initial capital contributions. See "Summary of Partnership Agreement—Capital Contributions," page 367

Purchase Price of Units

$50,000 per Unit payable in cash at time of subscription therefor. See "Summary of Partnership Agreement—Capital Contributions," page 367

Liability of the Limited Partners

See "Summary of Partnership Agreement—"Limited Liability," page 369

Transferability of the Units

See "Summary of Partnership Agreement—Transfers," page 370

Tax Effects of Ownership of the Units

See "Income Tax Aspects," page 358

Counsel to Partnership   Kirkpatrick, Lockhart, Johnson &
                                        Hutchison
                                        1500 Oliver Building
                                        Pittsburgh, Pennsylvania 15222
Accountants to Partnership   Arthur Andersen & Co.
                                        911 Wilshire Boulevard
                                        Los Angeles, California 90017

RISK FACTORS

In addition to summary of risks contained in the "Introduction," prospective investors should consider the following factors:

Research and Development Risks

The Partnership proposes to expend significant sums on research to develop various types of electronic equipment. The Partnership does not itself have the necessary scientific or engineering capability, other than through its General Partner, to undertake the research contemplated hereby and has contracted with GTI for research and experimentation services. The prospect of a Limited Partner's recovering any money invested in the Partnership is dependent upon the successful conclusion of this research. There is no guarantee that any cash will ever be available for distributions to the Limited Partners by the Partnership.

No assurance exists that any products, knowledge or information developed in the course of research, if any, can be commercially developed or exploited. It is possible that other individuals, corporations or entities, with substantially greater financial and technical resources than GTI, are engaging in research which is similar to that which the Partnership (and GTI as its research contractor) plans to undertake; accordingly, another research team might perfect and patent various types of electronic equipment which are comparable or superior to the projects contemplated by the Partnership before the Partnership has completed its research. In such a circumstance, the commercial development of information gained from the research may not be feasible, and the Partners' investment could be lost in whole or in part.

Similarly, refinements of existing technology which is currently utilized could result in the marketing of new products which could compete with any products ultimately developed as a result of the Partnership's research. The rate of technological change in this field causes an ever present risk that new research or development efforts undertaken by others could succeed at any time.

Unless and until there is a successful commercial exploitation of the research and development projects contemplated hereby, the property of the Partnership would not be readily marketable.

Additional Capital Contributions

The successful completion of the research on any one or more projects described herein may require funds in excess of those contributed to the Partnership by the Limited Partners. No assurance exists that such funds will be available to the Partnership. If such funds are required and are not supplied by the Limited Partners pursuant to the terms of the Partnership Agreement, GTI and/or other third parties may, but are not obligated to, provide such funds by investing in the Partnership. (See "Business of the Partnership—Research and Development Agreement").

Risks in Commercial Exploitation

No assurance exists that the products, knowledge and information, if any, resulting from the research will be successfully developed or exploited by the Partnership. However, the research projects identified herein reflect the corporate priorities and strategy of GTI, which believes on the basis of its preliminary analysis that commercial markets will exist.

If the knowledge and information resulting from the research meets the technical specifications established by the Partnership and GTI, the Partnership will participate on a royalty basis in the commercial exploitation of such research through the sale and licensing of any resulting products to GTI in accordance with the terms set forth in the form of license agreement attached to the Research and Development Agreement. While GTI, as the prospective licensee of the Partnership, believes that it will have adequate sources of capital to finance the commercial sale or use of any research products meeting the technical specifications, no assurance exists that such sufficient capital will be readily available when needed.

Lack of Marketability of Partnership Units

The Units in the Partnership which are held by the investors will not be readily marketable. Furthermore, transfers of interests as a Limited Partner are subject to substantial restrictions which impair the liquidity of the investment. The General Partner arbitrarily determined the purchase price of the Units; and no assurance exists that any Limited Partner will be able to obtain upon the sale thereof an amount equal to his original investment.

Responsibility of General Partner

The responsibility for the conduct of the business affairs of the Partnership rests exclusively with James K. LaFleur, the General Partner, who also serves as Chairman of the Board, President and Chief Executive Officer of GTI. See "Potential Conflicts of Interest." The General Partner is committed to the continuing management of GTI, and he may develop and manage additional research projects in the future, either for his own account or through additional partnerships. Thus, the General Partner will not be devoting all of his efforts to the Partnership. However, the General Partner will manage the affairs of the Partnership to the best of his ability, will use his best efforts to carry out the purposes of the Partnership and will devote such time as is in his judgment necessary to the business of the Partnership.

Tax Risks—Research and Development Expenditures

It is intended that a high percentage of the contributions of the Limited Partners will be used for research and development and related general and administrative expenditures. The Partnership will elect under Section 174(a) of the Internal Revenue Code of 1954, as amended (the "Code"), to treat such expenditures as expenditures which are not chargeable to capital account and to deduct such expenditures in the year in which they are paid or incurred. Consequently, a benefit to Limited Partners will be the application of Partnership income tax deductions against such partners' taxable income from other sources.

Because of the above-described use of the research expenditure deduction for federal income tax purposes, it is estimated that expenditures will be largest during the first two years of the Partnership (unless the Partnership finances thereafter additional research which is not currently contemplated). Accordingly, a prospective investor should anticipate that he will have substantial taxable income for at least 1980 and the two years immediately thereafter during which all such research funds are expected to be fully expended by GTI.

Although a substantial portion of the Partnership's funds will be paid to GTI in 1980 as required by contract, and is expected to be expensed by the Partnership as paid, there remains a possibility that the Internal Revenue Service will disallow such current deduction of prepaid amounts and permit deduction only as GTI expends such funds.

The General Partner will take steps which he feels are prudent to increase the likelihood that royalties received by the Partnership will be taxable as long-term capital gain; however, substantial questions of fact and law may affect such characterization.

No assurance exists that any deductions will not be challenged or disallowed or that there will not be adverse legislative or administrative changes, with or without retroactive effect, any of which could affect materially the income tax consequences to the Limited Partners. For a fuller discussion of these and other tax risks, see "Income Tax Aspects." In view of the importance of such tax consequences, prospective investors should consult their tax advisers with specific reference to their own tax situation.

TERMS OF THE OFFERING

Suitability Standards

Prospective investors in the Partnership should give careful consideration to the risk factors described above, to the fact that their entire investment may be lost, and to the limitations described above with respect to the lack of a readily available market for the Units and the resulting long-term nature of any investment in the Partnership. Only persons who have adequate means to assume such risks and to provide for their current needs and personal contingencies, who can afford to bear the possible full loss of their investment and who have no need for liquidity in this investment should purchase the Units.

Since one of the benefits to investors who purchase the Units and become Limited Partners in the Partnership consists of the current deduction of certain research and development expenditures made by the Partnership against taxable income of such investors from other sources, the Units may be purchased only by investors who in each of the years 1980 through 1982 expect to have income taxable for federal income tax purposes at the rate of 50 percent or more, after adjustments and deductions.

Since the transferability of the Units is restricted in many respects under the terms of the Partnership Agreement and federal and state securities laws, the Units may be purchased only by investors who have a financial net worth in excess of $250,000 (exclusive of home, furnishings and automobiles and the value of their interest in the Units). A corporation, partnership, trust or other entity which is a prospective investor must have a substantial net worth (in typical cases at least $500,000) or other assets or sources of income that are substantial in that the investor can bear the risk of loss of the entire investment as well as satisfy federal and state securities laws applicable to such investor.

In certain cases, a potential investor may use an investment adviser to satisfy securities law requirements relating to his sophistication, experience and understanding. A prospective investor or his adviser will be required to complete and execute an investment questionnaire to evidence his experience and sophistication and to execute a Subscription Agreement for the Units purchased by him.

It should be noted that the foregoing represents only minimum suitability standards, and satisfaction of such standards by a prospective investor does not necessarily indicate suitability.

Access to Information

Each prospective investor and adviser may inquire about any aspect of this offering. The General Partner has agreed upon request (i) to grant, prior to the consummation of the transactions contemplated herein, to each offeree of the Units and his or its representative(s) the opportunity to review additional documents and to ask questions of, and to receive answers from, the General Partner or person acting on his behalf concerning the terms and conditions of this offering; and (ii) to supply any additional information, to the extent the General Partner possesses such information or can acquire it without unreasonable effort or expense, necessary to verify the accuracy of the information set forth herein.

Plan of Distribution

The Partnership directly is offering the Units for sale privately, subject to prior sale and certain other conditions. The General Partner will not receive any compensation or commissions in connection with the sale of the Units. The Partnership will bear all legal, accounting and other costs, not expected to be in excess of $50,000,in connection with this offering, if all the Units offered hereby are sold, and $25,000 if the minimum number of Units (seven) are sold. See "Use of Proceeds."

Such costs, however, do not include any commissions which may be payable to one or more selling agents, who may be broker-dealers registered under the Securities Exchange Act of 1934, that may be retained by the General Partner on a "best efforts" basis to sell Units. It is contemplated that such selling agents would receive usual and customary commissions (approximately 8%) of the gross proceeds received by the Partnership with respect to the purchase of those Units sold through the efforts of such selling agents. It is not presently expected that commissions would be payable in connection with the sale of a minimum of seven Units. Any commissions for the sale of Units would be paid to the selling agent or agents retained at such time as prospective investors are admitted to the Partnership as Limited Partners.

The General Partner will place the contributions to capital of the Partnership by the Limited Partners in a separate escrow account pending completion of the Offering. If the General Partner does not accept subscriptions for seven Units offered by October 1, 1980 (unless such date is extended one or more times to a date or dates not later than October 31, 1980), the General Partner will return such contributions to each of the investors who subscribed for the Units and will terminate the Partnership. If, on the other hand, the General Partner accepts subscriptions for seven Units or more offered hereunder on or before the aforesaid date (as extended from time to time), the General Partner will transfer such payments out of escrow into the operating account of the Partnership for use in the Partnership.

The Units offered by the Partnership hereby will not be registered under the Securities Act of 1933 or any state securities laws. For Federal securities law purposes, this offering is intended to satisfy the conditions of Rule 146 promulgated by the Securities and Exchange Commission. Pursuant to the Subscription Agreement and the Partnership Agreement, each investor who purchases the Units will be required to represent that the Units purchased by him are being acquired for his own account for investment and not with a view to resale or other distribution. The Limited Partners may not sell, transfer or otherwise dispose of the Units for twelve months after their purchase (subject to longer periods that may be required under applicable state securities laws) and must hold them indefinitely unless they are hereafter registered under the Securities Act of 1933 or an exemption from registration thereunder is available.

The Limited Partners have no right to require registration of the Units under the Securities Act of 1933, and such registration is not contemplated. The transferability of the Units is further restricted under the terms of the Partnership Agreement. See "Summary of the Partnership Agreement—Transfers."

BUSINESS OF THE PARTNERSHIP

The Partnership was organized by the General Partner effective August 11, 1980 under the Uniform Limited Partnership Act of Delaware pursuant to the Partnership Agreement. The principal place of business of the Partnership is 4337 Talofa Avenue, Toluca Lake, California 91602, which is also the address of the General Partner. The telephone number of the Partnership is 213-985-9226.

The Partnership has been formed to sponsor the research as provided in the Research and Development Agreement. As a result of such sponsorship, the Partnership intends to exploit commercially (subject to the license arrangements with GTI) any product, knowledge or information derived therefrom meeting predetermined technical specifications and to receive a royalty based on sales of marketable products developed as a result, subject to minimum and maximum royalties.

Prior to the offering and sale of the Units, the General Partner contributed his rights and interest under the Research and Development Agreement to the Partnership, and the Partnership acquired the rights of GTI in and to the research projects pursuant to the terms of the Research and Development Agreement.

Research and Development Agreement

The Partnership has acquired certain rights to the research projects described below under "Research and Development Projects," but none has been reduced to practice or is presently at a point of technical development such that patents or patent applications could be prepared or filed.

In order that research and experimentation necessary to develop commercially useful products may be undertaken, the General Partner has organized the Partnership to sponsor research required to create and develop the various types of electronic equipment described herein. GTI has released and quitclaimed any rights in such projects to the Partnership. The Partnership has contracted with GTI for such research and experimentation as the General Partner in consultation with GTI believes is necessary or feasible. The Research and Development Agreement provides for a contractual research period ending on December 31, 1982 (subject to a right of the General Partner and GTI to extend such period up to 12 months). However, GTI's present research schedule contemplates that all research (which varies from Project to Project) will be completed in the fall of 1981.

GTI agrees to perform the research and experimentation services with respect to the Projects as shall be specified by the Partnership. GTI shall prepare, subject to the approval of the General Partner, a detailed time schedule with respect to each Project showing the anticipated research steps, their estimated costs, and the time required for performance of each research step, all prepared in accordance with recognized critical path method generally used by GTI and other research oriented firms. In addition, GTI shall prepare, subject to the approval of the General Partner, technical specifications for each Project.

The Partnership will pay GTI for its research and experimentation services an amount equal to the costs of the research plus a fixed fee equal to eight percent of the costs set forth in the specifications for each Project agreed to by GTI and the Partnership. After the completion of the Offering, the Partnership will prepay 80% of the estimated research and development costs plus the related fixed fee for Projects which are funded by the Partnership after the completion of the Offering made hereby. Thereafter, GTI shall be paid for any additional costs it incurs after submitting invoices setting forth such costs plus a fixed fee which cannot exceed eight percent of the costs as originally specified. Project costs shall be determined in accordance with cost principles applicable to cost-reimbursement type contracts under applicable Federal Procurement Regulations. Such cost determinations are subject to the approval of the General Partner. The advance payment of estimated research and development costs has been required in order to assure the availability of engineering and scientific personnel and specialized equipment necessary to meet the various research schedules.

GTI will provide staff and facilities the quantity and quality of which are suitable for the performance of the research services required, although GTI may subcontract any portion of such services to others and has contracted with Mr. Holly with respect to research related to the Computer Graphics System Project.

GTI shall continue to perform such services with respect to any specified research Project until such time as the General Partner determines, after consultation with GTI, either that a product satisfying the technical specifications agreed upon by GTI and the General Partner has been developed or that no such product can be developed, taking into account the availability of research funds supplied by the Partnership and other factors which the General Partner deems appropriate.

Unused research funds originally budgeted for a Project which has been terminated or which has been developed successfully may, in the discretion of the General Partner in consultation with GTI, be applied to the research and development of other Projects described below or to new Projects which, in the General Partner's judgment, can be funded with the unused or excess funds. Where, however, a material amount of research funds would be required (in excess of 10% of the research funds paid or payable to GTI), the prior consent of the holders of a majority in interest of the Limited Partners of the Partnership would be required. If there are any cost overruns which cannot be funded through the use of unused or excess research funds, the Partnership Agreement provides for a voluntary method of obtaining additional contributions. GTI is not obligated to advance funds under such circumstances. See "Summary of Partnership Agreement—Additional Contributions."

The Partnership intends to seek patent protection whenever feasible for any inventions resulting from the research it sponsors. It is presently contemplated that the General Partner, in his individual capacity, will be an inventor or joint inventor of all or most of such inventions within the meaning of the United States patent laws. For the Federal income tax implications of this, see "Income Tax Aspects—Treatment of Royalty Payments Under License Agreement."

If any Project results in the development of a product meeting the technical specifications agreed to by GTI and the General Partner, GTI and the Partnership shall be obligated to enter into an exclusive, all rights license to manufacture, use or sell such product. In addition, if a Project does not meet the technical specifications agreed to by GTI and the General Partner, the results of the research, whether or not complete, may be acquired by GTI on terms to be negotiated by GTI and the General Partner. If no agreement is reached, GTI would have a right of first refusal to acquire such research results on the same basis as contained in a third party's bona fide offer. If a Project does not meet specifications and cannot be sold, the Limited Partners would bear all risk of the investment in such project.

Until the execution of a license agreement with respect to any Project, the Projects and all information relating thereto shall be the sole property of the Partnership.

GTI shall have the right to terminate the Research and Development Agreement if the Partnership fails to fund the Projects. The Partnership shall have the right to terminate the Research and Development Agreement if GTI fails in a material way to meet the performance standards agreed upon by GTI and the General Partner with respect to two or more Projects.

The principal persons who will direct or perform the research contemplated by the Research and Development Agreement are as follows:

James K. LaFleur, age 50, is Chairman of the Board, President and Chief Executive Officer of GTI Corporation and has held such position since 1976. As of March 1, 1980, he owned beneficially 108,201 shares of common stock of GTI, or 4.98 per cent of the total then outstanding. Mr. LaFleur obtained a Bachelor of Science degree in mechanical engineering from the California Institute of Technology in 1952. Thereafter, he was employed by Airesearch Manufacturing Company from 1952 through 1956. During the years 1956–1959 he served as President of Dynamic Research, Inc. and its predecessor. Mr. LaFleur served as President of the LaFleur Corporation from 1960 until 1965 and thereafter through 1966 served as Chairman of the Board of that corporation. He was President of Industrial Cryogenics, Inc. during the period 1966 through 1975, a firm engaged in the design and construction of liquid methane and helium extraction facilities. From 1975 to the present he has been serving as Chairman of the Board of GTI. He is a member of numerous professional organizations and holds over 130 U.S. and foreign patents in various fields. In 1980 Mr. LaFleur received his M.B.A. from Pepperdine University, Los Angeles, California. Mr. LaFleur is married and has three children.

John C. Brittain, age 44, Corporate Vice President and Division General Manager of GTI's Clover Division and GTI's Electronics Division since 1976; prior thereto he was a plant manager at GTI's Electronics Division, operations manager of GTI's Circuits Division, and general manager of GTI's operations in Meisbach, Germany in 1974; he attended Allegheny College, Gannon College, Linclon Institute and the University of Pittsburgh Management Program for Executives and served in the United States Marine Corps from which he was honorably discharged.

Richard W. Cousins, age 60, presently the Vice President and General Manager for the Equipment Division of GTI; a graduate of Tri-State College of Engineering (1942) with a B.S. in Aeronautical Engineering, he also took courses in Industrial Education at Pennsylvania State University in 1947–1949; he holds several patents on items for the electronics industry and has expertise in high-speed equipment, furnaces, plating, laser, tooling, was involved in the development of the first tantalum-to-tantalum welding equipment for the tantalum capacitor industry and has been involved in the production of glass-to-metal seal products, precision film resistors and networks, precision welded products, formed metal products and plastic products for the electronic and automotive industries; he served in the United States Air Force and was honorably discharged.

Ronald Steffey, age 39, the Engineering Manager for the Electronics Division of GTI and is responsible for manufacturing engineering, quality control, application engineering and plant maintenance; a graduate of Fort Lauderdale University (1972) with a Bachelor of Science Degree in Technical Management, he is also a graduate of Pennsylvania Institute of Technology, receiving an Associate Degree in Mechanical Engineering and Mechanical Theory in 1969; he has been involved in Mechanical engineering and Design for the past 16 years; his credits include designing a fully automatic system to clean compact vehicles all the way through and including buses and tractor trailers; and he holds a patent on a piece of equipment that he has designed in this industry; during the past two years he has been involved in designing and manufacturing marking and handling equipment for the electronics industry, as well as high-speed welding and sealing equipment; he has been involved in the manufacturing of the first high-speed tantalum-to-tantalum welding equipment for the tantalum capacitor industry and has been involved in the production of glass-to-metal seal products, precision welded products, formed metal products, and plastic products for the electronic and automotive industries.

James C. Holly, age 31, is an independent consultant under contract with GTI to design and build a graphics terminal prototype capable of displaying in color three-dimensional shaded objects (i.e. computer generated imagery); a graduate of the University of Michigan (1971) he has been involved in computer graphics research for the past 13 years; his credits include designing a computer-aided drafting language, three-dimensional display software, and several advanced microprocessor-based games for the consumer market; he has done much independent study in the area of advanced computer graphics and has worked under several of the leading professionals in the field; and during his service with the United States Air Force, from which he was honorably discharged, he worked on projects involving real-time computer software systems.

During the term of the Research and Development Agreement, GTI, in its sole descretion, may change its research personnel as circumstances require, subject in the case of Mr. Holly to the terms of his contract.

Research Projects

The following three categories of Projects for which Partnership funds would be applied, assuming $970,000 (net of administrative and other expenses) is obtained as a result of the offer of the Units hereby, reflect the current research priorities of GTI. Estimates of the research and developmental costs to produce prototypes of the described electronic equipment have been developed by GTI personnel and consultants. GTI personnel and consultants have also undertaken to estimate the potential market for each of these products using their best current judgment as to feasibility, selling prices and marketing strategies. Because of the rapid changes experienced in the electronics industry, no assurance can be given that the preliminary market estimates or their underlying assumptions are now or will in the future prove to be accurate. See "Introduction" and "Risk Factors" elsewhere herein.

1. *High Speed Welder.* Since 1947, GTI and its predecessors have maintained a leadership position as a producer of welded parts because its equipment is versatile and can be adapted to meet individual customer needs. GTI has been taking productive steps toward increasing its productivity and stabilizing its costs. Although the welded business is volume sensitive, GTI programs have enabled it to maintain selling price and profit and keep abreast of double digit inflation. However, GTI believes that the time and need has come for still a faster and more versatile welding machine.

In order to increase penetration of the world market for two-piece welded electronic leads, GTI believes that it is necessary to develop and produce a welding machine capable of producing 1,000 pieces per minute of two-piece welds with the capability of welding dissimilar materials. An estimated $270,000 of capital would be required to finance the engineering effort and estimated material costs to develop in approximately 12 months a prototype high speed welder. Such a welder could be used by GTI in its own manufacturing operations. The ultimate market for two-piece welds would be the semi-conductor industry. Sales of two-piece welds over a six year period are estimated to range from $33,000,000 to $50,000,000.

   2.   *Computer Graphics System.*   This research project is intended to develop a low cost shaded real-time graphics system, which is presently not commercially available. The estimated research and development costs are $250,000 and estimated development period is approximately 15 months.

   Shaded real-time computer graphics systems, an area that has shown substantial growth in the past decade, are capable of displaying pictures of three-dimensional objects in color. High performance systems, priced in excess of $500,000, which are capable of displaying realistic three-dimensional pictures in real-time (at least 30 frames per second) have not exhibited substantial growth to date because of the enormous computation rate required to generate video data at a real-time rate. It is believed that recent developments in the semi-conductor industry, however, have allowed the development of a new type of graphics terminal which should have the performance characteristics of the expensive high performance systems at a much reduced price.

   Computer graphics systems could probably be sold to original equipment manufacturers (OEM's) which would incorporate the graphics system with their own systems or as turnkey (ready-to-go) products for specific applications requiring substantial investment by the user in software development. The principal commercial applications appear to be in pilot training by computer simulation, manufacturers using CAD-CAM (computer aided drafting-computer aided manufacturing), medical diagnosis and research, architecture, animation and art. Preliminary estimates of total sales over a five-year period range from $6,000,000 to $60,000,000.

   3.   *Marking and Handling Equipment.*   The need for innovative marking and handling equipment for electronic components including integrated circuits used within the electronics industry is seemingly inexhaustible. Most manufacturers have ongoing programs whose sole purpose is to increase productivity, thus creating a constant demand for more efficient and expeditious handling equipment. The Federal Government is increasing its demand that all products be marked and identified. This creates a major new need for fast and efficient marking systems.

   According to knowledgeable observers, at least half of the equipment sold to the electronics industry is custom-designed and built. However, the other half is purchased as standard equipment. GTI offers a complete line of standard equipment which would be enhanced further if an option such as *U.V. (ultraviolet) OVEN* was developed and offered for sale. In conventional marking U.V. inks are replacing heat sets and air dying inks because U.V. inks have a short drying time and low curing temperature.

The fastest growing segment of the semiconductor market is the integrated circuit (IC). GTI does not have a standard unit for handling and marking an IC. Single in-line packages (SIPs) and dual in-line packages (DIPs) originally developed for integrated circuits are also being used by resistor and capacitor manufacturers in producing networks. GTI could expand its standard line of handling equipment if an *AUTOMATIC HANDLING SYSTEM* could be developed for SIPs and DIPs to facilitate marking ease and speed.

Integrated circuits are generally transported within the factory and shipped to the customer in a device known as a magazine or tube. GTI could enhance its standard equipment if an efficient tube-to-tube handler were developed to facilitate ease of additional operations.

Many electronics firms have fully automated production lines. However, there is a great need for GTI to design and develop a simple *STAMPING (MARKING) HEAD* capable of easily being interfaced with customer's existing production equipment. An extension to the simple stamping head is the *SERIALIZED PRINT HEAD* for use by hybrid package manufacturers (a hybrid package is a combination of an integrated circuit and discrete component assembled into a single package) as well as an additional option in connection with GTI's other printing systems.

In the semiconductor industry certain devices require orientation for polarity. This simply means that one side of a device is positive and the other side is negative. An orienter positions each part so that they are the same. Although GTI presently has a machine capable of orienting axial leaded devices, the equipment line could be enhanced further if a new orienter were developed which was capable of becoming interfaced with other GTI equipment (in-line) as well as other (in-line) production equipment presently in place.

It is the intent of this research and development effort to develop appropriate equipment such as described above to enhance GTI's position in the marking and handling equipment field. The estimated research and development costs are $450,000. Preliminary estimates of total sales of all such marking and handling equipment over a ten year period range from $3,800,000 to $5,700,000.

The foregoing represents the order of importance, in the General Partner's judgment, of each research project to be undertaken. If less than $970,000 net proceeds from this offering is available for research and development purposes, the Partnership will sponsor research only with respect to those that it can fund generally in the order of priority presented. Any cost overruns will be financed, to the extent possible, by applying any unused research funds initially raised by the Partnership or by seeking additional voluntary contributions from the Partnership. See "Risk Factors—Additional Capital Contributions."

Other research projects could be added or substituted for the Projects described above, in the judgment of the General Partner, only where "surplus" research funds were available either as a result of a termination of an unsuccessful or unpromising project or a cost "underrun" encountered in developing a particular product which satisfies technical specifications. In certain cases, where a significant amount of research funds for a particular new project is required, the consent of Limited Partners holding a majority in interest of the Partnership would be required. No additional specific research opportunities have now been identified.

Manufacturing and Marketing Arrangements

The manufacture of the electronic equipment that is to be developed by the Partnership through the Research and Development Agreement requires special "know how" as well as a substantial amount of special purpose capital equipment. GTI believes that it is well positioned to undertake the manufacture and marketing of the electronic equipment that results from the research and development efforts.

As described above under the "Research and Development Agreement," GTI and the Partnership have agreed to enter into a license agreement or agreements with respect to all Projects which satisfy the technical specifications established for them. The form of license agreement attached as an exhibit to the Research and Development Agreement grants to GTI an exclusive license to make or cause to be made and to use and sell the licensed product throughout the world whether or not the licensed products are ultimately patented. GTI has the right to grant sublicenses. The term of all such licenses shall be until the expiration of the last-to-be-issued patent relating to the licensed product, or up to 17 years after the issuance of such patent or, in the case of licensed products not subject to patent protection, for the useful life of the invention incorporated in such licensed products. Because of the technological obsolescence factor in the electronic equipment field, it is not expected that insignificant sales would be generated throughout the entire term of each license agreement.

While the provisions of the license agreement are substantially uniform with respect to all the research Projects to be funded by the Partnership, the royalty provisions differ. Each of the described Projects has been assigned a separate annual royalty rate, a minimum royalty and a maximum cumulative royalty payout, as set forth in Appendix II to the license agreement.

The form of license agreement provides that GTI shall pay a minimum royalty on October 31, 1984 for Projects which have met the technical specifications of the Partnership and GTI designed to return the full amount of the Limited Partners' investment allocable to such Project. No license agreements will be entered into unless the research results in products satisfying such technical specifications.

Maximum cumulative royalties are calculated on a basis intended to yield a fixed return to the Limited Partners on the assumption that actual net sales will be significant and will be consistent with preliminary market estimates made by GTI and its consultants. There can be no assurance that such assumption will prove to be accurate.

Annual royalty rates are calculated on the basis of net sales of the marketable product resulting from the research, except in the case of the High Speed Welder where the net sales of two-piece welded leads are used as the sales base for computing the royalty as well as actual sales of such High Speed Welders produced by or for GTI.

The respective annual royalty rates, the aggregate minimum royalties and aggregate maximum cumulative royalties payable to the Partnership (net, in the case of the Computer Graphics System, of a royalty payable to a consultant to the Partnership) during the terms of the respective license agreements would be as follows:

	Annual Royalty Rate	Minimum Royalties	Maximum Cumulative Royalties
1. High Speed Welder	3%	$353,520	$1,286,832
2. Computer Graphics System	5	303,024	7,903,008
3. Marking and Handling Equipment	10	555,552	2,022,240

In the event that less than all of the research Projects generally described under the heading Marking and Handling Equipment are funded or successfully developed (e.g. technical specifications with respect thereto are satisfied), the minimum royalty and the maximum cumulative royalty described above would be reduced in proportion to the amount of research funds and allocable overhead costs directed to the development of that particular product. Reference is made to Exhibit D attached hereto for a more complete description of the allocation of the cash flow by the Partnership derived from royalty payments (if any) from GTI.

The form of license agreement provides that royalty payments are to be made quarterly, and appropriate certification and record keeping requirements are imposed upon GTI.

The Partnership agrees to file, at its expense, patent applications in the United States or elsewhere as it deems appropriate, although there can be no assurance that patents will issue with respect to all the research projects. GTI, as the licensee, agrees to take whatever actions are necessary to prosecute third party infringement of the patent rights. It is presently believed that Mr. LaFleur will be an inventor or joint inventor under U.S. patent laws with respect to all or most of the Projects that meet the technical specifications previously established. The income tax consequences to the Limited Partners of the receipt of royalty income under such circumstances is described under "Income Tax Aspects—Treatment of Royalty Payments Under License Agreement."

The Partnership shall have the right to terminate each license agreement if GTI fails to make any royalty payments within 30 days of the due date, or is adjudicated bankrupt or otherwise seeks the protection of the bankruptcy laws.

USE OF PROCEEDS

All of the proceeds from the sale of the Units will be used by the Partnership to satisfy the Partnership's obligations under the Research and Development Agreement and to pay certain of the expenses incurred by the Partnership in connection with the sale of the Units and in connection with the formation of and administration of the affairs of the Partnership, estimated as follows:

	Maximum Contribution	Minimum Contribution
Source of Funds		
Contribution of General Partner	$ —	$ —
Subscriptions from limited partners	1,200,000	350,000
Total	$1,200,000	$350,000
Use of Funds		
Research and development	$ 970,000	$270,000
Legal fees for organization of Partnership, offering of securities and operation for two years	50,000	25,000
Accounting fees for two years	15,000	5,000
Costs of administration for two years, including management fee to General Partner	50,000	45,000
Patent costs, including legal fees	32,000	4,000
Selling commission[1]	68,000	—
Miscellaneous	15,000	1,000
Total	$1,200,000	$350,000

[1]The above table indicates an estimated sales commission (at 8%) for the sale of 17 Units. However, no selling agent or broker/dealer has been retained by the Partnership as of the date hereof. If no selling commissions are ultimately paid by the Partnership, such funds will be applied to pay administrative and other expenses incurred or to be incurred by the Partnership or otherwise applied to research and development activities.

MANAGEMENT OF THE PARTNERSHIP

General Partner

The management of the Partnership is conducted by the General Partner, James K. LaFleur, in accordance with the terms of the Partnership Agreement. Mr. LaFleur will also be actively engaged in the research and development of the Projects. See "Business of the Partnership—Research and Development Agreement."

Mr. LaFleur, age 50, is Chairman of the Board, President and Chief Executive Officer of GTI Corporation and has held such position since 1976. As of March 1, 1980, he owned beneficially 108,201 shares of common stock of GTI, or 4.98 per cent of the total then outstanding. Mr. LaFleur obtained a Bachelor of Science degree in mechanical engineering from the California Institute of Technology in 1952. Thereafter, he was employed by Airesearch Manufacturing Company from 1952 through 1956. During the years 1956–1959 he served as President of Dynamic Research, Inc. and its predecessor. Mr. LaFleur served as President of the LaFleur Corporation from 1960 until 1965 and thereafter through 1966 served as Chairman of the Board of that corporation. He was President of Industrial Cyrogenics, Inc. during the period 1966 through 1975, a firm engaged in the design and construction of liquid methane and helium extraction facilities. From 1975 to the present he has been serving as Chairman of the Board of GTI. He is a member of numerous professional organizations and holds over 130 U.S. and foreign patents in various fields. In 1980 Mr. LaFleur received his M.B.A. from Pepperdine University, Los Angeles, California. Mr. LaFleur is married and has three children.

GTI Corporation

GTI Corporation, a Rhode Island corporation, whose executive offices are located in San Diego, California, is engaged through its three operating divisions in the manufacture of parts, components and processing equipment primarily for the electronic, automotive, computer, appliance and electrical markets in the United States and to a lesser degree in foreign markets, including Japan.

Its principal products, distributed primarily by means of manufacturer's representatives, include glass-to-metal seals, rolled pins, precision cut, formed and welded metal and glass components, production process and component handling and feeding systems, standard and custom metal and plastic parts and protective devices and both die and stamped and etched flexible circuit boards.

Management of GTI believes that GTI's major expertise at present relates to manufacturing sub-components for high quality discrete electronic components. Such components are required for application where high reliability and ability to withstand adverse environmental conditions are key requirements, which are characteristic not only of automotive and computer but military applications as well.

GTI faces competition in the sale of all its principal classes of products from manufacturers of competing products and from customers who choose to manufacture rather than purchase such products. Competition is based primarily upon quality, service and price.

For the fiscal year ended December 31, 1979, total sales were $20,866,000 and net income was $1,500,393, as compared to $17,603,000 in sales and a loss of $601,748 in 1978.

GTI is subject to the informational requirements of the Securities Exchange Act of 1934 and in accordance therewith files reports and other information with the Securities and Exchange Commission. Securities of GTI are listed on the American Stock Exchange. Information concerning directors and officers, their remuneration and any material interest of such persons in transactions with GTI, as of particular dates, is disclosed in proxy statements distributed to stockholders of GTI and filed with the Commission. Such reports, proxy statements and other information can be inspected and copied at the offices of the Commission in Washington, D.C. Copies of this material can also be obtained from GTI directly upon request.

FEES PAYABLE TO GENERAL PARTNER AND AFFILIATES

Management Fee

The General Partner will receive from the Partnership a management fee which shall be a guaranteed payment determined without regard to the income of the Partnership in the amount of $1,666.67 per month, constituting an annual fee of $20,000.

In addition, the General Partner shall be reimbursed for any expenses incurred by him directly on behalf of the Partnership, including all expenses in connection with the organization of the Partnership. The General Partner may use his own secretarial staff, supplies, telephone and similar support services in managing the affairs of the Partnership, for which he may obtain reimbursement from the Partnership for the proportionate amount of such services utilized by the Partnership.

Partnership Interest

As described under "Summary of the Partnership Agreement," one per cent of all income, gains, losses, deductions and credits of the Partnership will be distributed to the General Partner until the Limited Partners have received a return of 100 per cent of their initial investment in the Partnership. After that time, the General Partner will be entitled to receive 25 per cent of the aggregate income, gains, losses, deductions and credits of the Partnership for income tax purposes. The amount of royalty income that may be received by the General Partner in the event all the Projects become subject to license agreements is set forth on Exhibit D hereto.

Payments to GTI; License Arrangements

GTI will receive payments under the Research and Development Agreement, as more fully described under "Business of the Partnership—Research and Development Agreement," for research and development costs plus a fixed fee of eight percent of such costs as profit. In addition, under license arrangements described in this Memorandum, GTI will manufacture and market any commercially useful results of the research sponsored by the Partnership in consideration for a royalty payable to the Partnership, subject to payment of a minimum royalty and a maximum cumulative royalty. These royalties, both as to rate and amount, vary depending upon the Project which results in licensed products. Any sales of licensed products which would yield royalty payments in excess of the maximum cumulative amount will inure solely to the benefit of GTI as licensee.

POTENTIAL CONFLICTS OF INTEREST

The General Partner will be devoting only a portion of his time and attention to the Partnership's business, and he may participate in or organize or be affiliated with persons, firms, corporations or their business ventures which are engaged in substantially similar or competitive activities. At the present time, Mr. LaFleur is Chairman of the Board, President and Chief Executive Officer of GTI, whose business and relationship to the Partnership is more fully described under "Management of the Partnership."

The terms of the Research and Development Agreement and the form of license agreement are not the product of arm's-length negotiations, although the General Partner believes that he has allocated fairly and appropriately the risks and rewards inherent in the transactions described herein. See "Introduction." In addition, to the extent that the relationship between GTI and the Partnership in all phases of the research, development and commercial exploitation of the electronic equipment to be developed by the Partnership in conjunction with GTI is not completely defined or involves the exercise of judgment or discretion, the General Partner intends to resolve any conflicts fairly in accordance with his best judgment.

The Research and Development Agreement, for example, requires the General Partner to exercise his judgment in assessing GTI's proposed research plan, budget and technical specifications, in determining to modify said plan and specifications and in determining whether material deviations from said plan exist which could give rise to a right in the Partnership to terminate in whole or in part the research arrangements with GTI. In addition, there may be differences in opinion between GTI and the General Partner as to whether a product has been developed meeting the technical specifications agreed upon by GTI and the General Partner on behalf of the Partnership triggering the license arrangements, or whether or not technically satisfactory products can be developed. See "Business of the Partnership— Research and Development Agreement" and "Manufacturing and Marketing Arrangements."

Other conflicts and considerations appear elsewhere herein or are apparent, and prospective investors should review those matters carefully.

FIDUCIARY RESPONSIBILITIES OF THE GENERAL PARTNER

The General Partner bears a fiduciary responsibility to the Partnership and its limited partners. As a fiduciary, the General Partner is required to exercise good faith and integrity in his conduct of the business and affairs of the Partnership, consistent with the general duties and obligations of the General Partner as provided in the Partnership Agreement.

Not withstanding the fiduciary relationship, however, the General Partner has broad discretionary power under the terms of such Partnership Agreement and the Uniform Limited Partnership Act exclusively to manage the business and affairs of the Partnership; and, generally, actions taken by the General Partner are not subject to vote or review by the Limited Partners except to a very limited extent.

Furthermore, the liability of the General Partner to the Partnership and the Limited Partners is limited in certain respects by provisions in such Partnership Agreement, which exculpate the General Partner for actions within the scope of its authority.

INCOME TAX ASPECTS

Introduction

It is impracticable to review or comment here on all aspects of Federal, state or local tax laws which may have an impact on research and development partnerships. The following is a summary of some of the Federal income tax consequences to Limited Partners resulting from their investment in the Partnership. This summary is based upon the Internal Revenue Code of 1954, as amended (the "Code"), and regulations promulgated thereunder (the "Regulations") and existing interpretations thereof, any of which may be changed at any time by legislation or otherwise. Therefore, each prospective investor should review the income and other tax consequences of his investment with his own tax adviser.

Taxation as a Partnership

Kirkpatrick, Lockhart, Johnson & Hutchison, counsel for the Partnership, have rendered their opinion that the Partnership, if formed and operated in accordance with the Partnership Agreement and as described herein, will be classified for Federal income tax purposes as a partnership and not as an association under the current law and Regulations. (Such opinion of counsel is attached hereto as Exhibit C.)

Present Treasury Regulations provide that a limited partnership such as the Partnership will generally be treated for Federal income tax purposes as a partnership, rather than as an association, if it lacks at least two of the following four corporate characteristics: (1) centralization of management; (2) free transferability of interests; (3) continuity of life; and (4) limited liability. The opinion of counsel is to the effect that, under the terms of the Partnership Agreement and on the basis of the present financial condition of the General Partner, the Partnership lacks at least two of these corporate characteristics. The possibility exists, however, of a change in such Regulations, the amendment of which has already been proposed but withdrawn by the Treasury Department in 1977 and the validity of which has been questioned by certain judges of the Tax Court of the United States and others.

Status as a partnership means that the Partnership as such will not be subject to Federal income tax and each partner will therefore report, for Federal income tax purposes, his distributive share of the income, gains, losses, deductions and credits of the Partnership whether or not any actual distribution is made to such partner during his taxable year. A partner may use his distributive share of Partnership losses in any taxable year to offset his income from other sources to the extent of his tax basis in his interest which generally includes not only the amount of money paid for his Unit or contributed to the Partnership but also his proportionate share of Partnership liabilities as to which he is personally liable.

The Partnership will adopt the calendar year as its fiscal year for Federal income tax purposes and will elect to use the cash receipts and disbursements method of accounting.

It should be noted that the opinion of counsel referred to above is not binding on the Internal Revenue Service (the "Service") and no assurance can be given that the classification of the Partnership as a partnership will not be contested by the Service, or if contested, will be sustained in court. If the Service were to succeed in classifying the Partnership for Federal income tax purposes as an association taxable as a corporation, it would be taxed as a separate entity at corporate tax rates and any distributions made to partners would also be taxable to them, quite possibly as dividend income. Such classification as an association would also preclude the pass-through of losses to individual partners referred to earlier.

Increased Likelihood of Audit

The Service has recently increased its audit surveillance of "tax shelter" partnerships where losses are significant in any given year. It should be noted that if adjustments are made to the income tax returns of the Partnership as a result of an audit by the Service it is possible that returns of the Limited Partners will also be audited, with the resultant potential for adjustment of such partners' returns for items both related and unrelated to the Partnership.

Research and Development Expenditures

Section 174 (a) of the Code provides that a taxpayer may elect to deduct currently the "research or experimental expenditures" paid or incurred by him in connection with his trade or business. The General Partner intends to make such an election for the Partnership. The Treasury Regulations issued under the applicable Code section define such research or experimental expenditures to include costs incident to the development of new scientific processes and inventions or the improvement of existing technology. The Regulations further explain that the deduction is available not only for expenditures incurred for the costs of research undertaken by the taxpayer directly but also for the costs of research conducted on behalf of the taxpayer by other research organizations. In addition, the deduction is available for the costs of obtaining a patent, including attorneys' fees expended in making and perfecting a patent application. A taxpayer may not, however, deduct the amount allocable to the acquisition or improvement of land or depreciable property which is used in connection with the research or experimentation and to which the taxpayer acquires ownership rights.

The United States Supreme Court in the case of *Snow v. Commissioner*, 416 U.S. 500 (1974), held that a limited partner was entitled to deduct his share of the partnership's research and development expenditures even though the partnership had not yet offered a product for sale. The Supreme Court, in rejecting the position of the Service, concluded that the Congressional intent underlying section 174 was to stimulate research and make the same tax benefits available to new entities as were available to established companies which sponsored continuous programs of research.

In light of the foregoing, counsel has rendered its opinion, subject to assumptions and qualifications therein set forth, that, to the extent that such expenditures qualify as research or experimental expenditures under the

Code, payments made by the Partnership under the Research and Development Agreement may be the subject of an election to expense. Such opinion does not comment on the timing of such deductions.

The Research and Development Agreement requires the prepayment to GTI of approximately 80% of the total estimated research cost and related fee. No judicial decision or published Service determination exists with respect to the deduction of such "prepaid" Section 174 expenditures. Although a cash basis taxpayer is generally not entitled to deduct substantial advance payments made in one taxable year for service to be performed in a subsequent year, cases and Service rulings with respect to prepayment of expenses analogous to those for research and development indicate that such payments may be deductible under certain circumstances. Those circumstances include the presence of a binding obligation to pay for the services prior to the end of the taxable year in which the deduction is taken; the non-refundability of the payment; prepayment of the costs at issue being a customary business practice of the taxpayer and others engaged in similar businesses; the presence of an arm's length relationship between the taxpayer and the person or entity to which the payment is made; and, if the services at issue are being subcontracted by a related payee, the existence of an obligation to prepay the subcontractor.

Under the terms of the Research and Development Agreement, the "prepaid" portion of research costs must be paid shortly after the completion of this Offering and in no event later than December 31, 1980, and such costs are not refundable. Although the Partnership has no prior business history, a business purpose for the required prepayment may be found in GTI's need to undertake with assurance certain capital outlays required for it to perform the research called for by the Research and Development Agreement. The relationship between the Partnership and GTI cannot be considered "arm's length," since the General Partner is the President and Chief Executive Officer of GTI; however, the prepayment will be made pursuant to an agreement approved by GTI's disinterested directors. Moreover, substantial research and development services will be performed in the taxable year in which the payment is made and the balance of such services will be performed in the following year. Counsel has advised that deductibility of such an advance payment in the year in which it is paid will turn on questions of fact such as whether the payment materially distorts income. The General Partner believes that current deductibility of the payment contemplated by the Research and Development Agreement is consistent with existing authority and, subject to review of the situation at the time of actual payment, intends to expense such amounts as paid. Should deduction of a portion of such prepayment be disallowed with respect to 1980, such disallowed portion as qualifies as an appropriate research or experimental expenditure should be available with respect to 1981.

Because existing legal precedent is somewhat contradictory on this point, no assurance exists that any deduction will not be challenged, disallowed or allowed only in a year subsequent to the year in which it is taken. Further, no assurance exists that there will not be adverse legislation or administrative rulings, with or without retroactive effect, which reduce or eliminate the availability of a current deduction for research and development expenses to the Partnership and thereby substantially reduce the tax-shelter benefits to an investor in the Partnership.

Allocation of Partnership Income and Loss

A major advantage of a limited partnership form of ownership is the ability of the partners to allocate among themselves various tax consequences of the partnership's operations. Under the terms of the Partnership Agreement, even though the Limited Partners own a 75 percent interest in the Partnership and the General Partner also owns a 25 percent interest therein, 99 percent of the items of income, gain, deduction and credit of the Partnership, except as noted below, will be allocated among the Limited Partners in proportion to their interests in the Partnership and one percent of those items will be allocated to the General Partner until the point at which the Limited Partners have received distributions equal to 100 percent of their initial investment in the Partnership. Thereafter, all such items shall be allocated among all the Partners in proportion to their respective percentage interests in the Partnership.

Although the Code and Regulations permit special allocations of income and loss as described above, the Service may attempt to reallocate a portion of the Partnership's tax items among the Partners if it determines that the allocations set forth in the Agreement do not have "substantial economic effect"; that is, the Service may contend that the allocations do not actually affect the dollar amount of the Partners' shares of the total Partnership income or loss independent of the tax consequences. Since the test of whether an allocation has "substantial economic effect" is in part a question of fact, no assurance can be given that the Service may not challenge the allocation. It is believed that there is an economic justification for the special allocations contained in the Partnership Agreement because of the disproportionately high contributions of capital to the Partnership made by the Limited Partners. The Partnership has not requested an opinion of counsel with respect to whether such allocations will be recognized for Federal income tax purposes and by *Revenue Procedure 79–14* the Service has indicated that it will not issue advance rulings or determination letters as to whether special allocations have substantial economic effect.

Most of the recent rulings and cases dealing with special allocations involve tax shelter limited partnerships where substantial losses are allocated to the limited partners. Recent letter rulings give major consideration to whether the rights of the limited partners to distributions at the time of the liquidation of the partnership are adjusted so as to reflect the amount of losses (as well as other tax items) previously allocated to them in determining whether a special allocation has "substantial economic effect." The Partnership Agreement does provide for such adjustments upon liquidation and, therefore, the special allocations contained in the Partnership Agreement should be upheld upon an audit by the Service. If the Service were to succeed in reallocating a portion of either the Partnership's income or loss, the share of such items allocable to each Limited Partner could be reduced. This would also result in a change in the tax basis of the Limited Partners' Units, thereby affecting the recognized gain or loss on a sale of Units or on the liquidation of the Partnership.

Treatment of Royalty Payments Under License Agreement

The Research and Development Agreement requires that GTI and the Partnership enter into licenses concerning those Projects which achieve technological success; such licenses would result in the payment to the Partnership of royalties (see "Business of the Partnership—Research and Development Agreement" and "Manufacturing and Marketing Arrangements").

Where all substantial rights in a patent are transferred by a "holder" of such patent, Section 1235 of the Code authorizes the treatment of the royalties concerned as long-term capital gain. Although a partnership cannot qualify as a "holder," an individual partner who is either the "creator" of the patent or an investor whose contribution to the partnership helped to finance such "creator's" efforts may so qualify. The General Partner expects that the Projects will all involve patentable technology and he presently anticipates that he will personally qualify as an inventor or joint inventor with respect to all or most of the Projects. While the General Partner may not be an inventor or joint inventor with respect to the computer graphics system, the Partnership has entered into an agreement which would finance the efforts of the creator of this system. Subject to such assumptions, the General Partner is of the opinion that individual Limited Partners should qualify as "holders" within the meaning of Section 1235. The licenses referred to above are intended to convey all substantial rights in the Projects to the licensee. Thus, to the extent that the Limited Partners qualify as "holders," their respective share of Partnership income allocable to royalties received under the license agreements should qualify for capital gain treatment. Although the General Partner will take reasonable steps to increase the likelihood of capital gain treatment, any individual partner's qualification as a "holder" (corporate holders will not qualify under Section 1235) and the resultant prospect for capital gain treatment of royalties may turn on questions of fact which are not presently known and on legal questions as to which little direct precedent exists. Further, if the Projects ultimately include significant elements of non-patentable rights, Section 1235 may not be available as to those elements; in such event or if Section 1235 is unavailable, the Partners would have to look to the Code sections governing sale of capital assets generally, including Sections 1221 and 1231, to seek capital gain treatment. The determinative questions under those Code sections will be predominantly questions of fact, including, among other things, (i) the Partnership's having held the technology being licensed for a one-year period prior to the execution of a license agreement with respect thereto; (ii) the Partnership's not being characterized as holding such technology primarily for sale to customers in the ordinary course of its business; and (iii) the capital nature of the technology in the hands of the Partnership. At this time the Partnership's ability to demonstrate such facts cannot be predicted with any certainty.

Thus, there can be no assurance that capital gain treatment with respect to royalties received by the Partnership will be available to any investor or that there will not be adverse legislation or administrative rulings, with or without retroactive effect, which would preclude any investor's treatment of his allocable portion of Partnership income represented by such royalties as capital gain.

Treatment of Fees and Expenses

The General Partner believes that the management fees which he is to receive from the Partnership are generally comparable to fees for similar services rendered by parties billing at arm's-length and that they represent the fair value of the services to be rendered. The General Partner further believes that such services are necessary in the conduct of the business of the Partnership and, therefore, should be a deductible expense to the Partnership. The Internal Revenue Service may challenge the deductibility of all or a portion of these fees on the grounds that the fees are excessive or that all or a portion of the fees should be properly considered a nondeductible distribution to the General Partner.

The Partnership will pay certain other fees to the Partnership's professional advisers, principally for legal and accounting services. These services, particularly legal services, fall into a variety of categories, including organization expenses (amortizable over 60 months), syndication costs (non-amortizable) and tax advice (currently deductible). Although the Partnership will allocate these professional fees among the categories in a manner consistent with invoices rendered by its professional advisers, the Internal Revenue Service may differ with these allocations and seek to allocate such fees in a manner which produces fewer current deductions and/or fewer amortizable organization expenses.

Sale or Exchange of Partnership Interests

A sale or exchange of an interest in the Partnership by a partner is treated as though it were a sale or exchange of his proportionate part of the Partnership property. In the event of a sale of an interest in the Partnership, the gain realized for federal tax purposes by the selling partner is, in effect, measured by the difference between (1) the sum of the partner's portion of cumulative net losses, his cash distributions theretofore received and his net proceeds, if any, realized upon sale and (2) the partner's investment in his interest plus his proportion of Partnership income.

The income tax advantages referred to above will not be achieved if the Internal Revenue Service determines that the Partnership should be treated as an association for tax purposes and therefore be taxed as a corporation. In such a situation, the Partners, being treated as shareholders, would not be able to take advantage of the previously discussed tax benefits. In the event that in any taxable year the Partnership were treated as an association, whether because of a change in the law, or otherwise, then there would be no tax shelter benefits which could be used by the limited partners to offset income from other sources. Furthermore, if the loss of the Partnership's tax status occurred at a time when total liabilities exceeded the aggregate adjusted tax basis of its assets, a constructive incorporation resulting in a gain to the partners proportionately to the extent of the difference between such liabilities and such tax basis may be deemed to occur.

Other Tax Aspects

The Tax Reform Act of 1969, the Tax Reform Act of 1976 and the Revenue Act of 1978 made certain changes in the Code that may affect an investor's overall tax planning and his return from his investment in the Partnership. Some of the most significant changes are as follows:

(a) *Add-on Minimum Tax on Tax Preference Items.* A taxpayer is subject to an additional tax equal to 15% of the amount by which his aggregate tax preferences in any one year exceeds the greater of $10,000 ($5,000 in the case of married taxpayers filing separate returns) or one-half (or in the case of a corporation, an amount equal to) the amount of his income tax for such year computed without regard to the minimum tax and certain other provisions of the Code. No major items of tax preference are present in the Partnership, but the relationship of the add-on minimum tax to the alternative minimum tax (see below) should be considered.

(b) *Alternative Minimum Tax.* With respect to taxable years beginning after December 31, 1978, there is, in addition to the add-on minimum tax on tax preference items, an alternative minimum tax. The alternative minimum tax, which is applicable only to individuals, applies only to the extent that it exceeds the taxpayer's regular tax liability as increased by the add-on minimum tax. Thus, a non-corporate taxpayer must compute his regular tax liability and increase it by the amount of any add-on minimum tax liability. He must then compare this sum with the amount of tax computed under the alternative minimum tax. If the liability computed under the alternative minimum tax exceeds that calculated under the present regular income tax, as increased by the add-on minimum tax, the taxpayer must pay the greater amount.

Generally speaking, the tax basis for the alternative minimum tax is the taxpayer's taxable income for the year, plus (i) certain itemized deductions in excess of 60% of the taxpayer's adjusted gross income, and (ii) the excluded portion of capital gains (see below). This amount is then reduced by a $20,000 exemption, after which it is subject to the following tax rates: 10% on the first $40,000, 20% on the amount over $40,000 up to $80,000 and 25% on the amount over $80,000.

(c) *Modification of the Capital Gain Tax.* By reason of the Revenue Act of 1978, an individual may exclude from gross income 60% of his net long-term capital gain. The remaining 40% of net capital gain must be included in gross income and will be subject to tax at the otherwise applicable individual income tax rate. The excluded portion of capital gain is classified as a tax preference item for purposes of the alternative minimum tax (see above) but not for purposes of reducing the amount of personal service income which is eligible for the maximum tax (see below). The effect of these changes is to provide that the maximum tax on long-term capital gain of individuals is 28%. In the case of corporations, the corporate alternative capital gains tax rate is decreased from 30% to 28%. The alternative tax for capital gains of individuals, which had the effect of limiting the rate on the first $50,000 of long-term capital gains to 25%, has been repealed for taxable years beginning after December 31, 1978.

(d) *Maximum Income Tax Rate on Personal Service Income.* The Code limits the maximum income tax rate on personal service income in the case of individuals to 50%. Non-personal service income received by individuals is subject to tax rates as high as 70%. The amount of personal service income qualifying for the maximum 50% rate is reduced by the amount of the taxpayer's tax preference items during the taxable year. For 1979 and thereafter, the 60% net capital gain deduction, although treated as a tax preference item for certain other purposes such as the new alternative minimum tax, is not treated as such for this purpose. Any taxable income generated by the Partnership will be treated as non-personal service income.

There can be no assurance that Congress will not, in the future, enact Federal income tax legislation adversely affecting the tax consequences of investing in the Partnership. In recent sessions of Congress proposals which would have an adverse effect have often been made.

NO REPRESENTATION IS MADE HEREIN BY THE GENERAL PARTNER OR ANY OTHER ENTITY CONNECTED WITH THIS TRANSACTION AS TO THE DEDUCTIBILITY OF ANY EXPENSE OR THE TREATMENT OF ANY ITEM FOR FEDERAL INCOME TAX PURPOSES.

In addition, there exist potential state and local tax consequences of an investment in the Partnership, depending on the jurisdiction in which an investor is a resident.

These statements concerning the income tax effects of the Partnership merely summarize some of the tax consequences of investment in the Partnership. Furthermore, Treasury Regulations and current judicial interpretations are subject to changes that may result in modification of such statements. Each investor who considers the purchase of a Unit should, at his expense, consult his tax adviser with respect to all tax aspects involved in such purchase.

SUMMARY OF PARTNERSHIP AGREEMENT

The form of the Electronic Equipment Development Ltd. Limited Partnership Agreement dated as of August _____, 1980, to which all investors will become parties as Limited Partners, is attached hereto as Exhibit A. Set out below is a summary of certain of the significant provisions of the Partnership Agreement. This summary is qualified in its entirety by reference to the attached text. PROSPECTIVE INVESTORS ARE STRONGLY URGED TO READ THE ENTIRE PARTNERSHIP AGREEMENT FOR COMPLETE INFORMATION CONCERNING THE RIGHTS AND OBLIGATIONS OF THE PARTIES THERETO.

Interests in the Partnership

The Partnership consists of the General Partner who has a 25 percent interest in its capital and residual profits and the limited partners that have a 75 percent interest therein, allocated among the Limited Partners in proportion to the respective number of Units owned by each of them. Accordingly, each of the 24 Units would represent a 3.125 percent interest in the capital and residual profits of the Partnership. In the event that fewer than 24 Units are acquired by the limited partners, then the interest represented by each Unit would be increased accordingly.

The Partnership Agreement does, however, contain a variety of special allocations regarding the distribution of cash flow and allocation of profit and loss which substantially affect the return and tax effects of investing in the Partnership. See "Distribution of Cash Flow and Allocation of Profit and Loss" below.

Capital Contributions

In return for his 25 percent interest in the capital and profits of the Partnership, the General Partner has contributed to the Partnership his interest in the Research Agreement and all his rights and interest in all other agreements and arrangements concerning the development and commercial exploitation of any results of the research. The investors who purchase the Units and become Limited Partners will contribute to the Partnership the sum of $50,000 per Unit. Such contribution is payable in full at the time of the investor's subscription.

Distribution of Cash Flow and Allocation of Profit and Loss

The Partnership Agreement provides that, after the payment of all necessary fees and expenses, the General Partner may distribute to the Partners any cash or other assets not needed to carry on the business of the Partnership. All distributions to Limited Partners will be proportionate to the number of Units owned by each of them.

All such distributions and all tax allocations shall be made in accordance with the following special allocations. Ninety-nine percent of all distributions and all items of income, gain, deduction and credit of the Partnership will be allocated to Limited Partners and one percent will be allocated to the General Partner until the Limited Partners receive distributions in an amount equal to 100 percent of their initial investment in the Partnership. During this period the General Partner will receive one percent of such distributions and allocations.

Thereafter, distributions and tax allocations shall be divided between the Limited Partners and the General Partner, such that 75 percent of any such items are distributed and allocated among the Limited Partners and 25 percent is distributed and allocated to the General Partner.

Upon this dissolution of the Partnership whether as a result of the expiration of the term of the Partnership Agreement or upon the dissolution, resignation or bankruptcy of the General Partner, or otherwise, the remaining assets of the partnership may be sold and the proceeds distributed or the assets distributed in kind along with the retained profits of the Partnership as follows. First, any pre-existing undistributed income or profits will be distributed in accordance with the formula set forth above. Thereafter, the Limited Partners shall receive any such proceeds to the extent of their Capital Account balances in the Partnership, and then the General Partner shall receive an amount equal to his capital account balance. All remaining proceeds shall be distributed in accordance with the distribution formula set forth above.

Additional Contributions

The Partnership Agreement provides that the General Partner may determine that the Partnership has need for additional funds in order to complete, or develop new, research projects undertaken by the Partnership from time to time. In such an event, the General Partner shall give each Limited Partner the opportunity to provide such funds in proportion to his interest in the Partnership. No Limited Partner shall be under any obligation to make any such additional contributions. Those Limited Partners who do desire to make such additional investments may also proportionately invest therein in lieu of those Limited Partners who do not desire to make any further contributions.

If the current Limited Partners do not invest all the funds so required, the General Partner may offer the investment opportunity to third parties who shall then become limited partners with respect to such additional contributions. The raising of such additional capital shall not dilute the interest of the Limited Partners regarding their initial contributions to the Partnership and the assets acquired therewith. The plan of cash distributions and the allocation of profits and losses regarding such new contributions shall be comparable to the formula described above regarding the initial investments.

Management

The Partnership Agreement stipulates that the management and control of the operations and assets of the Partnership rests entirely with the General Partner who carries the power to act for and on behalf of the Partnership in all its business. No Limited Partner has any right to participate in the management of the business of the Partnership or to act for or bind the Partnership, although the General Partner may, at his discretion, consult with the Limited Partners regarding the business of the Partnership.

In the event that the General Partner deems it appropriate to apply the funds which are paid or payable by the Partnership to GTI pursuant to the Research and Development Agreement and are not utilized in connection with the Research Projects described herein, the General Partner may apply such funds to one or more other research projects in the field of electronic equipment development, pursuant to the terms of the Research and Development Agreement. However, the General Partner may not exercise this authority with respect to more than an aggregate of 10% of the funds paid or payable to GTI pursuant to the Research and Development Agreement without providing an opportunity to the Limited Partners owning a majority of the limited partnership interests then outstanding (exclusive of any such limited partnership interests owned by the General Partner and his affiliates) to object to such application of funds.

Limited Liability

No Limited Partner will be personally liable for any of the debts of the Partnership or be required to lend any funds, or contribute any capital to the Partnership, in addition to the contributions specified in the Partnership Agreement. Under the Uniform Limited Partnership Act as adopted in Delaware, the Limited Partners may be consulted regarding Partnership business decisions; nevertheless, the limited liability of any limited partner who actively participates in the management of the Partnership may be jeopardized to the extent that a third party reasonably believes him to be generally liable for the debts of the Partnership.

The General Partner bears general personal liability to third parties for the obligations of the Partnership, except as otherwise provided in the Partnership Agreement or the Research and Development Agreement.

Books and Records

The Partnership Agreement stipulates that the General Partner maintain the books and records of the Partnership and that each partner have access thereto at all reasonable times.

The General Partner will submit to every partner within 75 days after the end of each fiscal year (ending on December 31) a financial report showing the results of the operations of the Partnership for such year and other information, including income, gains, losses, deductions and credits for income tax purposes.

Transfers

Other than upon dissolution and reconstitution of the Partnership, the General Partner does not have any right to transfer an interest as a general partner in the Partnership.

The Partnership Agreement limits the right of the Limited Partners to transfer their interests in the Partnership in that, if any Limited Partner receives a bona fide offer to purchase all or any part of his interest in the Partnership, he must first offer in writing to sell such interest to the General Partner who then has an option for a period of 60 days after receipt of such written offer to purchase such interest upon the same terms and conditions as the bona fide offer.

The requirement that a Limited Partner first offer his interest or any part thereof to the General Partner before transferring that interest does not apply to transfers, subject to certain conditions, to an associate thereof as defined in the Partnership Agreement.

In the event of a transfer of any of the interests of a Limited Partner, the transferee becomes only an assignee of the Limited Partner and does not have the right of a substituted limited partner unless, with the approval of the General Partner, which can be withheld for any reason, he executes an addendum to the Partnership Agreement agreeing to be bound by all the terms and conditions thereof and to reimburse the Partnership for costs incurred in connection with any action taken by the Partnership to reflect the transfer under the Uniform Limited Partnership Act.

Termination and Liquidation

The Partnership does not terminate upon the death or incapacity of any Limited Partner. Instead, the Partnership will continue until July 31, 1990, or upon the earlier occurrence of any of the following: (i) the sale, abandonment or disposal by the Partnership of all or substantially all its assets (except pursuant to the Research and Development Agreement), (ii) the bankruptcy of the Partnership; or (iii) the death, legal incapacity, resignation or bankruptcy of the General Partner.

If a dissolution occurs because of (iii) above, the limited partners may elect to continue the Partnership and substitute a new General Partner for the remainder of its term in accordance with the Partnership Agreement.

In the event of a dissolution of the Partnership without a continuation of its business, the Partnership will be wound up and its assets liquidated and distributed, after payment of debts and obligations of the Partnership to creditors, among the partners in the manner set forth above. (See "Distribution of Cash Flow and Allocation of Profit and Loss.")

Upon the written consent of the General Partner and those Limited Partners owning 75 percent of the interests of all the Limited Partners in all portions of the Partnership, the term of the Partnership may be extended for periods not in excess of seven years. The term may be so extended more than once but not beyond July 31, 2020.

Amendments

The Partnership Agreement grants to the General Partner the authority to amend its provisions from time to time with the consent of those limited partners owning a majority of the interests held by all the Limited Partners in all portions of the Partnership, exclusive of any such interests owned by the General Partner and his affiliates. No amendment, however, may have the effect of removing the limited liability of any Limited Partner or increasing the obligation of any Limited Partner to contribute to the capital of the Partnership without his express written consent.

Power of Attorney

Pursuant to the Subscription, each investor who becomes a limited partner in the Partnership will appoint the General Partner, with full power of substitution, as his attorney to sign, swear to and record any amendment to the certificate of limited partnership of the Partnership as required under the Uniform Limited Partnership Act and to execute various other instruments.

LEGAL MATTERS

Legal matters for the Partnership related to this offering have been passed upon by Kirkpatrick, Lockhart, Johnson & Hutchison of Pittsburgh, Pennsylvania. This firm has served as general counsel to GTI for a number of years.

FURTHER INVESTIGATION

Statements contained in this Private Placement Memorandum as to the contents of the Partnership Agreement, the Research and Development Agreement, the form of license agreement or any other agreement or document referred to herein are not necessarily complete, and each such statement is deemed to be qualified and amplified in all respects by the provisions of such agreements and documents, copies of which are either included in the appendices hereto or made available for examination by prospective investors at the offices of the General Partner. Each prospective investor and his business and tax adviser are urged to examine all such agreements and documents in order to verify the statements contained herein.

No offering literature or advertising in whatever form will be employed in connection with the offer or sale of the Units except for this Private Placement Memorandum and the appendices attached hereto; and no person is authorized to make representations or give information with respect to the Units except for the information contained in this Private Placement Memorandum, the Partnership Agreement, the Research and Development Agreement, the form of license agreement and any other agreement or document referred to herein.

ELECTRONIC EQUIPMENT DEVELOPMENT LTD.

(A Delaware Limited Partnership)

LIMITED PARTNERSHIP AGREEMENT

Dated: August 11, 1980

Exhibit A

TABLE OF CONTENTS

Exhibit A *(Continued)*

Exhibit A *(Continued)*

375

ELECTRONIC EQUIPMENT DEVELOPMENT LTD.
(A Delaware Limited Partnership)

LIMITED PARTNERSHIP AGREEMENT

THIS AGREEMENT made and entered into as of the 11th day of August in the year 1980, by and between JAMES K. LAFLEUR, an individual maintaining a business address at 4337 Talofa Avenue, Toluca Lake, California 91602 (hereinafter sometimes called the "General Partner"), as general partner, of the first part,

AND

RONALD LUST, an individual maintaining a business address at 14761 Poway Mesa Drive, Poway, California 92064 (hereinafter sometimes called the "Nominee") as NOMINEE for those persons (hereinafter sometimes called the "Limited Partners") who execute and deliver the Subscription Agreement and Additional Signature Page in the form set forth [Exhibit A1] at the conclusion hereof (hereinafter sometimes called the "Subscription"), accepted by the General Partner in accordance with the terms and provisions hereof, as limited partners, of the second part.

WITNESSETH:

WHEREAS, the General Partner has negotiated an agreement (hereinafter sometimes called the "Research and Development Agreement") with GTI Corporation (hereinafter sometimes called "GTI") in the form set forth as Exhibit B attached at the conclusion hereof wherein GTI has agreed to make available to the Partnership all its rights in and information regarding certain defined research projects (hereinafter sometimes called the "Research Projects") for the purposes of permitting the Partnership to undertake research (which GTI shall conduct on behalf of the Partnership for compensation) concerned with the development of various types of electronic equipment in return for certain rights regarding the results of the Research Projects as are set forth in the Research and Development Agreement and in the form of license agreement attached as an exhibit thereto (hereinafter sometimes called the "License Agreements"); and

WHEREAS, the General Partner is willing to contribute his rights under the Research and Development Agreement and the License Agreements and in and to the Research Projects and the Limited Partners are willing to

Exhibit A *(Continued)*

377

contribute certain sums of cash to finance the cost of the Research Projects and/or similar research and the cost of organizing the Partnership; and

WHEREAS, the General Partner and the Limited Partners (hereinafter sometimes collectively called the "Partners") wish to join together in a limited partnership organized pursuant to the Uniform Limited Partnership Act of the State of Delaware (hereinafter sometimes called the "ULPA") for the purposes, generally, of carrying out the Research Projects and/or similar research and the development and exploitation of the inventions and discoveries, if any, resulting from the Research Projects (hereinafter sometimes called the "Assets").

NOW, THEREFORE, for and in consideration of the covenants contained herein, the parties hereto, intending to be legally bound, hereby agree as follows:

Article I

Definitions

Sections 1.01 Affiliate. As used herein, the term "Affiliate" shall mean, with respect to any General Partner hereunder, any Associate thereof except for the Partnership and any other Partner who shall be an Associate thereof solely by reason of his participation as a Partner in the Partnership.

Section 1.02 Additional Contributions. As used herein, the term "Additional Contributions" shall mean all contributions to the capital of the Partnership by current or future Limited Partners in accordance with Section 3.04 hereof.

Section 1.03 Associate. As used herein, the term "Associate" shall mean, with respect to any Partner hereunder, (i) the Partnership, (ii) any other Partner, (iii) any corporation, partnership or organization of which such Partner is, directly or indirectly, together with any Associate thereof, the beneficial owner of fifty percent (50%) or more of the equity securities thereof having voting control, or is an executive officer or director thereof, (iv) any trust or other estate in which such Partner or any Associate thereof has a substantial beneficial interest or as to which such Partner or any Associate thereof serves as trustee or in a similar capacity having control, (v) any individual, corporation, partnership, or organization which is, directly or indirectly, the beneficial owner of fifty percent (50%) or more of the equity securities of such Partner or any executive officer or director of such Associate, (vi) any substantial beneficiary of such Partner, (vii) any principal of such Partner which serves as agent thereof hereunder and (viii) any relative or spouse of such Partner or any Associate thereof, or any relative of such spouse.

Exhibit A *(Continued)*

Section 1.04 Capital Account. As used herein, the term "Capital Account" shall mean with regard to any Partner as of any date, the amount of cash and other property contributed by such Partner to the capital of the Partnership in accordance with the provisions hereof, properly adjusted to reflect (a) the distributive shares of such Partner of items of income, gain, loss, deduction, or credit of the Partnership, including, if such date shall not be the close of the fiscal year of the Partnership, the distributive share of such items of the Partnership for the period from the close of the last such fiscal year of the Partnership to such date, and (b) distributions by the Partnership to such Partner, including, if such date shall not be the close of the fiscal year of the Partnership, distributions by the Partnership to such Partner during the period from the close of the last such fiscal year of the Partnership to such date.

Section 1.05 Certificate. As used herein, the term "Certificate" shall mean the Certificate of Limited Partnership of the Partnership to be filed for record in accordance with the ULPA, in substantially the form set forth in [Exhibit B3] attached hereto and made a part hereof.

Section 1.06 General Partner. As used herein, the term "General Partner" shall mean James K. LaFleur, an individual, or any other individual, partnership, corporation or other entity which shall become a general partner of the Partnership hereunder.

Section 1.07 Initial Contributions. As used herein, the term "Initial Contributions" shall mean all contributions to the captial of the Partnership by the Limited Partners in accordance with Section 3.02 hereof.

Section 1.08 I.R.C. As used herein, the term "I.R.C." shall mean the Internal Revenue Code of 1954, as amended, 26 U.S.C.A. §§1 et seq., or any succeeding federal internal revenue law as from time to time in effect. Any reference to any section of the I.R.C. shall include the provisions of any succeeding internal revenue law, the subject matter of which shall correspond with that of such section.

Section 1.09 Limited Partner. As used herein, the term "Limited Partner" shall mean any person who shall execute a Subscription which is accepted by the Partnership and who shall thereafter contribute to the capital of the Partnership in accordance with the provisions of Section 3.02 hereof or who shall contribute to the capital of the Partnership in accordance with the provisions of Section 3.04 hereof or any successor thereof who shall become a substitute limited partner in accordance with the provisions hereof.

Section 1.10 New Units. As used herein, the term "New Units" shall mean the measure into which the interests of the Limited Partners shall be divided

Exhibit A *(Continued)*

with respect to any Additional Contributions to the Partnership in accordance with Section 3.04 hereof.

Section 1.11   Partner.   As used herein, the term "Partner" shall mean any General Partner or Limited Partner.

Section 1.12   Partnership.   As used herein, the term "Partnership" shall mean Electronic Development Ltd. (A Delaware limited partnership), the partnership formed in accordance with the provisions of this Agreement.

Section 1.113   Subscription.   As used herein, the term "Subscription" shall mean the Subscription Agreement and Additional Signature Page in substantially the form set forth in [Exhibit A1] hereto.

Section 1.14   ULPA.   As used herein the term "ULPA" shall mean the Uniform Limited Partnerhsip Act of the State of Delaware, Del. Code. Ann., Tit. 6, §1701 et seq., or any succeeding Delaware limited partnership law as from time to time in effect.

Section 1.15   Unit.   As used herein, the term "Unit" shall mean the measure into which the interests of Limited Partners in the Partnership shall be divided with respect to the Initial Contributions in accordance with Section 3.02 hereof.

Article II

Formation, Name, Offices and Purposes

Section 2.01   Formation.   The Partners hereby form this partnership under the ULPA.

Section 2.02   Name.   The name of the Partnership shall be ELECTRONIC EQUIPMENT DEVELOPMENT LTD. (A Delaware Limited Partnership).

Section 2.03   Offices.   The registered office of the Partnership in the State of Delaware is in care of The Corporation Trust Company, 100 West Tenth Street, Wilmington, Delaware 19801. The principal office of the Partnership shall be 4337 Talofa Avenue, Toluca Lake, California 91602. The Partnership may have such substituted and additional offices at such other locations as the General Partner shall, in his discretion, deem advisable.

Section 2.04   Purposes.   The purposes of the Partnership shall be as follows:

(a) To sponsor, support and finance the Research Projects;

Exhibit A *(Continued)*

(b) To apply for and obtain United States and foreign patent rights concerning the Assets;

(c) To develop and exploit the Assets to a sufficient state to permit determination of their commercial feasibility and marketability and to market or otherwise commercially exploit the Assets;

(d) To develop any machinery appropriate to the mass production of the Assets and to apply for and obtain United States and foreign patent rights with respect thereto;

(e) To license patent rights, copyrights and other rights with respect to the Assets and any related technology to GTI or other persons or entities on a royalty basis pursuant to the Research and Development Agreement, the License Agreements or otherwise; and

(f) To enter into, make and perform all contracts and other undertakings and to engage in all activities and transactions as may be necessary in order to carry out any of the foregoing purposses, including, but not limited to, the following: (1) to purchase, transfer, mortgage, pledge and acquire or exercise rights, powers, privileges and other incidents of ownership with respect to real and personal property; (ii) to borrow or raise monies without limitation as to amount, and to secure the payment of any obligations of the Partnership by mortgage, hypothecation, pledge or other security assignment or arrangement of all or part of the property of the Partnership; and (iii) to rent or acquire office space, to engage personnel and to do such other acts as may be necessary or advisable in connection with such offices and personnel.

(g) To undertake any of the above-described actions with respect to research regarding other projects in the field of electronic equipment development and any inventions and discoveries resulting therefrom in accordance with the provisions of Section 5.02(g) hereof.

The activities of the Partnership for these purposes shall constitute the conduct of a trade or business by the Partnership.

Article III

Capital

Section 3.01   Contribution by General Partner.   The General Partner has contributed to the capital of the Partnership and does hereby transfer, convey, set over and assign as a contribution to capital (a) all his right, title and interest in and to the Research and Development Agreement, the License Agreements, the Research Projects, and the Assets, (b) all his right, title and interest in all other contracts, agreements, and arrangements concerning the development and exploitation of the Research Projects and Assets and

Exhibit A *(Continued)*

all his developments and opportunities relating thereto; provided, however, that nothing contained herein shall be interpreted or construed as a contribution to the capital of the Partnership of any right, title or interest of the General Partner in and to any fee or expense reimbursement to which the General Partner may be entitled hereunder.

Section 3.02 Contributions by Limited Partners.

(a) The Limited Partners shall contribute in cash to the capital of the Partnership the aggregate amount of not less than Three Hundred Fifty Thousand Dollars ($350,000.00) and not more than One Million Two Hundred Thousand Dollars ($1,200,000.00) divided into seven (7) to twenty-four (24) equal Units, each representing a commitment for, and the contribution of capital of, Fifty Thousand Dollars ($50,000.00). For and on behalf of the Partnership, the General Partner shall receive such contributions of cash to the capital of the Partnership from any persons or entities who shall be admitted to the Partnership as Limited Partners upon their execution and delivery of the Subscription and upon the acceptance thereof by the General Partner. The Limited Partners shall severally pay such contributions to the Partnership with respect to each Unit in cash upon the admission of the Limited Partners to the Partnership.

(b) The Units shall be divided severally among the Limited Partners in accordance with the number set forth on the respective Subscription executed and delivered by each of the Limited Partners and accepted by the General Partner.

Section 3.03 Escrow Account.

The General Partner shall deposit the contributions paid in accordance with Section 3.02(a) in an escrow account separate and apart from any operating account until (a) the date when he shall have accepted Subscriptions for not less than seven (7) Units from the Limited Partners hereunder or (b) September 30, 1980 (hereinafter sometimes called the "Escrow Return Date"), whichever shall be earlier. In the event that the General Partner shall accept Subscriptions for not less than such seven (7) Units hereunder on or before the Escrow Return Date, the General Partner shall close such escrow account and shall transfer the contributions held in escrow thereunder to the operating account of the Partnership for use for the purposes of the Partnership as set forth in Section 2.04 hereof. In the event, however, that the General Partner shall not accept Subscriptions for seven (7) or more Units on or before the Escrow Return Date, the General Partner shall then close such escrow account and shall pay to each of the persons subscribing for the Units theretofore subscribed for the amount of the contributions made thereby plus interest, if any, actually earned thereon; and, upon the receipt thereof, each of such persons shall have no further right, title or interest in and to the Partnership, including but not limited to the Research and Development Agreement, the License Agreements, the

Exhibit A (Continued)

Research Projects and the Assets, and shall not be a Limited Partner hereunder. Notwithstanding the foregoing, the General Partner, in his absolute discretion, may at any time on or before September 30, 1980, extend (and thereafter re-extend) the Escrow Return Date for all the purposes hereof to a date or dates not later than October 31, 1980.

Section 3.04 Additional Contributions to Capital of Limited Partners.

(a) At any time and from time to time following the investment of the Initial Contributions provided for in Section 3.02 hereof, the General Partner may, in his discretion, decide that the Partnership has need of cash as an extra contribution to the capital of the Partnership in excess of the contributions by the Partners under Section 3.02 hereof. In such event, the General Partner shall call upon the Limited Partners to contribute within fifteen (15) days an aggregate amount, divided into equal New Units in the Partnership, equal to such total amount as the General Partner shall determine, pro rate in proportion to the number of Units then held by the Limited Partners. Any of the Limited Partners may decline to make any of such contributions to the capital of the Partnership.

(b) In the event that any Limited Partner shall decline or fail to make all or any part of such extra contribution to capital of the Partnership as indicated in Section 3.04(a) hereof, the General Partner shall thereupon call upon the other Limited Partners to contribute within fifteen (15) days thereafter the portion of such extra contribution to capital which any Limited Partner shall have declined to make. In the event that any of such other Limited Partners shall thereupon desire to contribute to capital of the Partnership in whole or in part such extra contribution to capital which any Limited Partner shall have declined to make, such extra contribution to capital of the Partnership shall be made by such other Limted Partners pro rata in proportion to the number of Units then held by each of them. Any of the other Limited Partners may decline to make any or all of such extra contribution to capital of the Partnership.

(c) In the event that the Limited Partners shall decline or fail to provide the full amount of extra contribution to capital as indicated in Section 3.04(a) hereof, after compliance with the procedures set forth in Section 3.04(a) and Section 3.04(b) hereof, the General Partner may, at his discretion, accept the portion of extra contribution to capital not provided by the Limited Partners and divided into New Units in the Partnership, from any other person or entity, including any person or entity with which the Partnership has contractual relationships. Such other persons or entities shall then become Limited Partners herein and shall have that percentage interest in the Partnership as provided in Section 4.03 hereof. Each of such new Limited Partners shall become a Limited Partner only by executing, in a form satisfactory to the General Partner, an addendum to this Agreement of Limited Partnership agreeing to be bound by all the terms and provisions hereof.

Exhibit A *(Continued)*

Section 3.05   The Nominee.   The Nominee shall act as nominee of the Limited Partners hereunder solely for the purpose of the execution and delivery of this Agreement for and on behalf of the Limited Partners and shall bear no obligation or personal responsibility for the contributions to capital of the Partnership by the Limited Partners hereunder; except, however, that the Nominee has contributed to the capital of the Partnership, as nominee for the Limited Partners hereunder, the sum of One Dollar ($1.00) for the purpose of effecting the organization of the Partnership.

Section 3.06   Confirmation of Capital Contributions.   The Partners shall execute and deliver to the Partnership, in form reasonably acceptable to the General Partner, any assignments and other instruments of transfer as may be deemed necessary to confirm and carry out the contributions to capital of the Partnership provided for herein.

Section 3.07   Use of Capital Contributions.   The aggregate of all the contributions to capital of the Partnership provided for herein shall be available to the Partnership to carry out the purposes of the Partnership, including payment of costs incurred in connection with the organization and administration of the Partnership, as well as fees to accountants, consultants, lawyers and broker-dealers for services rendered to the General Partner and the Partnership and all costs of syndication of the Units and any New Units subscribed for by the Limited Partners in accordance with Section 3.02 and Section 3.04 hereof.

Section 3.08   Advances to Partnership.   In the event that, at any time or from time to time during the term hereof, the General Partner has need of additional funds in excess of the contributions to capital of the Partnership indicated hereinabove for the conduct of the business of the Partnership or the payment of any of its obligatins, expenses, costs, liabilities or expenditures including, without limitation, operating deficits, the General Partner may, in his discretion, borrow such funds for and on behalf of the Partnership, with interest payable at rates then prevailing, from commercial banks or other financial institutions or other persons including Partners. Nothing contained herein shall be interpreted or construed to require the General Partner to advance any of his funds or other assets to or for the benefit of the Partnership except as provided in Section 3.01 hereof.

Article IV

Participation in Partnership Property

Section 4.01   Ownership by Partners of Partnership.   Each Partner shall have and own an undivided interest in the Partnership equal to his respective percentage interest in the Partnership in accordance with the terms hereof;

Exhibit A *(Continued)*

provided, however, that no Partner shall have any right of partition with respect to any property of the Partnership including, without limitation, the Assets.

Section 4.02 Percentage Interests in Partnership. Subject to the provisions of Article IV hereof, the initial percentage interests of the Partners in the Partnership shall be as follows:

Partners		Percentage Interest
General Partner		25%
Limited Partners		75%
	Total	100%

The percentage interest in the Partnership allocated to the Limited Partners shall be divided among them pro rata in proportion to the respective number of Units owned by each of them.

Section 4.03 Adjustment of Percentage Interests in Partnership. In the event that the General Partner shall, in accordance with Section 3.04 hereof, obtain cash as Additional Contributions to the capital of the Partnership, the precentage interests of all the Partners in the Partnership shall be adjusted and established in the the following manner. The percentage interests of the Partners set forth in Section 4.02 hereof shall be proportionately reduced such that the entire interests originally allocated by said Section 4.02 shall not longer constitute one hundred percent (100%) of the interests in the Partnership but shall constitute a lesser percentage equal to that percentage of the total contributions to the Partnership made by the Limited Partners (both as Initial Contributions and as Additional Contributions) which is represented by the Initial Contributions. The remainder of the Percentage interests in the Partnership shall be allocated to the General Partner and to the Limited Partners who make the Additional Contributins to the Partnership, subject to the provisions of Article VI hereof, as follows:

Partners		Percentage Interest
General Partner		25%
Limited Partners		75%
	Total	100%

The percentage interests of the Limited Partners resulting from their Additional Contributions shall be divided severally among them in proportion to the respective number of New Units owned by them. All distributions and all allocations for income tax purposes as set forth in Article VI hereof shall be made separately, in accordance with the formula set forth in this

Exhibit A *(Continued)*

385

Section 4.03, with respect to the interests resulting from the Initial Contributions and the interests resulting from the Additional Contributions.

Section 4.04 Withdrawals from Capital Accounts. Except as expressly provided herein, no Partner shall be entitled to withdraw any amount from his Capital Account in the Partnership; and no Limited Partner shall have the right to demand and receive interest thereon or property other than cash in return for any contributions to the capital of the Partnership. In the event, nevertheless, that, in accordance with Section 3.03 hereof, the General Partner shall not accept Subscriptions for seven (7) or more of the Units on or before the Escrow Return Date, as extended, the General Partner shall pay to each of the persons subscribing for the Units theretofore subscribed for the amount of the contributions made thereby plus interest, if any, actually earned thereon. Upon such distribution, the Limited Partners shall have no further rights or obligations hereunder and no further interest in the Research and Development Agreement, the License Agreements, the Research Projects, the Assets or any other property of the Partnership or the capital and profits of the Partnership.

Section 4.05 Limitation on Distributions. Except as expressly provided herein, the General Partner shall make no distribution of the property of the Partnership to any Partner with respect to his interest in the Partnership; and, notwithstanding anything contained herein, the General Partner shall make no distributions or take any other action in violation of the ULPA.

Article V

Management

Section 5.01 General Management. Except as set forth in Section 5.08 hereof, the management and control of the day-to-day operations of the Partnership and the maintenance of the property of the Partnership shall rest exclusively with the General Partner.

Section 5.02 Powers of the General Partner. The General Partner shall be hereby authorized and empowered to carry out and implement any and all the purposes of the Partnership; and, in that connection, the General Partner, or his authorized agents, shall, except as otherwise expressly provided herein, have all the rights and powers and shall be subject to all the restrictions of a partner in a general partnership. In tha connection, the powers of the General Partner shall included, without limitation, the following:

(a) To engage personnel;
(b) To engage attorneys, accountants, consultants or such other persons as he may deem necessary or advisable;

Exhibit A *(Continued)*

(c) To open, maintain and close bank accounts and to draw checks and other orders for the payment of money;

(d) To borrow money and to make, issue, accept and endorse and execute promissory notes, drafts, bills of exchange and other instruments of indebtedness, all without limit as to amount, and to secure the payment thereof by mortgage, hypothecation, pledge or other assignment of or arrangement or security interest in all or any part of the property then owned or thereafter acquired by the Partnership;

(e) To retain, at his discretion, broker-dealer(s) who will syndicate the sale of the Units and/or the New Units in accordance with Section 3.02 and Section 3.04 hereof, and to negotiate and pay a reasonable and customary commission to any such broker-dealer for performing such services;

(f) To incur such other expenses and take such other actions on behalf of the Partnership as he may deem necessary or advisable in connection with the conduct of the affairs of the Partnership, including the termination of any Research Projects covered by the Research and Development Agreement and the License Agreements; and

(g) To apply any funds, which are paid or payable by the Partnership to GTI pursuant to the Research and Development Agreement and are not utilized in connection with the Research Projects as described therein, to one or more other research projects in the field of electronic equipment development in the manner set forth in the Research and Development Agreement; provided, however, that the General Partner shall not exercise his authority under this Section 5.02(g) with respect to more than an aggregate of ten percent (10%) of the funds paid or payable to GTI pursuant to the Research and Development Agreement without obtaining the prior consent of the Limited Partners as set forth below. In the event that the General Partner desires to so apply more than ten percent (10%) of the funds so paid or payable to GTI to such other project(s), the General Partner may only do so after giving written notice to the Limited Partners as to the nature of the other project(s) which he so desires GTI to undertake pursuant to the Research and Development Agreement and the amount of funds he desires to so apply, and those Limited Partners who shall then own a majority of the total Units or New Units then outstanding (exclusive of any Units or New Units owned by the General Partner or any Affiliates thereof) within thirty (30) days following such notice shall not object in a writing or writings delivered to the General Partner to such application of funds.

(h) To enter into, make and perform such contracts, agreements and other undertakings as he may deem necessary or advisable for the conduct of the affairs of the Partnership, including, without limitation, the Research and Development Agreement and the License Agreements.

Notwithstanding the foregoing in this Section 5.02, the Partnership shall

Exhibit A *(Continued)*

not enter into, make, perform or modify in any manner which affects the interests of the Limited Partners in any material respect (as determined by the General Partner on advice of counsel) any contracts, agreements, undertakings and transactions with the General Partner or any Affiliate of the General Partner, except as expressly provided herein, unless the General Partner shall give notice in writing to the Limited Partners of the terms and provisions of such contract, agreement, undertaking or transaction, and those Limited Partners who shall then own a majority of the total Units or New Units then outstanding (exclusive of any Units and New Units then owned by the General Partner or any Affiliates thereof), within thirty (30) days following such notice, shall not object in a writing or writings delivered to the General Partner to such contract, agreement, undertaking or transaction.

Section 5.03   Fees Payable to the General Partner.

(a) In consideration for its services as manager of the Reseach Projects and/or similar research and Assets, the General Partner shall receive from the Partnership during the term hereof a management fee which shall constitute an expense of the Partnership and a guaranteed payment determined without regard to the income of the Partnership in accordance with Section 707(c) of the I.R.C. The Partnership shall pay such fee to the General Partner in cash within thirty (30) days of the end of each month commencing with the month during which the contributions of the Limited Partners are transferred to the Partnership's operating account pursuant to Section 3.03 hereof, in the amount of $1,666,67 per month, constituting an annual management fee of $20,000.00.

(b) The General Partner shall be reimbursed for any expenses incurred by him to the extent that such expenses are incurred directly on behalf of the Partnership, including without limitation all expenses incurred in connectin with the organization of the Partnership. The General Partner may utilize his own secretarial staff, supplies, telephones and similar support services in managing the affairs of the Partnership; in such an event, the General Partner may obtain reimbursement from the Partnership for the reasonable pro rata cost of any such services which are reasonably necessary for the organization and operation of the Partnership.

Section 5.04   Activity of the General Partner.   Although nothing contained herein shall require the General Partner, or his agents, to devote their full time to the conduct of the affairs of the Partnership, the General Partner shall use his best efforts in carrying out and implementing the purposes of the Partnership and shall devote to the conduct of the affairs of the Partnership such time and activity as he, in his discretion, shall deem reasonably necessary therefor.

Section 5.05.   Transfer of Assets and Other Acts Outside Ordinary Business of Partnership.   The General Partner shall not sell, convey, exchange or

Exhibit A *(Continued)*

otherwise transfer a material part of the assets of the Partnership unless he shall have first obtained the written consent of those Limited Partners then owning an aggregate of no less than a majority of the Units and New Units (exclusive of any Units and New Units owned by the General Partner and Affiliates thereof); provided, however, that no such consent of the Limited Partners shall be required (i) for the transfer of any such assets pursuant to the provisions of the Research and Development Agreement or any of the License Agreements or (ii) for the license of such assets to or for the benefit of any person or entity other than the General Partner, or any Affiliates thereof in accordance with the provisions of Section 5.02 hereof.

Section 5.06   Insurance Coverage.   The Partnership shall cause to be maintained insurance of the coverage and in the amount consistent with prudent business practice.

Section 5.07   Holding of Property.   Property owned by the Partnership shall be held in the name of the Partnership or in nominee name. Subject to the provisions of Section 5.02 and Section 5.05 hereof, the General Partner shall, in his capacity as general partner, have the right, power and authority, without regard to the term hereof, for and on behalf of the Partnership, to lease, sell, mortgage, convey or refinance any property of the Partnership, including, without limitation, the Research and Development Agreement, the License Agreements, the Research Projects and the Assets, and to create straw corporations to act as straw parties and nominees solely for and on behalf of the Partnership. In no event shall any party dealing with the General Partner with respect to any property of the Partnership, or to whom any such property, or any part thereof, shall be conveyed, contracted to be sold, leased, mortgaged or refinanced by the General Partner for and on behalf of the Partnership, be obligated to see that the terms of this Agreement have been complied with, or be obligated to inquire into the necessity or expediency of any act or action of the General Partner, or be obligated or privileged to inquire into any of the terms of this Agreement. Every contract, agreement, deed, mortgage, lease or other instrument or document executed by the General Partner with respect to any property of the Partnership shall be conclusive evidence in favor of any and every person relying thereon or claiming thereunder that (a) at the time or times of the execution and delivery thereof, the Partnership was in full force and effect, (b) such instrument or document was duly executed in accordance with the terms and provisions of this Agreement and is binding upon the Partnership and all of the Partners hereof, and (c) the General Partner was duly authorized and empowered to execute and deliver any and every such instrument or document for and on behalf of the Partnership. The manner of holding title to any property of the Partnership, or any part thereof, shall be solely for the convenience of the Partnership; accordingly, no spouse, heir, legal representative, successor or assign of any Partner shall have any right, title or interest in and to any

Exhibit A *(Continued)*

property of the Partnership by reason of the manner in which title shall be held; and all such property shall be treated as property of the Partnership subject to the terms of this Agreement.

Section 5.08 Meetings. The General Partner or those Limited Partners owning no less than twenty percent (20%) of the Units and New Units may call a meeting of the Partners for any reasonable time in Los Angeles, California, upon at least ten (10) days' notice to the other Partners. Such meetings shall be for the purpose of receiving the report of the General Partner provided in Section 8.03 hereof or for considering any action to be taken by the Limited Partners under this Agreement.

Section 5.09 Activity of the Limited Partners. Subject to the provisions of Section 5.02 hereof, the Limited Partners shall, as may be determined by mutual agreement of the General Partner and each Limited Partner, consult with and advise the General Partner as to the conduct of the Partnership's business. Notwithstanding the foregoing, the General Partner shall be under no obligation to seek or accept the advice of any Limited Partner.

Article VI

Distributions of Cash and Allocations of Profit and Loss

Section 6.01 Distributions.
(a) If after the payment of all necessary fees and expenses, the General Partner shall from time to time determine that any cash or other assets attributable to the Initial Contributions in accordance with Section 4.02 and Section 4.03 hereof are not reasonably needed to carry on the business of the Partnership and if the General Partner shall decide to distribute such cash or other assets, such cash or other assets shall be distributed to the Partners having an interest therein in accordance with their respective percentage interests then held in the Partnership with respect thereto as set forth in Sections 4.02 and 4.03 hereof; provided, however, that the General Partner shall receive no distribution under this Section 6.01(a) in excess of one percent (1%) thereof until the then Limited Partners (together with their predecessors in interest) shall have received an amount hereunder equal to one hundred percent (100%) of the Initial Contributions made by them (or by former Limited Partners who have transferred their interests thereto) as indicated in Section 3.02(a) hereof.
(b) If after payment of all necessary fees and expenses, the General Partner shall from time to time determine that any cash or other assets attributable to the Additional Contributions in accordance with Section 4.03 hereof are not reasonably needed to carry on the business of the Partnership and if the General Partner shall decide to distribute such cash and other assets, such cash and other assets shall be distributed to the Partners having an interest

Exhibit A *(Continued)*

therein in accordance with their respective percentage interests then held in the Partnership as set forth in Section 4.03 hereof; provided, however, that the General Partner shall receive no distribution under this Section 6.01(b) in excess of one percent (1%) thereof until the then Limited Partners (together with their predecessors in interest) shall have received an amount hereunder equal to one hundred percent (100%) of the Additional Contributions made by them (or by former Limited Partners who have transferred their interests thereto) as indicated in Section 3.04 hereof.

Section 6.02 Prohibition of Distributions. Except as expressly provided herein, the General Partner shall make no distribution of the property of the Partnership to any Partner with respect to his interest in the Partnership; and, notwithstanding anything contained herein to the contrary, the General Partner shall make no distributions or take any other action in violation of the ULPA.

Section 6.03   Partners' Shares of Tax Profits and Losses.
(a) For the purposes of Sections 702 and 704 of the I.R.C. and in light of the substantial economic effect attributable to the disproportionate cash contributions by the Partners to the capital of the Partnership in accordance with Section 3.01 and 3.02 hereof, the items of income, gain, deduction and credit of the Partnership attributable to the Initial Contributions in accordance with Section 4.02 and Section 4.03 hereof for income tax purposes for each taxable year of the Partnership, shall be allocated among the Partners having an interest therein as follows:

(i) For each fiscal year of the Partnership or fraction thereof through the Conversion Date as defined in Section 6.04(a) hereof, ninety-nine percent (99%) of such items shall be allocated to the Limited Partners pro rata in proportion to their respective Units in the Partnership and one percent (1%) thereof shall be allocated to the General Partner; and

(ii) for each fiscal year of the Partnership or fraction thereof after such Conversion Date, all such items shall be allocated to all the Partners having an interest therein pro rata in proportion to their respective percentage interests in the Partnership with respect thereto as set forth in Sections 4.02 and 4.03 hereof;

except as adjusted pursuant to any election made in accordance with Section 6.03(c) hereof.
(b) For the purposes of Sections 702 and 704 of the I.R.C. and in light of the substantial economic effect attributable to the disproportionate cash contributions by the Partners to the capital of the Partnership in accordance with Sections 3.01 and 3.04 hereof, the items of income, gain, deduction and credit of the Partnership attributable to the Additional Contributions in accordance with Section 4.03 hereof for income tax purposes for each taxable

Exhibit A (Continued)

year of the Partnership, shall be allocated among the Partners having an interest therein as follows:

(i) For each fiscal year of the Partnership or fraction thereof through the Conversion Date as defined in Section 6.04(b) hereof, ninety-nine percent (99%) of such items shall be allocated to the Limited Partners pro rata in proportion to their respective New Units in the Partnership and one percent (1%) thereof shall be allocated to the General Partner; and

(ii) For each fiscal year of the Partnership or fraction thereof after such Conversion Date, all such items shall be allocated to all the Partners having an interest therein pro rata in proparation to their respective percentage interests in the Partnership with respect thereto as set forth in Section 4.03 hereof;

except as adjusted pursuant to any election made in accordance with Section 6.03(c) hereof.

(c) In the case of distribution of property of the Partnership to any Partner or transfer of the interest of any Partner in the Partnership pursuant to the provisions hereof, the Partnership shall file the election contemplated by Section 754 of the I.R.C. in order to adjust the basis, for federal income tax purposes, of property of the Partnership in the manner provided by Section 734 and Section 743 of the I.R.C.

Section 6.04   Conversion Date.

(a) The term "Conversion Date," as used in Section 6.03(a) hereof, shall mean with respect to the Initial Contributions the date on which the then Limited Partners having an interest therein (together with their predecessors in interest) shall have received aggregate distributions in accordance with the provisions of Section 6.01(a) hereof in cash in an amount equal to one hundred percent (100%) of the Initial Contributions made by the then Limited Partners (or by former Limited Partners who have transferred their interests thereto) in accordance with Section 3.02(a) hereof.

(b) The term "Conversion Date," as used in Section 6.03(b) hereof, shall mean with respect to the Additional Contributions the date on which the then Limited Partners having an interest therein (together with their predecessors in interest) shall have received aggregate distributions in accordance with the provisions of Section 6.01(b) hereof in cash in an amount equal to one hundred percent (100%) of the Additional Contributions made by the then Limited Partners (or by former Limited Partners who have transferred their interests thereto) in accordance with Section 3.04 hereof.

Any allocation of income, gains, losses, deductions and credits for income tax purposes with respect to the fiscal year in which any Conversion Date hereunder shall occur shall be made in the ratio of the number of days in such year before and on and after such Conversion Date, except as expressly provided herein.

Exhibit A *(Continued)*

Article VII

Liability

Section 7.01   Liability of General Partner.

(a) Except as expressly provided herein, the General Partner shall have no personal obligation or liability for the return of all or any part of the contribution to capital of the Partnership of any Limited Partner; and, except as expressly provided herein, the General Partner shall have no personal obligation to contribute to capital of the Partnership or to loan any funds to the Partnership.

(b) The General Partner shall have no personal obligation or liability to the Partnership or any Partner by reason of any act of omission of the General Partner; provided, however, that such act or omission was performed in good faith, within what the General Partner reasonably believed to be the scope of the authority of the General Partner under this Agreement, without gross negligence or willful misconduct.

(c) The General Partner shall be entitled to indemnification from the Partnership, but not from any of the Limited Partners, for any cost, damage, liability or expense reasonably incurred by him arising out of or in connection with the business of the Partnership.

(d) Any liability of the Partnership, whether or not the General Partner shall bear any personal liability therefor, shall first be satisfied out of the assets of the Partnership (including the proceeds of any liability insurance which the Partnership may recover therefor) to the extent thereof.

Section 7.02   Limited Liability of Limited Partners.   The liability of the Limited Partners in all respects shall be limited to the capital contributions paid by such Limited Partners to the Partnership under the provisions of this Agreement except as specifically provided in Section 10.07(e) hereof.

Article VIII

Accounting

Section 8.01   Books and Records.

(a) The General Partner shall keep true, exact and complete books of account in which shall be entered fully and accurately each and every transaction of the Partnership. The books of account shall be kept on the cash receipts and disbursements method or the accrual method as the General Partner may, in his discretion, determine; provided, however, that, for federal income tax purposes, the General Partner shall make no election on behalf of the Partnership to capitalize any item which may reasonably be deducted as an expense and shall make every election on behalf of the Partnership to expense or amortize any item which may otherwise be cap-

Exhibit A *(Continued)*

393

italized or not amortized, including without limitation all research and ex-perimental expenditures as referred to in Section 174(a)(1) of the I.R.C.

(b) Such books of account, together with all correspondence, papers and other documents, shall be kept at such offices of the Partnership as the General Partner shall designate and shall be at all reasonable times open to the examination of all or any of the Limited Partners who shall be permitted to make copies of all or any part thereof.

Section 8.02   Fiscal Year.   The initial fiscal year of the Partnership shall begin upon the commencement of the term of this Agreement and shall expire on the December 31 thereafter; and each succeeding fiscal year of the Part-nership shall commence on January 1 and shall expire on December 31 thereafter until the termination of the Partnership. The fiscal year shall be the taxable year of the Partnership for income tax purposes.

Section 8.03   Annual Reports.   Within seventy-five (75) days after the end of each fiscal year of the Partnership, the General Partner shall cause to be prepared and transmitted to each Partner a financial report containing: (a) a balance sheet of the Partnership showing its condition at the close of such year; (b) a statement of income of the Partnership showing the results of operation during such year; (c) a cash-flow statement of the Partnership showing the cash receipts and disbursements of the Partnership during such year; and (d) a statement showing each Partner's share of the income, gains, losses, deductions and credits of the Partnership for such year for income tax purposes. Such cash-flow statement shall show separately: (i) cash dis-bursements of the Partnership, if any, other than for operating expenses of the Partnership; (ii) payments by the Partnership of principal, interest or other charges payable to the holder of any loan made to the Partnership; (iii) payments by the Partnership, if any, of taxes based upon or measured by income. The General Partner shall also cause to be prepared, filed and distributed to all the Partners all appropriate tax returns.

Article IX

Assignments

Section 9.01   Investment Representation.   Each Limited Partner shall ac-quire his interest in the Partnership for investment and not with a view to the transfer, resale or distribution thereof; and he shall not sell his interest within one year of its acquisition or sell or otherwise distribute such interest in violation of the Securities Act of 1933, as amended and then in effect, the regulations then promulgated by the Securities and Exchange Commission thereunder or any other applicable securities law or regulation. Each Limited Partner shall indemnify the Partnership, the General Partner and the Nom-inee against all liability, costs, and expenses, including without limitation

Exhibit A *(Continued)*

attorney's fees, arising as a result of any disposition by him of his interest in the Partnership in violation of this Section 9.01 or any applicable securities law or regulation.

Section 9.02 Transfers by General Partner. The General Partner shall have no right to transfer his interest as a general partner in the Partnership except as provided in Section 10.06 hereof.

Section 9.03 Transfers by Limited Partners.

(a) In the event that any Limited Partner shall wish to sell all or any part of his interest in the Partnership, then, as a condition precedent to the sale by such Limited Partner thereof, such Limited Partner shall give to the General Partner written notice containing a copy of a bona fide, legally enforceable written offer of a third party forthwith to purchase such interest for a consideration consisting solely of cash to be paid upon the assignment of such interest free and clear of all liens, encumbrances, equities and claims except as provided herein. For a period of sixty (60) days after receipt of such notice from such Limited Partner, the General Partner shall have an option to purchase such interest from such Limited Partner for the same price set forth in the bona fide offer contained in such notice hereunder. If the General Partner shall waive his rights hereunder or shall fail to exercise the option within a sixty-day period, then for a period of thirty (30) says thereafter, the option of the General Partner hereunder shall be suspended; and such Limited Partner shall have the right to accept the written offer to purchase such interest as contained in such notice and shall have the right to transfer such interest in accordance with the terms and provisions of such offer.

(b) Except as provided in Section 9.03(c), nothing contained herein shall prevent any Limited Partner from transferring his interest herein, in whole or in part, whether by will or intestacy, by inter vivos gift, by sale for consideration, by contribution to capital, by merger or consolidation, by distribution or liquidation or otherwise to any Associate thereof.

(c) Notwithstanding the foregoing in the Section 9.03, nothing contained herein shall be interpreted or construed to permit any Limited Partner (i) to assign, without the prior written consent of the General Partner, all or any part of his percentage interest in the Partnership to any individual person who shall be under twenty-one (21) years of age, to any non-resident alien individual or foreign partnership referred to in section 1441(a) of the I.R.C. or to any person who shall thereafter own less than one percent (1%) of the percentage interest in the Partnership within twelve (12) months of its acquisition; (iii) to cause a termination of the Partnership in accordance with section 708(b)(1)(B) of the I.R.C.; or (iv) to cause treatment of the Partnership for federal income tax purposes as an association referred to in section 7701(a)(3) of the I.R.C.

Exhibit A (*Continued*)

Section 9.04 Substitution of Partners. In the event of a transfer pursuant to the provisions of Section 9.03, any transferee shall become only an assignee of a Limited Partner in accordance with the ULPA and shall not have the rights of a substituted Limited Partner, unless, with the approval of the General Partner, which approval may be withheld for any reason, such transferee shall execute an addendum to this Agreement, agreeing to be bound by all the terms and provisions hereof, to assume all the obligations of the transferor Limited Partner hereunder and to reimburse the Partnership for any costs incurred in connection with any action taken by the Partnership to reflect such transfer under the ULPA.

Section 9.05 Treatment as Partners. No person other than the General Partner, any General Partner who shall become a successor limited partner, any succesor general partner, the Limited Partners and any substituted Limited Partners hereunder shall be considered a Partner hereof. The Partnership, the General Partner and each Limited Partner need deal only with the then General Partner and such Limited Partners or substituted Limited Partners; and they shll not be required to deal with any other person by reason of an assignment by any Limited Partner or by reason of his death or incapacity except as expressly provided herein. In the absence of a substitution of an assignee of a Limited Partner hereunder, any payment to a Limited Partner or his legal representative shall acquit the Partnership and the General Partner of any and all liability to any other person who may be interested in such payment by reason of any assignment or other disposition of an ownership interest in the Partnership by such Limited Partner.

Section 9.06 Tax Effect of Transfers.

(a) In the case of the transfer of a Partner's interest in the Partnership pursuant to any provisions hereof at any time other than the end of the fiscal year of the Partnership, the distributive shares of the various items of income, gains, losses, deductions and credits of the Partnership, as computed for income tax purposes, shall be allocated between the transferor and the transferee in the ratio of the number of days in such year before and on and after such transfer; provided, however, that in the event of a mutual agreement in writing executed by the transferor and the transferee and delivered to the General Partner prior to the end of such year as to any such allocations, any such items shall be allocated to either the transferor or the transferee on the basis of such agreement except as otherwise provided in section 706(c)(2) of the I.R.C.

(b) Any contribution to the capital of the Partnership hereunder shall not constitute a transfer of a Partner's interest in the Partnership hereunder; and, subject to the provisions of section 706(c)(2) of the I.R.C., any Partner who shall contribute to the capital of the Partnership hereunder in any fiscal year of the Partnership shall be considered to be Partner thereof from the commencement of such fiscal year.

Exhibit A (*Continued*)

Article X

Term and Dissolution

Section 10.01 Term. The term of the Partnership shall commence on the date of filing of the Certificate of Limited Partnership of the Partnership in substantially the form set forth on [Exhibit B3] attached hereto and made a part hereof (hereinafter sometimes called the "Certificate") in the office of the Secretary of the State of Delaware in accordance with the ULPA. Subject to the provisions of Section 10.02 hereof, the term of the Partnership shall continue until July 31, 1990, or until prior termination as provided herein.

Section 10.02 Extension of Term. Not later than ninety (90) days prior to the expiration of the term of the Partnership, the Partners, by written instrument signed by the General Partner and not less than those Limited Partners owning seventy-five (75%) of the Units and the New Units (exclusive of any Units and New Units owned by the General Partner or any Affiliates thereof) then owned by all the Limited Partners, may extend the term of the Partnership for a period not in excess of seven (7) years from July 31, 1990. The term of the Partnership may be so extended more than once; provided, however, that the term shall not be extended beyond July 31, 2020.

Section 10.03 Death or Incapacity of a Limited Partner. The Partnership shall not terminate and dissolve upon the death or legal incapacity of any Limited Partner. Rather, subject to and in accordance with the provisions of Section 9.03 hereof, the heir, legal representative, successor or assign of such Limited Partner, as the case may be, shall become an assignee of such Limited Partner in accordance with the ULPA and shall not have the rights of a substituted Limited Partner unless, with the approval of the General Partner, which approval may be withheld for any reason, such heir, legal representative, successor or assign shall execute an addendum to this Agreement as provided in Section 9.04 hereof.

Section 10.04 Dissolution. Subject to the provisions of Section 10.06 hereof, the Partnership shall be dissolved upon the occurrence of any of the following:

(a) The arrival of the termination date without extension thereof as stipulated in Section 10.01 and Section 10.02 hereof;

(b) The failure of the General Partner to accept Subscriptions for seven (7) or more of the Units on or before October 31, 1980;

(c) The sale, abandonment, or disposal by the Partnership of all or substantially all of its assets;

Exhibit A *(Continued)*

397

(d) The bankruptcy of the Partnership;

(e) The death, legal incapacity, resignation or bankruptcy of the General Partner.

For the purposes of this Section 10.04, the bankruptcy of the General Partner shall include the filing of a voluntary petition in bankruptcy or insolvency or a petition for reorganization under any bankruptcy law thereby, the consent thereby to an involuntary petition in bankruptcy or the failure thereof to vacate within sixty (60) days from the date of entry thereof any order approving an involuntary petition, the appointment for a receiver for all or substantial portion of the property thereof or any interest herein, or the entry of an order, judgment or decree for relief of the General Partner by any court of competent jurisdiction on the application of a creditor or approving a petition seeking reorganization or appointing a receiver, trustee or liquidator of all or any substantial part of the assets of the General Partner of any interest thereof herein if such order, judgment or decree continues unstayed and in effect for any period of one hundred twenty (120) consecutive days; and the bankruptcy of the Partnership shall include any of the same events with respect thereto as set forth herein with regard to the General Partner except for the filing of a petition for reorganization or the entry of an order, judgment or decree approving a petition seeking reorganization, neither of which shall constitute the bankruptcy of the Partnership hereunder.

Section 10.05   Resignation of General Partner.   Nothing contained herein shall be interpreted or construed as permitting the General Partner to resign as the general partner of the Partnership without the prior written consent of those Limited Partners then owning not less than seventy-five percent (75%) of the Units and the New Units (exclusive of any Units and New Units owned by the General Partner or any Affiliates thereof).

Section 10.06   Continuation of Partnership Business.

(a) If the Partnership shall be dissolved upon any occurrence indicated in Section 10.04(e) hereof, such dissolution shall have not effect upon the continuation of the business of the Partnership except as provided in Section 10.06(d) hereof. The Limited Partners who shall then own a majority of the Units and the New Units (exclusive of any Units and New Units owned by the General Partner or any Affiliates thereof) shall have the right, within thirty (30) days of such occurrence, to reconstitute the Partnership, the successor general partner of which shall be that person selected by those Limited Partners electing to reconstitute the Partnership hereunder. In the event of such reconstitution, each Partner, including without limitation the former General Partner, whether electing to reconstitute the Partnership or not, shall be deemed to assign one one-hundredth (1/100) of his interest in

Exhibit A *(Continued)*

the Partnership to the succesor general partner who shall own such interests as a general partner hereunder.

(b) In the event of a reconstitution of the Partnership hereunder, the person who shall become a successor general partner hereunder shall execute an addendum to this Agreement creating a new Partnership and agreeing to be bound by all the terms and provisions hereof and to assume all the obligations of a general partner hereunder; provided, however, that nothing contained herein shall be interpreted or construed to require such successor general partner to assume any liability arising prior to the date on which he shall become General Partner hereunder.

(c) In the event of a reconstitution of the Partnership hereunder, the former General Partner, or his heir, legal representative, successor or assign, shall become a successor limited partner hereunder with the same percentage interest herein formerly held as a general partner hereunder, less the one one-hundredth (1/100) thereof assigned to the successor general partner in accordance with Section 10.06(a) hereof.

(d) If the Limited Partners shall not elect to reconstitute the Partnership in accordance with the provisions of Section 10.06(a) hereof, the Partnership shall liquidate its assets, wind up its affairs and distribute the proceeds in the manner set forth in Section 10.07 hereof.

Section 10.07   Distribution on Liquidation.

(a) Upon the dissolution of the Partnership by means of occurrences described in Section 10.04 hereof without a reconstitution of the Partnership under Section 10.06 hereof, then, the General Partner in the case of the dissolution under Section 10.04(a), (b) or (c) and the person designated by those Limited Partners who shall then own a majority of the Units and the New Units (exclusive of any Units and New Units owned by the General Partner and any Affiliates thereof) or by a court of competent jurisdiction if not otherwise designated in the case of any other dissolution (hereinafter, in any case, sometimes called the "Liquidator") shall proceed to liquidate the assets of the Partnership, wind up its affairs and distribute the proceeds in the following order of priority:

(i) The Liquidator shall first provide for the payment of the debts and liabilities of the Partnership and the expenses of liquidation in the order of priority as required by law, and for the establishment of any reserves which the Liquidator shall deem reasonably necessary for any contingent or unforeseen liabilities or obligations of the Partnership. Such reserves may be paid over by the Liquidator to a bank or an attorney-at-law, to be held in escrow for the purpose of paying any such contingent or unforeseen liabilities or obligations and, at the expiration of such period as the Liquidator shall deem advisable, of distributing the balance in the manner provided in Section 10.07(a)(ii) hereof.

(ii) The Liquidator shall thereafter pay any balance of proceeds to the

Exhibit A *(Continued)*

Partners in cash or in kind in the following order of priorty. First, any pre-existing undistributed income or profits shall be distributed in the manner provided in Section 6.01 hereof. Second, the proceeds shall be distributed pro rata to the Limited Partners to the extent of the positive balances in their Capital Accounts. Third, the proceeds shall be distributed to the General Partner to the extent of the positive balances in his Capital Account. Any then remaining proceeds shall be distributed to the Partners in the same manner as provided for distribution in accordance with Section 6.01 hereof.

(b) A reasonable time shall be allowed for the orderly liquidation of assets of the Partnership and the discharge of its liabilities so as to enable the Liquidator to minimize any possible losses attendant upon such a liquidation. The provisions of Section 6.03 hereof relating to the allocation of income, gains, losses, deductions and credits shall be applicable during the period of liquidation.

(c) Upon the completion of the liquidation of the Partnership, the Liquidator shall furnish each Partner with a report showing the information required under Section 8.03 hereof for the period from the date of the last annual report prepared under Section 8.03 hereof to the date of the final distribution of the proceeds of liquidation of the Partnership; provided, however, that, if those Limited Partners then owning an aggregate of no less than a majority of the Units and the New Units (exclusive of any Units and New Units owned by the General Partner and any Affiliates thereof) shall demand in writing during the period of liquidation, such report shall be examined by such independent certified public accountants as such Limited Partners shall designate at the cost of the Partnership.

(d) In the event of the liquidation hereunder, each Partner hereby makes, constitutes and appoints the Liquidator, with full power of substitution, his true and lawful attorney for him and in his name, place and stead and for his use and benefit, to have, with respect to the property and assets of the Partnership, all the powers of a general partner hereunder as set forth in Sections 5.02 and 5.07 hereof. To evidence the appointment of the Liquidator as attorney-in-fact for the Partners hereunder, each Partner shall execute, acknowledge and deliver such other power of attorney or instrument as shall be reasonably requested by the Liquidator. The foregoing grant of authority shall be irrevocable and shall constitute a power coupled with an interest surviving the death or incapacity of each Partner and binding upon the heirs, legal representatives, successors and assigns of each Partner.

(e) No Partner shall be liable to the Partnership or to any other Partner for any negative balance in his capital account as such capital account is constituted immediately prior to the liquidation of the Partnership, except to the extent that such negative balance is attributable to an erroneous overpayment to any Partner or attributable to the breach by such Partner of his obligations under the provisions hereof.

Exhibit A *(Continued)*

400

(f) The Partnership shall terminate when all property owned by the Partnership shall have been disposed of and the net proceeds, after satisfaction of liabilities to creditors, shall have been distributed among the Partners as aforesaid. The establishment of any reserves in accordance with the provisions of Section 10.07(a) above shall not have the effect of extending the term of the Partnership.

Section 10.08   Firm Name and Goodwill.   For the purposes of this Agreement, no value shall be placed upon the firm name of the Partnership, upon the right to its use, or upon any goodwill attached thereto. In the event of the liquidation of the Partnership hereunder, the Liquidator shall assign such name and the right to its use to the General Partner, or any successor or assign thereof, in exchange for the payment of One Dollar ($1.00) therefor.

Article XI

General Provisions

Section 11.01   Binding Effect and Benefit.   This Agreement shall be binding upon, and shall inure to the benefit of, the parties hereto and their respective heirs, legal representatives, successors and assigns.

Section 11.02   Certificates, etc.   At the expense of the Partnership, the General Partner shall promptly prepare and execute all legally required fictitious name or other applications, registrations, publications, certificates and affidavits for filing with the proper governmental authorities, including without limitation any amendment to the Certificate, and shall arrange for the proper advertisement, publication and filing thereof for record where required by applicable law in the State of Delaware or any other jurisdiction.

Section 11.03   Power of Attorney.   Each Limited Partner hereby makes, constitutes and appoints the General Partner, with full power of substitution, his true and lawful attorney for him and in his name, place and stead and for his use and benefit, to sign, acknowledge, swear to, file and record any amendment to the Certificate in Delaware, required under the ULPA, and to sign, execute, certify, acknowledge, swear to, file and record any other instruments referred to in Section 11.02 hereof or required of the Partnership or Partners by law in Delaware or any other jurisdiction. The foregoing grant of authority, which shall be irrevocable and shall constitute a pwoer coupled with an interest surviving the death or incapacity of each Limited Partner and binding on the heirs, legal representatives, successors and assigns of each Limited Partner, may be exercised by any such attorney-in-fact by listing the name of any Limited Partners for whom such attorney-in-fact is acting and executing such certificates or other instruments with the single

Exhibit A *(Continued)*

signature of such attorney-in-fact acting for all the Limited Partners whose names are so listed.

Section 11.04 Partners' Relationships Inter Se. Except as expressly provided herein, nothing herein contained shall be construed to constitute any Partner the agent of any other Partner or in any manner to limit the Partners in the carrying on of their own respective businesses or activities.

Section 11.05 Notices, Statements, etc. All notices, statements or other documents which are required or contemplated by this Agreement shall be in writing and shall be either personally served upon the persons entitled thereto or mailed, postage prepaid, by certified or registered mail, return receipt requested, addressed to such person at his last known mailing address.

Section 11.06 Amendments. This Agreement and any part hereof may be amended at any time and from time to time by the General Partner; provided, however, that those Limited Partners then owning an aggregate of a majority of the Units and New Units (exclusive of any Units and New Units owned by the General Partner or any Affiliates thereof) shall agree in writing to any such amendment; and provided further, however, that no such amendment shall remove the limited liability hereunder of any Limited Partner in accordance with the ULPA, shall increase the obligation hereunder of any Limited Partner to contribute to the capital of the Partnership without his express written consent, or shall amend this Section 11.06

Section 11.07 Integration. This Agreement represents the entire understanding of the parties and supersedes and cancels any and all prior negotiations, understandings and agreements among the parties with respect to the subject matter hereof. Except as provided in accordance with Section 11.06 hereof, no termination, revocation, waiver, modification or amendment of this Agreement shall be binding unless in writing and signed by each of the Partners; provided, however, that any addendum to this Agreement executed in accordance with the provisions hereof shall not constitute a modification or amendment requiring a writing signed by each of the Partners, other than the amended Certificate filed in compliance with the ULPA, or any writing required by any other applicable law.

Section 11.08 Interpretation.

(a) Whenever in this Agreement reference is made to "this Agreement" or to any provision "hereof," or words to similar effect, such reference shall be construed to refer to the within instrument and all the attached exhibits as an integral part thereof, unless the context clearly requires otherwise.

(b) As used in this Agreement, any gender shall include any other gender

Exhibit A *(Continued)*

and the plural shall include the singular and the singular shall include the plural, all wherever appropriate.

(c) The table of contents and titles of the articles and sections herein have been inserted as a matter of convenience of reference only and shall not control or affect the meaning or construction of any of the terms and provisions hereof.

Section 11.09 Governing Law. Except as otherwise expressly provided herein, this Agreement shall be interpreted and construed in accordance with the laws of the State of Delaware.

Section 11.10 Arbitration.

(a) Any controversy, claim or dispute between the parties directly or indirectly concerning this Agreement or the breach hereof or the subject matter hereof, including questions concerning the scope and applicability of this Section 11.10, shall be finally settled in arbitration held in Los Angeles, California, in accordance with the rules of commercial arbitration then followed by the American Arbitration Association or any successor to the functions thereof. The arbitrator shall have the right and authority to determine how his decision or determination as to each issue or matter in dispute may be implemented or enforced. Any decision or award of the arbitrators shall be final and conclusive on the parties to this Agreement and there shall be no appeal therefrom other than for gross negligence or willful misconduct.

(b) All the parties hereto agree that an action to compel arbitration pursuant to this Agreement may be brought in the appropriate California Court and in connection therewith the laws of the State of California shall control. Application may also be made to such Court for confirmation of any decision or award of the arbitrator, for an order of enforcement and for any other remedies which may be necessary to effectuate such decision or award. All the parties hereto hereby consent to the jurisdiction of the arbitrator and of such Court and waive any objection to the jurisdiction of such arbitrator and Court.

(c) Notwithstanding the foregoing in this Section 11.10, however, nothing contained herein shall require arbitration of any issue arising under this Agreement for which injunctive relief is successfully sought by any party hereto.

Section 11.11 Counterparts. The parties hereto may execute this Agreement in any number of counterparts, each of which, when executed and delivered by the General Partner and the nominee for the Limited Partners, shall have the force and effect of an original; but all such counterparts shall constitute one and the same instrument.

IN WITNESS WHEREOF, the parties hereto have duly executed this Agreement under their respective seals as of the day and year first above written.

Exhibit A *(Continued)*

Witness: GENERAL PARTNER:

_____   _____(SEAL)
                                 James K. LaFleur

                                 LIMITED PARTNERS:

_____   _____(SEAL)
                                 Ronald Lust, as Nominee
                                 for the Limited Partners

Exhibit A *(Continued)*

SUBSCRIPTION AGREEMENT AND ADDITIONAL SIGNATURE PAGES

Electronic Equipment Development Ltd.
(A Delaware Limited Partnership)
4337 Talofa Avenue
Toluca Lake, California 91602

, 1980

Gentlemen:

As of the date hereof, I, the undersigned, whose full name is set forth hereinbelow, offer to purchase from you an aggregate of _____ ( ) of the units of participation as a limited partner (the "Units") in Electronic Equipment Development Ltd. (A Delaware Limited Partnership) (the "Partnership") organized under the Uniform Limited Partnership Act of Delaware pursuant to the Limited Partnership Agreement dated as of August 1, 1980, (the "Partnership Agreement") by and between James K. LaFleur as General Partner and Ronald Lust as nominee for the Limited Partners, for a purchase price of fifty thousand dollars ($50,000.00) per Unit in accordance with the provisions of the Partnership Agreement. In consideration thereof and intending to be legally bound, I hereby make the following representations and agree as follows:

1. I am familiar with the business and financial condition, operations and prospects of the Partnership, and with the Partnership's purposes of sponsoring research concerned with the development of various types of electronic equipment and the commercial development, licensing and exploitation of any inventions or discoveries resulting from such research.
2. I have substantial knowledge, skill and experience in business, financial and investment matters and am capable of evaluating, in conjunction with my profesional advisers, if any, the merits and risks of an investment in the Unit(s).
3. To the extent that I have deemed it appropriate to do so, I have retained at my own expense, and relied upon, appropriate professional advice regarding the investment, tax and legal merits and consequences of purchasing and owning the Unit(s). Each such adviser ("Offeree Representative") retained or relied upon by me in connection with the investment in the Partnership has been acknowledged by me in writing as my Offeree

Exhibit A *(Continued)*

405

Representative in connection with evaluating the merits and risks of the prospective investment in the Unit(s) and such acknowledgment was made by me after disclosure in writing to my by me Offeree Representative of all material relationships, if any, between my Offeree Representative or any of his Corporation or any of their affiliates which exists, is mutually understood to be contemplated, or has existed at any time during the previous two years. Each Offeree Representative retained or relied upon by me in connection with the investment in the Partnership has completed an Offeree Representative Disclosure Form and Certificate.

4. Neither the Partnership nor any person acting on behalf of the Partnership has offered, offered to sell, offered for sale or sold the Unit(s) to me by means of any form of general solicitation or general advertising. I have not received, paid or given, directly or indirectly, any commission or remuneration for or on account of any sale or the solicitation of any sale of the Unit(s).

5. I and my Offeree Representative(s), if any, have been given full access to all material information concerning the condition, operations and prospects of the Partnership and and of the propsed offering of the Unit(s) therein. Among other things, I and my Offeree Representative(s), if any, have received and examined a copy of the Private Placement Memorandum dated August 11, 1980 and any supplements thereto and the Partnership Agreement including, but not limited to, Article IX thereof. I and my Offeree Representative(s), if any, fully understand the limitations on transfer of the Unit(s) or any interest therein and the right of first refusal of the General Partner therein; and I and my Offeree Representative(s), if any, have had an opportunity to ask questions of, and to receive information from, the General partner and persons acting on his behalf concerning the terms and conditions of my investment in the Unit(s), and to obtain any additional information necessary to verify the accuracy of the information and data received by me. I am satisfied that there is no material information concerning the condition, operations and prospects of the Partnership or concerning the proposed offering of the Unit(s) of which I am unaware.

6. I have made, either myself or together with my Offeree Representative(s), if any, such independent investigation of the Partnership, its General Partner, and the matters mentioned in paragraph 1 above, as I deem to be, or my Offeree Representative(s), if any, have advised is, necessary or advisable in connection with this investment; and I and my Offeree Representative(s), if any, have received all information and data which I and my Offeree Representative(s), if any, believe to be necessary in order to reach an informed decision as to the advisability of investing in the Unit(s).

7. I understand that the purchase of the Unit(s) involves a high degree of risk. Among other risks, I understand that it is unlikely that any market will exist for any resale of the Unit(s).

8. I have reviewed my financial condition and commitments, alone and together with my Offeree Representative(s), if any. Based on such review, I am satisfied that I have adequate means of providing for my financial needs

Exhibit A *(Continued)*

and possible contingencies, and that I do not have any current or foreseeable future need for liquidity of the funds being utilized or to be utilized in the purchase of the Unit(s). I am capable of bearing the economic risk of the investment in the Unit(s) for the indefinite future.

9. If an individual, with respect to the year 1980 and the two years immediately thereafter, I expect to have income taxable for federal income tax purposes, some portion of which, after adjustments and deductions, will be taxable at 50% or more under present law, taking into account the effect of my purchase of the Unit(s); I also have a present financial net worth in excess of $250,000, exclusive of personal residences, furnishings and automobiles. If I represent a subscriber which is a corporation, partnership, joint venture, trust or other entity, such entity has a net worth in excess of $500,000, or otherwise has substantial assets or sources of income and expects to have substantial amounts of taxable income with respect to the year 1980 and the two years immediately thereafter, which, taken together, are more than sufficient so that such subscriber can bear the risk of loss of its entire investment in the Partnership.

10. I am acquiring the Unit(s) solely for my own beneficial account, for investment purposes, and not with a view to, or for resale in connection with, any distribution of the Unit(s). I understand that the Unit(s) have not been registered under the Securities Act of 1933 ("Federal Act") or the securities laws of any State (collectively referred to as "State securities laws") by reason of specific exemptions under the provisions thereof which depend in part upon my investment intent and the other representations made by me in this Subscriptions Agreement and Additional Signature Page ("Agreement"). I understand that the Partnership is relying upon the representations and agreements contained in this Agreement for the purpose of determining whether this transaction meets the requirements for such exemptions.

11. I understand the position of the Securities and Exchange Commission (the "Commission") that the statutory basis for the exemption under the Federal Act would not be present if my present intention were to hold the Unit(s) for resale (i) upon the expiration of any capital gains holding period under any applicable income tax statute, or (ii) in the event of a market rise, or if the market does not rise, or (iii) at a definite or indefinite future time upon the happening of any anticipated specific occurrence or contingency, including changes in the business or financial condition of the Partnership, of the electronic equipment industry, or in my financial condition. I also understand that the Commission takes the position that "changes of circumstances" may not be considered in determining whether the statutory exemption is available, and that the fact that the Unit(s) have been held for a particular period of time does not by itself establish the availability of the exemption from registration. I have no present intention of making any sale, assignment, pledge, gift, transfer or other disposition of any of the Unit(s) or any interest therein.

12. I understand that the Federal Act and the rules of the Commission

Exhibit A *(Continued)*

provide in substance that I may dispose of the Unit(s) only pursuant to an effective registration statement under the Federal Act or an exemption from such registration if available. You have advised me that the Partnership has no obligation or intention to register any of the Unit(s) thereunder, or to take action so as to permit sales pursuant to the exemption from registration provided by Regulation A under the Federal Act. Accordingly, I understand that under the Commission's rules I may dispose of the Unit(s) only (i) in "private placements" which are exempt from registration under the Federal Act, in which event the transferee will acquire "restricted securities" subject to the same limitation as in my hands, or (ii) pursuant to Rule 237 permitting negotiated sales (otherwise than through a broker or dealer) of a limited amount of securities, more than five years after the securities have been purchased and paid for, by noncontrolling persons of the Partnership upon compliance with the provisions of that Rule. As a consequence, I understand that I must bear the economic risks of the investment in the Unit(s) for an indefinite period of time.

13. I agree that I will not sell, assign, pledge, give, transfer, or otherwise dispose of the Unit(s) or any interest therein, or make any offer or attempt to do any of the foregoing, except pursuant to a registration of the Unit(s) under the Federal Act and all applicable State securities laws or in a transaction which, in the written opinion of counsel satisfactory to the Partnership, is exempt from the registration provisions of the Federal Act and all applicable State securities laws; and that the Partnership and any transfer agent for the Unit(s) shall not be required to give effect to any purported transfer of any of the Unit(s) except upon compliance with the foregoing restrictions. I further agree that I will not sell or transfer the Unit(s) for a period of one year after purchase.

14. *Pennsylvania Subscribers Only.* I understand that the Unit(s) have not been registered under the Pennsylvania Securities Act of 1972 in reliance upon a representation by me that the Unit(s) have been purchased for investment purposes. I will not sell, transfer or dispose of the Unit(s) except in compliance with the provisions of Section 203(d) of such Act and the regulations promulgated thereunder or in a transaction which is exempt from the provisions thereof. I UNDERSTAND THAT I HAVE THE RIGHT TO WITHDRAW FROM THIS AGREEMENT IF I SO ELECT, UNDER SECTION 207(m) OF THE PENNSYLVANIA SECURITIES ACT OF 1972, WITHIN TWO DAYS AFTER I EITHER EXECUTE AND MAIL THIS AGREEMENT OR MAKE A PAYMENT FOR ANY UNIT(S) OFFERED, WHICHEVER OCCURS LATER. I UNDERSTAND THAT IF I EXERCISE MY RIGHT TO WITHDRAW, I WILL RECEIVE FULL REPAYMENT OF ALL MONIES PAID BY ME.

MY WITHDRAWAL WILL BE WITHOUT MY FURTHER LIABILITY TO ANY PERSON. TO ACCOMPLISH THE WITHDRAWAL I UNDERSTAND THAT I NEED ONLY SEND A LETTER OR TELEGRAM TO ELECTRONIC EQUIPMENT DEVELOPMENT, LTD. (A DELA-

Exhibit A *(Continued)*

WARE LIMITED PARTNERSHIP) INDICATING MY INTENTION TO WITHDRAW. I UNDERSTAND THAT SUCH LETTER OR TELEGRAM SHOULD BE SENT OR POSTMARKED PRIOR TO THE END OF THE AFOREMENTIONED SECOND BUSINESS DAY. I UNDERSTAND THAT IF I AM SENDING A LETTER, IT IS PRUDENT TO SEND IT BY CERTIFIED MAIL, RETURN RECEIPT REQUESTED, TO ENSURE THAT IT IS RECEIVED AND TO EVIDENCE THE TIME WHEN IT WAS MAILED. IF I MAKE THE REQUEST ORALLY, I UNDERSTAND THAT I SHOULD ASK FOR WRITTEN CONFIRMATION THAT MY REQUEST HAS BEEN RECEIVED.

15. I have enclosed herewith my check payable to your order in the amount of fifty thousand dollars ($50,000) with respect to each of the Unit(s) subscribed for herein.

16. I hereby make, constitute and appoint the General Partner of the Partnership, with full power of substitution, my true and lawful attorney for me and in my name, place and stead and for my use and benefit, to sign, execute, certify, swear to, acknowledge, file and record any other instruments required of the Partnership or of the partners thereof. The foregoing grant of authority may be exercised by any such attorney-in-fact by listing my name along with the names of all others persons for whom such attorney-in-fact is acting and executing such certificates, instruments and documents with the single signature of the attorney-in-fact acting for all the persons whose names are so listed.

17. I acknowledge that the subscription herein may be rejected in whole or in part by you in your sole and absolute discretion. I UNDERSTAND THAT IF I AM A PENNSYLVANIA SUBSCRIBER, I HAVE THE RIGHT TO WITHDRAW MY SUBSCRIPTION WITHOUT INCURRING ANY LIABILITY AFTER I HAVE SUBSCRIBED FOR THE UNITS IF I ACT IN ACCORDANCE WITH THE PROVISIONS OF PARAGRAPH 14 OF THIS AGREEMENT. Otherwise, I further acknowledge that I am not entitled to cancel, terminate or revoke this subscription, any agreement hereunder or any power of attorney granted hereunder; provided, however, that if this subscription is not accepted by you by written notice of acceptance either hand delivered or deposited, postage prepaid, in the United States mail, addressed to me at the address set forth hereinbelow on or before October 31, 1980, this subscription and any agreement hereunder shall be automatically cancelled, terminated and revoked.

I hereby acknowledge that my execution of this Subscription Agreement and Additional Signature Page, upon its acceptance by the Partnership, constitutes the execution of the Partnership Agreement by me as a party thereto in accordance with all its terms and provisions with the same force and effect as if such terms and provisions were set forth herein verbatim.

WITNESS my execution hereof as of the day and year first above written.

SEE LEGENDS ON THE LAST PAGE HEREOF

Exhibit A *(Continued)*

409

Individual Subscription:

_____ (SEAL)
Signature

Social Security or Taxpayer
Identification Number:

Name _____
(Please Print)

Address _____

_____

_____

Telephone Number:

Entity Subscription:

(   )   - _____

_____ (SEAL)

Area Code   Number

Name of Entity

By _____
Signature

Its _____
Title

Address _____

_____

ACCEPTED on behalf of
Electronic Equipment Development Ltd.
(A Delaware Limited Partnership)

By _____

James K. LaFleur
General Partner

Exhibit A *(Continued)*

INDIVIDUAL ACKNOWLEDGEMENT

STATE OF   )
) ss:
COUNTY OF   )

On the _____ day of _____ , 1980, before me, the undersigned authority, personally appeared

_____ to me known (or satisfactorily proven) to be the individual who executed the foregoing Subscription Agreement and Additional Signature Page ("Agreement") and he/she acknowledged that the Agreement was executed by him/her individually as his/her own free act and deed for the purposes contained therein and that the statements made therein are true and correct to the best of his/her knowledge, information and belief.

IN WITNESS WHEREOF, I have hereunto set my hand and affixed my official seal.

                                       _____

                                            Notary Public

My Commission Expires:

_____

Exhibit A *(Continued)*

CORPORATION, PARTNERSHIP, TRUST OR OTHER ENTITY ACKNOWLEDGEMENT

STATE OF   )

)   ss:

COUNTY OF   )

On the _____ day of _____, 1980, before me, the undersigned authority, personally appeared _____ and known to me (or satisfactorily proven) to be _____ of _____ a corporation, partnership, trust or other entity ("Entity"), and he/she acknowledged to me that the foregoing Subscription Agreement and Additional Signature Page ("Agreement") was executed by him/her for and on behalf of the Entity for the purposes contained therein, that he/she was duly authorized to execute the Agreement for and on behalf of the Entity as the free act and deed of the Entity and that the statements contained therein are true and correct to the best of his/her knowledge, information and belief.

IN WITNESS WHEREOF, I have hereunto set my hand and affixed my official seal.

_____

Notary Public

My Commission Expires:

_____

Exhibit A *(Continued)*

THE UNITS EVIDENCED BY THIS AGREEMENT HAVE NOT BEEN REGISTERED UNDER THE SECURITIES ACT OF 1933, ("FEDERAL ACT") OR THE SECURITIES LAWS OF ANY OTHER STATE (COLLECTIVELY REFERRED TO AS "STATE ACTS"). THE UNITS MAY BE OFFERED FOR SALE, SOLD OR OTHERWISE TRANSFERRED ONLY IF EITHER AN EFFECTIVE REGISTRATION OR THE UNITS IS OBTAINED IN COMPLIANCE WITH THE FEDERAL ACT AND SUCH STATE ACTS AS MAY BE APPLICABLE OR IF THE UNITS ARE SOLD OR TRANSFERRED IN A TRANSACTION WHICH IN THE WRITTEN OPINION OF COUNSEL SATISFACTORY TO ELECTRONIC EQUIPMENT DEVELOPMENT, LTD., (A DELAWARE LIMITED PARTNERSHIP) IS EXEMPT FROM THE PROVISIONS OF THE FEDERAL ACT AND SUCH STATE ACTS. IN ADDITION, THIS AGREEMENT, AND THE LIMITED PARTNERSHIP AGREEMENT TO WHICH IT RELATES CONTAIN SUBSTANTIAL RESTRICTIONS ON TRANSFERABILITY WHICH RESTRICTIONS ARE FULLY DESCRIBED IN SUCH AGREEMENTS. *ANY TRANSFER CONTRARY HERETO IS VOID.*

Additional Restrictions for Pennsylvania Subscribers: THE UNITS EVIDENCED BY THIS AGREEMENT MAY NOT BE TRANSFERRED EXCEPT IN COMPLIANCE WITH SECTION 203(d) OF THE PENNSYLVANIA SECURITIES ACT OF 1972 AND THE REGULATIONS PROMULGATED THEREUNDER.

Exhibit A *(Continued)*

ELECTRONIC EQUIPMENT DEVELOPMENT LTD.

(A Delaware Limited Partnership)

CERTIFICATE OF LIMITED PARTNERSHIP

In accordance with the Uniform Limited Partnership Act of the State of Delaware (the "ULPA"), the undersigned, being all the partners (the "Partners") of ELECTRONIC EQUIPMENT DEVELOPMENT LTD. (A Delaware Limited Partnership), (the "Partnership") formed pursuant to the Limited Partnership Agreement dated as of August 11, 1980 (the "Partnership Agreement"), hereby certify as follows:

I. *Name of Partnership*. The name of the Partnership is ELECTRONIC EQUIPMENT DEVELOPMENT LTD. (A Delaware Limited Partnership).

II. *Character of Business*. The character of business of the Partnership consists of (a) the sponsorship of research concerned with the development of various types of electronic equipment; (b) the application for and obtaining of patent rights concerning inventions or discoveries resulting from such research; (c) the development and exploitation of such inventions and discoveries; (d) the development of any machinery appropriate to the production of such invention and discoveries and the application for and obtaining of patent rights concerning such machinery; (e) the licensing of any of the foregoing patent rights and other rights relating to such inventions, discoveries, and related technology, on a royalty basis; and (f) the entry into, making and performing all contracts and other undertakings and the engaging in all activities and transactions as may be necessary in order to carry out any of the foregoing business.

III. *Place of Business*. The registered office of the Partnership in the State of Delaware is in care of The Corporation Trust Company, 100 West Tenth Street, Wilmington, New Castle County, Delaware 19801. The principal office of the Partnership is 4337 Talofa Avenue, Toluca Lake, Los Angeles County, California 91602.

IV. *Partners*. The name and place of residence of each Partner and the designation of each Partner as a general or limited are as follows:

Exhibit A *(Continued)*

Name	Residence	Designation
James K. LaFleur	4337 Talofa Avenue Toluca Lake, California 91602	General
Ronald Lust, as Nominee	14761 Poway Mesa Drive Poway, California 92064	Limited

V. *Term.* The term for which the Partnership is to exist shall commence on the date of the filing of its Certificate of Limited Partnership in accordance with the ULPA, and will continue until July 31, 1990 or until prior termination or extension as provided in the Partnership Agreement.

VI. *Contributions of the Limited Partners.* The limited partners have contributed to the capital of the Partnership, in cash, the sum of One Dollar ($1.00) and will contribute thereto certain additional amounts, under certain circumstances and subject to certain conditions, as provided in the Partnership Agreement.

VII. *Additional Contributions of Limited Partners.* The limited partners will not be required to make additional contributions to the capital of the Partnership, except as referred to in Article VI hereof.

VIII. *Return of Contributions of Limited Partners.* No time has been established for the return of any contributions to the capital of the Partnership by the limited partners prior to the dissolution of the Partnership, and no limited partner has the right to demand or receive the return of any contribution prior to the dissolution of the Partnership.

IX. *Share of Profits by Limited Partners.* Subject the terms of the Partnership Agreement, the limited partners will receive a percentage of the profits of the Partnership of seventy-five percent (75%) and no other compensation by way of income, by reason of their contributions to the capital of the Partnership.

X. *Substitution of Assignee as Limited Partners.* The limited partners may not substitute an assignee as contributor or partner in their place except by first offering their interest in the Partnership to the general partner or, upon the approval of the general partner, by will or intestacy, by inter vivos gift, by sale for consideration, by contribution to capital, by merger or consolidation, by distribution or liquidation or otherwise to any associate of any limited partner as defined in the Partnership Agreement.

XI. *Addition of Limited Partners.* The general partner is given the right to admit as limited partners to the Partnership any persons who contribute to capital of the Partnership in accordance with the Partnership Agreement as well as any assignees of a limited partner as indicated in Article X hereof.

XII. *Priority Among Limited Partners.* No present or future limited part-

Exhibit A *(Continued)*

ner has any priority over any other limited partner as to contributions, compensation by way of income, or otherwise.

XIII. *Death, Legal Incapacity, Resignation or Bankruptcy of the General Partner.* The death, legal incapacity, resignation or bankruptcy of the general partner causes a dissolution of the Partnership; but, in the event thereof, the limited partners, under certain circumstances and subject to certain conditions, as provided in the Partnership Agreement, are given the right to continue the business of the Partnership by the designatin of a successor general partner.

XIV. *Right of Limited Partners to Receive Property Other than Cash in Return for Contributions.* No limited partner is given any right to demand property other than cash in return for his contribution to the capital of the Partnership. Upon dissolution of the Partnership, the general partner may distribute any or all of the assets of the Partnership in kind.

IN WITNESS WHEREOF, the undersigned partners of ELECTRONIC EQUIPMENT DEVELOPMENT LTD. (A Delaware Limited Partnership) have executed this certificate of limited Partnership as of this 11th day of August, 1980.

WITNESS: GENERAL PARTNER:

_____   _____ (SEAL)

                                           James K. LaFleur

WITNESS: LIMITED PARTNERS:

_____   _____ (SEAL)

                                           Ronald Lust, as Nominee

Exhibit A *(Continued)*

ACKNOWLEDGMENT

STATE OF CALIFORNIA   )
) ss:
COUNTY OF   )

ON THIS _____ day of August, 1980, before me, the undersigned authority, a notary public in and for the said county and state, personally appeared JAMES K. LAFLEUR, the general partner of ELECTRONIC EQUIPMENT DEVELOPMENT LTD. (A Delaware Limited Partnership) who is known to me (or satisfactorily proven) to be the person whose name is subscribed to the within certificate of Limited Partnership and acknowledge he executed the same for the purpose therein contained.

WITNESS my hand and seal this day, month, and year first written above.

                                                _____

                                                 Notary Public

My Commission Expires:

_____

Exhibit A *(Continued)*

ACKNOWLEDGMENT

STATE OF CALIFORNIA   )
) ss:

COUNTY OF   )

ON THIS ____ day of August, 1980, before me, the undersigned authority, a notary public in and for the said state and county, personally appeared RONALD LUST, as nominee for the limited partners of ELECTRONIC EQUIPMENT DEVELOPMENT LTD. (A Delaware Limited Partnership) who is known to me (or satisfactorily proven) to be the person whose name is subscribed to the within certificate of Limited Partnership and acknowledge he executed the same for the purposes therein contained.

WITNESS my hand and seal this day, month, and year first written above.

_____

Notary Public

My Comission Expires:

_____

Exhibit A *(Continued)*

418

Electronic Equipment Development LTD.

(A Delaware Limited Partnership)

RESEARCH AND DEVELOPMENT AGREEMENT AND EXHIBITS

Exhibit B

ELECTRONIC EQUIPMENT DEVELOPMENT LTD.

(A Delaware Limited Partnership)

RESEARCH AND DEVELOPMENT AGREEMENT

THIS AGREEMENT, made as of this —— day of August, 1980, by and between GTI CORPORATION, a Rhode Island corporation having its executive offices in San Diego, California ("GTI"),

AND

ELECTRONIC EQUIPMENT DEVELOPMENT LTD. (A Delaware Limited Partnership), having its principal office in Toluca Lake, California ("EED");

WITNESSETH:

WHEREAS, GTI desires to remise, release and quitclaim any right, title and interest in the subject matter of the research projects described in Exhibit 1 attached hereto (all such projects collectively referred to as the "Projects"), none of which has been reduced to practice or is presently at a point of development where patents or patent applications can be prepared or filed; and

WHEREAS, in order that the research and experimentation necessary to develop marketable products from the Projects may be undertaken, James K. LaFleur, the general partner of EED, had organized EED as a limited partnership pursuant to a Limited Partnership Agreement dated as of August ____, 1980 (the "EED Partnership Agreement"), for the purpose of raising capital to sponsor research and expermentation; and

WHEREAS, EED desires to contract with GTI for such research and experimentation under the terms and conditions set forth herein and to grant

Exhibit B *(Continued)*

to GTI certain rights regarding the results of the research related to the Projects;

NOW, THEREFORE, in consideration of the mutual convenants set forth herein, the parties hereto, intending to be legally bound, hereby agree as follows:

Article I

Quitclaim; Authority

1.01. GTI hereby remises, releases and forever quitclaims to EED any right, title and interest which it may have in and to the subject matter of each of the Projects.

1.02. GTI warrants that it has full authority and right to enter into this Agreement and the transactions and actions contemplated hereby.

Article II

Research Services

2.01. EED hereby agrees to retain GTI, and GTI hereby accepts such employment, for the diligent and timely performance of research and experimentation services with respect to the subject matter of such of the Projects as EED determines shall be undertaken by GTI. Such Projects shall be identified by EED at the time funds are released from escrow pursuant to the applicable provisions of the EED Partnership Agreement. To the extent any Projects are not undertaken and identified by EED, nothing contained herein shall preclude GTI from developing the subject matter of such Projects; EED hereby agrees to remise, release and quitclaim all of its rights in said Projects which are not undertaken and identified as aforesaid, and EED shall have no rights with respect thereto or to the results of any research and development undertaken by GTI or others.

2.02 GTI shall maintain a staff and facilities the quantity and quality of which are suitable to the performance of the research and development services called for hereunder, provided, however, that GTI may, in its sole discretion, subcontract any portion of such services as it shall deem advisable under terms consistent with the Specifications (as defined in Section 2.03(a)) applicable to each Project so subcontracted, and EED may retain one or more consultants to work with or under the supervision of GTI or any subcontractor hired by GTI with respect to any Project.

2.03. (a) As soon as practicable after the execution of this Agreement, GTI shall prepare and submit to EED for approval a detailed schedule with respect to each Project identified by EED pursuant to Section 2.01 showing the anticipated or required research steps, their extimated costs, and the time for performance of each research step in accordance with agreed upon

Exhibit B (*Continued*)

technical specifications, all prepared in accordance with a recognized critical path method generally used by GTI (such schedule and technical specifications sometimes herin referred to as the "Specifications"). GTI shall promptly make whatever modifications or changes in the Specifications with respect to each such Project recommended by EED, such Specifications so modified constituting the original scientific and budgetary specifications for each such Project.

(b) GTI shall furnish EED with periodic status reports with respect to each Project as frequently as requested by EED, but in no event less frequently than the tenth (10th) day of each calendar month during the course of the research and development hereunder, which report shall summarize the services performed during the preceding calendar month and the progress or lack thereof made with respect to each Project. GTI shall advise EED of the need for additional research funds above those described on the Specifications applicable to such Project.

(c) In the course of the research with respect to any Project, EED and GTI jointly may from time to time revise or modify the Specifications with respect thereto.

2.04. GTI shall continue to use its best efforts to perform research and experimentation services with respect to each Project in accordance with the applicable Specifications until such time as EED determines, after consultation with GTI, whether or not the Specifications with respect to such Project have or can be satisfied. Such determination shall be reflected in a writing signed by both parties hereto on the date such determination is made. If EED determines that GTI's performance of its research and experimentation services with respect to any Project materially deviates from the Specifications (as jointly revised from time to time) applicable to such Project, EED may refuse to authorize any further payment of research funds to GTI with respect to such Project and may terminate all further research by GTI with respect thereto. In the exercise of its sole descretion, EED may thereafter enter into a research contract with other qualified research persons, firms or entities and assign such Project to, or contract for the performance of research services with, such entity.

2.05. If research funds remain after the funds paid hereunder have all been allocated to the Projects, EED, with the consent of GTI, may add new research projects in the field of electronic equipment to this Agreement, which in EED's judgment can be developed with such surplus or unspent research funds.

2.06. If additional funds are required to continue or complete the research on any of the Projects or new projects contemplated by this Agreement, research funds which were initially allocated to a particular Project may in the sole judgment of EED be applied to other Projects, and the budgetary Specifications with respect to such other Projects shall be revised accordingly pursuant to Section 2.03(c). Neither EED nor GTI shall be obligated under this Agreement to advance additional funds to complete a Project so that it satisfies the Specification applicable thereto.

Exhibit B (*Continued*)

Article III

Invoices; Payments

3.01. EED agrees to pay GTI for its services hereunder an amount equal to the costs incurred by GTI in performing research and experimentation services hereunder plus a fixed fee equal to eight percent (8%) of the costs originally set forth in the Specifications with respect to each Project undertaken by GTI, all as follows:

(a) No later than 10 days after EED identifies the Projects to be undertaken by GTI pursuant to Section 2.01 and in no event later than December 31, 1980, an amount for prepaid research and expermentation costs equal to 80% of the sum of such costs as set forth in the Specifications with respect to each Project to be undertaken hereunder plus the fixed fee applicable thereto; and

(b) As requested from time to time by GTI, such costs in excess of the amount described in Section 3.01(a) as may be incurred by GTI in performing research and experimentation services as determined in the manner set forth in Section 3.01(c) plus a fixed fee equal to eight percent (8%) of such costs, provided, however, that the total fixed fee with respect to each Project to be undertaken hereunder shall not exceed eight percent (8%) of the costs originally set forth in the Specifications with respect to such Project.

(c) In connection with requests for payment under Section 3.01, GTI shall determine its costs in performing the research and development services called for hereunder in accordance with the cost principles applicable to cost-reimbursement type contracts under the then-current Federal Procurement Regulations. Such cost determinations are subject to the approval of EED. EED shall not be obligated to make any payments hereunder in excess of the total estimated research and development costs of the Projects undertaken by GTI on behalf of EED hereunder as set forth on the applicable Specification, except as otherwise expressly provided in this Agreement.

3.02. With respect ot payments under Section 3.01(b), GTI shall submit to EED a separate invoice for an amount equal to the costs in excess of prior payments made in accordance with the provisions of this Agreement actually incurred by GTI in the course of research and expermentation with respect to each Project plus a fixed fee as provided in Section 3.01(b). EED shall pay to GTI the invoiced amounts no later than ten (10) days after its receipt of each of GTI's invoices, provided that the provisions of this Agreement are otherwise satisfied.

3.03. In addition to the invoices required under Section 3.02, GTI shall concurrently submit to EED a reasonable detailed report setting forth the costs of services (plus fixed fee) performed during the preceding calendar month, calculated as required under Section 3.01(c), and in connection with the initial invoice submitted under Section 3.02, a reconciliation of the amounts

Exhibit B (*Continued*)

prepaid by EED under Section 3.01(a) with costs (plus fixed fee) actually incurred by GTI in accordance with the Specifications applicable to each Project.

Article IV

Assignment of Inventions

4.01. GTI hereby agrees, as part of its performance of the services called for hereunder, to disclose promptly to EED any and all inventions, discoveries and improvements with respect to the subject matter of any of the Projects on which it is working, whether or not such inventions, discoveries or improvements are patentable, made by GTI or any of its employees, consultants or persons with whom it has contracted and to assign to EED all such inventions, discoveries and improvements and any patents and patent applications relating thereto.

4.02. Whenever requested to do so by EED, GTI shall execute any and all applications, assignments or other instruments which EED deems appropriate or necessary to enable it to apply for and to obtain patents related to the subject matter of any of the Projects in the United states or any Foreign country or to protect EED's interest in any such patents or in the maintenance or enforcement of such patents, all at the expense of EED.

Article V

License Arrangements

5.01. Within ninety (90) days of the determinatin that the Specifications with respect to a particular Project have been satisfied, as provided in Section 2.04, GTI and EED shall execute and deliver a license agreement substantially in the form attached hereto as Exhibit 2 with such variations, additions, deletions and modification as are appropriate or necessary.

5.02. In the event that EED has determined, after consultation with GTI as provided in Section 2.04 hereof, that the Specifications with respect to a particular Project cannot be satisfied, the results, if any, of the research with respect to such Project, whether or not complete, may be acquired by GTI on terms to be negotiated by GTI and EED. If no satisfactory agreement can be reached within ninety (90) days of the date when it is determined that the applicable Specifications cannot be satisfied, GTI shall have a right of first refusal to acquire such research results on the same terms and conditions as are contained in a bona fide offer of a third party to purchase such research results. Such right of first refusal shall terminate sixty (60) days after written notice is provided to GTI by EED setting forth in reasonable detail the terms of such third party offer.

Exhibit B (*Continued*)

Article VI

Confidentiality

6.01. The Projects and all information relating thereto, including applicable Specifications, reports, drawings, schematics, or any other writings or materials ("Proprietary Information") shall, upon the execution of this Agreement, be the sole property of EED. GTI agrees to use its best efforts and to take all reasonable precautions, including such efforts and precaution as are fully commensurate with those employed by GTI for the protection of its own confidential information, to maintain strict confidentiality with respect to the Proprietary Information and to prevent disclosure thereof to persons other than those GTI employees and agents who require access thereto in order to fulfill the purposes of this Agreement.

6.02. GTI agrees to use its best efforts and to take all reasonable precautions to insure that those GTI employees and agents who are given access to any of the Porprietary Information shall make no further disclosure thereof either to other GTI employees or agents or to any other persons.

6.03. GTI agrees to make no use of the Proprietary Information except for the purposes stated in this Agreement.

6.04. Proprietary Information shall not include any of the following:

(i) Any information that appears in issued patents or printed publications in integrated form or that otherwise is or becomes generally known in the trade or becomes a part of the public domain other than through the actions or fault of GTI, its employees or its agents; or

(ii) Any information that GTI can show by written records came into GTI's possession without covenants of confidentiality from a third party under no obligation of confidentiality to EED.

GTI shall have the burden of proving that any information otherwise within the meaning of Proprietary Information comes within one of these exceptions.

6.05. The Provisions of Article VI shall survive the termination of this Agreement and shall continue in full force and effect for a period of two (2) years after such termination.

Article VII

Termination

7.01. This Agreement shall terminate on December 31, 1982, unless extended for one renewal period of no more than 12 months upon the mutual agreement of GTI and EED or unless it is earlier terminated in accordance with this Article.

Exhibit B *(Continued)*

7.02. In addition to the rights granted EED under Section 2.04 in the third sentence thereof, EED shall have the right to terminate this Agreement in the event of the failure by GTI to perform its research services hereunder with respect to two or more Projects in accordance with the Specification applicable to such Projects, unless the deviation from the applicable Specifications are not material in the reasonable judgment of EED.

7.03. GTI shall have the right to terminate this Agreement upon the failure of EED to make any of the payments required under Section 3.01 if such failure shall continue unremedied for thirty (30) days after written notice is given to EED by GTI.

7.04. Either party may terminate this Agreement upon an adjudication of the other party as bankrupt or insolvent; or the admission in writing by such other party of its inability to pay its debts as they mature; or an assignment by such other party for the benefit of its creditors; or such other party's applying for or consenting to the appointment of a receiver, trustee, or similar officer for any substantial part of its property; or such receiver, trustee or similar officer's appointment without the application or consent of such other party, if such appointment without the application or consent of such other party, if such appointment shall continue undischarged for a period of ninety (90) days; or such other party's instituting (by petition, application, answer, consent or otherwise) any bankruptcy, insolvency arrangement, or similar proceeding relating it under the laws of any jurisdiction; or the institution of any such proceeding (by petition, application or otherwise) agianst such other party, if such proceeding shall remain undismissed for a period of ninety (90) days; or the issuance or levy of any judgment, writ, warrant of attachment or execution or similar process against a substantial part of the property of such other party, if such judgment, writ, or similar process shall not be released, vacated or fully bonded within ninety (90) days after its issue or levy.

7.05. Either party shall exercise its right to terminate by giving written notice to the other party of its intention to do so upon the occurrence of any of the events listed in Sections 7.02, 7.03 or 7.04 hereof. This Agreement shall terminate as of the thirtieth (30th) day following receipt by the other party of such notice.

7.06. Upon the termination of this Agreement, GTI shall promptly return to EED any Proprietary Information relating to any Project with respect to which no license agreement has been executed, including copies or models of such Proprietary Information, and GTI shall thereafter have no further rights to or interest in any of the Projects or the subject matter thereof, except to the extent provided in any license agreement applicable thereto.

7.07. The parties hereto agree that, in connection with their mutual obligations to enter into one or more license agreements as provided in Section 5.01, the non-defaulting party shall be entitled to obtain specific performance or other equitable relief with respect to the enforcement of the obligations of the defaulting party. This right shall be in addition to, and not in lieu of, any other rights or remedies available at law or in equity.

Exhibit B *(Continued)*

Article VIII

Miscellaneous

8.01. All notices, requests and demands given to or made upon the parties hereto shall, except as other wise specified herein, be in writing and be delivered or mailed to any such party at its address which;

(i) In the case of GTI shall be:

GTI Corporation
10060 Willow Creek Road
San Diego, California 92131

(ii) In the case of EED shall be:

c/o James K. LaFleur, General Partner
4337 Talofa Avenue
Toluca Lake, California 91602

Any party may, by notice hereunder to the other paty, designate a changed address for such party. Any notice, if mailed properly addressed, postage prepaid, registered or certified air mail, shall be deemed dispatched on the registered date or that stamped on the certified mail receipt, and shall be deemed received the fifth business day thereafter or when it is actually received, whichever is sooner.

8.02. This Agreement shall be binding upon the inure to the benefit of the parties hereto and their respective successors, assigns and legal representatives; provided, however, that neither party hereto shall have the right to assign or otherwise transfer (by operation of law or otherwise) its rights or obligations under this Agreement (other than by subcontract as referred to herein) except with the prior written consent of the other party.

8.03. This Agreement may be executed in any number of counterparts, each of which shall be deemed to be an original and all of which shall constitute together one and the same agreement.

8.04. This Agreement shall be deemed to be a contract made under the laws of the State of California, and for all purposes it shall be construed in accordance with and governed by the laws of the State of California.

8.05. Wherever possible, each provision of this Agreement shall be interpreted in such manner as to be effective and valid under applicable law, but if any provision of this Agreement shall be prohibited by or invalid under applicable law, such provision shall be ineffective only to the extent of such prohibition or invalidity without invalidating the remainder of such provision or the remaining provisions of this Agreement.

8.06. This Agreement may not be and shall not be deemed or construed to have been modified, amended, rescinded, cancelled, or waived in whole or in part, except by a written instrument signed by the parties hereto.

Exhibit B (*Continued*)

8.07. This Agreement constitutes and expresses the entire agreement and understanding between the parties hereto in reference to all the matters referred to herein, and any previous discussions, promises, representations and understanding relative thereto are merged into the terms of this Agreement and shall have no further force and effect.

IN WITNESS WHEREOF, GTI has caused this Agreement to be executed by a Vice President and EED has caused this Agreement to be executed by its General Partner as of the day and year first above written.

ATTEST: GTI CORPORATION

_____   By _____
[Corporate Seal]   Vice President

WITNESS: ELECTRONIC EQUIPMENT
                                                         DEVELOPMENT LTD.
                                                         (A Delaware Limited
                                                         Partnership)

_____   By _____
                                                         General Partner

Exhibit B *(Continued)*

RESEARCH PROJECTS

The three research projects initially subject to this Agreement are as follows:

1. *High Speed Welder*—Design and development of a prototype welding machine capable of producing 1,000 pieces per minute of two-piece welds with the capability of welding dissimilar materials. Such a welder could be used by GTI in its own manufacturing operations. The ultimate market for two-piece welds would be the semi-conductor industry.

2. *Computer Graphics System*—Design and development of a low cost shaded real-time graphics system, which is presently not commercially available. Shaded real-time computer graphics systems are capable of displaying pictures of three-dimensional objects in color. High performance systems, priced in excess of $500,000, are capable of displaying realistic three-dimensional pictures in real-time (at least 30 frames per second). Recent developments in the semi-conductor industry have allowed the possible development of a new type of graphics terminal which is believed to have the performance characteristics of the expensive high performance systems at a much reduced price. Computer graphics systems could probably be sold to original equipment manufacturers (OEM's) which will incorporate the graphics system with their own systems or a turnkey (ready-to-go) products for specific applications requiring substantial investment by the user in software development. The principal commercial applications appear to be in pilot training by computer simulation, manufacturers using CAD-CAM (computer aided drafting-computer-aided manufacturing), medical diagnosis and research, architecture, animation and art.

3. *Marking and Handling Equipment*—Design and development of appropriate equipment, such as that described below, to enhance GTI's position in the marking and handling field:

(a) *U.V. Ovens for Printers*—Design and development of a prototype for an ultraviolet (U.V.) oven for use as optional equipment on printing equipment sold by GTI. The principal sales markets for such a product would be the electronics industry.

(b) *Serializing Print Head*—Design and development of a prototype having wide applications for hybrid package manufacturers as well as for GTI in connection with its other printing systems.

Exhibit B *(Continued)*

(c) *Tube to Tube Handler*—Design and development of a tube to tube handler system for integrated circuits which could be used as optional equipment on existing GTI products.

(d) *Orienter*—Design and development of a new orienter that is capable of being easily interfaced with a number of GTI's axial lead printers or other units for handling axial devices. It is intended that any marketable product developed would be offered as an option and not as a stand alone unit in connection with the sale of these GTI products whose principle markets would be the semi-conductor industry.

(e) *DIP and SIP Package*—Design and development of automatic handling of DIP (dual in-line packaging) and SIP (single in-line packaging) packages to be used on either a conventional marking head or a laser marking head for a wide variety of potential customers.

(f) *Stamping Head*—Design and development of a simple stamping head designed to stamp stationary objects in either a verticle or horizontal position. GTI believes that this equipment could be easily interfaced with customers' production equipment and would be able to print parts in line with other manufacturing processes.

Exhibit B *(Continued)*

Form of LICENSE AGREEMENT

THIS AGREEMENT made this _____ day of _____, 19__ by and between ELECTRONIC EQUIPMENT DEVELOPMENT LTD. (A Delaware Limited Partnership) ("Licensor"),

AND

GTI CORPORATION, a Rhode Island corporation with executive offices in San Diego, California ("Licensee");

WITNESSETH:

WHEREAS, Licensor is the owner of patents, patent applications and/or technology relating to the inventions described in Appendix I attached hereto which have been developed in accordance with certain technical and other specifications under the terms of that certain Research and Development Agreement dated as of August _____, 1980 ("Research and Development Agreement") between Licensor and Licensee; and

WHEREAS, Licensor desires to grant to Licensee, and Licensee desires to acquire, an exclusive license of all substantial rights in said inventions and any related patents, patent applications and/or technology for the lives of such patents, patent applications and technology;

NOW, THEREFORE, in consideration of the convenants herein contained, the parties hereto, intending to be legally bound, hereby agree as follows:

Article I

Definitions

1.01. Licensor means Electronic Equipment Development Ltd. (A Delaware Limited Partnership), or any person or entity which succeeds to substantially all of its assets.

Exhibit B *(Continued)*

1.02. Licensee means GTI Corporation, its successors and assigns.

1.03. The Invention means _____[insert project identification generally as described in Appendix I which has satisfied those certain Specifications established with respect thereto under the Research and Development Agreement] and any Imporvement thereto.

1.04. Commercialization means research, development, manufacture, quality control, assembly, testing, sale, use and/or servicing.

1.05. Patent Rights means (i) those patents and patent applications directed to the Invention and listed in Appendix I; and (ii) any and all letter patent, United States and foreign (including but not limited to patents of implementation, improvement or addition, utility model and design patents and inventors certificates as well as divisions, reissues, continuations, continuations-in-part, renewals and extensions of any of these) and applications for letters patent owned by Licensor and directed to the Invention.

1.06. Improvement means (i) in the case of patented items, any modification, which if unlicensed would infringe one or more claims of the Patent Rights; and (ii) in the case of unpatented items, any modification which substantially depends upon and makes use of the basic innovation, invention or discovery represented by the Invention.

1.07. Licensed Product means a product which incorporates the Invention. [Insert the following if the Invention is the High Speed Welder (identified as item 1 on Appendix I): Licensed Product shall be deemed to include all High Speed Welders produced by or for Licensee and all two-piece welded leads produced by or for Licensee after the date the License Agreement for such Invention is executed.]

1.08. An item of Licensed Product shall be deemed to have been sold (a) where the transaction is on an open account, when such item is invoiced; (b) at the time of payment when such item is paid for by the purchaser in advance of delivery; or (c) where the transaction is on consignment, when such item is paid for or when it is released from consignment.

1.09. Net Sales means the aggregate gross billings by Licensee, less the following items of expense to the extent to which they are paid or allowed and included in the aggregate gross billings in accordance with recognized accounting principles: (a) sales, use or turnover taxes on sales invoices; (b) excise taxes, customs duties or consular fees; (c) transportation and insurance on shipments to customers; (d) trade or quantity discounts (but not cash discounts); and (e) credits allowed for returned goods.

1.10. Proprietary Information means the Invention itself and any information relating thereto or to the Commercialization thereof, including all trade secrets, product ideas and concepts, technical information, inventions, whether or not patentable and whether or not recorded in any way, including engineering, scientific, practical information and formulae regardless of the stage of development, information for attributes and characteristics, uses and markets, assembling and manufacturing data and procedures, machinery and equipment design, information or materials including the processing,

Exhibit B *(Continued)*

sources and historical cost thereof, technical informatin included on drawings, blueprints, specificatioons, and other writings, all developed or in the process of development, but excluding any information disclosed in an issued patent within the Patent Rights.

Article II

Grant of License

2.01. Licensor hereby grants to Licensee the exclusive license to make or to have made for it, to use and to sell Licensed Product throughout the world, whether or not subject to Patent Rights.

2.02. Licensee shall have the right to grant sublicenses on terms not inconsistent herewith. Licensor shall promptly be furnished with a copy of each sublicense granted by Licensee.

2.03. The term of the license granted hereunder shall be (i) with respect to Licensed Product subject to Patent Rights a period of 17 years, or until the expiration of the last-to-be-issued patent within the Patent Rights, and (ii) with respect to Licensed Product not subject to the Patent Rights, for the useful life of the Invention incorporated in such Licensed Product.

2.04. Not withstanding any provision herein contained to the contrary, it is understood and agreed that this license is intended to constitute a grant of all substantial rights of Licensor in and to the Invention and related Patent Rights, if any. Any later final administrative or judicial determination that a provision of this or any other agreement results in the retention of a substantial right by Licensor for purpose of the Internal Revenue Code of 1954, as amended, shall have the result of deleting any such right retroactive to the date of this license.

Article III

Royalties; Minimum and Maximum Payments

3.01. In consideration of the grant by Licensor of the right to make, have made for it, to use and to sell the Licensed Product, during the term specified in Section 2.03, Licensee shall pay, in accordance with the provisions of Article IV hereof, royalties to Licensor with respect to Net Sales of Licensed Product sold by Licensee or any sublicensee of Licensee at the rate of ___ percent (___%) per annum [insert applicable amount set forth in Appendix II hereto], subject to the terms and conditions set forth in Sections 3.02. and 3.03, respectively.

3.02. Subject to the limitations set forth herein, Licensee shall pay to Licensor on or before October 31, 1984 ("Minimum Payment Date") roy-

Exhibit B *(Continued)*

alties of not less than $_____ ("Minimum Royalty") [insert applicable amount calculated in accordance with Appendix II] regardless of the Net Sales of Licensed Product by Licensee or any sublicensee of Licensee by such date. In determining the amount, if any, to be paid on the Minimum Payment Date, the following amounts should be totaled: (a) royalties (if any) previously paid pursuant to Section 3.01 with respect to the Licensed Product, plus (b) royalties (if any) paid in excess of the minimum royalty required to be paid pursuant to other license agreements to which Licensor and Licensee are parties, which excess has not otherwise been taken into account for the purpose of this Section 3.02 or comparable provisions in other license agreements. If such total is less than the Minimum Royalty payable hereunder, then Licensee shall pay an amount equal to such deficiency within 30 calendar days after the Minimum Payment Date. The Licensee may recoup any deficiency so paid by offsetting the amount thereof against any royalties otherwise payable to Licensor after the Minimum Payment Date under this License Agreement or under any other license agreement with Licensor.

3.03. Licensor shall not be entitled to receive royalties in excess of the maximum cumulative royalty of $_____ [insert applicable amount calculated in accordance with Appendix II] with respect to Net Sales of the Licensed Product. Upon payment of said maximum cumulative royalty amount to Licensor, this License Agreement and royalty abligations hereunder shall be considered to be fully paid, and no further royalties shall be payable to Licensor with respect to the continued manufacture, use or sale of Licensed Product by or for Licensee or any sublicensee of Licensee throughout the term hereof.

Article IV

Payment of Royalties

4.01. Except as provided in Section 3.02, payments required under Article III shall be made quarterly on or before the last calendar day of each April, July, October and January during the term specified in Section 2.03; the amount of each payment shall be determined by Net Sales of Licensed Product by Licensee or any sublicensee within the three month period preceding the month in which payment is required to be made.

4.02. Each payment made pursuant to Section 4.01, and any deficiency payment made pursuant to Section 3.02, shall be accompanied by a resonably detailed statement setting forth with respect to the preceding three month period or applicable period prior to the Minimum Payment Date, as the case may be, the quantity of Net Sales of Licensed Product sold by Licensee and any sublicensee and the payments due or previously paid Licensor with respect thereto.

4.03. Licensee shall keep regular books of account adequate to verify all reports and payments to be made by Licensee under this Agreement. Such

Exhibit B *(Continued)*

books of account shall be open at all reasonable business hours for inspection by Licensor or its duly authorized representative.

4.04. If this Agreement is terminated for any reason whatsoever, Licensee shall retain said books of account for a period of six (6) months after such termination and permit Licensor or its duly authorized representative to inspect them to verify all statements and payments required hereunder.

Article V

Patent Prosecution; Improvements

5.01. Licensor shall file patent applications in the United States and any other countries it deems appropriate with respect to the Invention as soon as reasonably practicable and shall take title to any patents which may issue thereon. The rejection of any claim, claims or all claims contained in any patent application within the Patent Rights shall have no effect on the rights and obligations of the parties hereto.

5.02. Whenever requested to so so by Licensor, Licensee shall execute any and all applications, assignments or other instruments which Licensor deems appropriate or necessary to enable Licensor to apply for and to obtain patents related to the Invention in the United States or any foreign country or to protect Licensor's interest in any such patents or in the maintenance or enforcement of such patents, all at the expense of Licensor.

5.03. If, during the term specified in Section 2.03. Licensor acquires rights in a patent for an Improvement, such patent automatically shall be included in the Patent Rights, provided Licensor possesses the right to grant thereunder a license of the same scope granted in Article II.

Article VI

Infringement

6.01. If, during the term of this Agreement, a third party infringes the Patent Rights, if any and to the extent applicable, Licensee shall take whatever actions are necessary, including litigation, to terminate such unlawful activity. Licensee shall have the right to name Licensor as party-plaintiff in any such litigation, and Licensor shall cooperate fully with Licensee. Licensee shall control the prosecution of any litigation, shall bear all the costs thereof and shall be entitled to retain any proceeds thereby recovered. In the event that Licensee fails to institute litigation to terminate unlawful infringement of the Patent Rights (where applicable), Licensor shall be entitled to institute and prosecute such litigation, naming Licensee as party-plaintiff, and in such an event, the parties shall share any proceeds recovered in accordance with their respective contributions to the cost of such litigation.

Exhibit B (*Continued*)

Article VII

Confidential Relationship

7.01. Proprietary Information is the sole property of and is confidential to Licensor. Licensee shall use its best efforts and will take all reasonable precautions fully commensurate with those it employs for the protection of its own confidential information, to protect Proprietary Information and to prevent disclosure thereof except such disclosure as is reasonably necessary or appropriate in commercializing the Invention.

7.02. Proprietary Information shall not include any of the following:

a. Any information that appears in issued patents or printed publications in integrated form or that otherwise is or become generally known in the trade or become a part of the public domain other than through the actions or fault of Licensee; and

b. Any information that Licensee can show by written records came into its possession without covenants of confidentiality from another party who is under no obligation to Licensor to maintain the confidentiality of such information.

Licensee shall have the burden of proving that any information otherwise within the meaning of Proprietary Information comes within one of these exceptions.

Article VIII

Patent Marking

8.01. Licensee shall mark all Licensed Product subject to Patent Rights manufactured or sold by it under this Agreement in accordance with the applicable statutes of the appropriate countries relating to the marking of patented articles and shall require corresponding conduct of its sublicensees pursuant to the terms of any sublicenses granted by Licensee.

Article IX

Remedies

9.01. Licensor shall have the right to terminate this Agreement upon the occurrence of any of the following events:

(i) the failure by Licensee to make any of the payments required under Article III hereunder within thirty (30) days of the date on which such payment is due;

Exhibit B *(Continued)*

(ii) an adjudication of Licensee as bankrupt or insolvent, or Licensee's admission in writing of its inability to pay its debts as they mature, or an assignment by Licensee for the benefit of creditors; or Licensee's applying for or consenting to the appointment of a receiver, trustee, or similar officer for any substantial part of its property; or such receiver, trustee or similar officer's appointment without the application or consent of Licensee, if such appointment shall continue undischarged for a period of ninety (90) days; or Licensee's instituting (by petition, application, answer, consent or otherwise) any bankruptcy, insolvency arrangement, or similar proceeding relating to Licensee under the laws of any jurisdiction; or the institution of any such proceeding (by petition, application or otherwise) against Licensee, if such proceeding shall remain undismissed for a period of ninety (90) days; or the issuance or levy of any judgment, writ, warrant of attachment or execution or similar process against a substantial part of the property of Licensee, if such judgment, writ, or similar process shall not be released, vacated or fully bonded within ninety (90) days after its issue or levy.

9.02. Licensor shall exercise its right to terminate in accordance with Section 9.01 by giving written notice to Licensee and any sublicensees known to Licensor of its intention to terminate. This Agreement shall terminate as of the thirtieth (30th) day following the date such notice is given.

9.03. Termination of this Agreement shall not affect the rights granted any sublicensees of Licensee, provided any such sublicensee notifies Licensor, in writing, at any time during the thirty (30) day period preceding the date of termination of this Agreement, of its intention to continue to exercise its rights under such sublicense and to pay such royalties as are provided therein directly to Licensor. The rights of any sublicensee to make, have made for it, to use or to sell Licensed Product shall terminate upon the date of termination of this Agreement unless such sublicensee notifies Licensor, in writing, within such thirty (30) day period, of its intention to continue to exercise its rights under its sublicense.

9.04. Within five (5) calendar days of its receipt of the notice called for under Section 9.02 of Licensor's intention to terminate this Agreement, Licensee shall notify each of its sublicensees, in writing, of the termination of this Agreement; of the date such termination becomes effective; and of the right of such sublicensee to continue to exercise its rights under its sublicense as provided in Section 9.03.

9.05. If termination occurs by operation of Section 9.01, Licensee and any sublicensees of Licensee who elect not to continue to exercise their rights under their sublicenses shall have six (6) months to dispose of its or their existing inventory of the Licensed Product and thereafter cease and desist the manufacture, use and sale of Licensed Product and any use of Proprietary Information.

Exhibit B *(Continued)*

Article X

Warranties

10.01. Licensor represents and warrants that any patent and patent applications within the Patent Rights constitute the entirety of Licensor's worldwide patent properties relating to the Invention.

10.02. If it is later determined by final decision of a court of competent jurisdiction that Licensor has transferable rights in a patent which contains claims that are infringed by Licensee's Commercialization of the Invention but which patent is not included in the Patent Rights, such patent automatically shall be included in the Patent Rights.

10.03. Nothing in this Agreement shall be construed as a warranty by Licensor as to the validity or scope of any patents within the Patent Rights or that any manufacture, use or sale by Licensee will be free from infringement of patents other than those comprising the Patent Rights.

Article XI

Miscellaneous

11.01. All notices, requests and demands given to or made upon the parties hereto shall, except as otherwise specified herein, be in writing and be delivered or mailed to any such party at its address which:

(i) In the case of Licensor shall be:
   Electronic Equipment Development Ltd.
   c/o James K. LaFleur, General Partner
   4337 Talofa Avenue
   Toluca Lake, California 91602
(ii) In the case of Licensee shall be:
   GTI Corporation
   10060 Willow Creek Road
   San Diego, California 92131
   Attention: Vice President

Any party may, by notice hereunder to all parties, designate a changed address for such party. Any notice, if mailed properly addressed, postage prepaid, registered or certified mail, shall be deemed dispatched on the registered date or that stamped on the certified mail receipt, and shall be deemed received the fifth business day thereafter or when it is actually received, which ever is sooner.

Exhibit B *(Continued)*

11.02. This Agreement shall be binding upon and inure to the benefit of the parties hereto and their respective successors, assigns and legal representatives. Licensee shall have the right to assign or sublicense its rights under this Agreement.

11.03. This Agreement may be executed in any number of counterparts, each of which shall be deemed to be an original and all of which shall constitute together one and the same agreement.

11.04. This Agreement shall be deemed to be a contract made under the laws of the State of California and for all purposes it shall be construed in accordance with and governed by the laws of the State of California.

11.05. Wherever possible, each provision of this Agreement shall be interpreted in such manner as to be effective and valid under applicable law, but if any provision of this Agreement shall be prohibited by or invalid under applicable law, such provision shall be ineffective only to the extent of such provision or invalidity without invalidating the remainder of such provision or the remaining provisions of this Agreement.

11.06. This Agreement may not be and shall not be deemed or construed to have been modified, amended, rescinded, cancelled, or waived in whole or in part, except by a written instrument signed by the parties hereto.

11.07. This Agreement constitutes and expresses the entire agreement and understanding between the parties hereto in reference to all the matters referred to herein, and any previous discussions, promises, representations and understandings relative thereto are merged into the terms of this Agreement and shall have no further force and effect.

IN WITNESS WHEREOF, Licensor has caused this Agreement to be Executed by its General Partner, and Licensee has caused this Agreement to be executed by its Vice President as of the day and year first above written.

WITNESS

ELECTRONIC EQUIPMENT DEVELOPMENT LTD.

_____   By _____
                                         General Partner

ATTEST:

GTI CORPORATION

_____   By _____
[Corporate Seal   Vice President

Exhibit B *(Continued)*

440

PROJECT DESCRIPTION

The following is a descripion of the Invention, as defined in Section 1.03 of the License Agreement of which this is a part.

[furnish brief description of the following project or projects more fully described in the Research and Development Agreement which satisfy the applicable Specifications, as defined therin, and thereby achieve technological success]

1. High Speed Welder
2. Computer Graphics System
3. Marking and Handling Equipment, including one or more of the following projects:

a. Ultra Violet Ovens with Printers
b. Serializing Print Head
c. Tube to Tube Handler
d. Orienter
e. DIP and SIP Package
f. Stamping Head

4. New projects (if any) developed pursuant to the Research and Development Agreement.

The patents and patent applications owned by Licensor with respect to the above Invention are as follows:

[furnish applicable information]

Exhibit B *(Continued)*

ROYALTY RATES

The following table sets forth the annual royalty rate to be inserted in Section 3.01, which is a percentage of Net Sales of all Licensed Product subject to this License Agreement sold by Licensee or any sublicensee of Licensee, and sets forth the aggregate minimum royalty and the aggregate maximum royalties payable to Licensor:

	Annual Royalty Rate	Minimum Royalty	Maximum Cumulative Royalty
1. High Speed Welder	3%	$353,520	$1,286,832
2. Computer Graphics System[1]	5%	$303,024	$7,903,008
3. Marking and Handling Equipment	10%	$555,552	$2,022,240

In the event that one or more but less than all of the six projects included under the Marking and Handling Equipment Research Project description in Appendix I become the subject of one License Agreement, the minimum royalty and maximum cumulative royalty payable with respect to Marking and Handling Equipment shall be appropriately reduced so that such amounts to be paid shall equal a portion of the amounts shown above based on the following percentages of originally estimated research costs and adminstrative costs allocable to each of the projects:

a. Ultra Violet Oven		7%
b. Serializing Print Head		7
c. Tube to Tube Handler		23
d. Orienter		15

[1]With respect to the Computer Graphics System, GTI shall pay EED any additional amounts which EED is required to pay to James C. Holly under the terms of a consulting agreement or any assignment thereof.

Exhibit B *(Continued)*

e. DIP and SIP Package	28
f. Stamping Head	20
	100%

For example, if projects a., b. and c. above are included under Section 1.03 of one License Agreement, the amount of the minimum royalty and the maximum cumulative royalties to be paid with respect to those three projects or inventions shall be an amount equal to 37% of $555,552 and $2,022,240, respectively (the amounts shown above under Marking and Handling Equipment) multiplied by the total number of Units or New Units then outstanding. The annual royalty rate would remain unchanged.

If any projects other than those generally described in Items 1 to 3 of Appendix I are developed pursuant to the provisions of the Research and Development Agreement dated as of July 31, 1980, to which this form of License Agreement is attached as an exhibit, an annual royalty rate and minimum and maximum cumulative royalties will be negotiated between Licensee and Licensor.

Exhibit B *(Continued)*

FORM OF OPINION

KIRKPATRICK, LOCKHART, JOHNSON & HUTCHISON

1500 Oliver Building

Pittsburgh, Pennsylvania 15222

August ____, 1980

Electronic Equipment Development Ltd.
4337 Talofa Avenue
Toluca Lake, California 91602

Gentlemen:

You have asked our advice with respect to several matters relating to the formation and federal income tax treatment of Electronic Equipment Development Ltd. ("Partnership"), a Delaware limited partnership, organized pursuant to the Limited Partnership Agreement dated as of August 11, 1980, between James K. LaFleur, as general partner, and Ronald Lust, as nominee for the limited partners, and the Cerificate of Limited Partnership as recorded on August ____, 1980 in the Office of the Secretary of the State of Delaware in File number _____.

As counsel for the Partnership, we have made such investigation of law, and have examined such certificates of public officials, certificates of the gerneral partner of the Partnership and such other documents and records as we have deemed necessary and relevant as a basis for our opinions hereinafter set forth. Based on the foregoing, it is our opinion that:

(i) The Partnership is a limited partnership duly organized, validly existing and in good standing under the laws of the State of Delaware.

Exhibit C

(ii) The liability of the limited partners in the Partnership is limited to the amount of the capital contributions paid or to be paid to the Partnership by such limited partners plus the amount of any distributions from the Partnership to the limited partners which represent, in whole or in part, a return of their capital contributions, plus interest on such distributions, provided that the limited partners do not take part in the control of the business of the Partnership (although the limited partners may consult with and advise the general partner as to the conduct of the Partnership's business).

In addition to the foregoing, you have requested our opinion as to the classification of the Partnership as a partnership and not as an association taxable as a corporation for Federal income tax purposes. Before rendering such an opinion, we wish to set forth the following qualifications and analysis regarding this matter.

Under the current provisions of the Internal Revenue Code of 1954, as amended (the "Code"), the regulations promulgated thereunder (the "Regulations") and existing interpretations thereof, an organization will be characterized as a partnership and not as an association taxable as a corporation for Federal income tax purposes unless it possesses more corporate characteristics than non-corporate characteristics. The Regulations specify the following four major corporate characteristics: (1) continuity of life, (2) limited liability, (3) free transferability of interests and (4) centralized management.

The Partnership should not be deemed to possess continuity of life because the death, legal incapacity, resignation, or bankruptcy of its sole general partner will dissolve the Partnership. However, this analysis is somewhat weakened by the fact that the limited partners who own a majority of the interests in all portions of the Partnership can reconstitute the Partnership by appointing a new general partner, under certain terms and conditions, if the Partnership is dissolved as indicated above. The Partnership should not have the corporate characteristic of limited liability because we understand and with your permission have assumed for purposes of this opinion that the general partner possesses substantial assets that could be reached by creditors of the Partnership. In addition, the Partnership should not be found to possess the characteristic of free transferability of interests because the partnership agreement prohibits a limited partner from transferring his interest to third parties (except to his associates as defined in the partnership agreement) without first offering the interest to the general partner, and a limited partner's assignee may not become a substituted limited partner without the approval of the general partner in his sole discretion. Thus, under existing definitions, the Partnership does not possess more corporate characteristics than non-corporate characteristics.

It must be noted, however, that early in 1977 the Internal Revenue Service issued proposed regulations, which, if adopted, would have significantly

Exhibit C *(Continued)*

altered the current Regulations governing the classification of organizations as partnerships by redefining the aforementioned corporate characteristics. Prop. Reg. ¶¶301.7701-1 to 301.7701-3, 43 Fed. Reg. 1038 (Jan. 5, 1977), *withdrawn* 43 Fed. Reg. 1489 (Jan. 7, 1977). Although these proposed regulations were almost immediately withdrawn, it is possible that the Internal Revenue Service may reissue the same or similar regulations at any time. If any such regulations were reissued and were applicable to the Partnership, it is quite possible that the Partnership would be classified as an association taxable as a corporation for Federal income tax purposes.

Subject to the foregoing qualifications, it is our opinion that the Partnership will be characterized as a partnership and not as an association taxable as a corporation for Federal income tax purposes.

You have further asked our advise with respect to the treatment for Federal income tax purposes of certain expenditures expected to be made by the Partnership. It is our understanding that such expenditures shall be made pursuant to the terms of a Research and Development Agreement dated as of August 11, 1980 between the Partnership and GTI Corporation (the "Research and Development Agreement").

The Research and Development Agreement provides that the Partnership will pay certain sums to GTI in exchange for the performance by GTI or by consultants supervised by GTI of certain research and experimentation services on behalf of the Partnership. Section 174(a) of the Code provides that a taxpayer may elect to deduct currently the "research or experimental expenditures" paid or incurred by him in connection with his trade or business. The Treasury Regulations issued under section 174 define such research expenditures to include costs incident to the development of new scientific processes and inventions or the improvement of existing technology. The Regulations further explain that the deduction is available not only for expenditures incurred for the costs of research undertaken by the taxpayer directly but also for the costs of research conducted on behalf of the taxpayer by a research insitute or similar organization. In addition, the deduction is available for the costs of obtaining a patent, including attorney's fees expended in making and perfecting a patent application. However, a taxpayer may not deduct the costs of aquiring a patent, model or process belonging to another person, or the costs allocable to the acquisition or improvement of land or depreciable property used in connection with research conducted on the taxpayer's behalf and to which land or property the taxpayer acquires ownership rights.

Costs deemed to constitute "research or experimental expenditures" within the meaning of section 174(a) may be deducted notwithstanding the fact that the taxpayer has not yet offered for sale a product resulting from such research and experimentation. The United States Supreme Court in the case of *Snow v. Commissioner*, 416 U. S. 500 (1974), held that such expenditures on the part of a partnership had been incurred "in connection with" the trade or business of a limited partner of the partnership within the meaning

Exhibit C *(Continued)*

of section 174(a) even though the partnership had not yet offered a product for sale. The Supreme Court, in rejecting the position of the Internal Revenue Service, concluded that the Congressional intent underlying section 174 was to stimulate research and make the same tax benefits available to new entities as were available to established companies which sponsored continuous programs of research.

In light of the foregoing, and to the extent that the services conducted for the Partnership by GTI Corporation pursuant to the Research and Development Agreement constitute the type of "research or experimental expenditures" to which section 174 applies, then the election provided by section 174(a) to deduct the costs of such services should be available to the Partnership.

This opinion is subject to the general qualification that new state or Federal laws dealing with limited partnerships could partially or entirely alter the accuracy of the opinions contained herein. Moreover, amendments to the Code or the Regulations, new judicial decisions, or changes in administrative policy could substantially affect or invalidate statements set forth in this opinion.

Very truly yours,

Kirkpatrick, Lockhart, Johnson & Hutchison

Exhibit C *(Continued)*

Appendix N

Where to File Partnership Certificates

The following list of where to file Limited Partnership Certificates in the various states is intended for use as a general guideline. Specific filing requirements should be verified with the respective filing office, as such filing requirements are apt to change. It should be noted that especially within the last several years there has been a gradual movement away from filing on a local or county level to filing on a state-wide level, most often with the Secretary of State.

Alabama	Code of Alabama, 1975, as amended, Title 10, Chapter 9, Article 1, Sec. 10-9-21 et seq.—file with the Judge of Probate of the county in which the principal place of business is located.
Alaska	Alaska Statutes, 1962, Annotated, Title 32, Chapter 10, Sec. 32.10.010 et seq.—file with the Recorder for the recording district in which the partnership is located.
Arizona	Arizona Revised Statutes, Annotated, Title 29, Chapter 3, Sec. 29-302 et seq.—file with the County Recorder of the county in which the principal place of business is situated.
Arkansas	Arkansas Statutes, 1947, Annotated, Title 65, Chapter 3, Sec. 65-302 et seq.—file with the Secretary of State.
California	West's Annotated California Codes (Corporation Code), Title 2, Division 3, Chapter 2, Sec. 15502 et seq.—file with the Recorder of the county in which the principal place of business is situated. If there are additional places of business or if the

	partnership owns property in other counties, the certificate should be filed with the Recorder of each such county.
Colorado	Colorado Revised Statutes, 1973, Annotated, Title 7, Article 61, Sec. 7-61-103 et seq.—file with the County Clerk and Recorder.
Connecticut	General Statutes of Connecticut, Revision of 1958, as amended to January 1, 1981, Title 34, Chapter 610, Sec. 34-10 et seq.—file with the Secretary of State.
Delaware	Delaware Code Annotated, as amended, Title 6, Chapter 17, Sec. 1702 et seq.—file with the Secretary of State.
District of Columbia	District of Columbia Code, 1973, as amended, Title 41, Chapter 4, Sec. 41-402 et seq.—file with the Recorder of Deeds of the District of Columbia.
Florida	West's Florida Statutes Annotated, Title 34, Chapter 602, Sec. 620.02 et seq.—file original with the Department of State and a certified copy with the Clerk of Circuit Court in the county where the principal place of business is located.
Georiga	Code of Georiga, Annotated, Title 75, Chapter 75-4, Sec. 75-403 et seq.—file original with the Clerk of Superior Court of the county in which the principal place of business is situated. If there are additional places of business in other counties, a certified copy of the certificate should be filed with the Clerk of Superior Court of each such county.
Hawaii	Hawaii Revised Statutes, as amended, Title 23, Chapter 425, Part II, Sec. 425-22 et seq.—file with the Director of Regulatory Agencies.
Idaho	Idaho Code, as amended, Title 53, Chapter 2, Sec. 53-202 et seq.—file with the Secretary of State.
Illinois	Smith-Hurd Illinois Annotated Statutes, Chapter 106-1/2, Sec. 45 et seq.—file with the Recorder of Deeds of the county where the principal office is located.
Indiana	Burns Indiana Statutes Annotated, Title 23, Article 4, Chapter 2, Sec. 23-4-2-2 et seq.—file with the County Recorder of the county in which the principal place of business is located.

Iowa	Iowa Code Annotated, Title 23, Chapter 545, Sec. 545.2 et seq.—file with the County Recorder in the county in which the principal place of business is located.
Kansas	Kansas Statutes Annotated, Chapter 56, Article 56-1, Sec. 56-123 et seq.—file original with the Secretary of State and a certified copy with the Register of Deeds of the county in which the principal place of business is located.
Kentucky	Baldwin's Kentucky Revised Statutes, Annotated Title XXIX, Chapter 361, Sec 362.030 et seq.—File with the County Clerk of each county in which a place of business is situated.
Louisiana	West's Louisiana Statutes Annotated, 1964, Title 11, Chapter 2, Section 4, Articles 2846 & 2847 et seq.—"Partnerships in commendam"—contract must be filed within six (6) days from the time of execution of the contract in the place where the principal establishment is situated with the officer authorized to record mortgages.
Maine	Maine Revised Statutes Annotated, 1964, Title 31, Chapter 7, Sec. 152 et seq.—file with the Secretary of State
Maryland	Annotated Code of Maryland, as amended (Corporations and Associations), Title 10, Sec. 10-102 et seq.—file with the Clerk of the Court in the county where the principal place of business is located.
Massachusetts	Annotated Laws of Massachusetts, Title XV, Chapter 109, Sec. 2 et seq.—file with the Secretary of State.
Michigan	Michigan Compiled Laws, Annotated, Chapter 449, Sec. 449.202 et seq.—file with the County Clerk of the county in which the principal place of business is situated.
Minnesota	Minnesota Statutes Annotated, Chapter 322, Sec. 322.02 et seq.—file with the County Recorder of the county in which the principal place of business is situated.
Mississippi	Mississippi Code, 1972, Annotated, Title 79, Chapter 13, Sec. 79-13-5 et seq.—file with the Clerk of the Chancery Court of the county in which the principal place of business is located.
Missouri	Vernon's Annotated Missouri Statutes, Title

	XXIII, Chapter 359, Sec. 359.020 et seq.—file with the Recorder of Deeds of the county in which the principal place of business is located. Also necessary to publish a notice as to specifics of the limited partnership.
Montana	Montana Code Annotated, as amended, Title 35, Chapter 12, Part 2, Sec. 35-12-201 et seq.—file with the County Clerk and Recorder of the county in which the principal place of business is located and with the Secretary of State.
Nebraska	Revised Statutes of Nebraska, 1943, as amended, Chapter 67, Article 2, Sec. 67-202 et seq.—file with the County Clerk of the county in which the principal place of business is situated.
Nevada	Nevada Revised Statutes, as amended, Title 7, Chapter 88, Sec. 88.030 et seq.—file with the Recorder of the county in which the principal place of business is located. If there are additional places of business in other counties, a certified copy should be filed with the Recorder of each such county.
New Hampshire	New Hampshire Revised Statutes Annotated, 1968, Title XXVIII, Chapter 305, Sec. 305:2 et seq.—file with the Secretary of State.
New Jersey	New Jersey Statutes Annotated, Title 42, Chapter 2, Sec. 42:2-6 et seq.—file with the Clerk of the county in which the principal place of business is situated.
New Mexico	New Mexico Statutes, 1978, Annotated, Chapter 54, Article 2, Sec. 54-2-2 et seq.—file with the County Clerk of the county in which the principal place of business is located.
New York	McKinney's Consolidated Laws of New York, Annotated (Book 38—Partnership Law), Article 8, Sec. 91 et seq.—file with the County Clerk of the county in which the principal office is located; a copy of the certificate must be published and proof of such publication filed with the original certificate.
North Carolina	The General Statutes of North Carolina, as amended, Chapter 59, Article 1, Sec, 59-2 et seq.—file with the Register of Deeds of the county in which the principal place of business is located.
North Dakota	North Dakota Century Code, as amended, Title 45, Chapter 45-10, Sec. 45-10-02 et seq.—file orig-

inal with the Clerk of the District Court wherein the principal place of business is located and a certified copy with the Secretary of State.

Ohio — Page's Ohio Revised Code, Annotated, Title XVII, Chapter 1871, Sec. 1781.02 et seq.—file with the Clerk of the Court of Common Pleas of the county in which the principal place of business is located. If there are additional places of business in other counties, the certificate should be filed with the Clerk of the Court of Common Pleas of each such county.

Oklahoma — Oklahoma Statutes Annotated, Title 54, Chapter 4, Sec. 143 et seq.—file with the Secretary of State.

Oregon — Oregon Revised Statutes, as amended, Title 7, Chapter 69, Sec. 69.180 et seq.—file with the State Corporation Commissioner.

Pennsylvania — Purdon's Pennsylvania Statutes Annotated, Title 59, Chapter 5, Subchapter B, Section 512 et seq.—file with the Department of State.

Rhode Island — General Laws of Rhode Island, 1956, as amended, Title 7, Chapter 13, Sec. 7-13-3 et seq.—file with the Secretary of State.

South Carolina — Code of Laws of South Carolina, 1976, as amended, Title 33, Chapter 43, Sec. 33-43-30 et seq.—file with the Clerk of the Court of Common Pleas for the county in which the principal place of business is located and with the Secretary of State.

South Dakota — South Dakota Codified Laws, Annotated, 1980 Revision, Title 48, Chapter 48-6, Sec. 48-6-3 et seq.—file with the Register of Deeds of the county in which the principal place of business is located.

Tennessee — Tennessee Code Annotated, Title 61, Chapter 2, Sec. 61-2-102 et seq.—file with the County Register.

Texas — Vernon's Civil Statutes of the State of Texas, Annotated, Title 105, Article 6132a, Sec. 3 et seq.—file with the Secretary of State.

Utah — Utah Code Annotated, 1953, Title 48, Chapter 2, Sec. 48-2-2 et seq.—file with the County Clerk of the county in which the principal place of business is located. If there are additional places of business in other counties, a ceritifed copy should be filed with the County Clerk of each such county.

Vermont	Vermont Statutes Annotated, as amended, Title 11, Chapter 11, Sec. 1392 et seq.—file with the Town Clerk of the town in which the principal place of business is situated.
Virginia	Code of Virginia, 1950, as amended, Title 50, Chapter 2, Sec. 50-45 et seq.—file with the Clerk of the county or city in which a charter for the conduct of such business would be required to be recorded.
Washington	Revised Code of Washington Annotated, Title 25, Chapter 25.80, Sec. 25.08.020 et seq.—file with the County Clerk of the county in which the principal place of business is located.
West Virginia	West Virginia Code, Annotated, Chapter 47, Article 9, Sec. 47-9-2 et seq.—file with the Clerk of the County Commission of each county in which a place of business is located and with the Secretary of State.
Wisconsin	West's Wisconsin Statutes Annotated, Title XVII, Chapter 179, Sec. 179.02 et seq.—file with the Register of Deeds of the county in which the principal place of business is located.
Wyoming	Wyoming Statutes, Annotated, 1977 Republished Edition, Title 17, Chapter 14, Sec. 17-14-103 et seq.—file original with the County Clerk of the county in which the principal place of business is located. If there are additional places of business located in other counties, a certified copy should be filed with the County Clerk of each such county.

Appendix O

EED Presentation Charts

EED

ELECTRONIC EQUIPMENT DEVELOPMENT LTD.

AN R & D LIMITED PARTNERSHIP

Chart 1

OUTLINE OF PRESENTATION

Introduction

What is an R & D Limited Partnership?

Who are major participants in this Partnership?

What is their background and how do they fit into the overall project?

What particular development projects are involved in this Partnership?

What are the major risks to the investors?

What are maximum potential benefits to investors?

Summary of presentation.

Question and answer session.

Chart 2

AN R & D LIMITED PARTNERSHIP

Composed of at least one general partner and one limited partner.

Devoted to the successful development of one or more marketable products.

Contracts with others to perform product development services.

Continues development efforts.

Provides tax advantageous investment opportunities.

Derives income from sale on licensing of successful products to an independent manufacturer.

Chart 3

**MAJOR PARTICIPANTS IN THIS R & D LIMITED PART-
NERSHIP ARE:**

James K. LaFleur

GTI Corporation

The Investors

Chart 4

GTI CORPORATION

Role:

Has assigned original product requirements to General Partner.

Will perform most of development effort.

Will license successful products from partnership.

Will guarantee minimum royalty payments if certain conditions are met.

Backgound:

Amex-listed company for 20 years.

$20 million in sales.

Serves electronic and automotive markets.

Three manufacturing locations.

Chart 5

JAMES K. LA FLEUR

Role:

Will act as General Partner.

Will control development effort.

Will probably be co-inventor on most projects.

Background:

Graduate of California Institute of Technology (B.S.M.E. in 1952).

Has managed technically oriented companies for 24 years.

Holds an M.B.A. from Pepperdine.

Holds approximately 130 U.S. & Foreign Patents.

Is currently President of GTI Corporation.

Is 50 years old, married with three grown daughters.

Chart 6

THE INVESTORS:

Will act as Limited Partners.

Will provide funds.

Will receive 99% of income/losses until investment is recovered.

Will receive 75% of income/losses thereafter.

No liability beyond original investment.

No management responsibilities.

Must qualify by virtue of net worth, income and business knowledge.

Chart 7

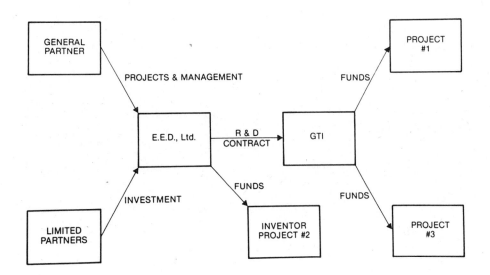

Chart 8

Summary of Relationships Between Participants—Stage I

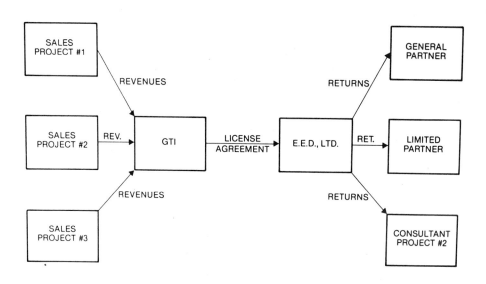

SALES PROJECT #1				GENERAL PARTNER
SALES PROJECT #2	REV.	GTI → LICENSE AGREEMENT → E.E.D., LTD.	RET.	LIMITED PARTNER
SALES PROJECT #3				CONSULTANT PROJECT #2

REVENUES · RETURNS

Chart 9

Summary of Relationships Between Participants—Stage II

PROJECTS IN THIS PARTNERSHIP ARE:

1. A high speed welder.
2. A computer graphics system.
3. Marking and handling equipment.

Chart 10

HIGH SPEED WELDING TODAY

Unique GTI Technology: Over 300 Welds Per Minute

Wide Variety of Dissimilar Materials Can Be Welded

GTI is Major Supplier in Growing Worldwide Market

Major Customers Include: I.T.T., Motorola, Hewlett-Packard, Siemens, Texas Instruments, R-Ohm

GTI HIGH SPEED WELDING TOMORROW

Three Times the Speed of Present Machines

Lower Labor Input

Automatic Packaging

Logical Extension of GTI's Experience

Chart 11

COMPUTER GRAPHICS TODAY

Confusing Interior Lines
No Shaded Surfaces
Cost $50K–$100K

GTI COMPUTER GRAPHICS TOMORROW

Hides Interior Lines and Surfaces

Full Color with Intensity Shading on Standard TV Monitors

Operates in "Real Time" with Free Movement of Objects Being Displayed

Cost: Comparable to Present Technology

Chart 12

ELECTRONICS PARTS HANDLING TODAY

Billions of Parts Handled Worldwide

Market Is Growing

Difficult to Handle Nonmagnetic, Glass, Plastic or Ceramic Parts

Labor Input Is High

Scrap Rate Is High

GTI PARTS HANDLING TOMORROW

Universal Carrier Strip-Handles All Types of Parts

Automatic Handling of Integrated Circuits and Hybrid Packages as Well as Discrete Components

Ultraviolet Ink Marks at Low Temperatures

Laser Marking for Precision Applicatons

Microprocessor Controlled Systems

Chart 13

THREE CATEGORIES OF MAJOR RISKS TO INVESTORS:

Legal Risks:

1. Partnership could be judged an "association" by IRS and "pass through" would not be allowed.
2. Deductions could be disallowed.
3. Limited liability feature could be breached.
4. Income could be judged "ordinary" rather than "capital gain."

Refer to Exhibit C for opinion of counsel relating to Items 1–3.

Technical Risk: Project objectives could not be achieved within budgetary and time limits allowed.

Market Risk: Projects even though successful technically might not sell. Income would then be limited to original investment.

Chart 14

Projects	Projected Total Capital of Partnership to be Applied to Project	Royalty Payable to Partnership as a Percentage of Net Sales	Minimum Royalty If Achieve Technological Success, to be Received October 31, 1984	Maximum Royalty Permitted by License Agreements
High Speed Welder	350,000	3%	14,583	43,749
Computer Graphics System	300,000	5%	12,500	250,000
Marking and Handling Equipment	550,000	10%	22,917	68,751
Totals	1,200,000		50,000	362,500

Chart 15
Summary of Maximum Potential Benefits to Investor
(One Unit or $50,000 Investment)

Refer to Exhibit "D" in Private Placement Memorandum for full details of potential benefits.

SUMMARY OF PRESENTATION

R&D Limited Partnerships were described.

Major participants and their roles, interrelationship and background was described.

Description of the three anticipated projects was given.

Major risks to investors were discussed.

Maximum potential benefits to investors were reviewed.

Chart 16

Sample EED Letters Indicating Acceptance or Rejection of Offeree

Electronic Equipment Development Ltd.
An R&D Limited Partnership

James K. LaFleur
General Partner

October 14, 1980

Dear Sir:

I am pleased to inform you that we have closed the private offering of units in Electronic Equipment Development, Ltd. The offering was fully subscribed and we have accepted your subscription for 1 unit for $50,000.00. I have enclosed a fully signed copy of the subscription agreement for your file.

I appreciate your interest in the offering, and I look forward to the sucess of the Partnership. The high speed welder and the computer graphics projects are presently underway and on schedule. The component handling project will be starting shortly. A detailed progress report will be prepared monthly starting in November.

Electronic Equipment Development Ltd.

By _____
James K. La Fleur, General Partner

4337 Talofa Avenue, Toluca Lake, CA 91602   (213) 985-9226

Electronic Equipment Development Ltd.
An R&D Limited Partnership

James K. La Fleur
General Partner

October 14, 1980

Dear Sir:

We have recently completed the private offering of units in Electronic Equipment Development, Ltd. with an oversubscription of the offered units. We appreciate your interest in the offering, and we regret that due to an excess of subscriptions we are unable to accept your subscription. Accordingly, we are enclosing your check for $50,000.00, representing the return of your previously tendered subscription.

With the success of this offering and the need for such research funds at GTI, it is our expectation that future offerings will be made by mid-1981. We welcome your continuing interest.

Electronic Equipment Development Ltd.

By _____
James K. La Fleur, General Partner

Enclosure

4337 Talofa Avenue, Toluca Lake, CA 91602   (213) 985-9226

IRS Form for Getting Employer Identification Number

Form **SS-4** (Rev. 11-81)

Department of the Treasury
Internal Revenue Service

Application for Employer Identification Number

(For use by employers and others as explained in the Instructions)

OMB No. 1545-0003
Expires 12-31-83

1 Name (True name as distinguished from trade name. If partnership, see instructions on page 4.)

2 Trade name, if any (Name under which business is operated, if different from item 1.)

3 Social security number, if sole proprietor

4 Address of principal place of business (Number and street)

5 Ending month of accounting year

6 City and State

7 ZIP code

8 County of business location

9 Type of organization (See instructions on page 4)
- ☐ Individual
- ☐ Trust
- ☐ Partnership
- ☐ Other (specify)
- ☐ Governmental
- ☐ Nonprofit organization (See instructions on page 4)
- ☐ Corporation

10 Date you acquired or started this business (Mo., day, year)

11 Reason for applying
- ☐ Started new business
- ☐ Purchased going business
- ☐ Other (specify)

12 First date you paid or will pay wages for this business (Mo., day, year)

13 Nature of business (See instructions on page 4)

14 Do you operate more than one place of business? ☐ Yes ☐ No

15 Peak number of employees expected in next 12 months (If none, enter "0"). ►
- Nonagricultural
- Agricultural
- Household

16 If nature of business is manufacturing, state principal product and raw material used.

17 To whom do you sell most of your products or services?
- ☐ Business establishments
- ☐ General public
- ☐ Other (specify)

18 Have you ever applied for an identification number for this or any other business? ☐ Yes ☐ No

If "Yes," enter name and trade name. Also enter approx. date, city, and State where you applied and previous number if known. ►

Date

Signature and title

Telephone number

Please leave blank ►	Geo.	Ind.	Class	Size	Reas. for appl.	Part I

For Paperwork Reduction Act Notice, see page 2.

Specific Instructions

Items 1, 2, and 3.—Enter in item 1 the true name of the applicant and enter in item 2 the trade name, if any, adopted for business purposes. For example, if John W. Jones, an individual owner, operates a restaurant under the trade name of "Busy Bee Restaurant," "John W. Jones" should be entered in item 1 and "Busy Bee Restaurant" in item 2. Enter the social security number in item 3, if you are a sole proprietor.

Note: *If a corporation.*—Enter in item 1 the corporate name as set forth in its charter, or other legal document creating it.

If a trust.—Enter the name of the trust in item 1 and the name of the trustee in item 2. Also, see instructions for item 10.

If an estate of a decedent, insolvent, etc.—Enter the name of the estate in item 1 and the name of the administrator or other fiduciary in item 2. Also, see instructions for item 10.

If a partnership.—Enter the legal name (not trade name) of the partnership, according to the partnership agreement, in item 1 and the first name, middle initial, and last name of a general partner in item 2. A general partner should sign this application.

Item 9. Governmental.—Check if or-

ganization is a State, county, school district, municipality, etc., or is related to such entities, for example: county hospital, city library, etc.

Nonprofit organization (other than governmental).—Check if organized for religious, charitable, scientific, literary, educational, humane, or fraternal purposes, etc. Generally, a nonprofit organization must file an application for exemption from Federal income tax with the Internal Revenue Service. Details on how to apply are in IRS Publication **557.**

Item 10.—For trusts, enter the date the trust was legally created.

For estates, enter the date of death of the decedent whose name appears in item 1.

Item 13.—Describe the kind of business carried on by the applicant. See examples below.

(a) *Governmental.*—State type of governmental organization, whether a State, county, school district, municipality, etc., or relationship to such entities, for example: county hospital, city library, etc.

(b) *Nonprofit* (other than governmental).—State whether organized for religious, charitable, scientific, literary, educational, or humane purposes and state the principal activity, for example: religious

organization—hospital; charitable organization—home for the aged; etc.

(c) *Mining and quarrying.*—State the process and the principal product, for example: mining bituminous coal, contract drilling for oil, quarrying dimension stone, etc.

(d) *Contract construction.*—State whether general contractor or special trade contractor and show type of work normally performed, for example: general contractor for residential buildings, electrical subcontractor, etc.

(e) *Trade.*—State the type of sale and the principal line of goods sold, for example: wholesale dairy products, manufacturer's representative for mining machinery, retail hardware, etc.

(f) *Manufacturing.*—State type of establishment operated, for example: sawmill, vegetable cannery, etc. In item 16, state the principal product manufactured and raw material used.

(g) *Other activities.*—State exact type of business operated, for example: advertising agency, farm, labor union, real estate agency, steam laundry, rental of coin-operated vending machines, investment club, etc.

Return both parts of this form to the Internal Revenue Service—your employer identification number will be mailed to you.

Appendix R

EED Progress Report

(Sample)

Electronic Equipment Development Ltd.
An R&D Limited Partnership

James K. La Fleur
General Partner

March 17, 1981

Dear Sir:

I am enclosing Progress Report #5 for the EED projects. The first three projects are all now out of the design phase and into the prototype fabrication phase. Although my early warning systems have alerted me to some potential budget overruns, I think these can be corrected. All in all, I feel everything is going well.

Sincerely,

_____

James K. La Fleur, General Partner

JKL/nt

4337 Talofa Avenue. Toluca Lake. CA 91602   (213) 985-9226

482

ELECTRONIC EQUIPMENT DEVELOPMENT LTD.

Progress Report: 5   Date: March 17, 1981

Red Flag Items:

1. The PERT network for the high speed welder is now forecasting a
    10% overrun in costs. I spent 3 days this month at the Electronics
    Division in Pennsylvania discussing this problem with the engineering
    and management personnel responsible for this project.

The forecasted cost overruns were traced to two problem areas: 1) The
fabrication of the ferris wheel, a key component in the design, was subcontracted at a cost of $37,000 vs. $25,000 estimated in the budget; and
2) The engineering design of the electronic control package ran over budget by $5,400.00.

As a result of these findings, some organizational changes were made to
give more direct responsibility to the project manager in charge of the
welder design. In addition some changes in the sequence of prototype
subsystem testing were made. While these changes will not recover costs
already incurred it is felt that tighter management control will reduce
costs in the future, hopefully bringing the project back on budget in the
months ahead.

Discussion:

1. General Partnership Business
a) The partnership tax returns and the K-1's were completed on sched-
    ule. The K-1's were mailed out to all partners on February 18, 1981.
    If you did not get yours or if you have questions, please contact me
    right away.
b) The K-1's were mailed as soon as possible to give each of you as
    much time as possible prior to preparing your own return. At the time
    I mailed them, however, the partnership had not received its Em-
    ployer Identification Number. The number has now been received.

483

For your records it is: 95-3568164. You might cross out "applied for" and write in this number in the upper right hand corner of the first page of the K-1 prior to filing your return.

c)   The partnership will file Federal, California and New York tax returns between April 1 and April 15. While the returns were completed I hold up filing them until I had the identification number as well as having no particular reason to file early.

2.   Project Status

a)   High Speed Welder (Project #1)

The problem with a potential cost overrun was discussed under the Red Flag Section above. During my three day visit to Pennsylvania several other technical areas that had concerned me with this project were discussed in some detail. As a result several small, but I feel important interim tests will be performed on various subsystems to try to detect any trouble spots (and correct them) before the complete machine is tested. For the moment, at least, I am comfortable with the project.

b)   Computer Graphics (Project #3)

I have included in this report one of Jim Holly's latest reports to me so that you can get some "flavor" for how this project is going. In simple terms Jim is in the process of designing ten separate stand alone computers which are designed to work together to create a three dimensional color picture. It's a complex project which is only made possible by the availability of the microprocessor and low cost memory chips. I think he is up to the job and I feel that the project is on time and on budget. A critical date is the last week in May, as you can see from his report.

c)   Non-Magnetic Lead Straightener (Project 3(a))

During my visit to Pennsylvania I watched this unit being assembled. The design looks good but a critical item is a zig-zag feeder chute that guides various electronic components into our machine. As the purpose of this entire machine is to straighten the leads of these components and then place them on a metal conveyor strip for further processing, it is obvious that we must assume the leads are bent to begin with and herein lies a problem. Zig-zag feeding chutes tend to jam when fed bent leads. I have been assured that this is a "special" chute that will not jam but . . . just to be safe, I have requested that a special test be run *now* to assure that this is true. If problems are encountered, we should have time to correct them prior to testing the completed system.

d) Non-Magnetic Printing System (Project 3(b)) and Packaging System (Project 3(f))

These projects were temporarily halted until I receive a test report on the zig-zag feeding chute as the success of these projects depends on that unit performing well.

Events:

1. K-1's mailed to partners on February 18, 1981.
2. 10% cost overrun on high speed welder forecasted.
3. As a result of this forecast, corrective action has been taken which should correct problem.
4. Work on projects 3(b) and 3(f) has been temporarily halted pending results of zig-zag feeder chute tests.
5. The character generator chip for the Computer Graphics project mentioned in past progress reports is in.

Enclosures:

1. Ron Lust's report to Mr. LaFleur dated March 13, 1981.
2. Dick Roessler's report to Mr. LaFleur dated March 12, 1981.
3. Jim Holly's report to Mr. LaFleur dated March 13, 1981.

James K. La Fleur, General Partner

JKL:nt
Enclosures

Appendix S

Blue Sky References

Alabama	"Securities Act of Alabama"
	1) CCH Blue Sky Reporter, ¶7101 et seq.
	2) Code of Alabama, 1975, as amended, Title 8, Chapter 6, Article 1, Sec. 8-6-1 et seq.
Alaska	"Alaska Securities Act of 1959"
	1) CCH Blue Sky Reporter, ¶8101 et seq.
	2) Alaska Statutes, 1962, Annotated, Title 45, Chapter 55, Article 1, Sec. 45.55.010 et seq.
Arizona	"Securities Act of Arizona"
	1) CCH Blue Sky Reporter, ¶9101 et seq.
	2) Arizona Revised Statutes, Annotated, Title 44, Chapter 12, Article 1, Sec. 44-1801 et seq.
Arkansas	"Arkansas Securities Act"
	1) CCH Blue Sky Reporter, ¶10,100 et seq.
	2) Arkansas Statutes, 1947, Annotated, Title 67, Chapter 12, Sec. 67-1235 et seq.
California	"Corporate Securities Laws of 1968"
	1) CCH Blue Sky Reporter, ¶11,101 et seq.
	2) West's Annotated California Codes, Title 4 (Corporation Code), Division 1, Part 1, Sec. 25000 et seq.
Colorado	"Securities Act"
	1) CCH Blue Sky Reporter, ¶13,101 et seq.
	2) Colorado Revised Statutes, 1973, Annotated, Title 11, Article 51, Sec. 11-51-101 et seq.
Connecticut	"The Connecticut Uniform Securities Act"
	1) CCH Blue Sky Reporter, ¶14,101 et seq.
	2) General Statutes of Connecticut, Revision of 1958, as amended, Title 36, Chapter 662, Sec. 36-470 et seq.

Delaware	"Delaware Securities Act" 1) CCH Blue Sky Reporter, ¶15,101 et seq. 2) Delaware Code Annotated, as amended, Title 6, Chapter 73, Sec. 7301 et seq.
District of Columbia	"District of Columbia Securities Act" 1) CCH Blue Sky Reporter, ¶16,101 et seq. 2) District of Columbia Code, 1973, as amended, Title 2, Chapter 24, Sec. 2-2401 et seq.
Florida	"Florida Securities Act" 1) CCH Blue Sky Reporter, ¶17,101 et seq. 2) West's Florida Statutes Annotated, Title 31, Chapter 517, Sec. 517.01 et seq.
Georgia	"Georgia Securities Act of 1973" 1) CCH Blue Sky Reporter, ¶18,101 et seq. 2) Code of Georgia, Annotated, Title 97, Chapter 97-1, Sec. 97-101 et seq.
Hawaii	"Uniform Securities Act (Modified)" 1) CCH Blue Sky Reporter, ¶20,101 et seq. 2) Hawaii Revised Statutes, as amended, Title 26, Chapter 485, Sec. 485-1 et seq.
Idaho	"Idaho Securities Act" 1) CCH Blue Sky Reporter, ¶21,101 et seq. 2) Idaho Code, as amended, Title 30, Chapter 14, Sec. 30-1401 et seq.
Illinois	"The Illinois Securities Law of 1953" 1) CCH Blue Sky Reporter, ¶22,101 et seq. 2) Smith-Hurd Illinois Annotated Statutes, Chapter 121-1/2, Sec. 137.1 et seq.
Indiana	"Indiana Blue Sky Laws" 1) CCH Blue Sky Reporter, ¶24,101 et seq. 2) Burns Indiana Statutes Annotated, Title 23, Article 2, Chapter 1, Sec. 23-2-1-1 et seq.
Iowa	"Iowa Uniform Securities Act" 1) CCH Blue Sky Reporter, ¶25,101 et seq. 2) Iowa Code Annotated, Title XIX, Chapter 502, Sec. 502.101 et seq.
Kansas	"Kansas Securities Act" 1) CCH Blue Sky Reporter, ¶26,101 et seq. 2) Kansas Statuttes Annotated, Chapter 17, Article 17-12, Sec. 17-1252 et seq.
Kentucky	"Securities Act of Kentucky" 1) CCH Blue Sky Reporter, ¶27,101 et seq. 2) Baldwin's Kentucky Revised Statutes, Annotated, Title XXV, Chapter 292, Sec. 292.310 et seq.

Louisiana	"Blue Sky Law"
	1) CCH Blue Sky Reporter, ¶28,101 et seq.
	2) West's Louisiana Statutes Annotated, Title 51, Chapter 2, Sec. 701 et seq.
Maine	"The Maine Securities Act"
	1) CCH Blue Sky Reporter, ¶29,101 et seq.
	2) Maine Revised Statutes Annotated, 1964, Title 32, Chapter 13, Subchapter 1, Sec. 751 et seq.
Maryland	"Maryland Securities Act"
	1) CCH Blue Sky Reporter, ¶30,101 et seq.
	2) Annotated Code of Maryland, as amended, Title 11 (Corporations and Associations), Subtitle 1, Sec. 11-101 et seq.
Massachusetts	"Uniform Securities Act"
	1) CCH Blue Sky Reporter, ¶31,101 et seq.
	2) Annotated Laws of Massachusetts, Title XV, Chapter 110A, Part 1, Sec. 101 et seq.
Michigan	"Uniform Securities Act"
	1) CCH Blue Sky Reporter, ¶32,101 et seq.
	2) Michigan Compiled Laws, Annotated, Chapter 451, Part I, Sec. 451-501 et seq.
Minnesota	"Regulation of Securities"
	1) CCH Blue Sky Reporter, ¶33,101 et seq.
	2) Minnesota Statutes Annotated, Chapter 80, Sec. 80.01 et seq.
Mississippi	"Mississippi Securities Law"
	1) CCH Blue Sky Reporter, ¶34,101 et seq.
	2) Mississippi Code, 1972, Annotated, Title 75, Chapter 71, Sec. 75-71-1 et seq.
Missouri	"Missouri Uniform Securities Act"
	1) CCH Blue Sky Reporter, ¶35,101 et seq.
	2) Vernon's Annotated Missouri Statutes, Title XXVI, Chapter 409, Sec. 409.101 et seq.
Montana	"Securities Act of Montana"
	1) CCH Blue Sky Reporter, ¶36,101 et seq.
	2) Montana Code Annotated, as amended, Title 30, Chapter 10, Sec. 30-10-101 et seq.
Nebraska	"Securities Act of Nebraska"
	1) CCH Blue Sky Reporter, ¶37,101 et seq.
	2) Revised Statutes of Nebraska, 1943, as amended, Chapter 8, Article 11, Sec. 8-1101 et seq.
Nevada	"Blue Sky Law"
	1) CCH Blue Sky Reporter, ¶38,101 et seq.
	2) Nevada Revised Statutes, as amended, Title 7, Chapter 90, Sec. 90.010 et seq.

New Hampshire	"Blue Sky Law"
	1) CCH Blue Sky Reporter, ¶39,101 et seq.
	2) New Hampshire Revised Statutes Annotated, 1968, Title XXXVIII, Chapter 421, Sec. 421:1 et seq.
New Jersey	"Uniform Securities Law (1967)"
	1) CCH Blue Sky Reporter, ¶40,101 et seq.
	2) New Jersey Statutes Annotated, Title 49, Chapter 3, Sec. 49:3-47 et seq.
New Mexico	"Securities Act of New Mexico"
	1) CCH Blue Sky Reporter, ¶41,101 et seq.
	2) New Mexico Statutes, 1978, Annotated, Chapter 58, Article 13, Sec. 58-13-1 et seq.
New York	"Fradulent Practices ("Martin") Act"
	1) CCH Blue Sky Reporter, ¶42,101 et seq.
	2) McKinney's Consolidated Laws of New York, Annotated, Article 23-A (General Business Law), Sec. 352 et seq.
North Carolina	"North Carolina Securities Act"
	1) CCH Blue Sky Reporter, ¶43,101 et seq.
	2) The General Statutes of North Carolina, as amended, Chapter 78A, Article 1, Sec. 78A-1 et seq.
North Dakota	"Securities Act of 1951"
	1) CCH Blue Sky Reporter, ¶44,101 et seq.
	2) North Dakota Century Code, as amended, Title 10, Chapter 10-04, Sec. 10-04-01 et seq.
Ohio	"Securities Act"
	1) CCH Blue Sky Reporter, ¶45,101 et seq.
	2) Page's Ohio Revised Code, Annotated, Title XVII, Chapter 1707, Sec. 1707.01 et seq.
Oklahoma	"Oklahoma Securities Act"
	1) CCH Blue Sky Reporter, ¶46,101 et seq.
	2) Oklahoma Statutes Annotated, Title 71, Chapter 1, Article 1, Sec. 1 et seq.
Oregon	"Oregon Securities Law"
	1) CCH Blue Sky Reporter, ¶47,101 et seq.
	2) Oregon Revised Statutes, as amended, Title 7, Chapter 59, Sec. 59.005 et seq.
Pennsylvania	"Pennsylvania Securities Act of 1972"
	1) CCH Blue Sky Reporter, ¶48,101 et seq.
	2) Purdon's Pennsylvania Statutes Annotated, Title 70, Chapter 1, Sec. 31 et seq.
Rhode Island	"Blue Sky Law"
	1) CCH Blue Sky Reporter, ¶50,101 et seq.
	2) General Laws of Rhode Island, 1956, as

	amended, Title 7, Chapter 11, Sec. 7-11-1 et seq.
South Carolina	"Uniform Securities Act" 1) CCH Blue Sky Reporter, ¶51,101 et seq. 2) Code of Laws of South Carolina, 1976, as amended, Title 35, Chapter 1, Article 1, Sec. 35-1-10 et seq.
South Dakota	"Blue Sky Law" 1) CCH Blue Sky Reporter, ¶52,101 et seq. 2) South Dakota Compiled Laws, 1967, Annotated, Title 47, Chapter 47-31, Sec. 47-31-1 et seq.
Tennessee	"Tennessee Securities Act 1980" 1) CCH Blue Sky Reporter, ¶54,155 et seq. 2) Tennessee Code Annotated, Title 48, Chapter 16, Sec. 48-1601 et seq.
Texas	"The Securities Act of 1957" 1) CCH Blue Sky Reporter, ¶55,101 et seq. 2) Vernon's Civil Statutes of the State of Texas, Annotated, Title 19, Article 581-1 et seq.
Utah	"Utah Uniform Securities Act" 1) CCH Blue Sky Reporter, ¶57,101 et seq. 2) Utah Code Annotated, 1953, Title 61, Chapter 1, Sec. 61-1-1 et seq.
Vermont	"Blue Sky Law" 1) CCH Blue Sky Reporter, ¶58,101 et seq. 2) Vermont Statutes Annotated, as amended, Title 9, Part 5, Chapter 131, Sec. 4201 et seq.
Virginia	"Blue Sky Law" 1) CCH Blue Sky Reporter, ¶60,101 et seq. 2) Code of Virginia, 1950, as amended, Title 13.1, Chapter 5, Article 1, Sec. 13.1-501 et seq.
Washington	"The Securities Act of Washington" 1) CCH Blue Sky Reporter, ¶61,101 et seq. 2) Revised Code of Washington Annotated, Title 21, Chapter 21.20, Sec. 21.20.005 et seq.
West Virginia	"West Virginia Uniform Securities Act, Acts 1974, Ch. 128" 1) CCH Blue Sky Reporter, ¶63,101 et seq. 2) West Virginia Code, Annotated, Chapter 32, Article 1, Sec. 32-1-101 et seq.
Wisconsin	"Uniform Securities Law" 1) CCH Blue Sky Reporter, ¶64,101 et seq. 2) West's Wisconsin Statutes Annotated, Title XL-B (40-B), Chapter 551, Subchapter I, Sec. 551.01 et seq.

Wyoming

"Uniform Securities Act"
1) CCH Blue Sky Reporter, ¶66,101 et seq.
2) Wyoming Statutes, Annotated, 1977 Republished Edition, Title 17, Chapter 4, Sec. 17-4-101 et seq.

Appendix T

Comparison Of Sec Exemption Rule 146 And Rule 506
(Including Text of Rule 506)

COMPARISON OF RULE 146 AND NEW RULE 506

	Rule 146	Rule 506
Aggregate Offering Price Limitation	Unlimited	Unlimited
Number of Investors	35 plus those purchasing $150,000 or more	35 plus unlimited accredited*
Investor Qualification	Offeree and purchaser must be sophisticated or wealthy (with offeree representative, if wealthy person is not sophisticated)	Offeree: none. Purchaser must be sophisticated (alone or with representative). Accredited presumed to be qualified.
Commissions	Permitted	Permitted
Manner of Offering	No general solicitation	No general solicitation
Resale	Restricted	Restricted
Issuer Qualifications	None	None
Notice of Sales	Form 146	Form D: 5 copies filed 15 days after first sale, every 6 months after first sale, 30 days after last sale
Information Requirements	Must furnish (unless offeree has access via economic bargaining power)	1. If purchased solely by Accredited, no information specified

Rule 146

1. Below $1,500,000—information may be limited to Part II, Form 1-A of Reg. A
2. Other offerings (a) (non reporting) information in registration available to issuer; unaudited financials if audit requirements unreasonable effort or expense (b) (reporting companies) recent Form S-1 or Form 10, definitive proxy statement and periodic reports

Rule 506

2. If purchased by non-accredited,
   a. non-reporting companies must furnish:
      i. offerings up to $5,000,000—information in Part I of Form S-18 or available registration, 2 yr. financials, 1 year audited—if undue effort or expense, issuers other than limited partnerships only balance sheet as of 120 days before offering must be audited—if limited partnership and undue effort or expense, financials may be tax basis
      ii. offerings over $5,000,000—information in Part I of available registration if undue effort or expense, issuers other than limited partnerships only balance sheet as of 120 days before offering must be audited—if limited partnership and undue effort or expense, financials may be tax basis

Rule 146	Rule 506
	b. reporting companies must furnish

b. reporting companies must furnish
   i. Rule 14a-3 annual report to shareholders, definitive proxy statement and 10-K, if requested, plus subsequent reports and other updating information *or*
   ii. information in most recent Form S-1 or Form 10 or Form 10-K plus subsequent reports and other updating information
c. Issuers must make available prior to sale
   i. exhibits
   ii. written information given to accredited investors
   iii. opportunity to ask questions and receive answers

*"Accredited" means:
1. Any individual whose net worth (or joint net worth with spouse) exceeds $1 million;
2. Any individual whose income exceeded $200,000 in the two most recent years and who reasonably expects his income to exceed $200,000 in the current year;
3. Any person who purchases at least $150,000 of the interests being offered, if (i) the total purchase price does not exceed 20% of the purchaser's net worth (or joint net worth with spouse), and (ii) payment consists of cash, securities for which market quotations are readily available, an unconditional obligation to pay cash or such readily marketable securities within five years, or cancellation of indebtedness;
4. Directors, executive officers, or general partners of the issuer or of the general partner of the issuer;
5. Certain institutional investors, including banks, insurance companines, registered investment companies, private business development companies, and certain large exempt organizations;
6. Any entity in which all of the equity owners are accredited investors.

RULE 506—EXEMPTION FOR LIMITED OFFERS AND SALES WITHOUT REGARD TO DOLLAR AMOUNT OF OFFERING
REG. § 230.506

(a) *Exemption.* Offers and sales of securities by an issuer that satisfy the conditions in paragraph (b) of this § 230.506 shall be deemed to be transactions not involving any public offering within the meaning of section 4(2) of the Act.

(b) *Conditions to be met.*

(1) *General conditions.* to qualify for exemption under this § 230.506, offers and sales must satisfy all the terms and conditions of §§ 230.501 through 230.503.

(2) *Specific conditions.*

(i) *Limitation on number of purchasers.* The issuer shall reasonably believe that there are no more than 35 purchasers of securities from the issuer in any offering under this § 230.506.

Note: See § 230.501 (e) for the calculation of the number of purchasers and § 230.502 (a) for what may or may not constitute an offering under this section 230.506.

(ii) *Nature of purchasers.* The issuer shall reasonably believe immediately prior to making any sale that each purchaser who is not an accredited investor either alone or with his purchaser representative(s) has such knowledge and experience in financial and business matters that he is capable of evaluating the merits and risks of the prospective investment.

[Adopted in Release No. 33-6389 (¶83,106), effective April 15, 1982, 47 F. R. —.]

Index